How can man achieve the good life?

Is the individual the most important fact of ethics? Or is the perception of the objective nature of things equally important? Mr. Jordan asserts that it is. He discards the relativistic and subjectivistic theories that have dominated modern ethics and makes a fresh approach.

Modern ethical theory has assumed the individual man as the basic fact. As a consequence, modern ethics has become a mass of data about the individual's character or personality—about his states of mind and their hypothetical causes and effects. The result is a maze of contradictions.

But Mr. Jordan formulates the principles of ethics without reference to the hypothetical individual. He rejects both the individualistic and the "social" presuppositions of modern thought. "Not man's wants or needs or states of mind but his actions are the material of ethics. For it is through action that man controls and changes himself and his relations to his fellows and to the natural and cultural world in which he has his being."

The ultimate problem of ethics is to find an objective ground for obligation, a ground within the nature of things. Either the basis of moral obligation lies in the substance of things—or there is no basis."

Ethical theory cannot be based on man set in isolation or on man set in the con-

fusion of "social" relations. It must be based on solid institutional structure. "The mere human being is no longer the center round which the universe revolves. Man does not have his whole being within his own skin."

Thus, ethics has its completion in politics. It deals with the ultimate relations that hold between two systems—nature or fact, on the one hand, and culture or values, on the other.

"The individual cannot be perfected, or indeed exist at all, outside the institutional relations: family, industry, education, religion, art, and politics." The moral individual is a corporate person— a man living in a scheme of institutions that completely express his purposes in accordance with the ultimate nature of things. Immorality is the destruction of, or failure to attain, corporate personality.

This book provides a statement of a coherent and original ethical theory. It is valuable both as an exposition of the philosophical background of ethics and as a criticism of contemporary thought and contemporary institutions. The discussion of the virtues and the analysis of the good and of the concrete problems involved in the realization of a good life are extremely clear and straightforward.

THE GOOD LIFE

THE
Good Life

By E. Jordan

THE UNIVERSITY OF CHICAGO PRESS

THE UNIVERSITY OF CHICAGO PRESS, CHICAGO 37
Cambridge University Press, London, N.W. 1, England
W. J. Gage & Co., Limited, Toronto 2B, Canada

*Copyright 1949 by The University of Chicago. All rights
reserved. Published 1949. Composed and printed by* THE
UNIVERSITY OF CHICAGO PRESS, *Chicago, Illinois, U.S.A.*

Table of Contents

PART I. THE FACTS OF THE MORAL LIFE

I. THE NATURE OF ETHICS AND ITS RELATION TO OTHER
    INTERESTS 3
II. THE ANALYSIS OF ACTION 17
III. IMPLICATIONS OF THE FACTS OF ACTION 28
IV. THE LAW OF MORALITY 58

PART II. THE NATURE OF THE
MORAL PERSON

V. THE COMPLEXITY OF EXPERIENCE 75
VI. THE BIOLOGICAL CAPACITIES OF THE PERSON . . . 86
VII. THE PSYCHOLOGICAL CAPACITIES OF THE PERSON . . 103
VIII. SOCIAL CAPACITIES OF THE PERSON 131
IX. THE MORAL PERSON—SUMMARY STATEMENT . . . 147

PART III. THE SUBJECTIVE OR
PARTIAL VIRTUES

X. THE PERSONAL VIRTUES 175
XI. SYMPATHY—VIRTUE AS PURE SUBJECTIVITY . . . 192
XII. GENEROSITY—VIRTUE AS OTHER REFERENCE . . 204
XIII. FRIENDSHIP—OBJECTIFIED FEELING 218
XIV. INTEGRITY OR PERSONAL WHOLENESS 233

PART IV. THE NATURE OF THE
MORAL WORLD

XV. THE WORLD AS A MORAL OBJECT 247
XVI. THE FAMILY AS ORGANIZED INSTINCT 270
XVII. INDUSTRY AS ORGANIZED WORK 288

XVIII. Education and the Organization of Intelligence . . 301

XIX. Religion and the Organization of Faith 314

XX. Art as Organized Beauty 324

XXI. Politics and the Unity of Life 338

XXII. The Moral Life as End-Object 358

PART V. THE OBJECTIVE OR PERFECT VIRTUES

XXIII. Wisdom or Objectified Knowledge 377

XXIV. Temperance—the Organization of Life 392

XXV. Courage—Institutionalized Active Attitudes . . 406

XXVI. Justice—the Order of Culture under Law . . . 414

XXVII. The Corporate Person and Objective Virtue . . 426

BIBLIOGRAPHY

Bibliography 445

INDEX

Index 449

Part I

The Facts of the Moral Life

Chapter I

The Nature of Ethics and Its Relation
to Other Interests

I. ETHICS AS THE SCIENCE OF ACTION

WHETHER ethics is to be called a science or not depends upon the meaning we attach to the terms. If by science we mean, as we ordinarily do, a reference only to the methods and procedures of what are commonly known as the natural sciences, then ethics is not a science. The purpose of science is to know, and its methods and procedures are adapted rather strictly and narrowly to the end of knowing the facts about man and the world in which he lives and the nature of his relations to his world. With the understanding of these facts and relations the purpose of science is achieved. But ethics, as the study is commonly understood, undertakes to go beyond the mere knowledge and understanding of the world to an interpretation of its meaning, and this meaning, when attained, gives rise to the demand for a certain type and degree of control over the world.

This demand for control leads us into reflections that are very complicated and difficult, and to arrive at a clear perception of its meaning is a large part of the purpose of the study of ethics. Ethics is then concerned with the relation of knowledge to control, and this relation rests on a knowledge of the nature of man and of the world in which he lives, together with a knowledge of the relations between man and his world. But its primary purpose is not to understand the relations as they are given in fact but as they are possible between man and the world, for it is this region of possible relations that imparts to action its ethical character.

Ethics has a special interest in these possible relations in that they suggest the conditions and the means through which man may effect a degree of control over his world. Ethics thus adds to the merely scientific purpose to know the practical motive to control, and it is this latter motive that distinguishes it from the sciences and makes it

3

the basis of all the cultural disciplines. Ethics then represents man's efforts to make over the world on a basis of a knowledge of it and in accordance with his wishes and purposes. This motive to reconstruct the world is the ethical motive properly so called, and this ethical motive becomes the central feature in the cultural disciplines of politics, law, religion, and art. It involves thus both the motive to know and the motive to control, and it is not always easy to distinguish the one from the other.

We may designate the interests these two purposes represent as the theoretical and the practical. The theoretical interest leads to such a knowledge of the world as it is able to attain; and, in attaining this knowledge, the purposes of theory are fulfilled. The practical interest undertakes to control the world and to reconstruct it along the lines suggested by the purposes of men. While the two motives should be clearly distinguished in thought, their various expressions run into each other and constantly overlap. The simplest way to state their most general relation to each other is to say that the practical interest, as expressed in action, always takes for granted such theoretical knowledge as is relevant to its purposes. As ethics is the characteristic expression of the practical motive, it will be well to notice the various forms of that motive.

A. Practical Disciplines

Ethics is both a theoretical and a practical discipline. Its purpose is to know and to control the world, as including man, and to determine man's relations within the world. What in detail is involved in the meaning of control we shall see as we go along. So far we have described it as merely presupposing a knowledge of the world. This does not mean that the practical purpose must wait until a competent knowledge has in every case been achieved. It means rather that in the pursuit of practical motives such knowledge as we possess must determine the direction which practical activity is to take. Also it means that in the absence of knowledge practical activity can only proceed without determinate direction. The practical motive of man is, then, the motive to *do*, to make changes in himself or in his fellows, or in his relations to his fellows, or in the world in which he lives and his relations to it. That is to say that the changes contemplated in the practical motive affect man in his natural or cultural being, or the world considered as a natural or cultural system, or the relations of man to the world.

The term "natural" refers to what man, his world, and their relations originally *are;* "cultural" refers to man, his world, and their relations after they have been modified by human action. The practical motive, then, always involves the relation between nature, as the external world system, and culture, representing man as he has re-created himself in the system of his institutions. It is this relation between nature and culture that lies behind and gives meaning to action. As a practical discipline, then, ethics is concerned with action, which constitutes its total and only subject matter. Action is grounded in knowledge and is directed toward the control of life and the conditions of existence with a view to their being transformed into the elements of culture.

Changes within the structure of either the natural or the cultural system are effected, for the most part, by modification of the outward relations between the two systems. Man as such and his institutions, and nature as such and its system, are not within man's power directly to change. Neither culture nor nature is therefore ever a direct object of the motive to change and control. But they may be contemplated with a view to control when we picture them in the system of their relations to each other. That is, these relations between nature and culture are the direct objects of action; they are also the means through which the natural and the cultural systems are to be changed and brought under control. For example, the apple is never the object of my action, but the apple as transformed into creative power is the object. In the long history of man these relations to his world have settled down into more or less fixed forms, and each of these forms represents a distinct type of practical activity. Also, each type of activity refers to a type of object that is its appropriate end.

We shall see that these forms of action are the basis of what we call the virtues, or established general types of action regarded as capacities of the actor, which we shall describe in their place. In the individual man these forms of action, or virtues, are known as habits and established traits and tendencies, while in collective life they are regarded as customs or traditions. We may here describe a number of the more important of these typic forms of action to illustrate the distinctions made above. It must be kept in mind that life as activity is, or continuously strives to be, a whole, and it is within this whole that these distinct motives have their meaning. When we regard these relations or fixed forms of action as realized in objects, they are the elements whose order makes up the structure of institutions. Institutions are then structured orders of objectified acts, or acts become objects of culture. The various ways, then, in which intelligent action transforms objects of nature into objects of culture represent the various kinds of moral activity, each of which is the subject matter of a distinct practical discipline. Following are some examples.

I. ECONOMICS AND ETHICS

Economic action is one of the typic forms of action, and the economic object is the object that appropriately ends this type of action. As we noted above, the relation between the knowing and the doing functions is a logical relation, that is, one as to which of the functions in a given instance is presupposed by the other. The virtues, or action types, have thus a logical meaning, and this meaning makes it possible to use them as ideas or categories and through these ideas or categories to form judgments about acts. There can be no temporal or historical or causal precedence, perhaps also no preference as a valuing attitude, given to any of the forms which the relation may take. Thus there can be no simplest or most primitive of the relations of man to his world or of culture to nature, no original form of action. If we consider the material basis of the relation, it becomes an economic fact. It can then be interpreted by categorizing it in terms of the wants and needs and impulses of the organism and their complementary objects in the system of nature.

Action with respect to physical objects regarded as counterparts of needs, etc., is thus the basis of economic science and is one of the elementary forms of the practical activity. Descriptions, then, in psychological terms of human needs and wants and motives, and, in physical terms, of natural objects and physical processes which more or less closely correspond to needs and wants, will constitute the subject matter of economics. And the activity through which these wants and needs are adapted to their appropriate natural objects and processes is economic activity, one of the elementary forms of practical life, and thus an important part of the content of ethics. The content of ethics is morality, that is, the total of the elementary forms of activity. A certain peculiar way or manner in which an act is carried on, as judged by the character of the object in which the act appropriately ends, is what we mean by the "morality" of the act; and this is a character, or may be, of all acts. This must be therefore quite obvious: all forms of activity are matters of content for ethics, and all the practical disciplines are in a profound sense subordinate to ethics.

2. RELIGION AND ETHICS

But a statement about the formal aspects of activity, when regarded as expressing the relation between the cultural and the natural, the human and the cosmic, may be considered a statement of the religious motive. Interpret the activity of food-getting or food-eating in terms of objects representing the ideal possibilities of life which it so strongly suggests, and it at once becomes a religious phenomenon. And the degree to which we idealize the actualities in the situation is the measure of its spiritual meaning and the basis, in thought, of the extraordinary symbolisms upon which the systems of spiritual meanings depend. It is through these symbolisms that ideal forces may be made vicariously effective in the actual world, and here the religious motive becomes a typical form of practical activity. It is therefore to that extent a part of the subject matter of ethics.

3. AESTHETICS AND ETHICS

We have noted that the difference between economic and religious activity is one of different interpretations of relatively simple fact. A still different interpretation is also true of the same fact, in that it includes the two just described and combines them in a new form. In economic activity we noted that the motive elements of cultural life, in the effort to control, connect immediately with their natural counterparts, or seek to do so; for example, hunger, as a life-need, leads directly to food, which is referred to the real world. In religious activity the connection of culture or "spirit" with its real objects is made by mediate or indirect methods and then deferred to the ideal in symbols. In the one case we immediately enjoy the natural object of our cultural purpose, that is, we eat the food; and in the other we contemplate and idealize it in imaginative perfection, make it an offering to the gods.

But these activities of enjoyment and contemplation are not necessarily separate motives. The persistent and pressing immediacy of the economic, and the deferred and ideal mediacy and remoteness of the religious, since both are at bottom subjective and lie within the inner consciousness of the agent, can be embodied together in an object that is both ideal and present. This is accomplished in the aesthetic object. In this the immediate and present is there as a natural object with the characters which our theoretical activity describes. And the ideal is there as the cultural form of the object which the practical activity can impose upon nature. How all this takes place is a matter of aesthetic theory and technique; but it illustrates how activity involved in the production and enjoyment of beauty is a form of the practical activity and so an element in the subject matter of ethics. Aesthetic activity is a necessary and natural part of practical activity, and this latter is the content of ethical theory.

4. LAW AND ETHICS

Thus the economic and the religious activities, as well as their combination in the aesthetic, come to their completion in an individual object which is concrete and recognizable as a whole of meaning. The aesthetic object is therefore the utmost of what the practical activity can do under the subjective limitations imposed upon it. It must realize in an object the total meaning of an act in so far as the act derives its meaning from its reference backward to its source, that is to say, so far as its meaning must be understood in terms of the inner conscious motives and purposes of the agent.

As an economic object it gets explanation in terms of its creation or possession by the agent, by its reference to his use or enjoyment. The object has no status of its own. As a religious object it is explained as merely a means to the "salvation" of the agent, that is, as a means to the maintenance of the agent as himself an independent object, and has no meaning by itself. And, as a consequence, the relation between the agent, as the active source of the economic or religious activity, and the object in which this activity finds its fulfilment is a mystery, is altogether beyond explanation. So, also, is the question of the relation of one active agent to another, and that of the relation of one completed object to another, quite out of reach of answer, so long as we remain on economic or religious grounds. The relations, then, of agent to act, of act to object, of agent to agent, and of object to object cannot be explained by the practical sciences which have for their purpose merely to describe them. The explanation of all these fundamental relations becomes the province of ethics in that phase of it in which these relations are to be regarded as constituting the basic structure and organization of culture. In this form they are the elementary materials of politicolegal systems and the subject matter of the "science" of law.

The question of the fundamental structure of the practical life then becomes one of the nature and connections of the various kinds of practical relations, where practical relations are always regarded as involving, as corollary questions, both the cultural subject or agent out of which action issues and the natural or cultural object in or upon which action issues; and this involves all situations of practical life. Action is to be regarded as the essential substance. In the subjective aspects of the practical relation the problem is one of the nature of that relation as unifying active motives in their individual form, that is, in a human being. It is the question as to how practical relations constitute the structure or makeup of the agent or person as actor. How the many active agents, now conceived as persons, can be brought together in the social whole of life and within the system of cultural objects, and their order there maintained, that is, how practical relations themselves in their system become genuine objects, is the problem of law. It is the law, then, that finally determines the moral object as a concrete fact, since it is law that finds a place for the concrete act within the total system of practical relations, upon which place the concrete objectivity of the act depends.

Objects now come to be contemplated as ends independent of specific subjective motives. They become, that is, objectives; and the meaning of ends lies in the fact that, as independent ends, objectives become the point of convergence of different subjective or personal motives, that is, they become objects for distinct and different agents. As things in nature these objects are necessarily exclusive of each other and conflicting in their reference to subjective motives. They are thus irrational except as it is the function of the law, as giving force to the ethical motive, to transform them into the means by which themselves and the subjective motives are reduced to harmony and order. The type of law thus called into being by the ethical act, and the kind of order which it contemplates, will depend upon the sort of interpretation necessitated by the nature of this fact of congruence or convergence of motives. Ultimately, however, there can be but one sense in which it is to be interpreted. The convergence must involve the overcoming of the conflicts of motives, at the same time preserving what in each of them made it capable of contemplating an end at all. It is this consideration of a unity of ends as the ideal of law that makes it necessary to include the system of civil law within the subject matter of ethics. Also, it is this demand that any law, if it is to be valid, must provide both for the harmony of individual purposes in the system of cultural objects and also equally for their realization as individual purposes that justifies morality in claiming authority over the law and that explains the phrase "the ethical basis of the law."

5. POLITICS AND ETHICS

Politics has to do with what is objective and public in the practical or moral relation. The ethical end which the law contemplates is itself conceived as an element within a larger objective whole. The end of the law is to effect the ultimate order of all agents and objects which the practical activity creates under the authority of morality. This system of all practical objects is the political body. It is created and maintained by law, where law is the dynamic power and original causality of the ethical end. But it is only as the law recognizes the authoritative command of morality that it creates this body in the state. It is also only as it is itself moralized that it maintains the state. As mere positive law it expresses itself fully in the authority and custom which characterized the ancient absolutisms and the modern power states, where morality is immature. It is only when morality dictates to the law the end that is proper to it that the rational state, principled upon freedom, is possible.

The law, therefore, is obligated to morality, and it is this obligation which gives it its compulsory power, when it has power. This obligation imposes upon the law a certain rigidity and fixity or inflexibility. It is the function of the political state, as the instrument and objective expression of moralized law, continuously to organize the ends of life into a system of permanent but dynamic objects which shall be maintained as both instruments to action and objectives of action for all persons who are capable of making use of them. Political activity is then a part of the content of ethics, and the basis of the state is that quality of active life which we have called "morality." What this peculiar quality is we shall see as we go on.

B. THEORETICAL DISCIPLINES

We have said above that the practical interest, as its varying forms are expressed in economic, religious, aesthetic, legal, and political objects, presupposes the theoretical. We must have knowledge of the world before we can control it. Rather we must have this knowledge in order to exercise intelligent control, and its importance cannot be too strongly insisted upon, since the quality and extent of our control of the world will depend upon the accuracy and the adequacy of our knowledge of its internal structure and its external conditions. But our interest to control must not enter into our quest for knowledge; the theoretical disciplines represent our pure disinterested curiosity in knowing for its own sake.

We can, however, classify the theoretical disciplines with respect to their bearing upon the practical interest. We have noticed that the practical relation connects two distinct but closely analogous regions, the subjective and the objective, the cultural and the natural. The subjective represents the element of life, mind, thought, etc., together with the structures that embody their historical and traditional forms, and may be broadly designated the human. The objective is that element in the practical relation which refers to the outward, the external, the extra-human and self-subsistent, the latter including those objective forms which man's action has created, and may be called the "cosmic element."

Theoretical disciplines may, then, with respect to their practical bearing, be divided into (1) human disciplines and (2) cosmic disciplines. Each of these will have a double reference because of the two poles of the practical relation to which it refers. This is indicated above where a certain objectivity is attributed to both as a result of the peculiar nature of action. The human disciplines are (*a*) psychology-biology, (*b*) sociology-politics, (*c*) history-methodology, and (*d*) logic-metaphysics. The cosmic disciplines are (*w*) physics-chemistry, (*x*) biology-psychology, (*y*) natural history–evolution, and (*z*) mathematics-metaphysics.

If we now note the complexity of the scheme of knowledge, and in particular how all the specific theoretical sciences seem to be coupled together in pairs, we are reminded again that we are making the classification from the point of view of the practical relation, since the terms of each pair are the terms of a specific form of the practical relation. And from this viewpoint the distinction drawn between the cosmic and the human is better stated as that between the natural and the cultural. In these terms the distinction will have a place of importance throughout this discussion.

C. The Natural or Cosmic Disciplines

The natural disciplines are important, as we have seen, in the fact that they define and classify, and ultimately reduce to hypothesis or postulate, the object in the first form in which it appears in the practical relation. This object remains always some aspect of the natural world, the world of physical reality. Hence, our knowledge of the moral object will always refer back to a ground in physics and chemistry, biology and psychology. It is then a moral obligation to possess this knowledge. This aspect of physical reality is an object, or an objective, because it is that in which the practical relation has realized the form of a subjective motive; it is that in which bare life and mere mind are objectified. As thus objectified, life and mind have a status in reality; hence judgments about them may be universal and so true or false.

But it is in their aspect of "value" that ethics is concerned with these objects of nature. As objects of nature they constitute the structure and substance of the valued or worthy life. Regarded as such, their description and classification develop the presuppositions and principles of natural history and evolution. Developed in accordance with philosophical method in mathematics and metaphysics, these principles become the ultimate postulate of nature as the substance of reality. But this latter topic is one that carries beyond ethics proper into metaphysics. Since the description and "evaluation" of the characteristics of nature that are of direct ethical significance are included in later chapters, no further discussion is called for here. Their discussion is to be found in the chapters on the biological, psychological, economic, etc., aspects of the person and in those on the institutionalized form of the industrial process.

D. The Cultural Disciplines

The human or cultural disciplines, then, express our knowledge of the subjective and internal and immediate aspect of the practical relation, that character of the practical relation which makes it an "experience." They indicate the knowledge which must be necessary and adequate if the practical relation is to be complete and effective on its human or spiritual or cultural side. This is the side of meanings, or, in popular phrase, of "values." But since the existence and worth of meanings are taken for granted in every practical relation as the ultimate reason for action, as well as in the type of theoretical judgment which gives them expression, the proper theory of "values" consists in the formulation of the metaphysics by which the necessity of this judgment is adequately expressed as a hypothesis or a postulate. This gives to aesthetics, as the philosophy of values, a place co-ordinate to that of the philosophy of existence—physics. Then in the moral object existence and value will be ever present characters, characters of everything that is real, and the discussion of them is a branch of metaphysics. Ethics assumes all this, especially in the synthetic judgment which asserts the existence universally of values, thus recognizing the logical compossibility of value with existence and also recognizing its task as that of defining and classifying all types of "values." What is therefore important about the cultural disciplines is that they represent the whole career of life and mind in the world and give an account of the products of life and mind as the latter are objectified in the value systems of institutions. And the importance of ethics with respect to the cultural disciplines lies in the fact that it tries to show how that career can be given unity of meaning both in the world at large and in the life of the individual.

These cultural disciplines, or representative ones of them, will be taken up for separate description in another connection.

II. ETHICS AS PHILOSOPHY

We have noted that ethics is not a science in the ordinary acceptation of that term. It is a practical discipline, in that it is more concerned with the control of reality than with merely knowing it. Ethics, that is, presupposes the knowledge of the world in all its aspects. And as ethics has for its subject matter the nature and meaning of the practical relation as universally expressed in action, the varied aspects of the world and the knowledge that comprehends them will constitute, in the problem they set up as to the relation between the world and the knower as moral agent, the task of an ultimate philosophical synthesis. It is this that we mean when we say that ethics is a form of philosophy and not a science. It must demand an answer to the problem as to the character and significance of the relation between nature and culture and must show, if the relation is to be found real, how the two factors constitute a total world such as can be conceived by us as an end in which life and matter, nature and art, "value" and existence, are not contradictories.

That these systems of meanings are, as given, essential contradictories, that is, that they are, in the nature of things and as facts of ordinary experience, incompatibles and incompossibles, is just the situation that makes action necessary. But it is also that which makes action intelligible. We act because some aspect of our world does not fit into the scheme of purposes; nature and grace, worth and crude being, mutilate each other at every juncture in experience; and the fact that action never more than partially equates the idealities of purposes with the coarse realities of nature and of life is the reason that action is always and continuously necessary. The same fact becomes the pattern of the persistent form of existence for men. Men will persist in trying to believe that reality is consistent and whole and satisfactory for them, even while it is gnawing their vitals away; but this is due to their persistent tendency to attach a predestinate existence to their ideal forms and ends, their tendency to believe that they can realize an object by merely thinking or feeling about it, can speak an object into being. But the only basis upon which finally to assume the reality of an object in any case is that the object is the reality or realization of an act. Objects remain mere things of and in nature until transformed in and through action. Existence as mere nature persists in obstreperous unreality. Mind, value, as not yet objectified in nature, "exists" only as an ever disappearing phantom. Each, existence and value, in the absence of action, infects the other with negation. It is in and through the act that mind and nature, value and existence, find their realization in their appropriate object. The practical relation objectifies in the act, and the act becomes the subject substance for all ethical thinking.

Experience as moral then becomes the adventure in which the objective is to bring together in mutual support the knowledge function and the control function in such a way as to make the appearances of present experience real for experiences to come. The duplicity of our world of fact determines that this question, as a matter of *practice*, that is, of ethics, should take two forms. In the one, it is the question of the *logical* control of nature and culture by knowledge, and its method is the critical analysis of these two realms of nature and culture regarded as the substance of the external world. In the other, the question is one of the *practical* control of the two realms by wisdom, the two realms being regarded as the content and stuff of the objective world. Its method is that of speculative insight, the method that sets up its perceptions and reflections as postulates and realizes them, in part out of the process by which they are set up, in part out of the realities presented to it.

III. THE SUBJECT MATTER OF ETHICS

We have seen that ethics has to do at every point with the facts of action, that action is the content about which all its descriptions and explanations are made. Action is the universal moral phenomenon, and all the concepts of ethics relate directly or indirectly to it; all of them state some aspect of the meaning of action. Such concepts as right, good, wrong, bad, freedom, obligation, and responsibility derive their ethical meaning from the way they relate to the facts of the active life. Even the concepts of person, agent, character, with all their intimate references to the inner subjective life, are, so far as they are ethical concepts, derived from the relations and circumstances of action in which their meaning is determined. There are points of view, to be sure, from which it is proper to assume person, character, etc., as ultimate, and to consider acts as derived from them. Thus it is proper to say, psychologically, that the acts of a person arise from the motives, intentions, impulses, and urgencies that can perhaps always be found as antecedent to an act. But it is also true that these mental states are parts of the general situation of fact within which the act occurs, and, if explanation consists in nothing more than finding this factual basis, then the careful listing and description of the facts is adequate explanation.

But it is questionable whether such procedure is what is meant by explanation. In ethics in particular, and in value considerations generally, an explanation must state the significance of the fact explained, and it is precisely this significance, as a part of the nature of the fact, and as distinguished from the abstract meaning-reference relation between physical or operational or linguistic entities which have no being outside their verbal definition, which is the point of interest in the explanation. As a consequence the meaning of a fact is not contained in the description of its surrounding facts, nor of its relations to them. These may vary almost indefinitely while the significant fact remains the same. An act of generosity does not lose its characteristic meaning merely by a change in the immediate circumstances within which it is performed. And while it is true that circumstances do have some influence upon the quality of an act, the act remains in essence the same throughout changes in its external conditions.

Generosity remains good universally and in principle, even though attendant circumstances in a given case determine that its effects are evil. We are not as yet in position to decide the question finally, but we can anticipate the principle: The moral quality of the agent, and the quality in general of the immediate circumstances within which an act occurs, are determined from a consideration of the universal characters of the act. It is, for example, a man's acts that determine his character *in principle*, and not his character that determines his acts except in their particular, external, and superficial aspects and features. As in any "science" of values we are concerned with matters of principle or norm, the peculiar moral phenomenon will be discovered within the universal nature of the act considered as the ground of principle.

We must therefore reject any interpretation of moral fact which rests upon the particulars of mere circumstance. We must rather insist that circumstance is capable of generalization toward principle only when viewed as a characteristic aspect of a something apprehended as universal and that the meaning of circumstance can be determined only by its reference to principle. Let us keep this in mind while we call attention to a particularist interpretation of ethical fact which has been of extraordinary importance historically but which now appears to be no longer a useful intepretation in the case of the contemporary setup of fact. This is the assumption of traditional ethical theory that all ethical attributes and distinctions derive from the metaphysical nature of the person and, in concrete terms, that all the characteristic qualities of action are determined by the states of mind of the actor or agent. It is not intended to suggest that states of mind are not important in moral considerations. What is denied is that all or any important ethical significance is derived from them. And it is further asserted that the importance of mental states is itself dependent upon other considerations and is discovered to be of very relative degree when compared with that of other facts.

Ethical and moral distinctions therefore depend not upon our states of mind but upon the independent fact of action. The same act may be adjudged good when regarded as the consequence of very different states of mind. It is good objectively and universally, and not relatively to the states of mind that precede or accompany it, *if it is good.* Saving a man from drowning is a good act even though done in malice, and it is not made good by being done from love or pity. States of mind in themselves have no inherent moral quality, even though it be true that there is no good in the absence of states of mind. The relation of states of mind to the moral quality is not one of cause or determining condition. There is no state of mind which by itself can determine the moral significance of any situation, even though it be true in a given case that the moral significance is itself a character of the state of mind involved in the situation. Morality is a matter of the nature and structure and relation and quality of objective fact, of the fact of action, within which all distinctions, including those of states of mind and their qualities, are to be discovered. It is the task of ethics as moral philosophy to lay bare this nature, structure, relations, and quality of those objective fact systems within which the moral quality appears.

Chapter II

The Analysis of Action

ACTION, then, is the fact which we have to investigate. It is the act, both in its general sense and as concrete fact, that is to be understood in the study of ethics. The fact of action is the whole subject of investigation. All the concepts and terms we may use in the investigation will get their meaning from their relation to action.

The practical relation, then, as universal, is the relation between nature and culture. When stated in its individual meaning, and in terms of experience, it has its instance in the act of a conscious individual. It is the generalized form of the relation of mind to its object under the peculiar conditions of control. In the concrete particular it is the expression of the unique relation of an individual to the circumstances that environ him, or the "response" of a person or agent to his environment. It is an instance of the kind of phenomena which make up the individual's conduct when conduct refers to the bearing of the agent upon his environment throughout his lifetime. By an act, in its simplest perceptual sense, we mean the fact situation referred to in the ordinary use of the word. But, when we come to make the fact situation usable for purposes of explanation, it must be restated in terms of a general definition. Considered as a definition, we may say then: An act is the assumption of the possibility of a real relation between a person and his world. Or an act is the assumption that a relation, created by and existing only in the contemplation, can be realized as a fixed objective bond between the agent and his world.

An act assumes, then, that a relation that is now only possible in the sense that it exists as a plan within a mind can be made real and fully expressed within the world beyond the mind. Or an act means that an object, which exists now only abstractly in the conditions and qualities out of which it can be produced, may be made to exist as the realization of these conditions. These definitions mean the same, and their differences of statement are due to the fact that they refer to the same facts from different viewpoints. In the first, for example, the door is closed now. As the opened door it exists for me now only in idea or plan, and its existence as fully real and objective depends upon the supposition that certain objective conditions will appear in the future. As such the opened door is what I take for granted or previse in plan when I venture to make certain movements, viz., those of walking across the floor and turning the handle; through these movements this plan becomes a realized consequence in the opened door as fact. In the second statement a pair of bookends lie in abstract possibility in the board before me, and their becoming realized is the meaning of the act that produces them in fact. The act as the mere plan or as projected in my mind is the assumption that the bookends can be made actual on my table. Later we shall see that it is only while the act is in this ideal form, and only so long and so far as it remains ideal, that it can be said to be subject to control; and the fact that the act can be controlled only before it exists will make complications for us on several occasions.

By these definitions we distinguish the mere potential act of the plan, which is ordinarily called the "act" of thought, or the "idea," sometimes the "purpose" or "intention," from the act properly and strictly so called. Thus action is distinguished from thought through the fact that the act presupposes a real, that is, an objective, overt, public relation, while thought contemplates a relation that is ideal and exists only in the symbols by which it is represented. It is true that thought objectifies its relations and conditions in the "act" of think-ing, but it objectifies them on a basis of ideal possibilities and in ab-stractly logical and universal terms. Its significance for us lies merely in leading us to see that, logically, there is a fundamental difference between thinking and action and that the one cannot be reduced to the other. Yet action and thought are identified in the object which is the objective of both. It is thus only in a figurative sense that we may speak of an act of thought, if action is to be taken in the usual sense as referring to changes in the real external world. In the genuine prac-tical act the ideal relation at its basis is realized in the sense that it is embodied or incorporated in an object for which it is an appropriate structure and thus becomes a permanent feature of the world.

Action thus always implies changed conditions in the world of cir-cumstance as the demonstration that it is real, and any falling-short of this effective change brands the act as ideal and at best only the ex-pression of a plan or an empty setup of mental states. The relation as ideal or objectified in thought can exist thus only as a plan, only as a projected and anticipated structure, and as lacking appropriate ex-

ternal or physical objects for its complete expression. It is characteristic of action considered as the ultimate moral fact that it must have
this overt objective expression, that it incorporate and embody itself
as a part of the stable world. It is this reference to the real world that
constitutes the meaning or value of an act. The facts of action, and
the objective conditions under which action has meaning, constitute
the whole field of ethical discussion. Every concept and every term
that is necessary to the discussion of morality, including terms and
concepts which directly implicate mental states, have their meaning
in their reference to the act, and the act has meaning only as it is
realized in objects. The subject matter of ethics is therefore extremely
complex, as can be shown by an example.

A man stands on the street corner waiting for an approaching street-
car. The car is coming at its usual rate of speed a block away, when
suddenly a child runs onto the track directly in front of the car. The
car is close upon the child, and the man sees that in all probability it
will be crushed to death before he can intervene to save it. Let us
suppose that he nevertheless makes the effort. He reaches the child
just in time to toss it off the track when he is himself caught and both
his legs crushed off. The man, let us say, is a very competent railroad
trainman, and it is because of his competence and his alertness in this
peculiar work that his value as a person lies, and it is his competence
that enables him to save the child. He has been working in his present
position only a short time, not long enough to take advantage of the
insurance scheme his employer has established. He goes to a hospital,
where he remains for several months under the care of expensive sur-
geons. His peculiar capacity, the ability to perform the duties he has
especially fitted himself for, is now gone. His savings are spent, and
he has a wife and two small children. On the other hand, the child
whom he saved is the child of dissolute parents who allow it to grow
up without the ordinary care, and it has perhaps not only picked up
ineradicable moral habits from its gutter associates but is also physically diseased, so that it is almost a foregone conclusion that it could
never grow up to competent manhood.

Now, this setup of circumstance is typical of the experience of all
of us every day. It is true that we are not generally aware of the far-
reaching consequences of the ordinary occurrences of our everyday
experience; but the consequences are there nevertheless, and our example differs from the ordinary only in that events which would in
most cases be drawn out over a stretch of years occur in rapid succession and in a few moments. But the long process through which

the child in the gutter is passing to complete moral and physical disability is just as sure and as easily observable as the quicker process by which the man loses his legs. The conditions of the child's moral disintegration and of the man's mutilation are always present and imminent. In any case both the child and the man are brought to a condition of complete incompetence, the one of them because of the bad general conditions in which he is being brought up, and the other in part perhaps because of the very goodness of his character and circumstances of his past life. For we may attribute the heroic act of the man to quick moral sensitivity which he acquired as a child from cultivated parents and favorable conditions, just as we may attribute the child's carelessness to his lack of training and the untoward conditions surrounding his home.

But suppose we should now undertake to discuss the "right and wrong" of the situation above described. That is, we pass from facts to their interpretation or meaning. We should perhaps agree at once that the act of the man was right, for, we assume, it must always be right to save life regardless of the type or quality of that life. We should agree also that it is wrong that the child was permitted to roam the streets or that it was allowed to grow up without restraint or training. But the child's parents both work or are perhaps dead. Or they may be drunk, never themselves having had a decent training. But the man's act in saving the child was noble, we assume, even though the result is the bringing to an end of his own competence. The man will now himself be obliged to see his own children grow up without proper care and training, for he can no longer support them or send them to school. We seem to be quite certain as to the right and wrong in this kind of situation until we begin to ask questions, and then our certainty vanishes. The man did a good deed, but all or most of the consequences were bad. He did it out of good will, we say, and acts done from good will must always be good. But it is not certain that he does the act from good will; he may have done it from malice or hatred or for a reward. And these motives do not necessarily issue in good acts and are supposed generally not to.

How much do we know about such situations? When we start tracing the connections of the various elements in the situation, where should we stop? If we find that the child is defective because of the dissolute life of its grandfather, how much should that fact weigh in our attempt to estimate the right and wrong of the question? And if we find, as we shall, the questions about personal characters and capacities become inextricably confused with problems of social relations, what is to be our standard of judgment? For example, is it the child's bad habits, or his bad heredity, or the bad social conditions in which he lives which should determine our judgment? Can we assume that, in general, we already know the distinction between the right and the wrong, that is, we know the principle by which we determine the nature and status of acts, and that a knowledge of right and wrong in this sense is a common possession of every rational being? If we can assume this, we shall all of us give the same answer to the question— the man performed a heroic act, let us say, for it is always good to save life.

But let us change the circumstances a little and say that the man and the child were both killed. Then we must amend our judgment to say that it is the will or the attempt to save life that is uniformly good. But then assume that the man saved the child (or tried to) for the sake of a Carnegie hero medal. Or he did it through vanity or to obligate the child's parents to himself. Or, perhaps, there was no *reason* or conscious motive at all for his act; he did it for the same reason that he smokes a cigar after dinner or laughs at a cripple who hobbles down the street. All we seem to know about an ethical situation is that something somewhere is right (or wrong); what and where the right or wrong is we do not know.

All our ready answers to the question of good and bad, right and wrong, etc., may turn out to be quite useless as explanations of the facts of human action; and, when we consider the complexity and confusion of human relations at the present moment, we may well fear that we know very little about them. For it is quite evident to anyone who thinks at all that the relations of men to each other, whether moral, social, industrial—and all these are moral and practical—are in a very unsatisfactory condition, are very imperfectly understood, and that some way should be found by which the conditions of active life could be altered. That is to say, it may very well be that the facts involving action are too complicated and intricate for the ready application of any of our standards. And it may be that our terms "good," "bad," "right," etc., are not applicable to specific situations at all but only to large social or cultural conditions, or possibly only to hypothetical states of mind of the actor at the moment of action. Perhaps right, for example, has no meaning for a specific case of action but has meaning only in the way of a principle by which the one who judges of action makes up his mind or determines the attitude from which his judgment is to proceed.

Let us here return to our illustration and examine the case with three considerations in mind: (1) this sort of situation as illustrative of much of the life of the ordinary man is very important; (2) our ready-made solutions to the problems involved do not indicate that we know much about it, do not understand what it means; and (3) common knowledge and ethical theory help us little in such situations.

1. The importance of such a situation does not lie in its rarity, for it is really typical of the fact situations in which the average person lives, though perhaps a little more spectacular than the ordinary. A man may have a habit of driving too fast; ordinarily we think little about it, but he and others are nevertheless in constant danger just as serious as that which threatens the child on the car tracks. Or a young woman may tolerate an improper suggestion from her escort and treat it as a joke; but in reality the impulse to tolerate such a suggestion is as charged with disaster as a physical threat to life, and the quality of the suggestion is not changed merely by the fact that it is never realized or that its consequences are deferred. That such situations are vital in the life of the individual is obvious; but what we do not clearly see is that they have a large part in determining the form and structure of society as the permanent condition within which persons will have their only opportunity to act.

2. The same is true of the second consideration. We really know very little about the more important types of conduct and equally little about the conditions in nature and culture upon a knowledge of which their interpretation or meaning depends. It is true of course that our knowledge of the nature of life and conduct and the world we live in is significant and increasing every day. But it is for the most part technical knowledge, knowledge designed to aid us in the achievement of specialized "practical" purposes; that is to say, a knowledge of situations which are narrowed and specialized to the point of almost total misrepresentation, and a knowledge which might give us the broader insight from which we may hope to reach a comprehensive view of our larger purposes is almost totally absent. As a consequence we appear to have become convinced that moral judgments merely refer to the fitness of our actions to the accomplishment of our narrow individual ends, this fitness being determined in terms of our own individual impressions and convictions, with no regard as to whether the ends are objectively worthy or otherwise. Or, if we consider the question of the worthiness of our ends, we tend to decide it on the theory that that is worthy which satisfies our desires or otherwise supplies us with what we want. And in this case what we consider ourselves to need, or what we want, however noble and

unselfish and generous, is yet some object which has meaning only in terms of individual states of mind, our own or someone else's. Whether our "wants" or "needs" are themselves justifiable we seldom inquire, and when we do consider the question we usually answer it on the principle that what we want is justified by the fact that we want it. But on such a principle no morality of any kind is possible at all, as has been demonstrated by our contemporary commercial system.

Most modern ethical theory proceeds on the assumption that the secret of the nature of an act can be discovered by investigation into the inner consciousness and "will" of the individual actor, so that ethical reflection has given way to psychological description. Even where the "results" of action are made the criterion, the results are themselves referred for their moral significance to the subjective estimate of an interested individual. But we begin to see that on this principle of subjective individualism no morality is possible; no basic ethical judgment can be derived from the distinction of one man from another, even the "good" man from the "bad." More recently the opposite method of social investigation has taken the place of psychological discussion. But this social method does not seem to be essentially different, since the social body is treated merely as a collection of individuals. The moral quality does not derive from the mere numerical complexity of human relations.

3. So that, even in those cases where we make serious effort to resolve the problems of our conduct, it can be questioned whether the presuppositions and concepts of ethical theory to which we resort are not misleading or possibly false. If we take as an instance the famous theoretical question as to whether the moral quality of an act is determined by the "motives" or "intentions" of the actor or by the "results" of the act, it seems possible to show that an ordinary act, such as we perform every day, is not fully comprehensible in such terms at all. Nor does any doctrine of "conscience" better withstand criticism, for it seems not always possible to determine exactly what the motives or intentions of a given act are, and there is often no way of showing that a given event is the necessary result of the act which it follows. Nor are the pronouncements of conscience always consistent, and sometimes they are not even intelligible. And on grounds of general theory it is necessary to assume that an act and its object are not related as cause and effect, so that prediction of results is not possible. Yet the knowledge of results is useful only when it can be had before

action takes place and before the results exist if the act is to be under control.

It may therefore very well be that our "convictions," which represent, on the whole, mere social precipitations of old ethical theories, give us really no insight into problems of conduct but merely serve to confuse our minds with respect to the very things upon which our ideas should be clearest. It appears then, that for experimental purposes at least, we might profitably approach the facts of our life-activities directly as we know them and ignore, in so far as may be possible, both the stagnant formulas of historical or traditional theory on the one side and the rather too scientifically abstract but bumptiously confident pronouncements of recent ethical theorizing on the other. Perhaps Plato and Aristotle may after all be the safest guides; we may appeal also to our own good sense, recognizing the precarious existence of such a function and the risks involved in its knowing itself when appealed to.

So we come back to the facts and to the meanings which we can derive from them by direct observation. From the point of view of ordinary common sense, the primary and original fact in any question of human life and human relations is the fact of *action* itself. Men act, and this fact is so important that it may be regarded as the basis of all the distinctions that may be found necessary for the theory that morality requires. Just what is involved in these distinctions, how, for example, an act differs from an instance of fact which we characterize as mere movement, is a question which involves the most difficult theoretical analysis. There is a sense in which it is true that the distinction of action from movement involves all the real differences in the world. In any case, the rest of what follows in this book may be looked upon as an attempt to explain action, this attempt being, for us, the special task of ethical theory. This fact of an ultimate difference between action and movement finally disposes of any claims to a causal ethics or to the assumption that an adequate ethics can be constructed upon a basis of scientific presuppositions. An act is not a caused event, nor is it as such the cause of any event; it is not a cause in any sense at all, although it includes or implies causes in every case. If acts or their issues were caused events, there could be no meaning attached to control in the sense required in morality. The relations of action to caused events is one of the standing problems of metaphysics. The nature of an act can then only be approached by logical or speculative methods, by inferences based upon the systems of derivative categories which are necessary to make the concept of an act intelligible. The study of ethics then is the study of the meanings of such concepts, such, for example, as agent, end, purpose, good, right, etc., all of which have been found necessary to make the notion of an act intelligible. The act is not a mere perceptible fact; its presence and essential nature must be inferred from presented movement situations and the conceptual reference which each situation involves. This makes logic the ultimate method of explanation in ethics. This we shall illustrate.

The fact that the man in our illustration accepted a course of action which involved the possibility of danger and injury to himself means for him—whether consciously or not at the time of the event does not here concern us—that some things are preferred to others. This implies that events in themselves have meaning, that meanings may be distinguished on a scale of relative worth, and that a selection of grades or degrees of worth may be made with respect to purposes, where purposes connect once more with objective situations. That is, we can pass from an act to its interpretation and remain on strictly objective ground all the way. This objective idea of worth and the preference based upon it is the logical ground of meaning for the concept of end. We shall not stop here to examine all the implications which this involves. But the fact that anyone, or in any case competent persons, would have acted in the same way in the presence of the same circumstances means that, in general, some things are in themselves preferable to others. They are objectively preferable in the sense that their distinction and acceptance depend on inherent qualities, qualities which have their unique characters not in their mere attribution to an abstract mind or thing or "substance" but as inhering in such a thing considered as a material presupposition of an act. We do not act because we prefer; we prefer because we act, since the act in ideal plan or design is the basis of the distinction of objects upon which the preference depends. Action is the ground of preference. This indefinite fact, that people do prefer some things to others as a consequence of active life, becomes refined, by processes we need not here inquire into, to the status of the principle of distinction between the *good* and the *bad*. Good and bad, that is, are, as judgments, products of the act of distinction in preference, where preference itself rests on the design of an object, and refer for their objectivity and their truth to the characters and relations of the object involved in the preference.

Also, the fact that we persist in our preferences and maintain the distinction between good and bad means that the distinction is objective and thus can be, or is believed to be capable of being made, ultimate and permanent. That is, there is implied also the *end* as the objective ground of preference and as that which makes all our "goods" of the same type, or furnishes a criterion for the evaluation of goods. That which gives to the concept end its meaning is, then, the logical necessity of a ground concept to which all terms which express essential or relational aspects of action can be referred. As a logical ultimate it is necessitated or postulated by the fact of action.

So also the persistence of the distinction between preferred objects to the point of involving ends means that the multiplicities of acts are unified in the concept of actor or agent in the same necessary way that goods are unified in end, and this unification of acts becomes generalized into the common notion of *person*. But it is clear that the act does not get its intelligibility from its reference to the person— the person rather gets its meaning from the act, is a logical derivative from the fact of action.

So all the meaning that we require for "person" at this stage is the fact that the concept serves to enable us perceptually and imaginally to envisage a point of view from which acts can be consistently thought about, just as end gave us conceptually such a point of view; that is, "person" furnishes us with a subject to which we may refer judgments which express the meanings of acts. But its relational ground is logical and not factual. For these judgments are, as such, objective and ideal universal acts, acts which do not require specific reference to, or inherence in, any designatable point of reference; they are, that is, judgments whose internal meanings are their own objects. Such judgments require a specifiable subject therefore only when their pragmatic relations to other judgments are in question. For other and merely descriptive purposes later "person" will be found to mean something much different from this. But here what we require is a logical device which will show that acts are substantive events, so that "objective" judgments may be made about them. Extension and refinement of these elementary concepts of end and person in their derivative relations to action give us the derivative and methodological notions of "right," "wrong," "motive," "intention," "purpose," "ideal," "means," etc. And a more profound analysis of the concept of end results in the formulation and postulation of other more speculative ideas like "object," "objective," "good," "bad," "means," "world," "the good," etc.

But persons, ends, and acts, the latter being the fact from which the other two are derived by implication, are the simple and elementary concepts at the basis of all our thought about conduct. The rest of the concepts used or useful ethically are derived from them, and their function is to render the original concepts clear for specific kinds of circumstances and situations of thought and life.

We shall find that it is the problem of theoretical ethics to make these ideas clear in their relations to each other so as to show that they form a system consistent enough to satisfy the intelligence and to interpret the meanings of the ideas in connection with the facts presented to us by a world which makes the demands upon us that our actions are in practice designed to satisfy. It is necessary, however, in the interest of being sure that our thinking shall remain close to the requirements of experience, that we undertake to state as clearly as possible what are the fundamental assumptions that the facts of action require us to recognize. This is the task of the next chapter.

There is, however, one further characteristic of action which it is desirable to consider here. It is generally assumed that ethics deals in some exclusive way with the good, that the good is the whole content of ethical discussion. And we have spoken of the life of action as the good life and have defined ethics as the "science" of action. Then apparently, if these statements are consistent, there must be some sort of identity between action and the good. But if by "the Good Life," considered as an ultimate object, we mean the active life-system as embodied in an appropriate world, then goodness, as the quality attaching to individual acts, will refer to that feature of the act by which it is related to the whole and by which it is known as a constituent of the whole incorporate life-system. The goodness of an act is just this quality in it by and through which the act is given a place and function in the total life-system, and the question of the presence or absence of this quality in connection with a given act may become one of extraordinary importance and difficulty because of the lack of knowledge of the total life-world. It is the complexity and intricacy of this life-world relation which makes the morality of a given act so extremely difficult on occasion to determine. And it is our almost total ignorance of some aspects of this relation that makes many of our acts appear to be leaps in the dark, and it is the imperfection of all our knowledge, even the most "scientific," an imperfection which cannot perhaps be overcome, that makes all our acts exhibit the character of adventure.

Chapter III

Implications of the Facts of Action

THE previous chapter has shown us that, in order to describe the facts of action, we had to make use of a number of terms which are in common use in the discussion of questions of conduct. It appeared also that many of the difficulties of the discussion arise from the fact that these commonly used terms are not clearly defined and thus involve us in many kinds of ambiguity. It was suggested that the working-out of consistent meanings for the system of concepts which are found necessary in developing a consistent account of action and in tracing the relations in which action is involved would give us all the theory that an elementary discussion of morality would require. We are, in this chapter and the next, concerned therefore with the task of describing these elementary conceptions and of pointing out some of their more elementary relations. We shall discuss as theoretical concepts (A) person, (B) world, and (C) the relation of person to world. And under each of these heads it will be necessary to make clear a number of subordinate conceptions. Also, as practical concepts or concepts of practice, we shall in the following chapter describe freedom, obligation, and the good life and will find a number of subordinate ideas under each of these heads that will require comment. The system of all these conceptions as expressed through a statement of their logical relationships will constitute what for us is ethical theory.

I. THEORETICAL CONCEPTS OR CONCEPTS OF FACT
A. Person

In the causal and mechanical terms in which it is commonly described person means that center of energy and purpose out of which an act issues. It is taken as an existing fact, and the perception of it is regarded as furnishing all the explanation that could be required. But a little reflection will show that the person is not fully represented when it is treated as merely the cause of acts, since no connection between the act as an overt fact and the "will" which is supposed to cause it can be observed. It would be better therefore, if we had to restrict ourselves to the causal point of view, to define person as that which enables us to conceive and describe an act in terms of its origin, since acts do not have their beginnings within the facts of observation. If we stick to causes, we must remember that a cause can never be observed to be the producer or originator of an act, so that, if it is action we wish to understand, we shall have to give up causes and try to find an explanation of action in some other idea.

We have already seen in the preceding chapter that the description of the nature of the person does not explain the moral quality of the act, as the causal theory seems to imply. What is truer to the facts of experience is that the act explains the person, that the concept of person gets its meaning from the nature and character of actions. The act is taken as an original fact, itself the source of description of the person, while it itself is not conceived to be derived from any source. It is the starting point of all explanation. The human being then is not a moral agent because he is an object of perception and a physical phenomenon. His morality is derived from his action, not his being. The concept of person is not simple and is perhaps the more confused in that it bulks large in traditional theory. The theory of the person as we have inherited it from the past centuries presupposes an entity whose being and character are immediately known and, as known, can be taken as the basis of explanation of all the concepts necessary in the discussion of morality. All explanations of the nature of the person refer, that is, to its own internal and exclusive characters; and not only this but all questions of the nature of the relations that persons normally stand in are settled by a reference to the supposed inner and unique nature of the person. The theory has many ways of describing this supposed inner nature, but most of them depend upon and emphasize its negative characteristics. The person is a distinct, unique, exclusive being, that is, it is what it is by virtue of not being something else or of being different from other things. But it is a principle of logic that a thing cannot be represented in terms of what it is not.

This method of representing the person through specialized and negative characters developed some very interesting types of theory in ethics, and these theories were partly successful in formulating the major problems that arise out of the facts of action. Since they all depend upon a negative viewpoint, they are all analytic in method and quantitative in results; hence they give us only a limited view of

the whole nature of the person. We shall here review some of them
briefly.

I. THE PERSON AS MENTAL STATE OR MENTAL CAUSE

Thus the fundamental problems of right, good, justice, etc., were,
in traditional theory, problems of finding and describing specific
types of inner character of the person—an experience—and this inner
experience was always found to be some characteristic or capacity
which was exclusive and peculiar to the individual. It was a "voice"
of reason, of God, or of conscience, or some specific type of pleasure
or "sense" which only the individual person involved could experience or exercise or understand. But it was represented as that which
originates acts. This as a rule divided ethicists into rationalists and
empiricists, depending on what type of mental state was regarded as
cause, and ethical theory seldom advanced beyond the descriptive
account of mental states. But, as mental states are as such instable, the
accounts showed great variation. All the types of ethical theory,
since they derive all explanation from the inner essence of the person,
must find the reality of the person in some sort of state of mind. But
on this assumption of the inner nature of the person as its basic concept, theory was limited to investigations in epistemology and psychology, and its method was analytic and descriptive. The problem
of obligation, for example, was pictured as one of finding an experience, preferably a feeling, which was unique among experiences in
just the capacity to make the actor take his duty seriously. In any
case obligation was nothing more than a very special feeling that
could be found, in the case of the person who had it, by methods of
psychological observation. And, since it could only be "found," its
nature was a mystery, and the theorist had to be content with describing it; it could not be explained. We shall see that obligation has
a logical, not a psychological, ground.

With such a view as to the nature of the person it is not surprising
that ethical thought frequently tended toward skepticism, in one
direction, or to mysticism in the other. The fallacy behind all the
different types of theory is the presupposition of the exclusive and
unique person with a mystical, or a causal, theory of the nature of an
act. The person was something which could exist by itself and could
be known only through its own inherent nature. The act of the person
could have no explanation except that which consists merely in pointing out its origin in the mystic depths of the person, and these mystical depths were generally personified and set up as some kind of

self-originated being which was designated as will, the peculiar characters of which were the inexplicable powers of spontaneity and freedom. It is this mystification of the idea of the person that is responsible for most of the difficulties of ethical theory and for much of the confusion of moral practice. In other words, it is "individualism" in ethics that is the basis of nearly all its fallacies; even the mystical notion of an act that flows autonomously out of the inwardness of the "agent" is due to the assumption of the unique individual.

But it is evident that right, obligation, and the other fundamental concepts are meaningless when stated in such terms as individualist theory proposes. It is not a question of whether a being has or does not have within his own nature a "capacity" for action or for right or for obligation, or whether he has or has not an experience of some specific kind. In any case it is not a question as to whether an individual has or has not, or is or is not, a particular kind of mental state; it is only indirectly a question of mental states at all; right, obligation, etc., cannot be expressed in such subjective mysteries. It is a question rather of what these notions mean in terms of the actualities of fact in the world that is there before us and in our relations to that world; what facts there are for all of us to see, which can give these terms meaning, and by and upon which our experiences would appear to be occasioned. It is a very large part of any competent discussion of the problems of ethics to explain the relations of the fundamental concepts of morality to these outward facts of nature and culture, for they get their meaning primarily from these natural and cultural objects and relations. And these relations are not intelligible when stated in terms merely of the individual or of collections of individuals and certainly not in terms of the individual's mental states alone. They are intelligible only when regarded as elements of the structure of the world, and regarding them in this way is metaphysics. We shall have to come back to this question again and again.

2. THE PERSON AS PHYSICAL CAUSE

But attempts to avoid an ethics based upon the supposed unique individual and his mental states have generally not been successful. It may therefore be worth while at this point to notice how important previous attempts to recognize the objective nature of ethical facts and relations have gone astray. These attempts fall into two sorts: (*a*) naturalism and (*b*) utilitarianism. We shall try to show that both fail, but by different kinds of attempts to rationalize the same mistake.

And we are here interested only in their treatment of the moral person.

a) *Naturalism.*—The mistake that both theories make is in assuming that the person is primarily a physical cause. For naturalism the causation of the person is directed toward the "preservation of the race" in its essential expression and, incidentally, toward the "self-preservation" of the individual. In the first the method is primarily an appeal to biology, and the person or agent is supposed to be explained, and his moral characters determined, when his place in the class or series of his species has been located and described in terms of organic capacities. The individual is thus a cause with reference to the species, in that his filling the place in the series makes the species a unity or whole and thus intelligible. The species would fall apart if one element were removed, so the individual is the necessary "link" which causally binds the species into an effective whole. This conception of species organization becomes the major concept of moral or "social" order, and on this principle is developed the "organic" theory of society.

Naturalism is thus a fruitful and interesting viewpoint in many ways; it emphasizes the fact that the person as an individual is a causal agent and has a cosmic or world place. But it mistakes in conceiving this place as that of merely a material or physical block in the system, an instance of causal energy whose sole purpose is merely to hold itself or the whole together. Naturalism has also done a lot of very useful work in the analysis of elementary fact, the facts upon which ethical distinctions finally depend, and to this extent its results are all true as far as scientific results can be true; it errs only when it insists that the causal or natural efficiency of the person is the essential and only basis of its ethical nature. This means, of course, that a genuine ethical system is not possible at all for any naturalistic theory. Naturalism stops just this side of the field where ethical principle normally holds. And this makes obvious the fact that ethics is not a science.

b) *Utilitarianism.*—This second type of interpretation of the person as physical cause makes a similar mistake. For it the person's moral nature is disclosed in the kind of effect he can produce in objective facts; that is, the person's morality is judged by types of changes he can make in the environing circumstance, the environment being conceived broadly as including the mental life of the agent with that of his fellows. It has thus and for this reason been the most potent, and in many ways the most beneficial, reform movement in the history of mankind. It has seized upon this basic truth: The good of man lies largely outside himself within the environing circumstance from and out of which he must make his destiny. But its mistake lies in having given a narrow and superficial meaning to this outer world. It has assumed that (1) this world is made up for the most part, and altogether as far as ethics is concerned, of physical or material and psychological things and that (2) these things and their moral quality can be properly judged only by some assumed unique relation they have to specific mental states.

The first assumption, while definitely limited, has, historically, been very successful. It has given us the "industrial age" with the myriads of tools and "conveniences" which have made life for us, in prospect and possibility, at least, easy and comfortable. And this has been a very great boon, or will turn out to be, when we have understood it and have learned its real moral significance, viz., that this world of things constitutes merely the basis in mechanism upon which all real moral goods are to stand. But the second assumption is wrong. The significance of these mechanical and physical facts upon which life is based does not lie in their relation to specific mental states or to mental states at all. It is this assumption that has transformed the industrial age into the commercial age and has plunged the practical life into chaos. As against this standpoint, it is not the primary purpose, for example, of the wheat we produce, that it should be made into bread in order to give us either physical energy or the mental state of satisfaction of hunger. The satisfaction is not the end at which the act is aimed, nor is any mental state the end of any act, for such "states" are of the nature of processes and cannot be ends. For under the influence of that satisfaction men will not work, so the idea of mental states as ends of acts is self-contradictory. It is not the moral purpose of the automobile to give us the thrill of moving fast; in that way lies danger. We do not yet know what the automobile is morally good for; hence we say it has no moral purpose but only an economic purpose and is thus made to sell and to thrill and kill people. Thus we see the weakness of utilitarianism. It is a practical contradiction—its acts work out to an end which negates the intent out of which the act is supposed to arise. But both naturalism and utilitarianism are right in so far as they see clearly that the foundation of morality is laid down solidly in the facts of the external world by the co-operation of the forces of nature and of culture. Both fail when they undertake to build on that foundation. So traditional theory has no adequate concept of the person.

B. The World as an Ethical Postulate

It is this solid foundation of life as laid down in the facts and systems of nature and the institutions of culture that we call the moral world. This idea of the world as an object and instrument of thought is co-ordinate in meaning and importance with that of the person. Both ideas are implicates of the fact of action. But the idea of the world as a basic ethical concept has either been neglected by ethical thought or has been misunderstood. It must therefore, before we are through with it, be explained in detail, and its various directions of ethical meaning and influence must be brought out. But its three general characteristics are what we are interested in here. These three characteristics are the basis of the objective features of action, and we must keep in mind that here we are engaged in laying bare the implications of the facts of action. The three universal facts of action, from the point of view of the external world upon which action depends, are (1) the world as stage for action, (2) the world as instrument of action, and (3) the world as the corporate whole or end of action. We must briefly explain each of these in turn.

1. THE WORLD AS THE STAGE FOR ACTION

The "natural" "origin" of man means, as an ethical fact, that he is by his own constitution already fitted into the scheme of physical nature from the beginning, and this means that every human action of whatever sort rests upon a foundation of natural conditions. That is, action rests upon a physical basis in the facts of the natural environment; but it also means that it rests upon a presupposition of natural conditions in the logical sense that, if one is going to think about it or describe it or theorize about it, one must recognize these natural conditions as fixed element of fact to which his thinking must conform. Action, therefore, in any sense of the term, presupposes a world as the place where it happens and further assumes that this place of action is objective and overt to the thinker as well as to the actor. The world must therefore be taken as given in the external natural and cultural circumstances; and, while the existence of change and growth within these circumstances has equally to be recognized, the change and growth must be recognized as also fixed characters of the given or ordered world. There is a sense therefore in which every act presupposes that the world will remain what it is relatively to the act, will remain what it is while the act is in process. In the absence of this presupposition an act can hardly be conceived. This fact would seem so obvious that it is hardly worth mentioning; but it is, after all, an important part of the most distressing fallacy that has beset ethical thinking throughout its history.

While it is true that the world in which an act takes place is one of change and growth and process, this change and process are only of the circumstance and not of the substance of the act. The act is effected within and through movements at every step, but the movements are accidental and instrumental to the act, which has its substance in the unity and identity with its appropriate object in an end. That is to say, the movement which lies at the basis of an act is not of the nature of a process, although it contains processes within it. The essential difference is that the process is an instance of infinite continuity and can have no end either in the sense of a limit or of that which gives it wholeness of meaning. The movement which constitutes an act, on the other hand, has its meaning at every step in the end in which it consummates; its end is present throughout as that which makes it possible for the act to embody or objectify itself. The end is there at the beginning in the plan which gives direction to the movement, and it is there as the ordered whole which defines the object in which the act is completed.

Evolutionary and scientific theories almost invariably fall into this fallacy of process: they confuse the process of action with its substance. This is closely related to the mistake of assuming that all ethical reality is a matter of mental "states," which are, of course, mental processes. Every moral situation involves action, and this action must be real; it must, that is, realize itself in the overt and objective facts of nature and culture, and any condition that falls short of this realization is a "mere" idea or state of mind, an empty and meaningless "good" intention. Moral action, then, and all action in the strict sense is moral, *takes place*, that is, realizes itself in the world that is the common stage for all moral agents. And this must be kept in mind for both factual and theoretical considerations; it must not be neglected at any point in ethical thinking or practice. The "idealism" which can define action in pure "spiritual" terms is mere superstition.

2. THE WORLD AS INSTRUMENT OF ACTION

The world is just as necessary, as a moral fact and presupposition, when we think of it as the instrument through which action is accomplished. It seems trivial to say this. Yet we all unconsciously take it for granted that the more important types of moral action are not instrumented by physical and cultural things but that they can somehow be negotiated without the intervention of these external things. As a matter of fact most of us, when we undertake to observe or reflect upon our morality, tend to ignore the more basic natural conditions of our lives, even developing a contempt for them when they refuse, as they always do, to be overlooked. We then find the "things of the world" a hindrance or obstacle to the good life, and we attempt either to overlook and ignore them or to despise them and disallow them a place in the good life. We assume as a matter of fact that a crippled or diseased man, or a poor man or a hungry man, may be as "good" as a man with a sound body and equipped with the material means, property, etc., to action. For is not his heart right, his motives good? We do not question the morality of a man with a wooden leg, or with consumption, or one who is temporarily drunk; we say that these are physical misfortunes and that the man's character is not, or need not be, influenced by them. But this is true only on the assumption that character is some mysterious spiritual entity and no part of the natural man; or, we assume that the natural man and his capacities are no part of the ethical man; or we say that the real man is his character but that his character is ideal and has nothing to do with such facts as wooden legs and disease and poverty. But these reflections of ours turn out to be contradictory when we look at them closely, and in confusion we confess, if we are honest, that we do not know what we mean when we talk of goodness and character, etc., in the absence of the conditions through which the acts may be performed by which character and goodness are realized.

But it is necessary that we see this question in its larger aspects. It is obvious, when we come to think of it, that morality involves things as instruments, external material and cultural things, that is, just as much, and as significantly, as it involves characters and intentions and mental states. In fact, we know, once we think of it, that our mental states, our right heart, our good motives, etc., are of little moral consequence except as they are somehow correlated into ordered wholes and given objective expression in things, for it is only as such ordered masses of things that they can be made effective in any way. Even a spiritual influence must become external, must be made flesh and dwell among us and assume a form within the world of things if it is to be effective; it must have a body even if a "body spiritual." Also we know that the order of even our mental states must be more or less independent of us as individuals, must be, that is, extended and projected so as to integrate us with others into "social" bodies. And a social body is an external cultural thing, a fixed structure in the world, a fact of order, independent of mind or states of mind, and close to the order of nature. Just so we know, upon reflection, that isolated things are as inconsequential as isolated mental states. Then the importance of things, including minds and persons, is seen to lie in the extent and manner in which they are by action incorporated into masses in such orderly fashion that they may be corporately effective. That is to say, it is the organization of things into large common instruments of action for all individuals that is finally important. For example, the house in which an individual is born may be full of books. But the individual may nevertheless grow up in ignorance despite the books, and the chances are heavily against his ever using them. That is, books must be made the center of a host of other objective physical things in the cultural institution of the school before they can be the means to the individual's education. Things organized as instruments become opportunities, ways to the good life.

Then the moral functioning of the world of things is made possible through its being made into institutions, which, as such, become moral opportunities, that is, instruments to significant action for individuals. How this is done, it is not the place to inquire here. It is the fundamental problem of politics and jurisprudence. But when we speak of things as having a moral function, or of morality as involving things, we mean that there can be no morality in the absence of things as instruments for action and that these things acquire their moral capacity only through their being ordered into large objective wholes to which all persons have access and within and through which the individual's capacity for action is realized. It is this fact that gives us the moral basis of institutions. Institutions that do not perform these functions are dead husks of an effete culture, and they must be made to give way to a better type. We must repeat, and with emphasis, that there can be no morality in the absence of this incorporate institutionalized world as the instrument of action; and, while the precise meanings we shall find it necessary to attribute to these terms must be allowed to appear as we go on, we could not go on without first getting this viewpoint clear in our minds.

3. THE WORLD AS CORPORATE WHOLE OR END OF ACTION

But not only is the world of things necessary as instruments with which the agent acts. It is also and in a profounder sense true that the world of things, natural and cultural, is in some aspect or detail the object of every act. By this we mean that every moral act tends to come to an issue in its appropriate object in some fact or event within the objective world. It is true that much recent discussion of ethical questions seems to assume that action may be endless, that is, that it is the sort of movement that can be interpreted without reference to any object within which it might issue, that action or "life" is its own purpose and explanation or has its meaning in its mere process. But this is purely subjective; ends are themselves thought of as "purposes" and confused with states of mind. This is also often the view of the ethicist whose thought is colored by aesthetic motives; and it must be confessed that ethical motives and aesthetic motives lie close together in human nature. Also it is sometimes said that action issues in an object merely for the purpose of getting a fresh start, to another object or to another movement or another "experience," and so on, in-definitely. It is even sometimes said that every object must find its reality in experience, to realize which is to canonize one as an idealist. And then there is the older utilitarian who argues that action issues in satisfying feeling. Now from no possible point of view can any of these be right; they are all inadequate.

Then moral action, all action, that is, issues in and is realized in an object; and that object is the object that it is, not merely because it is for the actor an objective, or because his intention is realized and objectified in it, but because it is a part of the total object, the whole order of all objects that make up the natural and cultural world. No object has its reality in the mere reference to the subjective motive that is realized in it: this is the fatal fallacy of private property. It is only this total or complete object, that is, the order of all objects, the world, that is the final issue or end of every moral act, and it is from the point of view of this total object that the morality of every act and the status of every object are to be judged. Every moral act tends to constitute the state. Even acts that apparently affect only the inner character of the actor are to be so judged. For the character which they modify is itself to be considered real only by virtue of its re-lations to this objective world. In the absence of the latter the char-acter is an empty abstraction; it is real and becomes actualized only through its acts, and its acts mean nothing until they issue in the factual world. This is the meaning, when it has any, of the often repeated demand that ethical knowledge be "practical"; and it is this motive, as a confused feeling in an ignorant but sensitive mind, that makes the "practical" man often engage in "social reform" or in "betterment." But he conceives reform and betterment in subjective terms of welfare, and the latter in terms of hedonic feeling. If he could but see the fundamental fact clearly, he could go on from this vague feeling to a really objective ethics where his reforms and meliorative methods are proved futile.

But let us go on with the explanation of the moral object. Of course the total world is not in every case the object at which the individual consciously aims. It is not the object at which the individual consciously aims in many cases; possibly it is never so for many persons. But this only reminds us that it is not the aim of the actor, not his intention or purpose or motive that determines the morality of an act, no more, in fact, than that it is the "results" that determine the morality of the act. What is the moral function of the intention or motive we shall inquire in the proper place. Acts are objective dynamic relations within the structure of the world and not states of mind of individuals. And it is this objective character, this relation of an act and its appropriate object to the world the act tends to constitute, the cosmic relation, that is the basis of the moral quality of the act. These larger generalizations we shall take for granted throughout, leaving their justification to the consistency of the account that we can base upon them.

But the object of an act means two things. It means, first, the isolated circumstance with which or upon which the act issues, or is expected to issue, when the act is abstracted to its most immediate movements. This we may call the immediate object of the act. For example, when I go to the bank to deposit money with the intention of buying an automobile, then the automobile is my object. We will not stop to argue whether the real object is not the pleasure that the automobile will bring, or the pleasure of saving, or the self-satisfaction from having done my duty. All these are psychological motives associated with the act, or may be, in any case. But the object of the act, the one reason for the act as the basis from which the act can be explained, is the automobile itself, and there may very well be no clearly defined psychological associates involved at all. This is the simple or immediate object of the act, and, so far as it can be interpreted in isolation from other similar objects and acts, the act is good or bad in proportion as the automobile does or does not perform the function of completing the action directed toward it. We do not, of course, mean the usefulness or utility of the automobile; not the goodness of the automobile to us, but its goodness as an instance of its kind. Utility in such a case is either a merely psychological factor or, at best, an economic factor. It is not by itself a moral consideration at all. What

is meant in ordinary language when we speak of the object of an act
is that external fact or thing in which the act appropriately comes to
end, and this meaning satisfies ordinary practical and reflective purposes equally well. When I am hungry, my action has meaning
through its relation to food and not to my subjective feeling of want,
or to any purpose or motive or aim, as those terms are ordinarily
interpreted.

Yet the question with respect to my buying the automobile goes
deeper. We spoke above of the act considered as an isolated fact. It
will sooner or later turn up as, "Ought I buy an automobile?" and
this will not be answered by determining merely whether the automobile will or will not perform the function of completing the act
of saving money. This determines whether the automobile is a good
or a bad instance of the machine considered merely as a representative
of a type. Here "good" and "bad" are adjectives referring technically
to the machine. But the real questions of goodness and badness refer
morally to the *act of buying* and are adverbial or modal attributes of
the total situation in which the act is involved, and the "oughtness"
lies in this modality. And this total situation turns out to be, when we
follow it to its end, the entire human world. This is the second meaning of the object of an act—where the object becomes an objective.
And it is this that is the real object of the act: the act as issuing in a
specific object makes differences within this total world, and, if the
difference is of one sort, we call the act right or good. If it is of
another sort, we call it wrong or bad. The moral quality of an act is
then determined by the kind of world it tends to create and maintain; and this reference to the world, this cosmic implication, sub-
stantiates the act. The problem of ethics as a genuine objective or
philosophical discipline is to determine, in principle, the nature of
these differences and to find the place which they occupy in the
structure of things. Ethical speculation is thus objective, disinterested,
impersonal.

The fundamental difficulty of the problem lies in the fact that the
objective difference which an act makes in the world does not exist
until after the act has taken place, whereas the possibility of control
of the act implies that the difference can be adequately known before
the act takes place. This gives the awkward situation: We cannot
know whether an act is right or wrong until after it is done; but our
responsibility for its rightness or wrongness must be determined before we act. By this latter, that is, the reference to responsibility, we
do not refer to the actor's intention, or to any of his mental states,

as will be explained later. We must know the objects to be created by an act before we do it if we are to control it, that is, to determine the movements and processes necessary to the production of the issue contemplated. Also we must know the outcome in some sense in advance of its existence if we are to think the outcome consistently into the structure of things. All this, the determining of appropriate movements and processes, together with the reflective fitting of the outcome into the structure of things, is involved in the concept of control, which is one of the major categories of morality. Here is then presented a problem which, from the point of view of practice, is irrational—which makes moral action an adventure in every case. So long and so far as action is moral, its outcome can never be predicted. This, as we hope to see, will demand a far-reaching modification of our traditional ideas of responsibility and obligation. From the point of view of theory, the problem is purely a speculative one, and the reference to experience can never be more than a reminder that our thought must somewhere come to grips with reality in the basic natural and cultural world. From the point of view of practice, then, ethics ends with results that are merely probable; not probable in any statistically computable sense but absolutely uncertain; there is no way of obtaining *any* advance insight into the final nature of an act. And adventure, chance, as purely exploratory, becomes a major concept of ethical practice, and experimentation is its method. Hence in method and theory, the experimentation is within logical conditions, so that ethics is purely speculative, and its issue in this direction is metaphysics.

The three speculative categories of ethics are, then, person, world, and action, the latter expressing the metaphysical relation and thus the real synthesis between the two former. That is, action is the ultimate substantive fact, and person (agent) and world (object) are logical and practical implications of it. Person and world are not then primarily facts but hypotheses or postulates referring to substantial natures or essences manifest in the fact of action, and conclusions respecting them can only be abstractly demonstrated, never proved. Proof applies only to the circumstances of action, so that in ethics considered as moral theory it has only a subordinate place.

II. PRACTICAL CATEGORIES OR CATEGORIES OF ORDER

We have just discussed the speculative categories of action, or the implications of the fact of action that determine the direction which thought must follow in making action intelligible. These concepts are shown to represent real elements in the nature of things, just as action itself has substantial being, and its implicates are thus parts of the structure of the world. Here we have to discuss the practical categories—categories, that is, that are seen to be implicates of the fact of action when action is considered as a process, so that the characteristics of process enter into their meaning. They all refer to the relation between person and world taken as a dynamic fact, in which the movement or change in mode of the one in respect of the other is the chief element of meaning. That is, for example, person has its meaning in the relation between itself and its world, and the relation is substantiated in an act; so that the act is the meaning of the person and is thus a value objectified. All the practical concepts involve change and process, but they also imply the constancy of the relation in which change takes place, so that the change itself is substantiated. We must remember that action is the characteristic relation between person, as actor or agent, on the one side, and world, as object or end, on the other; and, since this relation is a constituent or constitutional bond, it is, as such, a substance with the same objective status in reality as the person and the world. But the objective character of the act lies in the fact that the interchange of quality and mode between the person and the world is universal. We mean by this that person and world as facts of experience can be understood only when we think of them as always and everywhere connected with each other through the act and recognize that they can be thought only as connected by an act in which their relation is apprehended through the interplay of their qualities. The act is thus the great fact which ethics has to try to comprehend. The practical postulates are all implicative derivatives from the speculative concepts named above, and they all have for that reason the same factual and logical characters as those concepts. But their reference to the fact is from a different angle. They are all to be understood as affected by the positive factual character of probability in their empirical aspects, and are all speculatively uncertain or hypothetical in their reflective aspects, in that the act can in no concrete case ever be determined by or through the particulars of the empirical situation. Hence the theory of these practical concepts is burdened with extreme difficulty.

Here, however, we are interested merely to classify them and to state their descriptive characters and relations. They may be divided into two general types on the basis of the distinction made above. They are either (A) logical, that is, determined by and within the continuous reference to the thought process in which their meaning and content lie or (B) empirical, or methodological, by which it is meant that their meaning and content are derived descriptively from the simple facts of action as observed in the life-process. Both classes are practical concepts in the large sense that they deal with the life of action. This allows of describing the former as theoretical concepts in the sense that they are the concepts that deal with the *theory* of action, that is, they are necessary media by which we represent an act to thought, even though they are *practical* in the sense that they deal with action as actual.

Perhaps a better way of distinguishing these classes is to call the first or logical categories the "categories of freedom" and the other or empirical categories the "categories of obligation." The first are categories of freedom because they all may be regarded as derived from the "spontaneity" of the person regarded as an effective agent. Here the spontaneity of the person means no more, nor less, than the dynamic relation between the person and his act, where the act can be regarded as the term of the relation because of the fact that by virtue of its nature as substance it constitutes itself an identity with the agent. The categories of obligation are distinguished by the fact that they all imply this logical and metaphysical necessity with which the act, because it is real, binds the person to the world. It is this bond of logical necessity that in practice is the root meaning of obligation, just as it is the possibility *in thought* of negating the bond in a specific instance of action that constitutes freedom and that makes freedom primarily a concept of theory rather than one of practice in the strict sense. Freedom then is the possibility of thinking an alternative to an act while the act is held as a plan in contemplation before it is given expression in movement.

A. The logical concepts, or concepts of freedom, are (1) end (object, objective); (2) preference; (3) choice; (4) good-bad. We shall take these up in the order given.

1. END

As a practical category, and thus having in mind the processes of action, with special reference to the possibilities of alternative acts and thus of control, end is to be thought of as that point at which the processes of action are to come to their fulfilment and brought to a close. It is thus an ideal limit for thought, since a process can have no completion. End is here, therefore, the object. The distinction between object and objective must be kept in mind: object is a pure speculative concept and the end for thought; objective, a pure practical concept and the end for action. That toward which action tends, and, as such, is in thought completely statable in terms of its descriptive characters, is an end as an objective. For its complete descriptive nature cannot be known in fact until all the processes of the action which create it are completed and so eliminated, since it derives its qualities in part from those processes.

It is for this reason also that an end can only be anticipated but never known in the fulness of its nature; that is, it can be known only a priori in terms of its universal in thought relations but not in its qualities in intuition. But the objective, in addition to having all the characteristics of an object, is also the completion of the process through which the agent directs active processes toward the end. In this capacity the objective, as an end, is "ideal" in the sense that its perceptual characters can be formally anticipated, since the object is precisely the substance in which the qualities as mental states inhere. The objective is here necessitated by the qualities that appear in mental states, because mind can never apprehend its states as substances that can be the bearers of the qualities that appear in them. I can, that is, image or previse the object toward which I immediately feel my organic functions tending, and the object is experienced as identical in nature with the perceptual characters through which it is imaged. This feeling comes to me perhaps as the summary of the sensations connected with my movements and is the emotional glow in which, or on which as background, the objective is pictured in my mind. It is thus the basis of every practical consciousness and probably also of every "cognitive" state. It is not necessarily "conscious," so my ends, even in their essentially moral characters, may not be known to or by me. As such summary of sensory and active functions, and as the consciousness of them, this feeling is an important factor in the control of action, that is, in the case where action itself is made an objective. It is also and as well the occasion and the content stuff of the idea systems through which action may be made intelligible. I mean that an act can be controlled only from the point of view of the end toward which it tends; but also the ideas which in the cognitive function effectively fit the act into the objective world system are replicas or images of this objective.

It is because of this dual nature of the end, as both the objective in which action is completed and the plan which gives anticipatory meaning to relevant ideas, that the thought-processes and the active processes can be made to agree or conspire to the completion of an act. Every act, that is to say, is prefigured in the structure both of nature and of culture, just as nature and culture, as objects, are implicit in the act which creates them. This is most perfectly instanced in the work of art, where "idea" and "object" are indistinguishable. For this reason it seems probable that it is only in aesthetic theory that the basic assumptions of the theory of knowledge can be stated. For the same reason, also, the basic concepts of both logic and ethics rest upon the more primitive ground of aesthetics. Also this duplicity of the end is, it may be, though we do not argue it here, the ground of the correspondence of ideas with "objects" in the knowledge process. The concrete meaning of end as moral objective will have to be left to come out by degrees as our story develops.

2. PREFERENCE

This is the postulate by which in experience we undertake to state the relative worth of ends from the point of view of the subjective nature of the agent. The possibility of a series of ends of different degrees of worth is itself due to what we have just described as the dual nature of ends. It is this dual nature that makes preference possible and choice real. For preference and choice are merely subjective representations of the two phases of the duality. Preference is thus a central concept in all value considerations, but it is to be kept in mind that it has a genuine logical status only as an implicate of the dual nature of ends. That is, differences of worth are real in that their objective grounds imply a difference of logical status.

But the idea of preference has not been as yet very clearly worked out. The difficulty with most theory is that, in the notion of preference, too much emphasis is put upon the abstractly conscious or subjective aspects of ends. The problem of value theory, so far as it relates to preference, is thus to establish the objective status of preference. This will show, when it is worked out, that preference has an objective basis only in the relations which hold between the systems of nature and culture as instanced in action, and in action as implying ends; and it is only upon this objective basis that preference as a mental process in the individual and as a private claim can be shown to be real. The objectivity of preference can only be effectively formulated in aesthetics, because only in aesthetic theory can we avoid the dominance of interest, which as the claim to subjective privacy has wrecked most recent value theory. If we are to have an "axiology," the laws of preference must be objectively grounded; we must avoid merely psychological considerations if we are to find or create a logic of value. In its general aspects value theory presupposes a metaphysics and a reference to the structure of the universe as that structure becomes a necessary postulate of thought. Then the practical problem, always, it must be remembered, first a problem for thought and thus of theory, is to formulate, from elementary practical principles which have been established in pure theory, maxims of action-direction which shall be of special pertinence to empirical ethical questions in that they exhibit the comparative status in the objective sphere of worth that is to be occupied by the objects toward which action tends to move. It is a problem, that is, of showing logically how objects are, or become, ends. It is therefore axiomatic that an ethical theory, or *any value* theory, cannot be made consistent which does not go beyond the subjective states of individuals.

But theory will have to go far beyond empirical fact if preference is to be accepted as also a practical postulate of ethics. A consistent theory of ethical values will therefore be objective in a way in which the subjective empirical motives of the individual will appear as of no categorial consequence, will bear, that is, no reference to principle. It will show that, unless there can be formulated a universal principle by which the preferences of the individual can themselves be judged evaluatively, our theory of values is merely empirical, and no real laws can be laid down for the guidance of our thought with respect to values. And it is precisely at the point where values and preferences are experiences that guidance is required; experience cannot be the guide to logic here, since it is experience itself that is to be controlled. Individual preferences are the fact to be explained; they are not standards of explanation. If values represent genuine experiences, then, there must be objective principles by which distinctions among them may be reduced to order, at least in theoretical outline, since such distinctions among experiences are themselves intelligible only through principles rationally determined in advance. Preference, we may therefore conclude, has an objective practical ground in the dual nature of objectives, which dual nature is theoretically demonstrable as the essential principle of logical structure in real objects. And at this point it is clear that a principle of logical structure is also a cosmological principle.

We may say, then, that the "relativity" of ends to each other is a real implicate of the principle of ends and the ground of preference. For, it is a statement of the principle that ends are mutually relative because of the fact that an end is both an object and an objective and thus necessitates a system of stadia or grades of ends of different value.

3. CHOICE

Choice is the subjective maxim which the individual accepts in lieu of this undiscovered objective principle of preference. But, as it thus has no ground, choice is the *consciousness* of chance. Choice, for the individual, will, so far as his experience is concerned, always therefore be "principled" in chance, the manifest contradiction which is life. Practically, in the empirical realm, then, the life of the individual is dominated by accident, which, with reference to the good life, we call adventure. Subjectively, then, the criterion by which we distinguish values is choice. As a purely empirical concept, nothing could be done with it except to use it to describe the occasions upon and the circumstances within which it occurs. But if it is to be used as a theoretical concept to develop the grounds of practice, choice must be shown to have at least an indirect reference to principle, and it is as a possible theoretical concept that it interests us here. We must accept then the task of finding the element of principle that is implied in the meaning of choice.

If we take the usual statement of the meaning of choice as involving, on the one side, a set of objects among which the individual must express a preference and, on the other side, in the consciousness of the individual a set of conflicting motives, with the added assumption of some sort of correspondence between the subjective motives and the alternative objects, we have, speaking descriptively, nothing more than the ordinary complex situation of fact in the like of which science is content to find uniformities. From this point of view it is sufficient to say that the choice, as a resolution of the situation, is merely the operation of the strongest motive. But it is clear that this is a mere shifting of the problem, for it is at once a question as to what makes one motive stronger than another. For such a problem, then, the empirical method is of little use, since the facts that might explain why one motive will prevail over another are no longer in existence as facts; they lie submerged in the substance of history. The real explanation is therefore not accessible to the empiricist and must come from other sources. And there seems no escape from the conclusion that the "choice" is connected with the individual's history, with that history manifesting its evidences in the individual's character. But character is not an empirical fact, nor is history. (The choice depends upon the history and character of the chooser.) So there is no approach to such matters except the speculative one of inference, and the subjective and scientific approach must be given up.

Choice is a theoretical concept, then, in that its principle lies in the logical relations between the factually objective situation, with its distinction into corresponding systems of "alternatives" and "motives," on the one side, and the ideally objective character and history of the agent, on the other. The character and history of the agent are equally objective with the "facts" but are not directly available to experience. As a strictly psychological question, the facts of choice indicate merely a specified and specialized instance of causation, the "choice" is merely a psychological case of determined relations, a perfect instance of pure determinism and mechanism. So chance, the basis of real choice, in a psychological situation, is absent. "Free choice" is therefore meaningless when the phrase is taken to represent a subjective situation. But the relations between objective fact and the history and character of the individual, which are also objective facts, are not fixed; they are logical relations, not determined but speculatively determinable and therefore free. They can never be false or unreal, because they could only be determined as false by the same logic that has given them a prior determination as true and a status in reality; but the price of their necessity and truth is their empirical inaccessibility; they can be known but are not knowable to direct experience. These relations are the ontological ground of freedom, the substance of life.

This is not the place to go into the detail of meaning of that freedom. But we may remark that the least that it means is that neither the status of external fact nor the given arrangement, or any arrangement, of psychological motives determines the peculiar relation that lies at the bottom of choice. This relation is one of principle, universal as a relation of objects and objectives, and choice becomes a logical concept upon which practical rules and maxims may depend. Choice as the instance of freedom is thus the substance of the act, the ground upon which all practical reality is intelligible. But it has no relation to the caprice of the individual as it is represented in the empirical theory.

4. GOOD-BAD

Objects set apart by their principled relation of choice, referred, that is, to a relation between a fact situation and a history, are distinguished as good or bad. And it is the meaning and purpose of good-bad thus to individuate and substantiate the act, since as a maxim of choice and preference it expresses the principle of the duplicity of ends. This concept of objects principled by choice is the ground of the objective reality of the good in the Platonic sense. But it is the generic good, or good as principle, which comprehends bad, that alone can be thus substantiated. That is, the ground of the good is the principle upon which rests its distinction from the bad, or the good and the bad are grounded upon the fact that their distinction rests upon the principle of duality of ends.

In a concrete situation the principle good-bad becomes the practical maxim better-worse. The purely relative nature of better-worse makes it a maxim which can be used in ordinary experience; the agent can decide a question of better-worse without raising the question of the absolute good-bad and thus can act more or less intelligently where he could not act at all if he had to wait for a determination of the principle. And this is possible because the maxim better-worse refers not to the agent's interest but to some empirical situation which is taken as a proximate end. Better-worse then becomes the empirical maxim upon which the agent acts, while good-bad remains the principle in accordance with which he must think his way through the situation in which he is called upon to initiate action. Good and bad thus become objective elements in the structure of the world. They are then "real." Such questions as in what sense they are real, or in what degree they are real, or any other question as to the specific or individuate actualization of the good or bad as real, are problems for metaphysics, the metaphysics of ethics. But the point for us here is that good and bad are neither mysteries nor mere psychological facts; they are principled facts, they have their factuality in the principle that states the duality of nature in the end through the distinction of object and objective. They can be argued about, and true and false judgments may be made of them, and these judgments can be evaluated by the methods of logic. What we want to emphasize here is that good and bad have real meanings and to point out that the real meanings are neither in the scientifically determinable facts of presented situations nor in the psychologically demonstrable sets of motives of individuals.

The theory of good and bad, then, is neither a natural science, as the naturalists would declare, nor is it psychology, as most modern ethicists assume. Good and bad are not the "unanalyzable" entities of realistic philosophy or the unentiated analyses of idealists. The theory of good and bad is a philosophical statement of principle of the whole meaning of objective situations as including psychological motivation. It goes on from this principle, and by it, to determine the status in the world which this meaning occupies with respect to a history. Good and bad then are cosmic realities. They depend upon "situations" and "motives" only for their individuated actuality as particulars in experience, and even then only through a reference to a history; but they are not qualities or characteristics of situations of fact, and certainly not motives of anything. Good and bad are real relations in which fact situations and motives stand to the whole of their circumstance; they are not relations within such or any kind of situations. Good and bad are cosmic implications of objects as objectives. The theory that gives them meaning is ethics. For purposes of practical action, however, good and bad will always be more or less adequately stable in terms of better and worse, which thus become the maxims of concrete action.

We see, then, that choice operates as a principle, and in its operation objects are set apart from each other in stages or grades of relative worth. The principle of distinction in every case is the relation in which an object stands to the whole of its circumstance, the wholeness of circumstance being the object itself represented as an objective. We distinguish objects thus graded as good or bad, the good object representing one that choice has been compelled to accept or affirm as against another which is negated as worse; and the bad object, one that is rejected by the act of choosing as against another which is held as preferable. It is to be remembered that choice is not a mere psychological process in the individual. Choice is the reference of fact to a history and involves principle. Objects distinguished as good are thus properly regarded as differing in some final and objective way from those that are distinguished as bad. This difference, as an objective relation of things, is regarded as the basis of the distinction by which the difference is defined. Good and bad then is an "absolute" distinction, no object that is good can be judged as bad, nor can an object that is bad be included in the class of good objects, so long as they are referred to the same relation to the whole, that is, to their cosmic relation. Their goodness and badness as empirical characters depend on the choice that distinguishes them; but the choice is dictated by the objective relation to the whole in which they stand. They are made what they are by the dictated choice, and, so long as they are referred to the choice as principle, their qualities cannot be interchanged. The reason is that, while the objects are distinguished by the choice, the distinction is recognized as depending upon the qualities of the obejcts, and the qualities of the objects are functions of the relations of the objects to their appropriate whole, so that the choice itself has its objective ground. But, when goodness and badness appear in another act of choice, their qualities may be different, and what by the former choice was good may become for the latter choice bad. I may choose a piece of wood as good material for a support for a growing plant, but I would recognize at once that it is bad for a handle for a tool. When referred to objects (materials, motives, characters), the designations "good" and "bad" are absolute, and I cannot apply both to any object so long as I refer the object to a given choice as principle.

But there is a sense in which "good" and "bad" are relative terms. And it is this relative use of the terms which leads to their distinction as absolute. I may say that two pieces of wood are both good for a handle, and, when I choose one, I do not designate the other as bad. It is still good, but the first is said to be better. Thus the relative values of two objects referred to the same choice may be regarded as both positive in quality and the objects as such good, and I distinguish them by the principle of better. In the same way one of two objects is said to be worse than the other, while both are bad so long as referred to the same choice. For another and different choice the two objects pronounced good might be bad, and the two pronounced bad might be good. Good and bad then are absolute when referred to the same choice, but of good objects the one may be better or worse than the other, and of bad objects, the one worse or better than the other. "Good" and "bad" thus are relative terms when regarded from the point of view of the empirical qualities they represent, but both are absolute by the choice that applies them to objects.

Better and worse, then, are adaptations of good and bad made necessary in the application of good-bad in particular cases. They are the "schemata" of the categories good and bad.

Good and bad, then, are theoretical concepts, since they are the determinations of objects which I must make when I undertake to think them in relation to choice, and thus to explain them in their general relations to action. But in actual action where the problem is not as to their status in thought but as to the adaptation of the qualities of objects to the various moments of action, good and bad give place to better and worse which become practical maxims for the guidance of action. Good-bad, better-worse, and the whole list of ethical categories are symbols of values in action, just as the concepts of logic are symbols of values of objects determined in thought and the concepts of aesthetics are symbols of values of objects determined in feeling.

B. Empirical concepts, or concepts of obligation, are (1) purpose, (2) correct-incorrect, (3) expedient-disinterested, (4) obligation, and (5) right-wrong. Empirical concepts are derived from the practical maxim of better-worse and correspond closely to the logical categories described above.

I. PURPOSE

The logical relation which we determined upon as the meaning of choice and which grounds freedom becomes a dynamic or productive relation in cases where ends are attained, that is, in cases of genuine or overt action, where process is reduced to order and goods are produced. This dynamic relation is, under these conditions of production, called purpose. This is an empirical concept or a concept of method rather than a real concept or concept of theory, with which latter it is usually confused. That is, purpose is not a cause, as is too often assumed. It does not produce results, is not a cause in the efficient sense, and does not stand in the series of process, as the meaning of cause implies when it is used to indicate succession as the ground of the beginning-to-be of events. Purpose is a point of view for the interpretation of fact. But it is necessary to state what is meant by this point of view. It does not refer to psychological attitudes, nor to any subjective facts; it is not merely the directing the attention of conscious beings in a given direction. It refers an object to a principle, the concept of which is used as a criterion or maxim for the value estimation of that which is so referred. Thus the "purpose" operating within the Euclidean geometry is the necessity that every geometrical object be referred to the principle or law of the system of hypotheses or assumptions which makes that geometry rational and which thereby becomes the ground of every geometric object as well as the criterion of the truth or falsity of every proposition that has its meaning in that system of geometry. Euclidean geometry is thus a purposive system, a system governed by purpose, in this sense: it is made intelligible and internally consistent by the relation that states its reference to the system of cosmic principles upon which it stands. It has its being in its intelligibility.

Any active situation can be thus interpreted and only thus. What we call "conduct," or any instance in the life of a human being, or any characteristic or function of a rational being, such as a geometrical system, a state, or a work of art, can be explained in this way and only in this way. The act of a man as purposive is then made intelligible by a reference to the man's history, his character, and his world. It has its being also in the same reference; the act is the principle of identity within the conditions which it presupposes. The act or "life" of a work of art in expressing beauty is purposive in that it is made intelligible by reference to its appropriate system. The "science" of aesthetics describes that system or will do so when it has been created.

An act is a purposive act when it is consistently referable to the system of its conditions and where the latter are reduced to principle. That is, the man's character, stated in terms of the probabilities with respect to typic acts as determined from his history, together with the circumstance of the world in which that history has its setting and embodiment, as these are individuated within the circumstances of his present situation, constitutes the principle of purpose, reference to which furnishes the only judgments that can be pronounced upon his acts. The concept of purpose thus furnishes a basis upon which to assess the degree of moral quality involved in an act and, as such, offers suggestions with respect to preparation for action in the future. It is thus a practical, a regulative principle, a principle of method, in relation to the control of action; but it is not to be forgotten that it is nonetheless a concept of pure speculation in its logical derivation.

Purpose is not then a psychological motive or intention or any mode of any sort of the individual mind. It is a factor in the structure of the world, that, namely, which expresses the continuity of the part-elements in a whole. It is a concept of order and, as such, essentially objective.

2. CORRECT-INCORRECT

Where the relation in which I stand to my nature-culture world is specialized in any way and reduced from universality for any reason, it is called a technical relation. I judge the specific situation with reference to another partial situation and note, for example, their agreement. I say that the situation that is the subject of my judgment is correct, that is, it stands in the limited and specific relations that its partial nature implies. This is a moral relation; it is right (moral) adjectively to be right (correct); and it is wrong in principle to be technically wrong. But *that it is right* in a technical sense may itself be in principle wrong. Technical rightness may vary with moral rightness in almost any way. Hence it is a moral relation in a different sense from that of substantial right. A relation of correctness implies agreement, fitness, appropriateness in some particularized way, between two partial situations, or between a partial situation and a whole taken in some limited aspect. This same relation, however, considered as technically right, or the whole fact, including the relation and the two situations between which it holds, may be judged, often must be judged, as wrong. That is, the relation of correctness may be judged with respect to the sort of reference it makes to the whole of which its terms are parts. This judgment is a pure moral judgment, whose content is a technical judgment which latter may or may not be morally right.

Five dollars is the correct price to pay for a pair of shoes. But it may very well be wrong that the price of shoes is five dollars. Shoes that can be sold for five dollars because they represent sweated or child labor may be technically correct, good shoes, "worth the money"; all contractual obligations involved in the process of their production may be scrupulously met; yet five dollars is a wrong price for the shoes. The total shoe situation is not fit to enter into a moral world; it ought not to exist. The reply that we must have shoes, or cheap shoes, that men must be rewarded for their labor, skill, risk, etc., misses the point entirely. We must have shoes, cheap, good (techni-cally), promptly, etc., but all these are subordinate to the demand that shoes be right; meaning by this that the whole shoe situation, production, distribution, consumption, must be appropriate to the total cultural world which defines the shoe and creates the need for it. Men must have shoes along with groceries, art, religion, political competence; and all these must be reciprocally so interrelated as to make a rational and satisfying whole. In any case where shoes inter-fere in any way or degree with this total result the shoes are bad.

A judgment of correctness is thus not universal; its validity is de-rived from a more inclusive relation, and its morality is vicarious and derived from relations with which it is confused. All "economic" re-lations are of this sort; none of them can be universal without a com-plete transformation of their content; there can never be, therefore, any formulation of economic "principle" that is true, or any eco-nomic "policy" or "system" that can be satisfactory. All its "laws" are false; it is not therefore merely nonmoral, as it claims, but immoral in every phase of its being. It is not *necessary*, not necessitated in any aspect of human nature or in any human purpose; it is *compulsory* once you accept a certain set of assumptions which are false and a cer-tain purpose which is immoral.

3. EXPEDIENT-DISINTERESTED

An act may be expedient when it is neither technically correct nor morally right. It may, for example, be expedient for me to give money to this beggar. He may rob me or burn my house if I do not. But it is not correct to do so, since the act does not establish a relation of fit-ness between him and me, and it is not right, because it contributes nothing toward the fitting of his condition of penury and my opulence into the whole world of human relations.

It would be correct if it contributed to my self-esteem for having done him charity, and this correctness would be right, provided charity were right. Yet action from expediency is frequently right. It is perhaps the basis of what is commonly called "prudence," and prudence is a recognized virtue. Yet expediency is a moral relation only where one is unable, from ignorance, compulsion, or other cause, to do right; but it can never be right to be unable to do right. Expediency is only right "under the circumstances." But in many cases, at least, there must—the compulsion is moral—not be such circumstances. Expediency is thus only a derived virtue, extremely limited in its scope. And prudence is probably not a virtue at all. The fact that expediency is, practically, a very dangerous attitude does not concern its theoretical status; what ignorance may do in the name of expediency is not a question of principle. But as a "practical" attitude of adapting moral principle to present necessities, it has given us our very flexible commercial system, with consequences that are readily observable. The expedient thus seems to be an extreme development of the technical, the consequence which appears always to come from moral compromise in the interest of the "practical." It is to be observed that it was a "practical" age of great technical development that emphasized prudence as a virtue. It is not surprising that for it now any virtue may "cut the corners."

The attempt to make disinterestedness, regarded as the extreme opposite of expediency, the rule for the specific act merely reduces the argument to absurdity, since a disinterested act is either unconscious or not the act of a person; that is, it is self-contradictory.

4. OBLIGATION

Right, correct, expedient, etc., suggest conditions within the cultural whole, external, objective conditions, under which action can be complete, that is, such as can answer all reasonable questions as to its principle and as to the nature of its issue. They also suggest, each in its degree, the fact that the nature and significance of an act are functions of its own implications with respect to the total system in which the act occurs. In simple language this means that the circumstances of an act, the sets of environing conditions within which the act takes place, themselves not only constitute the content of the act but also determine its implications outward, that is, its objective or objectifying conditions. The chief of these outward or objective conditions is the undetermined object within which the act issues. This identity in nature between the system of conditions, partly subjective, within which the act occurs, and the system of objective conditions into which the act issues, the identity, that is, of means and end, is the objective completeness of the act, the completeness which the act has when looked at from the point of view of its own structure or constitution.

It is this last character which enables us to define obligation in non-subjective terms, that is, which enables us to define obligation in terms other than those which make an exclusive reference to the supposed subject from which that act issues. In other words, it frees the doctrine of obligation from the limitations and contradictions of individualism and the superstition of a unique will. Also, it is this objective completeness of the act, in which both actor and object or end are details, however important, which is the ground of the universality and objectivity of moral judgments. It is the reference which every moral judgment makes to an objectively complete act that implicates the system of the universe, in so far as that system is to be regarded as active, in so far, that is, as the system of the universe can be taken as the ground of culture.

Now this bond of identity within the act which unifies means and end, agent and object, substance and circumstance, is precisely the relation which is the essence of objective obligation, and which, when regarded merely from the point of view of the self-consciousness of the agent, is called the "feeling" or the "sense" of obligation. What we want to see here is that this subjective "feeling" or "sense" is, from the point of view of a consistent and objective morality, of very little consequence. The significance of fundamental matters like obligation, freedom, etc., lies far beyond the reach of private feelings; and unless these terms mean more than the mere psychological facts of private consciousness, then an associationist or hedonistic ethics is the best that can be had. The ultimate problem of ethics is to find an objective ground for obligation, a ground within the nature of things; the basis of moral authority lies in the substance of things, or there is none.

5. RIGHT-WRONG

Thus in the fitness or appropriateness which the principle of obligation enables us to posit between any given or proposed action and its factual basis in the objective system, which includes the character of the agent, the agent's history and the natural-cultural world as the substantial locus of that history, we have the idea of right. It must of course be kept in mind that the agent's character is his history, biological and cultural, as that history has taken substance in its circumstance, the environing world. Thus the system of ground conditions of moral action is reduced to the status of a principle. The whole of this situation, condensed to principle, and specified to the situation to which it refers, constitutes the content of every moral judgment. That is, the content which every moral judgment expresses is the metaphysical implications of an act. That content is the natural-cultural whole which every act and every judgment implies. It is the point of reference of every moral distinction.

Right is, then, the concept of balance and consistency and appropriateness within the constitution of this whole. Wrong is a reference to the lack of balance and inner harmony within this total logical situation. It is merely the obverse of what is properly called right, with which in its objective reference it is identical in meaning. Briefly, and with scientific abstractness which is never quite true, we could say that right, for me, refers to an act that is consistent with my character. However, my character is not a point of final reference, and itself requires a justifying status within a larger whole. Right is not thereby a private relation in which I in any peculiar way stand. The content of biological and cultural history, and the world-circumstance in which we live, are very largely "common" to all of us. Common, that is, in that it is the generative substance which constitutes man a species; not common in the sloppy phrase that we share its benefits in the way of acquisitions or emotional possibilities, which sharing has no moral significance. And for persons of the same race, nationality, etc., this community of culture in history and status in the world approaches identity. Of course there are individual differences. But these are not under any circumstance matters of right except as they imply specific differences among corporate forms of individuality; they are, as referring to human "individuals," almost exclusively either matters of technical function or of advantage derived from circumstance through accident, on the principle of chance described above. So a moral judgment is "universally valid"; that is, it refers to relations within the real or objective world and not merely to the individual or other object which happens to be the occasion of its expression or the occasion of its reference. Obligation is thus that character of an act which gives the act status in the nature of things. The "individual" agent's obligation is then to know the objective implications of his action.

Chapter IV

The Law of Morality

WE SAW in chapter ii that the elementary concepts of ethics are act, actor, and end. In chapter iii these concepts become more broadly generalized into the notions of person, world, and the end regarded as the unity of person with world in a realized act. We have seen also that the concept of actor or person is a synthetic notion derived by inference from a historical series of acts and that it is also a substance necessitated in the universality of judgments about acts. The concepts "world" and "end" have a similar status. From this point of view acts are in their own nature independent substances and as such may be regarded, when necessary, as subjects of which persons are predicates. On the other hand, acts, or types of acts, may be regarded as attributes of persons, meaning by this that the act, as the expression of a causal relation, is made intelligible within empirical situations by reference to the person as its source or point of origin. This means that, depending upon the logical purpose involved, acts may be regarded as substances with persons as attributes, or persons may be regarded as substances with acts as their attributes.

We may, then, with respect to an empirical situation, speak of the person as acting and of the act as following from the person. Acts, or types of acts, are then interpretable as capacities of persons, and we shall find this useful in the definition of the virtues. And yet we must not forget that it is the act that is the primordial fact, and the person, which we tend to think of as the source and origin and "cause" of acts, is a derivative corollary from that fact. The primary quality of the act is goodness or the good when we think of the act as realizing the relation of the person to his world, and in this sense we can think of the good as the objective basis of the personal character. With this restatement of the relations of the act, the actor, and the end, and assuming for descriptive and empirical purposes the prior position of the person, so that types of acts may be regarded as his attributes, we may formulate the law of morality thus:

The good life posits a person or actor endowed by nature and by culture with all the capacities that are possible to him, with these capacities developed to their fullest possible degree; the person living in a world so organized and ordered as to guarantee to the person full and free access to all the means and instruments necessary to the adequate and appropriate expression of his capacities and to the realization of his acts in satisfying objects.

The meaning of the various ideas in this law will come out as the discussion proceeds. The words are to be taken to mean what they mean to common sense, a simple description of the status of the ordinary human being considered as a moral agent and living in the world that is known in ordinary experience.

There are certain questions about this law that must be resolved in order to establish its right to function as the basis of explanation of moral fact. These are the questions of (I) the ground of the law, (II) the authority of the law, (III) the status of the law as a practical postulate, and (IV) its status as a categorical imperative.

I. THE GROUND OF THE LAW

The question of the ground of the law involves two issues: that of (x) its origin and (y) its validity.

x) Let us note some theories with respect to the origin of the law.

1. The simplest of these is perhaps the assumption that all moral distinctions derive from experience. There is a wide variation in the meanings of this very ambiguous word "experience," but it usually refers to the functions of perception, or to habituation or the consciousness of the individual, or, in social and historical relations, to custom and tradition. Now, the difficulty with the empirical philosophy in ethics is that the part of it that is true is too simple to serve as a principle of explanation, and the rest of it irrelevant to ethics if ethics means the explanation of action. To say that the ground of the moral relation is experience, either as individual perception, or habit, or consciousness, or even as social custom or tradition, is merely to say that the basis of the meaning of morality lies in simple fact. And this perhaps nobody would deny. But the theory goes on to tell us *which* fact is the elementary moral fact, and this is trivial. Moreover, the empiricists themselves do not agree as to what fact is elementary. The ground of morality is not a type of fact, but the principle or law of all fact in that aspect of fact by which it relates to the substantive action. The fact does not determine the law, as in natural science, but the law determines the fact through the relevance of the fact to action, which

relation of relevance is determined by the law itself. Morality is thus the principle, or an aspect of the principle, in accordance with which facts *are;* it is prior to the facts in so far as any type of fact may be specified. It is the peculiar function of moral action to determine the typic character of a fact antecedently to the existence of the fact. The kind of house I build is settled upon before the house exists. And if we mean to speak of fact in general, then we have given up the point, for facts are not facts except when specifiable.

This type of theory is peculiarly unfortunate in its "social" aspects. The attempt to find principle in the detail of facts within human association by the ordinary concepts of psychology and positive science has made something very like nonsense of sociology and "social ethics." The theory that the ground of the moral law is experience is, however, true; but it is not true in any empirical sense. The basis of moral law, as of all law, is fact; but it is not a "fact of experience," and the question of the nature of the peculiar relation of law to fact does not begin to be stated when expressed in ordinary empirical terms. We shall see below in what sense this is true.

2. The origin of the moral law, with the supposition that its origin is its proper ground, is often said to be in the reason, or in some other specific aspect of active experience, as feeling, or sense. This is correct in the sense that it is only in so far as mind in some form and in some way enters into a situation that the situation can be said to be moral. But it is certainly not true that an antecedently existing reason must operate to create the moral situation, as the doctrine of the spontaneity of reason seems to assume. The reason itself is not explicable in this abstract sense, although the rationalist view is right in insisting that a moral situation must be intelligible. The same remarks apply to feeling and sense; the ground of the moral law is not mere psychological fact.

3. The view that the moral law has its origin in God or in some other source outside the world is attempting to state a profound truth, viz., that the ground of moral law is outside of and beyond the private world of the individual in whose experience the moral situation occurs. But this is merely a reference to the fact that the particular moral situation has its meaning in a wider whole which is nevertheless of the same kind with itself. Yet the insight that the present detail of moral experience is not self-explanatory and that it refers beyond to a more inclusive whole is profound.

4. All the theories then have a common element of truth. This can be stated in the proposition that the moral law has its origin in the total fact or that morality has its whole meaning in the facts for which

its principle provides the law. But since the law is itself a large element in the fact, the statement that the law has its origin in fact is seen to be not a solution but a mere statement of the problem. This total fact is in some aspect doubtless an experience; it is a social experience, as recognized in custom or tradition; it is rational, for what could not be understood could not be moral; and the fact has or comprehends the characters of feeling and sense; it is beyond the individual and impresses him from without, that is, it is objective circumstance; in sum, the ground of the moral law is the total fact within which all being lies. What this means we shall see farther along.

y) The ground of the moral law is sometimes said to lie in its validity, that it has its being in its own truth. The validity of the law rests upon different bases according to different accounts.

1. Its validity is said to be a matter of correct transmission through social heredity or through tradition. This is a somewhat primitive view, and its cogency depends upon the genuineness of the tradition. The difficulty with it is that it is really a form of the empirical theory.

2. The moral law may be claimed to be based on its reasonableness as shown in its internal consistency. But this is the fallacy of deriving the validity of a judgment from the judgment itself, instead of from the reality from reference to which the judgment derives its meaning. The validity of the law lies in the faithfulness with which it expresses the ultimate fact of this meaning.

3. The moral law may be said to have its basis in the veracity of a personal lawgiver and the revealed will of the lawgiver as recorded in documents or otherwise. This is right in so far as it insists upon the importance of the person in the fact system whose description the law is intended to state. But it overemphasizes the personal element, making the person the sole ground. It also confuses validity with authority and is characteristic of an early absolutist organization of life. Its strong point practically is its capacity to maintain discipline and order, but it is not conducive to freedom.

4. What all these theories are trying to state is that the moral law has truth for the intelligent being because of its objective necessity as a universal formulary of the total fact, which we saw above was the meaning of the question as to the origin of the moral law. What is meant here by objective necessity is simply the fact that the moral law as we have stated it is a faithful formulation of the essential relations of life as it is actually lived. It is simply true of the total fact of active life and requires no other recommendation to enforce its claims upon the intelligence.

II. THE AUTHORITY OF THE LAW

The question of the authority of the law is in most respects similar to that of its ground, but here the emphasis is placed upon the necessity of finding reasons for our respect for the law within the experiences from which the law was formulated. That is, a more direct reference to experience is involved. The authority of the law may be based (*x*) on its utility or (*y*) on its reasonableness.

x) Utility may be explained as a matter of (1) pleasure-pain, (2) perfection or self-realization, (3) rewards, or (4) self-consistency. These require only brief explanation. If we begin with (1), the theory runs to the effect that the moral law, and moral concepts in general, are true because they are useful in affording the individual, or all individuals, experiences of pleasure or a balance of pleasure over pains. We do right in every case because we believe that in so doing we, or some other person or persons in whom we are interested, will experience pleasure or at least avoid pain. The experience is, generally speaking, uniform in quality from the simplest pleasant feeling to the condition of sustained happiness, and the fact of pleasure is the ground of authority for all moral concepts. Pleasure is then, in the utility theory, the great fact which we named above as the basis of the origin and validity of the law. But this is questionable; the fact to which the moral law refers contains all the possible experiences, many of which are of equal or greater value than pleasure and cannot be equated to pleasure and pain in any sense. Pleasure is not the whole of the good, even if we grant, which we need not do, that it is an essential part of every concrete good. This pleasure theory is perhaps the most widely held ethical conviction within the experiences of men, and the element of truth in it is almost universally recognized.

The difficulty with the "pleasure theory," or hedonism, is that there are facts of quite obviously genuine moral significance of which it is not true. It is not true of these facts in either of the forms of hedonism; neither in the assumption that pleasure is always the motive to action nor in the assumption that pleasure is the object at which we aim.

2. The doctrine that the authority of ethical concepts rests on their contributing to the perfection or self-realization of the individual would not usually be classed as a utility theory. In so far, however, as perfection and realization are to be thought in terms of individual experience, it seems to be a utility view. It is the individualism of the theory that makes it so universally plausible, that is, its justification of

the covert egoism that lies at the basis of individualism, and any attempt to subject moral concepts to individualistic assumptions seems to be a utility view. I do not see that the vision of myself as sensually happy differs, in principle, from my notion of myself as some austere model of perfection. The sensuality and the austerity are both useful to me, and it seems to be equally their utility that recommends them. It is hard to see how any moral theory of the isolated self as ultimate principle can be consistent with the demand for objectivity in morals. The very concept of law implies some entity outside the self to which the self must defer, unless we are to think of the self in absolutist individualistic terms as exclusive reality and in itself the law. But this makes it inconsistent with any possible explanation of social life, which is as obvious a fact as the individual. The law does contemplate the perfecton of the individual, but only through and in relation to other aspects of the real. The individual cannot be perfected outside the institutional relations; he does not have his whole being within his own skin.

3. The authority of the moral law as based on utility is sometimes expressed in the doctrine of rewards. This is not the same as the simple pleasure theory, since rewards may be in terms of objects of any kind of interests. The religious doctrine of salvation is a case in point, in which rewards are not necessarily in terms of pleasure. Here again we have to say that many of the objects enjoined upon us by moral law are not rewards in any sense and in many cases do not imply merit in us. The food I find in the forest is a good regardless of whether I have earned it. Its goodness is not a reference to me as an individual at all.

4. It is possible also to express utility in terms of a sort of self-consistency or self-respect or self-reference which may take many forms. The old Stoic notion that a man should stand foursquare even against destruction; the extreme hedonist position that a man should enjoy even at the expense of the whole world; the attitude of utter selfishness of, for example, the miser or the money-grubber—these may be the consequences of a utility view of the self-consistency and self-respect which is assumed to lie at the basis of the individual character. But another view may also interpret what is called integrity as a utility view, even when it takes the form of extreme nobility. As a matter of fact almost any ethical attitude may be superficially consistent with the utility theory, and this fact, viz., that the utility theory does not draw careful distinctions, is the main source of its weakness.

y) But authority may be based on rationality as well as on utility. And rationality in this connection may mean a variety of things.

1. Rationality may involve tradition and wont interpreted as a sort of purposive principle in the universe which humanity and all other existences are striving to work out. This makes morality a sort of destiny, or something less worthy in the idea of the inevitableness of economic or social law. It acquires a certain profundity in oriental moral fatalism. But it does not seem possible to give it the precision and definiteness of meaning that the moral law demands; it remains an abstraction.

2. A similar notion of rational destiny may be conceived to be the principle of the individual life. The individual himself is supposed to be a universal principle and the basis of the law's authority. It is he who legislates the law, and the law has authority simply as an expression of his will. This extreme form of individualism is now seen to be contrary to the facts, but it has had an enormous influence in recent times.

3. Rationality, regarded as what satisfies God, or some mystical principle external to the world of moral fact, often is made the basis of the authority of the moral law. Logically, this is the reference of facts and particulars to their universal as the ground of their being and, when stripped of narrowly human motives, becomes the final correct authority. But it must be stated clearly, and this requires another statement.

4. The ultimate authority of the moral law is due to the fact that the law is the law which the facts of reality, by possessing the character and constitution that they do possess, enforce upon the intelligence. The law of the triangle is inherent in the structure and constitution of the triangle, is a description of the facts of that constitution. The law of the expansion of gases is an expression of what it means to be a gas. Similarly, the law of moral goodness is a description of the constitutional structure of the good—a statement of the meaning of that whole of fact in which every moral concept finds the ground of its meaning. This statement is of course formulated in universal terms, as are the statements about triangles or gases, and the law refers to individual experience in the same way that the law of the triangle refers to the individual triangle. If the difficulty is raised that the man can ignore the moral law, while the triangle cannot ignore its law, the answer is that the triangle can ignore its law by ceasing to be a triangle. That is to say, the question of goodness here becomes identical with that of truth and reality—a true and real

triangle is one that conforms to the law of triangles. In the same way, the man who ignores or violates the moral law denies or negates himself as a human fact. He ceases to be a man and becomes something other than a moral being.

III. THE MORAL LAW AS A PRACTICAL POSTULATE

As an expression of the nature and constitution of the moral agent, and as a statement of his relations to his world in terms of the facts of his everyday experiences, the moral law implies the concept of freedom with its obverse aspect of obligation. As a practical postulate this concept of freedom-obligation derives directly from the concept of action when action is regarded as the form of all constructive relations between person and world.

x) Freedom has in the thought and experience of men acquired a variety of meanings. Among these we may distinguish (1) the freedom of indifference, (2) freedom of the "will," (3) rational choice, and (4) the total effectiveness of the moral agent, or what in subjective terms we have called the agent's integrity. These call for brief discussion.

1. Indifference is the form of freedom in the hypothetical case in which the freedom of the agent leads to acts without connection or continuity with his constitution or history. It is of course self-contradictory in the fact that it attempts to imply that an act can occur while all its conditions or constituents are under the domination of chance. But chance cannot be made to mean anything in the absence of some reference to a part of reality which is essentially lawful in nature and where chance has no force. Hence the freedom of indifference is practically meaningless. It does, however, have an element of meaning for theory when it implies that there may be features of an event that effectually resist conformity to law. In this sense indifference is equivalent to the postulate of real chance, the assumption that there is an aspect of reality which in the nature of things maintains a constant cleavage between the logical substance of law and the physical substance of reality. Thought in its substantial form as law never identifies wholly with things, as it does in its adjectival form in perception. It is implied further that this elemental difference between thought as law and the world of things is the metaphysical ground of the continued necessity of action—no action could be conceived to be possible in a world which conformed in all details to the requirements of the forms of thought. This means that there will always be some aspects of reality that defy rationalization,

that are beyond the reach of thought in the sense that thought will never be able to impose a complete order upon them. Hence action is always a necessity. This incorrigibility of the world and the continuing necessity for action seems to be an insight with the great religions—God is the incomprehensible being that cannot be expected fully to conform to thought. Here the physical necessity of action and its logical necessity become the same. Indifference thus refers to that determinate indeterminacy which makes the idea of "determinism" so persistent.

Another instance of the meaning of indifference is that of the agent when in a position to ignore or to refuse consideration of his circumstances when contemplating action. It is true that many things are indifferent to the will in a given case, in that the will is under no constraint to attend to them, and this fact seems to suggest the possibility that the will may be "free" of all circumstance or coercive externality. But it cannot consistently mean this, for the simple reason that one fact may be ignored only as against another which is not ignored, and this suggests that, with respect to objective circumstance, freedom is largely a reference to the fact of choice. The negation involved in ignoring circumstances may give us a suggestion for the explanation of the "negative freedom" which has become so prominent a feature of individualism.

2. Freedom may refer to the assumption of a special capacity of the agent of which the will is the peculiar expression. In any literal sense of these terms psychology has disposed of this assumption by reporting that there is no evidence of the existence of such a capacity and that all the valid facts which have been attributed to it can be explained better on other grounds. But as a reference to the elemental urgency of life, which cannot be ignored in the discussion of action, this idea of a special capacity is important. In fact, this primitive biological urge represented as controlled in its direction of expression by the equally primitive perceptual consciousness is as near a "bottom" as can be found in fact for any theory about will. And the fact that the "capacity" cannot be "found" merely means that the doctrine has the wrong conception of the nature of will, insisting that it must be a natural fact when it is rather a cultural and specifically a logical fact. That is, the "will" can be found neither as a capacity of body or mind; it is not a describable quality or adjunct of either. But as the idea of the substantial ground of the relation between body and mind, as made obvious to experience in the fact of action, that is, as a logical object, the will is there, and there is this important factual con-

sequence of its presence, viz., that the fact of action cannot be given definite locus in experience or thought except on the acceptance of the will as being there. It may of course be a mere "transcendental illusion" due to the dominance of the category of cause in our experience, but we cannot avoid a belief in the factuality of the will. A movement can be "located" or given a status in thought on the postulate of the body in relation to other bodies; neither action nor movement can be made intelligible by reference to mind alone. But an act in the concrete instance is intelligible as an expression of the relation between mind and body, and on no other basis. In general, and as a matter of principle, an act is intelligible only as an expression of the relation between mind-body on the one side and the nature-culture world on the other. Will is, then, as fact, this mind-world relation taken as a whole, mind-body being an instance in concrete fact.

3. It was noted above that the active being, when in the presence of varied circumstances, may ignore some facts in favor of others. This is the situation known as choice, and it is important in that it stands at the point where action is entered upon and where the direction of the course of action is determined. But this is clearly either the work of the "reason" in the sense that possibilities are compared, or the work of habit or automatism built up from previous experience. Freedom in this sense then refers merely to the act of the intelligence and is the traditional "rational freedom" of the old theories. It is a significant view of freedom, perhaps the one nearest true. But it is also one in connection with which many very difficult problems arise, most of which center around the question how the intelligence can make its pronouncements effective; a question for which there is no final answer short of a complete account of the political process of legislation.

4. The doctrine of "rational freedom" thus needs restatement and extension in order to be satisfactory. And with restatement it becomes the doctrine of objective freedom. It appears to assume a power of intellect by itself to determine action. At this point it may be well to state what is meant by determining action. It does not refer to cause as the condition of the coming-to-be of events—acts are never caused. Action is fact, and it would be absurd to inquire as to the cause of a fact. When, therefore, we speak of our rational freedom as determining action, we mean merely that intelligent choice among given or proposed ends and means on occasion determines which of them is more appropriate as fixing the direction and course of action with respect to our major goals. The more appropriate direction is open

for the entrance of the urges of life, and "will" has made a "choice." It is thus the determination of the direction and course of action that is the work of the will, and determination means no more than that, of presented alternative courses, one is more acceptable to the intelligence than the rest, and the life-urges flow out through it.

Now, when we observe the facts, we note that the ends at which we arrive in action are not always the ones that choice had singled out. Sometimes the end attained is not recognized at all as one that had been aimed at, or possibly not recognized as among those from which choice has been made. So the direction action is to follow is not perhaps in any case merely a question of choice or intelligence or reason. What is more nearly true is that the direction and course which our action pursues are determined by our whole character together with forces from our environment. Our capacities upon which direction depends are the possibilities of the movement of the organism, augmented by the whole historic past of our experience. Every putting-forth of effort by an intelligent being becomes an experience and achieves a direction because of the medium of intelligence and historic experience within which the effort takes place. The accumulated mass of these experiences collects a momentum of energy which becomes a capacity or power to do the act prefigured and designed within the structure of the experience type. The total mass of experiences, together with the direction given each type by intelligence, has itself an internal design, and this design, as exhibited in the tendencies to action of the whole organism and conditioned by its circumstance in nature and culture, is the "will" of the moral agent. The will is thus the expressed or expressible effectiveness of the whole being of the agent or person. Every act is the act of the whole self. Thus we see that the will is real after all and has substance, a substance necessitated in the design of the active experience, and therefore a "spiritual" or logical substance.

From the standpoint of freedom we thus see that law means will, and will means intelligent design within the structure and constitution of existence. Will and design are not mystic powers with which certain types of being are mysteriously endowed. They are the substantial essences of things to which description of the facts of experience necessarily drives us if we are to make our descriptions intelligible. They are thus logical entities, conceptual structures determined in and by thought, and hence have a status in the objective world where they have power to determine that a mere object shall also be an objective.

y) By "obligation" is meant the tie or bond that maintains the continuity and identity of the person with his world. It is a synthesis of all the cosmic implications of his whole character. It may be observed in four stages ranging from compulsion to responsibility.

Freedom is in principle the relation of the active agent or person to his world, the relation considered from the point of view of the inner nature of the person in its aspect as ground of effectiveness. Possibilities of action within the nature of the person are, in their typical forms, capacities of the person. All these capacities, taken in their total effectiveness for determining the course and direction of action, constitute the subjective will of the person. The exercise of this will constitutes his freedom. Limitations of personal freedom depend either upon internal defect of will, a breach of design in the will's constitution, or upon absence or inappropriateness of external conditions, as these conditions constitute a world as the arena and instrument of action. The relation of the active being or person to his world, regarded as a limiting bond necessitated by the condition of his freedom, and considered from the point of view of the nature of this external world, we shall call obligation. The external world here does not mean the physical world alone, but the world of nature-culture, the external world considered as the total objective world of which the physical world is only a part. It means all that is outside of and beyond the person when in the attitude to will an act, and hence might better be called the impersonal world. Obligation has a structure of its own and a variety of forms which we shall briefly examine.

1. Obligation in its lowest and most immediate form is compulsion. In the presence of his objective or impersonal world the person on occasion stands in utter helplessness. Any act he may elect to perform with respect to it will be designed in pure chance and its outcome shrouded in absolute uncertainty. To attempt to use intelligence in such cases is wholly futile, or, if it has any effect, perhaps reacts upon the person with adverse and generally disastrous, sometimes fatal, consequences. In such cases what appear to be the consequents of action have no intelligible relation to any act that precedes them. There are acts that end in the blue in utter disregard of any appeal to intelligence; not even can a trace of them be found in the character of the actor. In the purpose to act in such cases we find ourselves standing alone in a world of blank nothingness. In such cases the only character of the act that is possible of description is pure uncertainty, chance without the vestige of a ground. Such situations are, of course, morally inconsequential, but they are not negligible. The obligation of the person in such cases is to recognize that obligation is meaningless, in which case he will at least be free of regrets and self-accusa-

tions for evils in causing which he had no part. In the presence of earthquakes, possibly of politics, certainly in some aspects of sex, there is nothing whatever to be done, and the only rational act that is possible in the circumstances lies in the recognition of irrationality.

2. There are cases apparently irrational, however, where there are certain possibilities of action. In these a certain rough estimate of probabilities is possible, and the degree of uncertainty can be guessed at with such clarity as to aid in the design of an act. It is not the probable "results" of the act that are the object of the estimate; it is the probability of success of the act in attaining conformity to the design of the act as prefigured in imagination before the act is expressed. This prefiguration is an expression or representation of the structure of external or objective circumstance transformed into what it will be if the act is carried out. But it is not a result or an anticipated result. The success of the act that is estimated is expressed in terms of the inner consistency of this prefigured form or design, the latter recognized as embracing certain objective elements of chance. It is not that the agent anticipates the result, but the *act* as he sees it embodied in the more or less appropriate circumstances before him, that moves his will and formulates his purpose. To suppose that this embodiment should come as a result of anticipation is absurd. And the chance element lies largely in the degree of appropriateness of embodiment which circumstance offers to the designed act.

This form of obligation, in its subjective aspects, may therefore be called "faith" or "belief." My beliefs bind me to the forms of certain action types. They determine, therefore, my persisting active attitudes. But this, so far, is a purely subjective feeling, which, to be made real, must be brought by intelligence into the presence of the possibilities of objectification as these are determined within the outlying circumstances. It is to that outer realm that obligation always refers.

3. When our persistent active attitudes have been tested in experience to the point where they appear appropriate to their corresponding object forms, they themselves become objectified and a constituent part of the world of circumstance. They take their place within the world of fact, and science and knowledge may now deal with them as with other types of object. They are the practical objects of the cultural life, as, for example, courage, charity, friendship, justice, as embodied in appropriate institutions. Our relation to these objects is called "duty." It is no longer sufficient to look upon designed acts as representing mere probabilities. They are now certainties, and the acts are entered upon without hesitation. It does not matter that in former ages these objects have been personified and have had attrib-

uted to them all the powers and capacities which belong in and to the character whose act they objectify. This is a common enough failing even now for all of us in some connections. But the personification is due to the effort we make to insure genuine objectivity to the objects of our designs. So that if we say that God is at the bottom of our sense of duty it is merely to assure ourselves that action with respect to duty has a real status in the structure of things and that it is capable of setting up real objects in the world beyond our present reach.

Obligation is duty then when acts are complete, and where completeness means the perfect appropriation between the designs of the act and the structure of the objects in which the act is realized.

4. When the degree of appropriateness between the system of our design-types and the order of objects in the world of circumstance is relatively high, we feel responsibility. Responsibility is then the relation between our character as the totality of our capacities and the total world structure as we know it. It is, subjectively, the sense of oneness with the conditions of action which impels the person to effort. He is aware that he has the key to the proper form and quality of the world within his own character, and his duty and his conviction impel him to realize that form. It is the conviction of the zealot that he has the ideal image of his object within him that drives him to act in its behalf. He does not distinguish between its purposes and his own; he is therefore disinterested and impersonal. It is to no purpose to argue that he is ignorant and mistaken and possibly dangerous. When he becomes intelligent, his responsibility, as his integrated oneness with the world, is the very basis of his morality, is his morality, his objective freedom. In this conception of the unity of the integrated character with the rationalized world maintained throughout the changes of time we have the total meaning of cultural existence. That the meaning is never complete or absolute is due to the fact that the changes of time are not mere changes; time has a content. It is our relation to this system of conditions to action, which we perceive as without us, that gives meaning to our freedom and our obligation. It is inevitable, but it is not inexorable. The existence of chance makes it capable of change, and change gives us the opportunity of choice. But we are tied to our world with bonds of identity, and our feeling of recognition of this bond is the imperative that is categorical.

It is the statement of this relation of obligation or responsibility in terms of a simple description of the facts of life that constitutes the law of morality as stated at the beginning of this chapter.

Part II

The Nature of the Moral Person

Chapter V

The Complexity of Experience

WHAT is commonly called "experience" is the total life of activity, the thought, feeling, and volition of the whole self. But these words do not mean very much as commonly used. The difficulty is due to the fact that the terms are ambiguous; they look in two directions at the same time. They point in one direction toward what are called "facts," and in the other toward what are called "values." In spite of the difficulty there is in the attempt to point out the real differences between fact and value, we have reached a place where some workable distinction is necessary.

I. EXPERIENCE AS FACT AND AS VALUE

The distinction seems to imply, first, that between mind and what is not mind. Values appear to belong to the mind-life; facts to the world of nature outside. Also, the meanings of both mind and nature seem to rest upon relations that must be assumed to hold between the two after their distinctness has been recognized. Apparently, then, the fact that a significant distinction can be made between mind and what is not mind implies some kind of relation between them. So the attempt to isolate in thought either mind or nature rests upon a relation that is supposed to connect them. Mind and nature are then correlative terms. But since correlative terms are determined by an abstract relation, which is certainly not the relation involved here, they are better described as analogical terms, and their relation a relation of analogical identity. In this case the relation is taken in the sense that each of its terms is included as a part of the content or meaning of the other. Life or mind or experience considered as fact, then, is what life or mind or experience, considered as value, must take for granted as a necessary logical basis or substructure on which to complete its own meaning. That is, experience, when we think of it in terms of value, is not intelligible until after we have presupposed experience as fact and as its necessary analogue.

The relation between fact and value is then one of mutual implication, so that the act of inference can pass from either to the other with equal necessity; which of the two is to be taken as premise and which as conclusion will depend upon the logical structure of the individual object which the two terms and their correlation constitute in a given instance. We make our experience, as a value, mean something by referring it to an analogical basis in what is not an experience. But neither is fact intelligible in the absence of its analogical relation to value. Then we may say that experience as fact is what is necessary to make experience as value real, and experience as value is necessary in order to make experience as fact intelligible or to give it meaning. The relation between fact and value is then one of constitutional mutuality, since each is implied as a necessary element of structure in the other, that is, the two terms are analogues of each other and, with their relation, constitute an individual.

That in a given situation, then, which suggests that the situation is real is to be regarded as fact, and that in the situation that makes it mean something is its value. But this seems to be merely substituting "real" and "meaning" for "fact" and "value," and these terms are no more immediately clear than the others. By "real" we ordinarily mean that which is given or presented to us in intuition as a part of the system of things and forces outside us, and by "meaning" we refer to the system of things and relations in that aspect in which it bears a special reference to us as human and to the system of our accomplishments in institutional life. Both reality and meaning thus appear to have their essence in their reference to our minds or to the systems of objects which have been created as embodiments of our purposes. But this interpretation of everything in terms of its relation to man is not justified, and its contradictory character manifests itself in each of the value disciplines at the point where it attempts to find a basis in metaphysics for its basic assumptions. Thus ethics must find a good in the nature of things as the ground of the human good; aesthetics must find a beauty in nature as the archetype of all experienced beauty; religion must find an existent God behind its good God; and so with all "sciences of value." Since a value has its fact analogue as a logical necessity of its nature, the explanation of a value will inevitably involve the setting-forth of the logical structure of a fact if the explanation is to represent the value as real. And this representation of a system of logically structural relations which of necessity carry the implication of being—this formulation of metaphysical ground—has no reference to mere mind or to the merely human.

The tree that stands in the forest is a fact and a value within the natural system and is there related to other facts and values all of which are capable of being presented in experience. When I look at the tree and think of it in terms of its beauty or usefulness, or in any terms relating it to the experiences of men as expressed in institutions, it becomes a subjective value. Of course the tree is both fact and value; the terms are not exclusive but represent two ultimate analogical attributes of everything that is real. Fact and value then in the ordinary processes of description refer to different and distinguishable, but complementary and interrelated, realms; the one to the system of objects and relations called "nature," and the other to the systems of objects and relations called "culture." But the analogical identity of nature and culture as the ground of the reality of both and as the structure of the real must not be overlooked if we are to keep contact with the metaphysical principles upon which the discovery of truth depends. For practical, that is to say ethical, purposes this is equal to saying that fact and value represent an original and objective distinction and are to be regarded as data; that is, they are terms which for the present purpose do not require analysis into simpler terms, or which, under the limits of present purpose, cannot be so analyzed. And in any case, however ultimate, they could only be analyzed out of their cosmic unity, each could only be shown to be real by tracing the logical necessity of its relation to the other. This means that fact and value are themselves elements, and as such are the end products of analysis, not the subject matter of analysis. Then the place to look for their meanings is in the complex system of nature and culture from which they are derived, and where those meanings will themselves be found to be constituent ingredients of the cosmic system.

Any concrete or real instance of life or experience is thus always found as a combination of elements from the realm of nature, which are necessary to make it "real," or which guarantee it "reality"; together with other elements from the realm of culture, which are equally necessary to make it intelligible or to give it meaning. In the superficial language of descriptive science, and in the language of common appreciation, the former are facts, and the latter are values. This does not mean that fact and value are two kinds of facts; it does mean that fact and value are two descriptive and constituent characteristics of everything that is real. The full explanation of their relation can be adequately given only in the logical determination of the aesthetic object, where their relation is one of mutual implication and analogical identity in the substance of beauty. That is, since we must put a thing into terms of experience if we are to talk "scientific" about it, any instance of experience has within it, directly or by implication, both elements of fact as the guaranty of its reality, and elements of value as guaranty of its intelligibility. These two kinds of elements and the realms they imply are always present together and supplement each other in ways that do not require, except for the most extreme purposes of theory, to be distinguished. The theory which distinguishes them does so and can only do so by demonstrating their necessary analogical relations to each other—relations that are necessary in that they constitute the reality which fact and value both imply.

An experience, then, is an instance of reality that exists in nature, qualified so that it also has value or worth, which thereby subsists in the realm of culture; both characters of factuality and worth are immediately perceptible, because they are, together, the objective basis of all perception. Experience is then a term of purely subjective connotation. It is not involved as a term in the logic which depicts a metaphysical structure, because for metaphysics experience is merely one among other elements of the reality. Factual and worthful characters are both necessary as presuppositions in order that experience may have any meaning at all. That is, fact and value are logical implicates of a world which must be presupposed in order to make the notion of experience mean anything. We could not think of a being as having experience for which one of its states is exactly like another or for which any state is homogeneous in characteristic quality. There must be an ultimate distinction as the basis of experience, and the distinction that is ultimate is that of fact and value. And, when we speak of an ultimate distinction, we are reminding ourselves that difference is the criterion of reality so far as our method involves analysis. It is necessary to define experience in this objective way in order to avoid the absurdities of definition in terms of mental states and the "insides" of hypothetical or actual individuals, which always ends in subjectivist contradiction.

This character of experience by which it is made to represent the unity of nature with culture in a real world is called the personal character. Experience, as objective, is, then, personal.

II. EXPERIENCE AS CULTURE

An experience is a representation as an individuate instance of a fact that has worth or value, with the relation between fact and value made the basis of a reference to reality in perception. The absence of the perceptual reference to reality, which absence can be represented only in imagination, leaves the object complete and real, but not known. The two factors in any object that can be real *and* known are the factual and the worthy, or better, worthful, since worthy seems to imply mere capability of possessing worth. As combined in their peculiar unity, their identity by analogy, they constitute the real that has to be taken for granted in connection with every act and every thought of any rational being, if act or thought are themselves to be intelligible, that is, have objective meaning. That is to say, such notions as life, existence, action, purpose, etc., have significance only when such objective meaning is presupposed for the term "experience," since only by this presupposition of objective meaning can experience have any meaning at all. What must be avoided here is the assumption that experience need involve no more than mere inner presence to mind of some affectation or modification of the mind itself, some "mental state." Such an "experience" is a pure abstraction, and in the absence of some element of fact can be given no meaning. But, having presupposed this unity of fact with worth in a reference to the real, anything rational becomes possible to both thought and action, and the structures of existence and culture have been erected upon this basis. Thought becomes the process of progressively rendering explicit the logical (ideal) consequences that the unity of fact and value entails; and life as action becomes the system of processes by which these ideal consequences are created factually into existences by being given concrete relations with elements of fact in nature.

But the concrete result or consequence we have here of the operations of thought and action is an individuate instance of the objective unity of fact and value, and this instance is what we know in experience as the person. The person is then the instance of reality, or a case of reality instanced in experience. Fact and value in their unique identity are regarded as prior to or distinct from person, that is, as a logical presupposition upon which person rests, fact and worth in identity constitute abstract being, and this being with concrete factual and value characteristics is what we mean by reality. Reality instanced is then the person, and the logical function of instancing, or the act as instance, is an experience.

The person is then, in a fundamental sense, an element or unit of reality, *the* element or "point of view" from which the world is and is made intelligible. But intelligibility means, abstractly, nothing more than that fact and value are, on occasion, compatible and consistent within a personal experience and, as such, are elements of meaning.

For a person, then, a fact is a value or is valued, and it is a fact because it is valued; and a value is a fact in the sense that it necessarily implies fact, and it is a value only because it has fact as ground. Their distinction becomes, for intelligence, the basis of their unity. Concretely, intelligibility means that value represents that attribute of this whole or unity which we call dynamic. From this point of view life and experience are action. It is to fact in space and time and their identity in nature that we are to look for the basis of the static or fixed or place-occupying characters of things. This is the realm of reflective thought.

The person, then, as the presupposed basis of intelligibility, is this unity of fact and worth in its character as active thought, the creative or moral agent. So values connect immediately with what comes to be known as the life of action and thus become the topic specifically of morality. For ethics, then, we see once again that the fact of action implies the person, and the person becomes the first major topic for ethical discussion. But it is suggested here also that all life and experience are personal in nature; and every judgment we employ in ethical discussion is a judgment that asserts or implies the existence and value of a person, is, therefore, a judgment of individuality. But at the same time every ethical judgment asserts the world as the ground of personal existence, asserts the world, that is, as the logical structure of individuality, and thus proclaims the person an ultimate object. And as a consequence every ethical judgment is universal and objective and therefore a corporate judgment. Experience, then, is complex, all the differences in the world are, abstractly, differences in or for experience. Not differences *of* experiences, however; this is the fallacy of subjectivism. So all the complexities of life and nature refer us to the person. We shall see later that concretely some differences go beyond or back of experience, as immediately known to be humanly or individually personal, to its impersonal or objective or logical ground in the world. But, since all reality is individuate, this merely defines a higher type of person.

There are, thus, types of persons, and we must examine some of the more important forms. Persons are (A) individual and (B) institutional. Individual persons are (1) natural or (2) social. Institutional persons are (1) quasi-natural, (2) fictive, or (3) corporate.

A. Individual Persons

This is the person as thinker, in which experience in its completeness becomes reason or thought. The person as individual and as a concept of pure theory is limited strictly to the function of thinking, since thinking is the only act of which the individual is capable that does not also complicate his activity with that of other individuals. Objectively, thinking is the only act within which the individual can complete an object. All his ends are ends only in that they are means, that is, technical objects, instruments, so far as his act is overt. The individual in the traditional sense is an abstraction of thought, both in the sense that thought in its reference to objects reduces the object to its elements and in the sense that the processes employed by thought can only be conceived as centered in an isolated source. The only thing that the individual, as an individual, can do is to think; and, conversely, the only thing that can think is an individual. But this becomes complicated when we ask whether thought ever takes place without being involved with other forms of experience. The assumption that it is always involved with other forms of experience leads to the conception of the institutional person. The two types of person must be distinguished. The act of the individual is, then, so far as purely his own and so far as objectively complete, the act of thought.

I. NATURAL PERSONS

The natural person is the organism, or the organic individual as the scientist conceives it. This is the individual described in terms of such qualities and characteristics as relate it only to other individuals in the species. The scientific interest draws a picture of the individual which is constructed for the most part of these abstract relations, and it is difficult to imagine in such terms the active life of the individual in the form in which that active life is expressed in morality. The active life of the individual, the life that is the subject matter for morality in so far as it is strictly the life of the natural person, is described in the chapters on the biological and the psychological aspects of the person, and the discussion need not be repeated here. But we may remind ourselves that the natural person is the individual person of the traditional theory, and that the proper locus of such individuals is the realm of nature, just as the locus of species, as higher personal types with organic form, is the realm of culture. The attempt of science to find a strictly naturalistic interpretation of species has constructed the theory of evolution, and the neglect of the cultural element or the value element necessarily involved in the concept of species has left the doctrine of evolution inconclusive and contradictory on several, perhaps all, points. The attempt at a naturalistic and evolutionary ethics shows this contradictoriness conclusively.

For morality, then, the natural person is the person of biological functions, and with respect to action these functions become for ethics mere abstract capacities and capabilities, since in the nature of the case they can never be complete in an object, and since the functions are interpreted with reference to the natural objects which form the environing circumstance of the natural person. In no case are these functions acts, the natural person can only move, since they by nature are infinite continuities and can never end in an object. They are at best technical processes and issue in a means or tool.

Then the one and only genuine *specific* function of the natural individual is thought, and the issue and proper object of the natural individual's activity is hence in every case a plan. The individual can act only as he expresses himself in thought in the formulation of abstract forms of objects, which may serve as practical plans; or as thought creating ideal objects as imagination giving form to feeling in art; that is, the individual can act only in creating ideal patterns and designs or in fashioning tools in anticipation of objects. Both of these individual acts are incomplete from the moral point of view, since they do not objectify in nature. Action implies the possible unity of nature with culture, and to accomplish this unity is beyond the natural individual's powers. Even for reproduction, in the sense that reproduction is the condition of continuity in the species, the natural individual requires a cultural medium as a condition of morality. The plan itself, as formulated, or the work of art as designed, is then a factor in a fictive person, and its description is given later. But it is, as conscious plan, merely ideal, to be realized, and this also will have to be explained later. The facts with respect to the natural person are described in the biological and psychological sciences. But with respect to the theory of the natural person the sciences can have little to say.

2. SOCIAL PERSONS

This refers to the rather indistinct sets of species relations that bind individual persons into the more or less loosely ordered social "bodies." If, however, the integration of individuals reached the point of complete functional embodiment, the result would be an institutional person. These social or civic "bodies" are attempts to individuate masses or "groups" of natural individuals into a functioning whole. This cannot be done. It is the attempt to do what can be done in the way of integrating individual persons into collectivities or aggregates. There is no need to go into an elaborate description here, since as accurate a description as is possible is given in the traditional political theory of democracy. What is to be noted is that such bodies as can be represented by this method are of little moral consequence, since they are essentially unstable and tend continually to disintegrate. The reason for this is that individuals are collected together on a basis of their states of mind, which are individual rather than species functions, and hence the "collectivities" are mere aggregates without material unity. They are not competent persons because of this lack of material unity or body, without which their functions cannot be energized, and they represent personality on the halfway stage between the natural individual and the institutionalized person. They may have some value in a mere "practical" way, but they have little or no ethical significance.

B. Institutional Persons

This is the person as actor, or agent, the creator of genuine objects, the realizer of ends in their full actuality. Just as experience in connection with the natural individual means the inner reference of self-consciousness, so experience in the case of the institutional person is the cultural purpose functioning as history. An institution is then, subjectively considered, a form of experience objectified in history. Experience is therefore made objective, rendered independent of chance and change and time considered as limitations, while chance and change and time are under all conditions except thought limitations for individual persons. History is experience made objective and universal, and as such it is both the medium in which institutions live and their substantive content. It is as such the substance of the life of institutions, just as nature and consciousness are the stuff of the life of individual persons. Objectively considered, an institution is a system of things objectively ordered with respect to an end. It is as so objectively ordered that the institution can act and thus be a moral person. Institutional persons are (1) quasi-natural, (2) fictive, or (3) corporate. We will describe these briefly.

1. QUASI-NATURAL PERSONS

These are concrete organizations of things established under the influence of history. History in this connection is regarded as objective experience operating through the instrumentality of a specialized natural function and its corresponding structure. Thus the family is such a person—the organization of historic experience around sex and biological structure. The best instance, and perhaps the only perfect instance, is the family in all its various forms. A small economic or religious group where the basis of its unity is primarily some natural or organic need, as, for example, food, sex, security, etc., is also a good instance, the principle being, in every case, the immediate dependence upon some aspect of the natural order. These will require to be described in detail in later chapters.

2. FICTIVE PERSONS

These are instanced in what we in common speech call "ideals," plans, convictions, etc., only we must insist on their empirical reality; they are just as real in ordinary experience as is any other type of person. When I say that my conscience, or my faith, will not permit me to do this or that, I know what I mean just as clearly as in any other case, and you know what I mean also. That is to say, ideas, forms of thought and experience, modes of behavior, objects imaged in abstract futurity, even persistent hopes, fears, etc., come, in the experience of the race, to be organized entities and, as such, take a place in the structure of life as a historically continuous fact and perform a function there just as an organ takes its existence, form, and function from the matrix of life considered as a naturally continuous fact in the species. And ideas, forms of thought or feeling, purposes of will, persistent fears, stereotyped forms of action, become organized in the life-tissue of civilization just as a liver becomes organized in the body of a species of animal that eats a certain type of food.

It is futile to say that these are experiences and must therefore have no part in the fixed structure of the world. They are experiences, in the same sense that every form of existence that has its nature determined by its dependence upon a previously existing form is an experience. The father in an adoption is the father of the child only through the continuous personality of a formal structure of law and custom, and this personality is more real, in the history of civilization, than any natural man. The fictive person is equally important for morality as for law and religion, and, as legal experience and religious experience are aspects of the moral life, it must be regarded as a moral person.

3. CORPORATE PERSONS

The experience of the race, or of any historically persisting division of the race, has the faculty of finding or creating for itself a body in which it takes permanent lodgment and abode. The experience in the race as a whole of certain types of ideal realities has made itself permanent in the characteristic objects of, for example, religion. The experience of these ideal realities under peculiar local conditions has given itself the form, for example, of the Buddhist religion. The experience of specific realities in religion has embodied itself in a peculiar ritual, which has become a part of the life of the race. The same process, with other types of ideal reality, has gone on in politics, law, industry, and in every generalized aspect of experience. Bodies thus created are called "institutions," and specific individuals or persons within this type are called "corporate persons." Discussion of the moral aspects of the corporate person will occupy us in Parts IV and V.

The corporeity of experience, then, necessitates not an analysis of individual experiences into their myriads of conscious qualities or states of mind but a distinction of the types of persons reference to which will distinguish the major forms that experience may take in the process of life. Different forms of action may then be explained by reference to their corresponding types of person, and from this the organization of life may be represented in terms of its more important elements of structure as found in institutions. This will enable us to avoid the hopeless attempt to explain the complex structures of the moral life and culture by trying to show how individuals are brought together into social and institutional bodies. It is at this point where ethical individualism has so signally failed; it cannot explain the complicated structure of life as it appears moralized in political, legal, religious, and aesthetic institutions.

In the succeeding four chapters we shall give a somewhat detailed discussion of the capacities of the natural or individual person.

Chapter VI

The Biological Capacities of the Person

I. THE BODY AS ACTIVE ORGANISM

THERE are certain capacities for action that belong to the person simply by virtue of the fact that he possesses a body. The body is therefore an important detail in the life of action—as a moral phenomenon the body is the most important single fact in the life of the person. The moral aspects of the physical life have been neglected, for our interest in the physical life has been predominantly economic and has not been such as would emphasize those aspects of it upon which the possibility of moral living depends. The physical powers of life are many and varied, and we shall have to select some as typical. But the larger general types of action that characterize the body seem to be three: (A) the power to work, (B) the power to reproduce, and (C) the power to play. All these are of course to be interpreted very broadly as we take them up severally.

A. THE POWER TO WORK

From the point of view of the simplest and most immediate activity of the body, we should probably find the biological function of restitution the most important. By this we mean the power to restore and nourish the part of the organism when the part has been injured or lost. In the literal sense of the term this capacity is perhaps possessed in the most fully developed degree by the lowest organic forms, and it seems to be a function of the species rather than a power or capacity of the individual organism. Thus the more important of the body functions, at least the more immediate, are taken care of by "nature" or "instinct" operating as a function of the corporate life of the species. The power of the body to re-create and sustain itself is what we mean by work in its simplest form. This involves the procuring of certain kinds of materials from the environment and the changing of them in such ways as will make them readily usable by the body.

As this process of procuring and "processing" of materials is in modern life highly organized, there arises in connection with it a number of problems, which in their technical aspects are economic but in relation to the principles involved are strictly ethical problems. In this aspect of principle the organism is a moral fact. The right functioning of the body as a moral instrument depends upon conditions within it, upon conditions within the environment, and upon the relations of the body to the environment. We shall enumerate some of these problems.

a) Specifically, the health of the organism is the most important moral problem here. As the health of the body depends very largely upon the nature of the materials taken from the environment, the control of these materials becomes an important matter. Whether lands are to be used to produce wheat or opium is of great consequence morally. It matters much to the condition of the human body whether we use coal to make electricity for use in the work of industry and the home or use it to make profits for small groups of men. But the difficult thing in connection with bodily health is the maintenance of the right balance between work and play and the control of the nature and quality of the food supply. The moral imperative is that the balance of the work process with the conditions of the body and with the conditions of the environment be steadily maintained in order that the body may be able to function to the best advantage. An unhealthy man is so far not a morally good man, and that persons be physically in good health is a moral necessity.

b) The mental attitude of the worker is a moral problem. This is closely related to health, since it depends in a large measure upon physical health. But it also depends upon many other conditions, such as sanitary and aesthetic conditions in the natural environment and cultural conditions in the social and industrial environment. Good work cannot be done under depressing aesthetic conditions. The sordid ugliness of some factory conditions will inevitably result in morbid mental attitudes. One of the worst features of our machine civilization is the noise it makes. It is not possible to maintain a healthy attitude of mind where noises are so intense and varied as they are in many industries. The most pressing problems of the moral life today are the removal of the more ungainly types of ugliness from the visible environment and the elimination of noises that are excessive both in quantity and in quality from the world of sounds. How the world of nature and the physical aspects of the world of culture are to affect the senses and the sensibilities of persons is perhaps the most difficult problem we are called upon to face, since the character and makeup of our minds and attitudes directly depend upon these sensuous conditions. It is not of course meant that sights and sounds can or should be made always pleasing. But the best evidence of the right sort of effect is the uniform experience of pleasantness.

c) The opportunity to work, in the shape of access to appropriate tools, etc., constitutes a difficult problem which has only lately been recognized. The poverty that is so much lamented is not always a question of food and clothing and shelter and the things that contribute to physical comfort. Most often the cause of moral collapse is the lack of the chance to do something worth while, and this is a matter of access to the tools and materials which worth-while action always involves. The young person who has shown himself capable of intellectual and cultural activities but who has no chance to acquire the necessary training, or, having acquired the training, still lacks the "job," while he sees others no more deserving or capable with access to the use or abuse of the opportunities which he lacks, soon comes to a state of mind that is really dangerous to himself and the community in which he lives. There is of course no guaranty that every capable person will grasp the opportunities presented to him, but even where he fails to do so the reason is likely to be found in the failure of some other aspect of the person's natural or cultural world. He may lack the seriousness of purpose necessary to accept his opportunity, but this argues the failure of his family or his school training or the too aggressive influence of some institutional force like a corrupt theater or a diseased industry. In any case the person must have access to such tools and means as he can use significantly, and as a principle this admits of no exception. Even the incapable person has the right to demand the means by which his powers may be developed, or shown incapable of development, or at least this right is to be exercised in his interest.

d) Conditions of work, hours, speed, sanitary and aesthetic conditions of surroundings, involve a reference to the organization of industry within which most work is carried on. The control of such conditions can be effective only through the control of the organization of the institutions within which work is carried on, and this control should be exercised by those agencies which wield the moral authority of the cultural whole. It is futile to expect the mining industry to find the conditions under which it can organize and manage itself in the interest of the moral purpose. No private industry has ever done this, and it is not in the nature of industry to do it. It is equally hopeless to leave the question of the proper organization of the family to the family itself. The organization of the institutions through which the moral purposes of men are to be achieved is the peculiar function of that agency which represents the whole moral good, the state, the agency which gives opportunity for expression to all the capacities and interests of men. In the last analysis the special problems that grow out of the work function are questions for all of us as operating through corporate political agencies and cannot be met otherwise.

e) Closely related to (*b*) is the question whether the purpose in the mind of the worker is concordant with the purpose for which the work is performed. There is a large batch of problems which center around the disposal of the objects which the work activity produces. Ordinarily, or generally, when work is done under conditions that satisfy moral requirements, the person who performs the work is not interested in the disposal of the objects produced further than in the desire that the object should be used to express the purpose which has been incorporated in it in the process of its creation. A plow should plow and a picture should please, but the person who creates the plow or the picture is not concerned about who is pleased or whose utility has been served. The interest in the disposal of the products of work is not a proper personal interest of the worker, further than is implied in the recognition of the principle that the object should be used to express its own inherent purpose. To dispose of created objects in the interest of specific persons is not a moral function; rather it is an immoral function except when the "interest" of the person is taken to mean a reference to his capacities to produce and enjoy without the implication of control in any other way. And even this disposal of the object is not a personal but a public function. When therefore the person who creates an object of use or beauty sees it diverted from the expression of its proper use or beauty under inappropriate forms and conditions, when, for example, he sees the object controlled with reference only to its sale, he regards the object as prostituted and his own purpose in producing the object foiled. The creator of significant objects is likely to make trouble when he sees these objects become mere pawns in the sale process, for which there appears to be no moral warrant on any ground. Or when the object is made the instrument of control over the lives and prospects and opportunities of persons who have, or want, nothing to do with the object or its creation, it is easy to see that it has become perverted to an instrument of the profoundest injustice. The man who manufactures pills, that is, controls their production, and who uses the pills to buy up the most attractive areas about the city and prevent their becoming parks can never appear just to the chemists and workmen who created the pills for the purpose of bringing health and happiness to suffering people; nor does it seem just to people who suffer for lack of pills because their price is made prohibitive in order to build a high fence around the areas which should have been public parks. Nor does this misuse of land appear just to the farmer, who naïvely believes land should be used to produce food, textiles, etc. These and the controls which they imply are once more political questions which arise out of work.

f) Perhaps the same point as (*e*) is implied in the relation of the individual's work to the institutionalization of the processes of work. This is the problem of the organization of industry, a question best stated in connection with the corporate person later. It is the very difficult question as to the worker's recognition of the part which work activity plays in the organization of the industry to which the work belongs. It also involves the fitting of industry into the scheme of moral institutions. How to fit yourself and your work and its product into the institutions with which they connect most immediately, and through these institutions to fit yourself and them into the total structure of the good life, is precisely the question of politics as it faces the individual. This is complicated further by the question as to what specific types of political machinery will be the most appropriate means through which to express the political relation. While therefore we are unable to envision the work of the person in its larger and essentially moral relations, there is little wonder that the work process is in fact muddled in confusion. Few persons as yet see it in the light of these larger principles upon which alone it could be made effectively and righteously satisfying. One thing seems clear —work is essentially a public function and so long as we continue to subject the work process to the demands of sale and private control by interest it will remain in confusion, and the products of work will satisfy nobody.

B. The Power To Reproduce

This is the power to replace the organism as a whole, when considered from the point of view of the unity of the organism, but to replace it as a part when the organism is considered as an aspect of the species. As an aspect of physical strength or power of the individual, it has no direct "social" implications, and the control of the function looks backward to instinct as the mind of the species rather than forward to control through institutions. Between these two control functions there is of course no place left for any mysterious "social" force, and the reference to the latter is better avoided. Reproduction is thus an individual function designed to replace individuals as wholes, depending for its proper performance upon instinct, and the only control that has historically been exercised over it is that which restricts its scope and the numbers of individuals produced, and these results have been obtained by institutionalizing the function within aesthetic and religious forms. The peculiar emotional condition normally attending the reproductive process is not of great moral consequence, since it is largely a result rather than a cause and attaches to the process regardless of the moral quality of its expression.

Persons, even moral agents, may "choose" mates because of this emotional condition, but the "choice" will stick and establish a permanent arrangement or not, largely depending upon the mutual respect of the persons concerned in the "choice," and respect grows up later out of their more rational and prosaic common activities and interests. And, even where the mutual respect is present, the "choice" is likely to be temporary if the instinctive and organic relations between the two are not appropriate. The "love" therefore that remains permanent is better described as a function, first, of the organic and physiological fitness of the persons involved and, second, as a function of the institutional life of the family or the community. That is to say, such a feeling is a genuinely aesthetic consequence of the public organization or institutionalization of forms built up around the instinct by the influence of cultural history. There is, therefore, little meaning that can attach to the prevailing romantic interpretation of love, the cultural consequences of which are morally negative. That the emotional reaction, being a pure feeling, is not, of itself, capable of institutionalization, and has of itself no form that can be appropriately objectified so as to render the emotion permanent or stable, is demonstrated in the history of some important religious systems.

The moral aspects of reproduction, then, are seen clearly only when the process is recognized as of organic and instinctive origin and nature, for on these characteristics alone can there be built up an effective system of control. Emotion is not subject to direct control; the only way to deal with it is through the organic and instinctive processes upon which it depends, and this is best done by imposing upon the processes and their emotional expression an aesthetic form in the institutions of culture. That is to say, these processes can themselves be controlled only by elevating them to the status of functions of cultural institutions. With these facts in mind certain suggestions may be formulated.

a) The health and cleanliness of the organism is of first consequence.

b) This is closely connected with the injunction that a healthy attitude of mind is to be maintained. This depends for the most part upon a competent and adequate knowledge of the function being made a part of the education of young people, removing the mystical veil of secrecy which has been thrown over it for ages.

c) The opportunity for clean social contacts between the sexes should be maintained at all times, with no segregation.

d) The providing of appropriate cultural conditions surrounding youth. This is fundamentally a question of the adequate and proper institutionalization of the forms of common life, a good home, a competent school, a decent community decently governed, a clean material environment, streets, parks, industrial and other buildings. All these should be not only clean and cleanly managed but also as genuinely beautiful as they can be made. The standard by which the appropriateness of cultural conditions is determined is thus aesthetic. This means that the extent to which conditions can be made beautiful depends upon the physical quality of those conditions, not upon the condition of the public treasury, certainly not upon the caprice of a private owner, nor the whims of social reformers.

C. The Power To Play

This is to be taken in a very much broader sense than is commonly given to play. It involves two forms, both of which are of fundamental importance. These are recreation and art, the first including both the notion of physical and mental restitution and the deliberate interest in welfare. The second includes the appreciation of beautiful things with the developed sense of its importance, and the recognition of the significance of beautiful things as elements in the structure of the world. That is to say, abstractly, play includes all those activities which involve, either consciously or not, the restoration of the whole individual considered as a part of the larger whole of the world he lives in.

Play is therefore essentially creative, that is to say, an activity which goes beyond the mere productive and reproductive functions, which have in view the life of the individual considered independently of his relation to his world. For play, the relation of the agent to his world is the precise point of interest. It contemplates the organization of those relations into permanent systems which shall be as appropriate as possible to the physical conditions of human action. These objective systems are the institutions of life, and play is the essentially institution-building activity of man. The adequate theory of play is thus the aesthetic theory of comedy. Play is of great importance morally, since it is play as continuously creating and maintaining an institutional structure which makes the continued life of meaningful action possible. Since this is true, all, or nearly all, of our actions should be dominated by the play motive, and it is important that we understand what the play motive involves. We therefore undertake to point out the features that are characteristic of play, for these constitute its moral significance.

a) Play elevates the physical acts of the organism to forms of art. Why is this moral? Because morality implies first a physically competent person, and a person whose acts are not beautiful in form fails by so much of being a competent moral agent.

b) An act is not moral until it is technically correct, and it is correct only when it is perfectly adapted to the material it works on. This adaptation is effected by playful experimentation, that is, experimentation with no utility motive.

c) An act imposes upon its material (if appropriate to it) the forms of the ideas which motivate the act. So the act is essentially the setting-up, in overt forms, of the ideas that constitute or make up the mind. It is in this way that action is the instrument of identification of mind and body and thus the causal agency behind institutions. It is a causal agency because the institution comes into existence as the unforeseen and unintended embodiment of the ideas; it is the unmediated expression of the form of the ideas and not of their content, so action in play is the creation in purposeless activity of bodies fit for these ideal forms. It is thus that play, as purposeless or free experimentation, is the institution-building function.

Thus the three forms of biological or physical activity, work, reproduction, and play, are the fundamental types of action for human beings. Work is fundamental, because it sustains the person in life, also gives him his knowledge of and control over the materials of his world. Reproduction is fundamental because it effects the continuity of the species and thus creates the conditions upon which action can have permanent effects. Play is fundamental because it is the inventor of new types of action, and at the same time provides for the fitting-together of acts and their objects into the institutional structure of life. Play is here used in the broad sense which includes art and the objective forms of religion and represents the highest form that is reached by human action.

II. THE BODY IN HEREDITY

The life of the body is essentially continuous. This continuity is mediated through work and play and reproduction and extends in all directions. It extends from body to body laterally or contemporaneously, and as a consequence there is a physical continuity connecting, through the forces and materials of nature, all bodies that exist at the same time. This continuity is created and maintained by action. There is likewise a temporal or serial continuity among bodies, so that bodies of one time continue into the bodies of other preceding and succeeding times. This linear continuity is also effected by action. Hence the continuity of life is a moral question. The actions that create and maintain the continuity of life in time are the expression of the capacities that effect the unity of the body, and we enumerate and describe them here. We justify attributing moral quality to these biological functions on the ground that anything essential to action is of moral consequence; and action in every case depends on, and is mediated through, these lower biological functions.

1. TROPISM

This is an internal act of the organism in the sense that it always takes place within an organ, and there are no obvious connections between the organism and the environment involved. But the function of the tropism is to constitute the organ, and the function of the organ is to mediate a connection with the environment. So far as action is to be regarded as conduct, that is, as tending to modify the environment of the actor, tropism is merely to be taken for granted as a tool that is given, to be worked *with* and not *upon*, and is an instrument pure and simple.

Tropism is thus primarily merely the presupposition of spontaneity or autonomy within the organism and has a logical rather than a factual meaning. It is an assumption made necessary in order to enable us to distinguish action from movement, as it is an obvious fact that the movements of living things differ fundamentally from the movements of nonliving things. A purely physical movement is one that must be thought as unoriginated and infinite; an act is a movement than can only be thought as implying an origin, and, as a consequence, an end. Tropism thus enables us to take for granted that we are dealing with a movement that has an origin and whose origin we can point to with some degree of precision; that is, we can establish a locus for the movement, and so a direction. It is this assumption of originated or original movement that we mean by spontaneity or autonomy, and it is autonomy that distinguishes action from movement. So as originating within the organism, tropism endows the organism with spontaneity. We have here then for the first time the idea of a body that can move itself. Primitive theory here presupposed a "soul" or "spirit" as the cause of movement; we are presupposing an element of constitutional structure as "cause"; and there is little or nothing to dictate a preference in the use of words. But in the fact that it involves only the organism, individuality and a separate integrity cannot be thought for this "soul," nor can its spontaneity be regarded as a cause. The one important feature of tropism in this connection is that instances of it can be combined into complex and continuous structure, and thus action attains the formal character through which it is explained.

2. REFLEX

Structurally, the reflex is a complication of tropisms, and the important matter from the point of view of action is to explain how tropisms can be combined in more complicated forms. There is the same difficulty in understanding how separate impulses of movement can be brought together in a continuous force, also in seeing how separate particles of matter combine in a larger body. But the tropism makes the matter simple. The difficulty is overcome by assumption, and the assumption of the nature of tropisms makes it possible to connect them into composite wholes. The only ethical importance of reflexes, as of tropisms, is that they are the mechanical presuppositions of action, the assumptions that are necessary in order to distinguish actions from movements.

3. VOLITION

It has been shown that we of necessity make certain assumptions about the body and its movements in order to explain the fact of its spontaneity. But we can get the same result more directly by saying that, since the body as a matter of fact does originate movement, is, that is, an agent, it must have a capacity to originate movement. We can then give to this capacity an appropriate name. This we do when we speak of the will. But we complicate the matter very much by connecting the will with the mind, which we think of as distinct from the body, and then by speaking of the will as acting upon the body. But it would appear simpler to say that the will at least, whatever may

be true of the "mind," is just that capacity within the body to originate movements. In this statement we recognize that the body is a
highly organized structure and that by virtue of this organization it
possesses peculiar attributes. This would at least avoid the confusion
of assuming that the body and the mind and the will are a set of distinct things or entities and also avoid the absurdities and contradictions involved in the effort to describe relations among them which
cannot be found as matters of fact.

The will, then, let us say, is just the fact that movement originates
in certain types of situation, and that it characteristically does so upon
the situation's becoming conscious in certain ways of the appearance
of qualities and forms in the external world, the body itself being
regarded as a part of this external world. We have seen already that
certain qualities of actions justify us in speaking of the body as conscious; so the assumption of the power to originate movement is
merely an extension of the interpretation of the fact upon which we
postulate the consciousness or "mind." The fact upon which we postulate both consciousness and will is the substantial structure which
we find in the body's organization. This fact of substantial structure
will be useful to us later in dealing with corporate forms of will. The
fact that living bodies have the capacity to originate movement upon
the occasion of their being aware of the presence of qualified circumstances in the environment we shall call "will" or "volition."

4. HABIT

Another capacity of the body which is of great importance for
action is the power to modify itself, under the influence of a given
form of action, so that a new action may be performed and even
originated without the intervention of consciousness as in the case of
will. The form of an act comes to be imposed upon the structures
directly involved in its production, so that these specialized structures
acquire the capacity of spontaneity which is originally a function of
the body as a whole only. Thus we have in habit an instance of complete co-operation of mechanism and spontaneity, but limited by the
characteristic attributes of the involved structures. We can say either
that an act has its origin in spontaneity and becomes mechanical
through repetition; or we can say that the original capacity to act
derives from the tendency to uniformity of movement as grounded
in the stability of organic structure.

In any case a fact generally overlooked is that, once a habit is
formed, it becomes one of the conditions of the elementary structure

out of which a new type of act is derivable, and it is only "creatures of habit" that possess the higher types of spontaneity and the higher types of organic structure. And the development of a habit means that the organic life as a whole has become reorganized about the new act as a center, so that the internal structure of the active organism is modified by each established action-form. The development of a large number and variety of acts that have thus become mechanized reconstructs the organism upon a more complicated plan, and this again means an increased capacity in the agent for new types of action. Thus we see the unique character of the agent in the fact that his habitual stability and his spontaneity have a common ground or that each may be regarded as grounded in the other. The distinctive thing about habit is that it involves the isolated organism or the organism as unrelated or as only incidentally related to other organisms. The specific function of habit is to relate the organism to its world. It is only when we discuss custom as an extension of habit, and as thus implicating new factors, that we are concerned with the relations of organisms to each other.

5. CUSTOM

Custom, at the least and with reference to individuals, is habit extended to the relations of individuals. It is not merely the collective sum or result of the habits of individuals. Custom is the habit of the corporate human whole, and has its origin in the activities of that whole. It is the habit of the "social" organism, if we are to understand that the "social" organism is not made up merely of individual human beings. Just as action in the organism presupposes a system of parts which are, of themselves, inactive and incapable of action, so the "social" or corporate body presupposes an inert structure or instrument through which its action is mediated. And the inert masses of the "social" body are made up largely of human individuals, which are parts of the mechanism through which the will of the whole works. This "social" or corporate will is thus not a summary or a mystic fusion of the wills of individuals; in fact, the wills of individuals have little or nothing to do with this will of the corporate whole. The "social," or better, corporate public body is built on a basis of physical things, some of which are natural structures, and some are artificial or cultural structures. These physical things are of two types mostly, although all kinds of physical things enter in. The two types are human bodies as the major natural structure, and property objects as the cultural structure. These two types of bodies constitute the skeleton of the public body. That is to say that these two kinds of body are the instruments through which the acts of the public or corporate whole are mediated. The custom that is real is thus not a "social" phenomenon; it is the "custom of the constitution," the latter being the structure of the corporate body of life, which is structured in physical things.

When we ask just what constitutes the "mind" or will or spontaneity of the corporate whole, we have a story to tell similar to that of the mind of the individual body. In any case the mind of any body, and so therefore of the corporate body, is the spontaneity of the organization of the objects which make up that body. The bodies of men and property objects, when organized together, create their corporate spontaneity, which operates through their relations to each other as these relations are objectified in institutions and which constitutes an integrated spontaneous effectiveness that is independent of the minds or wills of individual men.

Thus we see that, when we undertake to describe the physical capacities of the person, we are led through the necessities of the case to consider the corporate body of humanity as the great person which, as end, dictates the directions of activities that are essential to the realization of individual persons and individual purposes.

III. THE BODY AS AN END

We have here the general problem as to how far and in what ways intelligence can be brought to bear upon the life and activity of the body, and how far and by what means can the life of the body be controlled or directed by deliberation toward the ends that intelligence sets up for it. We assume that the body as the physical fact of our existence is also the physical basis of our culture and that every good that we may contemplate in any relation of life will rest upon a physical basis. The problem of most difficulty here arises from the assumption that the body and its life-activities belong within the scheme of natural mechanism, and this scheme is supposed to be proof against any interference by intelligence or any other outside influence.

The question is, then, can the future destiny and development of the body be controlled or modified by our taking thought about it, and, if so, by what means, and, if not, what is to be our attitude to the physical life. When we reflect how great is the importance of the physical life in the scheme of culture, we see how essential it is to do everything that can be done in the way of promoting its development and providing the conditions upon which its development depends. One thing is clear: that if the cultural life depends upon the bodily life, then the bodily life should be cultivated for its own sake, since it constitutes a basic or intrinsic good. Then our question is: Is there any way in which the body and its life-functions can be modified in the direction of general ends? Is the body properly an object of control in the interest of the good life? There are two or three ways in which these questions can be answered affirmatively.

1. NUTRITION

Nutrition is one of the body functions that can be controlled. There are two important problems connected with proper nutrition of the body. One is the economic and industrial problem of providing that sufficient food be produced and equitably distributed, and the other that food be properly adapted to the requirements of the health and development and maintenance of the highest possible degree of physical life. What we have to say here applies not only to food but also to shelter and clothing, etc., and, when we speak of food, we have in mind all the necessary physical goods.

How the proper amounts, qualities, etc., of physical goods are to be produced and distributed is a problem of industrial technique, with the control element vested in political authority, and is better discussed in connection with the institutional aspects of those questions. The principle is, however, clear; production and distribution of goods are functions which should be regulated with respect to the idea of the whole good. They are therefore functions of the corporate person as expressed in legislative activity. The food and shelter and clothing necessities of mankind are too important and too difficult to be successfully met by each individual for himself or by any individual or individuals for the whole. With respect to the physical necessities the individual is quite helpless during the culturally formative period of his life, as well as during the period of his physical development. And it begins to be evident that the sustenance and maintenance of life throughout all periods is a function of the corporate whole if it is to be properly and effectively done. It is clear, therefore, that providing the physical goods to persons is a function of the corporate body, since it cannot be done consistently with the requirements of right and good by any other method.

The second question is in its technical phases essentially a matter for medical science and hygiene. Questions of the amounts and kinds of foods necessary for the most perfect maintenance and development of the physical capacities for all periods of life are technical questions in a peculiarly important way. But the same is true of clothing and shelter. The problem of maintaining the physical well-being of the moral agent is, however, one which can be solved only by the corporate whole and under its authority. For I cannot have health, food, clothing, shelter, beauty, strength, and intelligence except under conditions that guarantee to all men the same to the limit of their capacities, and the individual's isolated powers and capacities do not constitute an important part of those conditions. The one essential condition is that all our interests and activities and possessions are subject to the rule of the right and the good, and this expresses a character of the whole.

This of course means that all matters of welfare are properly to be determined by the public corporate purpose, and technically implemented in and by corporate instruments and agencies, under corporate public authority.

2. PHYSICAL TRAINING

Here the greatest difficulty comes from confusing the purpose of training with exercise and health, on the one side, and, on the other side, with "sport" and aesthetic activity.

a) Physical training is not exercise, not, that is, activity exclusively in the interest of health. In exercise we are interested in an activity for some reason other than the activity itself. We are interested in running to develop the "wind." Now in physical training what we want in these activities is merely to perfect the activities themselves; we want to know how to make running a perfect physical activity. The moral good here is determined by a pure aesthetic standard. Of course it is true that once the capacity is perfected it can be utilized in many ways—work, sport, exercise, etc.—but the purpose of physical training is the training of our physical capacities on the simple conviction that a trained and developed capacity is good, and its goodness lies in the kind of acts it can perform. That we may later use the capacity for other purposes is another and a different motive, and must not be confused with the pure purpose to be capable.

b) On the other side, we confuse physical training with aesthetic activity and sport. By "sport" we shall mean here activity entered into and maintained for pleasure, either the pleasure inherent in the activity or in its associations. By "aesthetic activity" we mean disinterested activity or activity for the sake of the perfection of its object. On the latter definition it is difficult to distinguish clearly between aesthetic activity and what we indicated above as activity with the pure moral purpose to be capable, which we identified with physical training. But the distinction is real nevertheless. Physical training is interested in the capacities of the individual as specific capacities, and its purposes are fulfilled when these capacities have been perfected to their highest degree as single capacities. On the other hand, aesthetic activity is interested in an act as a part of a whole of form—a form that is the perfect expression of a design. But these distinctions do not mean that the activities may not be pleasurable in their training, or that they may not be contributory to or even essential aspects of a whole of form; activities may or may not be of these classes. What must be true if it is to be physical training is that the activities involved be performed for their own sake and for their own sake alone, for their technical perfection as acts. That these acts may be used in other connections of sport or art or health is secondary and incidental. Physical training seeks a perfect body—perfect from the point of view of the technical competence of each of its capacities. This is the moral good of the physical life, which is the foundation of all goods for any ethical system which hopes to be complete.

3. EXERCISE

We have already indicated something of the nature of physical exercise. Its primary purpose is the maintenance of the condition created by training and the co-ordination of the various details of training into a general physical competence of the whole person. There are several things that exercise is not, on these terms, and we may indicate some of them. It is not of course necessary to mention the confusion of exercise with the maintenance of social standing through golf, dance clubs, etc., since this, again, deceives only practical people. Exercise is not properly a corrective for diseased or disturbed conditions in the physical life; and while taken with other measures it may be useful in this connnection, it is useful only as incidental to something else. Its real purpose, as we have said, is the maintenance of the body in the general condition of training. But this is a rather complicated function, and it is difficult to describe it without encroaching upon other matters.

There are, however, some characters that may be mentioned. It is not possible to distinguish the actual well-being that comes with exercise from the aesthetic and other pleasurable qualities of the activity, whether these qualities be intrinsic or attaching to it by association. I do not know, for instance, precisely what it is that has such value to me as I walk along the river. I feel the exuberant energy of the walking, the rare feeling of the air laden with sounds and scents, the forms and colors continuously spread before my eye, the buoyant or sad memories that arise from I know not where. All these are parts of the meaning of the exercise, but I do not know in what way any one of them contributes. The conclusion seems to be that it is precisely the function and meaning of exercise to combine and unify in my experience just these features, and it appears that nothing else will serve to that end. And if we remember that we mean by a "full or general physical competence" of the body or of the whole person just this type of co-ordination of capacities to act, together with their accompanying capacities to feel, we shall have the moral equivalent of the aesthetic meaning of the physical life.

4. BEAUTY

There is yet another moral characteristic of the body-life which may be stated in the maxim that the body must be beautiful. This frankly recognizes that physical beauty of person is a moral obligation. But until we have learned the very many things that are involved in saying that such-and-such a thing is beautiful, or that something is obligatory, until we know what such expressions mean, it will be best to postpone the discussion of this topic.

Chapter VII

The Psychological Capacities
of the Person

I. THE RATIONAL OR KNOWLEDGE FACULTIES

THE characteristic capacity of the person as a natural agent is the power to act and as a cultural agent the power to know. It is around the knowing function that the various powers of action are organized, and thus the moral character of the individual is built up. Hence it is necessary, in the interest of the good life, to get clear conceptions as to the nature and mode of functioning of the knowing powers, to see what they are and what is the specific work of each. There are four activities of mind that are regarded as phases of the knowledge function, each in its own special and peculiar way, and we shall briefly describe them. It must be kept in mind that each of these, while primarily a knowing function, has other interesting forms of expression which will not concern us here. Each of them has an important part in aesthetic activity, for example, but we are here interested in them as knowing functions with special reference to their bearing on action. Knowledge is the most important of the capacities of the moral person as a natural individual, just as wisdom, as we shall see later, is the fundamental capacity of the moral person in his corporate form.

There are four characteristic knowledge faculties: (A) perception, (B) memory, (C) imagination, and (D) reason. Let us examine the significance for action of each of these.

A. Perception

As a strictly knowledge function, perception is the act of mind in which objects are given in experience. It is not our purpose here to give an extensive account of the psychological processes involved. Our concern is rather with the objects of experience which are formed in perception. Perception is not the process of merely combining isolated sensations. As a matter of fact there are no such isolated elements in experience. What are called "sensations" are qualities distinguished within a perceived object. That red, a sweet scent, a velvety feel, etc., should mean rose would never occur to us from sensation alone. It is only when by an act of the mind in perception these qualities are experienced together as making up a whole that an object appears. The qualities are given with the object, as characters of what from the first is an object. Now, for all practical purposes, that is, for all situations where action is the first consideration, this object is of most concern. For it is with reference to an object that all types and all aspects of action, all distinctions concerning action in any case, are to be determined. It is true that in ethical thinking actions are frequently judged with respect to the mental states that are involved in them or that precede or follow them; but it is just this mistaken reference to mental states that makes so much of ethical reflection futile.

So perception is the faculty which gives us objects. The object is the point of reference not only for all distinctions of actions but also for all judgments about actions. And, as action is the subject matter of ethics, it is necessary that we understand as fully as possible the nature and practical status of the object. In our attempt to explain the function and status of the object we may proceed through certain distinctions. The object may be considered as (1) thing; (2) purpose; (3) goal; (4) tool; and (5) end.

I. THING

When the object is considered as a thing, we have the object of perception as a mere problem of knowledge. That is, our interest in it is limited strictly to those of its properties and relations through which it is known; and by its being known, in the simplest case, we mean its merely standing in the presence of consciousness without relations and with no qualities except those given immediately in sensation or derived by memory from sensation. This is the object regarded as "concrete"; but, formally, the same is true of the abstract or logical object, which is merely what is known in thought without direct reference to sensation. Its relations to the mind that knows it are its sole determinants. Both are *objects*, however; they are there, whether in consciousness or in thought, and are distinguishable from the mental processes in which they appear. That is to say, the object as thing is a pure object of cognition, and its importance for action is fully stated when we say that, as an object of cognition, it is merely presupposed in and by our active attitudes. We have to take it for granted, when we contemplate action, that the objects involved in the action are there and are known. If I go to town, I must know the road, which car to take, etc., before I start, or at least know other objects through which these are to be learned. The object as thing is for ethics, therefore, of only theoretical importance, but in this sense it must be understood, since all other meanings of the term are derived from and depend upon its meaning as an object of cognition.

2. PURPOSE

The object as a purpose is the object pictured to the mind in terms of the active attitudes which accompany its cognition. That is, an object is known, or formed in the mind in any case, within a matrix of feelings or upon a background of feelings, emotive urgencies, incipient desires—in fact, all the stuffs of which mind is made up. Hence it will often be determined as to a good many of it characters by the peculiar qualities and arrangements obtaining among these different stuffs. When the character of the object is obviously determined by a combination of these subjective factors with a strong bearing in the direction of desire, we say that our mental attitude is one of interest and that the object of the interest is a purpose. As almost any object may be thus colored, and as almost every one is to some extent so colored, the purposive character of objects is not of much consequence. The media through which an object is experienced cannot be, from the point of view of action, at least, the basic materials of the object, otherwise objects could be made by mind "out of whole cloth." But as the primitive mental urgencies are often supposed to be connected as causes with the objects of action, all we mean by purposive objects is that objects may be connected with mental states much in the same way that they are externally connected with each other as cause and effect. That is, object and mental state may stand in relations of sequence.

It must be remembered, however, that a cause does not *make* or produce its effect. The interpretation of objects as purposes gives us therefore no real insight into the nature of objects; it merely tells us something about the uniformity of a relation in which objects frequently stand in abstract perception, more particularly when they stand in consciousness in the abstract status of contiguity in space and time. Merely to describe objects as purposes, therefore, or to discuss their qualities by reference to factors of mind, is unimportant; at most it can tell us universally that objects are such as can and do stand in relations of many kinds to the act of mind by which they are cognized and through which they have the characters that

constitute them objects of knowledge and at the same time determine their strictly objective relations. Objects as things and purposes
are largely therefore mere hypothetical derivatives from psychological distinctions; and this assures us that little of ethical importance is
to be expected from psychological theory. The following three distinctions give the real practical or ethical significance of objects.

3. GOAL

The importance, such as it is, of the psychological or purposive
urgencies connected with objects lies in their capacity to integrate
themselves in a fairly clear cognition of an "ideal" object. By this is
meant nothing more than that an object may be imaged or prefigured
in the mind as if it were lying in some set of relationships other than
those given in the present perceptive or space-time scheme. And, in
the case of the "ideal" object, the relational setup is a framework
made up of just the subjective emotive and volitional elements of the
background within which the cognitive process moves. The cognitive process, that is, can formulate the object within an environing
circumstance made up of the present mental materials within and
among which it moves, and can and does substitute this scheme for
the scheme of space and time as the latter is given in sense. This is
what is meant by the popular idea that goals and "ideals" are postponed to a distant region and a far-off date. But they are not merely
set up in futurity; they are pictured as the kinds of thing that can
occupy a real objective scheme which differs from the present space-
time scheme, a structure that is obviously objective yet of the same
stuff as the mental motives which purposed it. It is through the idea
of objects as goals that all *motives* to action are explained. An act
would remain a mere movement except for the possibility, pictured
in an ideal object, of a goal that identifies or may identify in substance with our present actuality and that carries the conviction that
the realization of this identity is dependent somehow upon a modification of present actuality by our own energies and efforts.

A goal is, then, the substance of our present experience transferred
to an imagined situation in which that substance can be objectified
and materialized. We make the future, considered as the plan of a
system of possible objects, out of our own life-stuff when we prefigure goals and think them as connected with our inner urgencies
and energies. On any other view an act would be either a mere movement, which has never been nor can ever be explained, a mere fact to
be merely accepted; or a pure irrationality, a fact to be accepted be-

cause forced upon us but condemned in the acceptance. The latter alternative can make a good psychological case for itself when it resolves action into instinct and intuition, but it can never explain conduct or the existence of objective cultural values. The most difficult problem with respect to action, and one which must be solved before any ethical quality can attach to action so as to make it over into conduct, is just this, of showing *how* an *act* is intelligible; and it can only be done through the psychological and logical elucidation of the act of mind that recognizes an object as a goal and that sees the relations that distinguish a goal from a mere object as themselves part of the objective structure of things. Naturally we do not mean goals in the cheap sense of "objects of desire." There are no objects of desire; there are objects only of cognitive acts. What is meant by objects of desire is the state of empirical confusion in which there can sometimes be noted a correspondence between desire and kinds of abstract things which are not yet clearly cognized. It is not action that we can connect with our desires and other passions; the essence of an act is its intelligibility; in so far as our overt expressions are dependent upon these mere "states" of mind, they are movements and have their meaning only in terms of the merest possibility—that is, they are the abstract physical conditions of action. A goal is, on the other hand, the object of a cognition that is capable of being developed into a type of judgment, which judgment becomes the basis of any post facto evaluation of the act or any estimate of its status as an ethical phenomenon. A consistent ethical theory must be strictly speculative and rationalistic at every point, for it is dealing throughout with objects and hopes to describe the design of a world; it can and must leave it to the psychologists to describe mental, or rather psychological, processes.

4. TOOL

The implement by use of which we make connection between the mental substance and the ideal objective world is the tool, or as commonly called in ethics, the means. When we picture to ourselves the difference between the unsatisfactory present of our experience, itself represented to us as an object in the scheme of externality, and the logical opposite which we set up as a plan or goal, the volitional and emotive urgencies, which are there presented as mere materials, immediately suggest to the act of distinction how to define and prepare an act in which the difference between the actual and the ideal can be overcome. It is this mass of emotive urgencies that suggest to me that this rough board has a pair of bookends in it; in being the passive and massive stuff of my cognition they color the act by which I distinguish board from bookend with the design of the act that creates the bookends out of the board. This is the act of will; not the capricious expression of energy by a mystical power—there is no "will" in this sense—but the mere prefiguring in "feeling" of a way or procedure by which the differing states might be brought together.

The will is thus the advance image of an act at the moment when the act is merely implicated in the design or setup of present mental content and before cognition has given the setup or design definition in outline or definiteness of form. It is a form of consciousness, a low but basic form, in which the content is taken from the contrast of mental factors without any specific objective reference. It is for this reason and in this sense that acts of pure will are sometimes said to be blind; they have not as yet in any degree anticipated their normal outward connection. And they cannot do this for the reason that the prerogatives of anticipation and of objective reference belong to cognition. So there are no objects of will as such; what are sometimes called "objects of will" are really objectives of the intelligence; the will "act" is the formulation in subjective consciousness of the scheme of an overt act, and this formulation is effected by the confluence of the urgencies of feeling, desire, emotion, etc. When the conflict of these elements is cognized as an object, we speak of "a will." There is thus neither a mental substance nor a peculiar act that may be called will, certainly not a power or "agency" in the sense of a center of potential energy. The term is not nominative but descriptive; and there is no fact of action that can be explained by reference merely to "the" will. Action, indeed, must be explained in all its intricacies before any notion of will can be made intelligible. Acts do not "proceed from" the "will."

What is really significant in this connection is that, when an act is prefigured by "will," what really happens is that the intelligence cognizes an object as a means and as one through which the act itself may be realized. But it must be understood that it is a means to an act and not a means to an end. The doctrine that ends are results of the use of means, which are abandoned directly the results or "ends" are achieved, is what has justly brought theoretical ethics to ill repute. From this mistaken point of view ends are really indistinguishable from effects, and acts of will from causes. But this distinction is foundational for ethics, and we are not recognizing it when we merely obscure it by painting it over with colorful "valuations." Means are objects in their own right, just as ends are objects in their own right. Both are objectives, and in the same sense neither is a cause. A means is an end in itself in that it is the means through which itself is realized as end. The distinction between means and end is not, therefore, the conception of two objects, the one becoming or leading to the other in which it finds its total meaning; the doctrine that the end completes or realizes or justifies, or is related in any other way to, the means, in the sense that the means is incomplete as an object and derives all its meaning from the end, is as faulty as the doctrine that the means is a cause or mere instrument to the end. For it misconceives the nature of the relation between means and end. It is not the means that is completed in the end but the *act*. Means and end are two co-ordinate phases of the same end. The means is the practical objectification or implementation *of an act,* the expression of the act in overt and external form, the object in which the act finds its body. It is designed in cognition as the body appropriate to an act formulated in "volition." It is the end of the act in the sense of that in which the act is complete or is given full overt expression. And it must not be confused with the end as the issue of a mere process of energy expenditure, which is end in the sense of the abstract limit or point of cessation of motion. The end is not a result, in any sense, of anything. Nor must either means or end be confused with the mere "tool" which the act uses as a condition of its "action." This is the kind of confusion upon which depends the "utility" ethics and the ethics of pragmatic instrumentalism.

The tool or means is an object of cognition and differs from other objects of cognition only in that it is designed after the form of an act to serve as the physical expression or embodiment of the act. The act is formally complete in it, as the image of beauty is complete in the picture or statue. It is, therefore, a type of end and is an independent object in the sense that it is not a mere corollary of an end otherwise determined. And there is no part of its meaning that can be expressed in terms of use or usefulness.

5. END

But while means are ends, ends are also means. The object that embodies an act solidifies the act to permanent form, and the act thus acquires a determinate place in existence. As such, it is the type or pattern for all acts similarly "willed." It therefore terminates the effort toward further design of objects, since objects may now be produced in its image. It is the end in the sense that it is the limit to the further development of the expression of the act it represents, except in so far as the act may be indefinitely reproduced or repeated after it as pattern. The system of such acts objectified in the objects in which they are rendered permanent as means and ends constitutes the structure of culture. Culture as the order of acts and objects thus determined has two phases: it constitutes the established system of institutions as the medium or arena within which all action takes place and it is the sum of all objects that embody individual acts as the instruments or patterns to succeeding acts of the same kind. The first is the system of political society; the second, the institution of property.

The end (ultimate), then, of every act is, first, to embody itself in an object appropriate to its design or form or pattern and to make that object permanent; and, second, to create and maintain the system of such objects as the structure of the cultural life and the universal condition of all acts. When we speak therefore of action with reference to ends, we mean that the act finds its meaning ultimately in this system of culture. Also when we refer to the right and the good as standards of judgments about acts, we mean to refer to the cultural system in some of its generalized aspects; and we indicate, by using the terms "right" and "good," a place or locus in that system to be occupied by a typical object or a set of qualitative conditions to which the object must conform. The right as standard, for example, is the constitutional or constitutive element of structure within the cultural whole to which acts must conform if they are to contribute to the creation and maintenance of that cultural whole. The right may then be regarded either as a matter of fact or as a matter of principle; it may be discovered through analysis of the factual content of culture, or it may be derived logically from interpretation of the form of the cultural system as implicated in the structure and form of individual acts and objects which are statable in judgmental form. It is for this reason that legal and political, or economic and religious, concepts of right and good vary so widely as they do. Economic and political thought normally follows the content of the right, while religion and law usually insist upon its formal character. It is the function of ethical theory to provide a general synthesis of all these points of view to the end that their respective claims may all be harmonized.

The importance of perception, then, lies in the fact that it gives us the object, which the other cognitive functions develop and realize, and it is through the object that the important distinctions in ethics are all made.

B. Memory

If we were interested primarily in the psychological aspects of these mental functions, we should have to start from the assumption that they all are essentially only distinguishable phases within the unity of mind. Thus if we regard perception as the elementary knowing function, then memory, imagination, and reason would be only developments of it. So, also, if perception is the faculty of objects, then memory, imagination, etc., are various stages in the definition of objects in experience and represent the various forms of objects in the world. There will thus be a correspondence between the different mental stages and the various types of objects. Memory corresponds in general to the thing of perception as a pure cognitive object. It represents the element of continuity and solidity and permanence in experience which makes possible the stable historic world of culture. Memory is essentially the function, or set of mental processes, through which the objects of perception are made permanent elements of the life of the individual mind and, through it and its expression in action, fixtures of the total structure of culture. Ordinarily we think of it as a purely subjective process limited to the private life of the individual, in which case it is the learning, retention, recall, recognition, etc., of the individual in his efforts to establish some elementary degree of order among his mental states. This process is commonly described in psychology as the whole that memory means, but for purposes of morality what appears as real in our minds and as having existed through more than one presence to consciousness must be real in some sense and independent of its presence in any given moment of conscious experience. This independent object, the object as beyond and outside the present of consciousness, is a postulate of action and an assumption necessary to the continuity of experience as effected in memory. We saw in an earlier chapter that object in this sense is a logical implicate of action, that is, is necessary to make the fact of action intelligible.

Memory is thus the operation, in the present of the individual experience, of the past as that past has been reduced to cultural form in the objects of history. In the mere present of perception, when regarded as a function of mind, the mere data or details of the given are brought to a synthesis in a purely subjective form. This subjective form is known as a mental state, and the most characteristic of its qualities is its instability. It is this limitation of their consciousness to the mere present of mental states which marks the distinction of the lower animals from man. The animals live thus in the present, and their conscious life is maintained only so long as the intensity and quality, etc., of the mental state can be preserved. The man, however, lives beyond his present and can establish the permanent structures of his life upon elements which need not be in consciousness in the present at all. That is, the present of consciousness rests upon an objective past, as that which has been but is not now experienced, but which nevertheless so operates within the present that it can, as occasion requires, appear as consciousness in any given state or moment. The object of memory, therefore, as the past established in a system of cultural objects, mediates between, establishes universal connections among, the several instances of consciousness, and in this way lays down the condition for the unity of the mind-life as a whole and, at the same time and through the objective implicates of perception, makes intelligible the continuity of the objective or external world. And in the same way the memory object maintains the continuity of the mind-life with the external world, which is the empirical ground of the metaphysical assumption that matter has the capacity for memory.

In this conception of a continuous world we have the necessary ground or objective reason for an act, since an act would be meaningless if it did not presuppose that it is possible to secure real or permanent results, and permanent results are possible only in a stable world. The system of all these permanent or stable objects is culture. Thus the past and its object that are given in memory and that thus operate to unify experience are not the mere psychological or mathematical past and object but the cultural past and the cultural object. That is, it is the past with a history, the past that has preserved within its own substance the content of the myriad presents. The unity of the various presents is thus founded upon characters of the whole that are discoverable in every present experience, so it is memory operating as this historical past that first gives us universals. Memory is then the condition not only of objects and of a stable world but, through its universals, also the ground of the principles by which the world is made intelligible, and action in, on, and for that world justified.

But, once in possession of universals, the mind is freed of the mere blind functioning in it of historical content. The uniformity and regularity of conscious presents and of the stable objects which presents imply, as the formal basis of the universal, may now become an element within the conscious present and thus become an object; the *relations* of presented contents are now taken charge of by the active consciousness, and mind now thinks. Thus it comes to possess a method by which it passes from the mere variety and quality of its content to the significance or value of that content, and with this method assumes control of its own activities. That is, it can now act *with reference* to an object, and a future condition becomes the cause by which the present details of action are shaped and directed. With a degree of possible control from within over the operations of mind, the memory becomes the next more complex and higher form of mind-life which we call "imagination."

C. IMAGINATION

Imagination is also an extension and development of the earlier stages of mind. Just as memory extends the meaning of the elementary present of experience by connecting it with the past, so imagination extends it in the direction of what is future and possible, what is not yet realized or established. Imagination determines the object, that is, in terms of what it can be, or in terms of objects that are designed by new changes in the subjective life. The content of the subjective life is, as we say, notoriously instable, and of itself cannot maintain any given form. But the changes within this content, for the very reason of their instability, will hit upon object-forms which have not been realized and thus effect the unity of these newly designed forms with the old forms. These projected object-forms, held in mind as abstract designs, are what we know as *plans*. Imagination is then the planning function, the process in mind whereby the forms and designs of objects are prefigured before they are given concrete reality in and through action. The form or design of an object in mind is thus the plan of an act, and the form becomes shape and the design becomes structure through the ordinary processes of action. The thought becomes an object, the act a deed. The act as plan is thus the "cause" of the designed object, since it is one in nature with it, and in this act of unity life becomes "creative." But such terms would be regarded as rather out of place in ethical discussion; the common terminology would describe these processes and results in terms of phases and aspects of the "will." Imagination is thus the cognitive phase of will or the volitional phase of thought, and through it the transition from thinking to doing, from the functioning of thought to the execution of objects in action, is readily made.

D. Reason

To bring all the functions of thought and action into consistent relations with each other, so that life may operate as a whole, is the ethical function of the reason. Its logical function is to demonstrate the continuity of nature with culture, thus proving that culture is the designed objective or end which nature is destined to attain. Since the giving objective effect to the connection between nature and culture, world and mind, is essentially the meaning of action, the function of reason is, as a theoretical problem of ethics, to exhibit the continuity of the act as a rational and intelligible whole. That is, reason has the task of showing that an act is justified, that is, made an instance of right in the appropriateness of the relations of unity in which an idea as a plan is objectified in nature. As this is a cogent demonstration, at the present stage of knowledge, only when limited to the instancing of the unity of culture with nature in an act, we can have only inductive evidences of the unity, and, since obviously such evidences are not conclusive, action remains adventure. The act is therefore, in the sense of its ultimate objectification, capable of interpretation only on the "law" of chance. This adventure and the chance of being right in the sense defined above is thus the only rational justification of a moral act. If I do the act, I *may* learn from it not only worthful things as to the how of action but also reasons as to the why. But I may also wreck the world or destroy myself; I can say that I shall know the truth if I understand the will only when I can be sure I know the will; and this means that an act and its will can be right only in so far as knowledge justifies it. But while to intelligence action must always involve adventure, it is the task of intelligence also to know as fully as possible what are the conditions and probable consequences of the adventure in any given case. It must know something definite about the nature of the risk. It must protect the adventurer against the risks of ignorance and folly in so far as possible.

II. THE AFFECTIVE OR CONATIVE FACULTIES

We have seen that, so far as morality is a matter of the individual and his capacities, the capacity to know is the most important function of our nature. An act is, in the last resort, an act of mind, or, if we prefer, an act can only be distinguished from a movement by the presence in it of cognition. Knowledge thus lies at the root of action. But we noticed also that the act of cognition, or the phenomenon of knowing, presupposes also a ground within which it occurs, that the act of mind is unintelligible except we conceive it as bodied somehow in its nonmental circumstance. For us at this juncture and within the limits of psychological presuppositions, this ground or circumstance within which mind acts and lives is the complex of affective and sensory material which constitutes the bulk and stuff of experience at any moment. This material is the product of the myriads of contacts of our bodies with the external world, welded and fused together with the organic effects of the responses of our bodies to these contacts, the capacity of the body to have contacts and to respond presupposing the presence of some degree of elementary spontaneity. Our responses modify these contacts in such ways as to change, repeat, or prolong their physiological effects, and these changes of the effects of contacts constitute them affects, the mass of which taken together being what we call the affective life.

Feeling is, therefore, the total sum of effects of the contacts of the body with nature, with the cognitive elements of the sensory contacts blended into the whole. It implies merely, as pure or abstract feeling, the total of organic receptivity, and it is thus, substantially, passive and is properly called passion. But we have seen that the merest presupposition of life, as the total of organic functions in the way of urgencies toward the repetition of contacts, implies the active principle of cognition. Then the elementary life of passive feeling and the primordial activity or spontaneity of elementary cognition in sensation, imply each other; and the relation of feeling, as the background of cognition, to cognition, as the primary active intelligibility of feeling, is an intimate and internal one. It is a relation logically of mutual implication and factually of interpenetration. This relation is the only real identity we know and can be described only in terms of aesthetic principles. Thus feeling is not only a premise for the cognitive act but is also the material or substance from which the cognitive act, as a practical act, derives a consequent or creates an existent, just as the act of thought extends and expands its premises into a conclusion. All this is logically necessary in order that an act may be conceived to produce a result beyond what is given in its conditions; an act must contain within its original design the conditions of its objectivity, otherwise there could be in the life of action only the eternal and infinite sequence of events with each event exactly like the rest, as in the case of causation. An act must "get somewhere," must issue in something, and the issue must be qualitatively and functionally different in character from any or all of its antecedents or "causes." I say that this is necessary if an act is to be intelligible as distinct from movement, and if action is not to be intelligible, and not totally distinct from movement, there is not only no ethics but also no morality, and action is an illusion.

There is, then, behind every act that background of feeling which supplies not only the arena and stage for the act but also the material or stuff out of which the act is to be made. It is this feeling-stuff that gives to the act its connection with existence, and through it acts are enabled to realize or materialize themselves, to have objects. Acts give themselves a body in existence which is derived from the feeling-stuff within which they originate, the common *primum* of both life and nature. It is the function of the reason to direct the abstract process of embodiment in such ways as to issue in a designed form, that is to say, an individual.

Feelings are meaningless when regarded as "springs to action," since there is no meaning to the expression "springs to action," except in the case of spontaneity in cognition. Besides, feeling is *in substance* passive, and nothing arises from it except when it is vitalized from without. Feeling is not a cause but a material; and in any case action has no cause, lying as it does in another realm than cause.

A. Will

An act which implies existence is will. We noted above that an act need not imply existence and that this logically uncircumstanced or free act is precisely what we mean by cognition. But there is no act without a ground and an object, and the act of cognition has both in the feeling substance. This act of cognition thus comes to full expression in imagination in the prefiguring of plans. This is the function of active design. It would be tempting to discuss it here, especially in connection with the passive design with which it is to be correlated in aesthetics and which gives us the concept of form; the two together giving us the elementary concept of designed form or formed design, the basic principle of aesthetic theory. But aesthetic activity transcends existence; moral activity transforms it; both are objectified through it. It is this transformation of existence by morality that we are concerned with here in the discussion of will.

All affective and conative experience, in fact, experience as such, implies intelligence, and any statement about such experience, even the most simply descriptive, will take for granted the presence of intelligence. We may go on to describe the facts, then, with this assumption accepted as behind everything we say.

But before we come to the moral act as an expression of will, we

must further define the act of will, must name the species to which
the moral act belongs. The act of will, the act that implies and transforms existence, is an instance of the practical act in general. As such,
the act of will is the distinctive motive in a number of different types
of act, the difference of type being determined by which functions
of the unity of character predominate in a given case. If thought in
its analytical form prevails, the act will be scientific, or practical in
the utility sense; if feeling without the impulse to form prevails, the
act will be religious; the sense of form will determine the act as
aesthetic, etc. Thought in its unrestricted free motive to know is the
logical or pure cognitive "act" and differs generically from the practical act in any form, although an element of cognition is always
present in the latter. It is the direction given to the cognitive aspect
of the act that determines the type of practical act in any case. The
moral act is that practical act whose direction is determined by the
fact that the world of existence, as given in the cognition that formulates its design, is to be transformed or brought under direction and
control. The different types of agency through which the act of direction or control is exercised will determine the peculiar methodological techniques of the different forms which moral theory will
take on.

Now this somewhat abstract account of the meaning of the moral
will introduces us to one of the famous historical questions of ethical
theory. This is the question as to which one of the distinguishable
psychological "motives" present in the control of action it is that gives
to the process its peculiar moral quality. This inquiry about "motives"
was really a research intended to find the peculiar function which cognition always has in the act of will. The great variety of possible "motives" found was due to the mistaken assumption that the empirical
was the proper method of research, whereas the only adequate method
in such a connection is the speculative. The question has been debated
for ages, and all the prominent factors of mind have been shown to be
involved as "motives" in a moral act, with the emphasis now upon
this, now upon that factor. The rationalists have argued that it is the
presence of the reason in an act that makes it moral. The will is for
them a rational will. The sensationalists claim that we have a peculiar
sense or perception that discloses to us the moral quality. For them
will is an apprehending rather than a discriminating function.

Voluntarists argue that there is a unique and distinctive faculty of
action, a motive faculty called the will, as if the mere factual character of will could be personified; and that acts derive their moral qual-

ity from its influence. Others say that we discover the moral quality from "experience," and then go on to great lengths to explain that experience means pleasure and pain or some other empirical quality assumed to be elementary and so self-explanatory. It has been a very famous and very useful argument for centuries and has resulted, among other things, in at least clarifying to some extent the complexities of psychological fact involved in action, especially in distinguishing the characteristic attitudes of mind which action may involve. But it has not finally answered any questions. This inconclusiveness of the research for the motive brought into relief another famous ethical argument, viz., whether it is the "motive" or "intention" of the agent, or any character of the agent at all, or whether it is some external "results" of the act, that determine the moral quality of the act; all this has been argued almost without ceasing for many generations. These psychological questions came to be central for all ethical theory, in the sense in which we moderns are familiar with them, with the rise of modern individualism and subjectivism, and their ethical importance is to be judged upon a basis of a frank and critical estimate of the cultural significance of this modern subjectivist movement.

It is to be kept in mind that what is sought in all these questions is how we are to explain the element of direction that is obvious in all acts of will.

It is to be our final conviction that these questions as to what faculty is involved are not of major importance. Or, if important, their importance rests on other grounds than those assumed in the questions themselves. We shall assume, on the question as to which mental faculty it is that determines the direction of a will act and hence its moral quality, two things: in the first place, the significance of a thing is usually not determinable from a mere knowledge of its point of origin, from merely knowing where it comes from; second, that it probably is not true that the various forms of human expression can be referred each to its peculiar mental faculty, and, even it if could be so referred, this mere reference would not constitute an explanation. As to the famous question of intention versus results, we offer these comments: (1) The argument has assumed that motives and intentions are distinguishable psychological functions, and it seems doubtful that they are. It seems rather to overlook what appears to be the one sound result of psychological investigation, that is, (a) that the mind-life operates as a unity and not through specialized functions; (b) that it comes very near putting the worst possible interpretation on the theory of the creative power of mind, apparently assuming that external circumstance is under the control of psychological causes; (2) it assumes a correspondence generally between types of circumstantial fact and forms of mental act; that is, it assumes that a given sort of external collocation of events will or should uniformly follow upon the occurrence of a certain frame of mind.

But there seems little reason to accept any of these propositions. Indeed, the facts seem to indicate quite other conclusions. There are, however, positive results to be noted in connection with these arguments. (1) They have helped to show the extraordinary complexity of the mind. (2) They have emphasized the importance of the study of the relations that are possible between human cultural purposes and the world of circumstance in which those purposes are to be given form—they have emphasized, that is, the problem of control and have shown, by implication, at least, that "will" is largely a reference to the psychological aspects of this problem of control. (3) They have emphasized the importance of "results" and have shown that a large factor in the problems of morality and in the direction of will is the question of the nature of the external world. But they have contributed little or nothing to the formulation of principles. All these latter results have summed up in a tendency to turn the attention to the objective world as the basis of explanation of ethical questions and away from the excessive preoccupation with the inwards of experience which has been characteristic of modern thought in all its forms. This change seems to be altogether to the good.

Questions of "will," therefore, are complicated and difficult. The one thing will unambiguously means is that there is an important relation of a practical sort between the subjective life and the external world, and the importance attributed to will implies the conviction that the world is, at least to some extent, such as can be modified favorably to the subjective purpose. But the problem is to be approached on other grounds. If it is true that in the concept of will there is involved a strong reference to the external world or the element of nature, then it will be necessary to give up the assumption that will is merely a psychological phenomenon. And here we suggest that will, when considered as effective agent, involves subjective factors only in the sense that such factors are an ingredient part in the total person to which the agency is referred. The essence of will is this external reference, this reference to the objective world which we find logically necessary to give to the concept of person or agent the integrity implied in its being the center to which action is referred. And the reference of action to the integrity of the agent is necessary to make it intelligible. Hence we are merely recognizing this universal objective reference, this finding the meaning of agency in its implication of a world objective to the agent, there in the nature of things, and to be recognized as a matter of fact when we define will as the total effectiveness of the natural-cultural system which constitutes the person or individual. This will or agency is neither "mind" nor "body" but the synthesis of both under their appropriate universal, the assumption of the possible unity of the person with his world in the dynamic phase of that unity. And the directive factor in this agency is just the knowing which is constituted of a blend of the apprehensions of the sensory contacts which the unity of the person with his world implies. There are distinguishable degrees of this knowing factor, and we shall describe some of them.

B. Desire

From a practical viewpoint, will is a question as to how far and in what ways the qualities of objects affect the form and tone organization of the conscious life. The traditional theory has it that desires are inherent urgencies within the mind toward external things, and seems to assume that they can be controlled by exercise of the fiat of the mystic will. But there is no such will; or, rather, such a will makes the question of agency meaningless. Of course it is true that the subjective quality as it is experienced and the urgency as it is felt are internal to us and that they are mental phenomena pretty much as any other internal facts are. But this must recognize that desires can be all that is necessary to class them as mental without giving them all the qualities that other mental facts possess. They are not, for example, acts of cognition, although cognition is present in them. They are also not a characteristically active function, and the older notion of them as "passions" is perhaps the more appropriate. They seem more closely akin to the elementary feeling background within which cognition takes place, and as such are to derive their explanation more from their relations with external events than from any assumed spontaneity of mind. Whether this be true for descriptive psychology, is, however, not the point we require.

It appears certain that some sort of correlation exists between the "desires" and the qualities of external objects and that the nature of desire is involved in that relation. What the relation is is not clear, but it seems to reduce the desire to a form of sensation, where it is not an active function at all, since sensation here seems to be taken in abstraction from perception and a mere impress from objects. Desire is then a mere hypothesis necessitated in grounding the idea of control of action and is based on the nisus toward externality which is present in all awareness. It is this fact that is important to ethics for the purpose here is that of control. The control of desire then, or the control of action with respect to desire, is to be effected through the disposition of external objects. Reflection upon our desires as psychological phenomena is not likely to be conducive to significant action; besides it gives to them a nature and an importance which they do not possess and develops the peculiar subjectivity of the moral introvert. But the interpretation of control and direction in terms of the disposition of the things involved in action makes the idea of control at least intelligible. The theory of desire then seems of peculiar importance in the explanation of conduct only when it gives justification for the hypothesis that grounds the idea of control upon the objective reference which desire seems to imply.

C. MOTIVE, INTENTION, PURPOSE

We noticed above the psychological and traditional aspects of these functions. They are all attempts to designate, within the subjective life, the characteristic which is of peculiar moral value. But they all fail because of the fallacy imposed upon them by our subjective-individualistic viewpoints. They all attempt to find the morally important factor by isolating it as a particular function within the mental life, thus isolating the person or agent from his world of objects. But as this is a complete negation of any significant meaning for the agent, since it denies to him any possibility of action, it reduces the subjectivist-individualist theory to complete absurdity. It is here, in the point of method, that our criticism must be final. There is no peculiar moral faculty, as there is no isolated moral agent. Both conceptions are contradictory. There is no single power of mind or will or peculiar type of psychological fact, or any combination of mental powers, involved in an experience which alone makes the experience moral. No motive, or intention, or purpose can, as such, be isolated or given an unambiguous meaning as the mere subjective ground of an act, so the effort to determine the source of the moral act, or the peculiar quality of the moral act, in any or all of them will always be futile. It is never possible to know, with precision, either by the agent himself or by the "observer," what in a given case is the motive, intention, or purpose. And this means that they are all hypotheses that fail to convert themselves into grounds because they cannot exemplify themselves in fact. They can therefore explain nothing, because they are themselves unintelligible. It is not possible for the person who experiences them to distinguish them clearly in his own mind, and he can, on occasion, be seriously mistaken as to what his motives, etc., are. They are known most clearly by those who observe them from the outside, which suggests once more that the important facts of morality are objective and are not to be discovered within the depths of the soul.

We shall attempt to explain in the following section the moral functions represented in the psychological motive, intention, purpose, etc.

D. The Inclination to Ends

All these confused and contradictory psychological theories impel one finally to raise the question: Is there, within the nature of the moral person or agent, a faculty or power or character which drives or directs him toward ends and the objects and objectives which his life implies and requires? Is there an ultimate "spring to action," or principle of spontaneity, or autonomy, in the person which impels him onward and holds his efforts within the limits which must not be too widely transgressed if his life is to be continued and furthered and made worth while? It is clear that any intelligent discussion of such questions will have to be pitched on higher ground than that represented by psychological analysis. They are among the ultimate questions of the moral life, and it is doubtful whether psychological analysis will contribute much to their formulation. The same applies to sociological and anthropological attempts to explain the active life and to formulate its meanings. To attempt to explain the meaning of human action on a basis alone of the relations among individuals or persons, however collected in groups we may conceive persons to be, will forever remain futile, for the obvious reason that much of human action, and much that is most important, is impersonal and nonindividual in every sense so long as the sociological conception of the nature of the person or individual is retained. For similar reasons, the attempt to show that human action is a function merely of the movements of nature, in a biological and naturalistic fashion, will turn out to be nonsense. And yet the question of a metaphysical principle or agency operating in human life, either "from within" or "from without," not, indeed, as discontinuous with nature, or as having a purely human origin and implication, will not down. And this suggests that all the assumptions from which we have been accustomed to approach the problems of ethics are either false or inadequate or made vicious by overemphasis.

Whether a basic hypothesis that will avoid these weaknesses can be developed is the problem for ethical theory. It is here suggested that the negative premise from which investigation must start is a sweeping rejection of the subjectivism and individualism which has governed ethical thinking throughout the entire period of "modern" thought. The human factor is only one of the factors in the eternal substance of things. And of the human the psychological and the subjective, or the merely natural, is a still smaller part. That everything significant in the human world should come from the motives and intentions and purposes, or the wants and needs and instincts, of human individuals or of individuals in group relations is merely absurd. There are many other factors involved in the good life. And ethics must somewhere make contact with these other factors before it can rid itself of the tissue of theoretical contradictions in which it has become involved.

We shall see below reasons for believing that one factor operating in human life "from the outside" is the corporate structure of human life itself. This corporate agency exerts its influence upon life and action through the institutions which life itself has created. And this power exerted by the corporate structure of institutions upon the life-situation is probably the largest and most important factor in determining the action of the moral agent. And this power or influence is not exerted through the minds or motives of men. It is implemented within structures of its own creation and is directed to objects and situations in which the subjective element is negligible. The direction or trend of movement of institutions is practically free of the influence of individuals, however "great." The "will" of the individual is rather dominated by "outside" forces, and these outside agencies are the more specifically moral "faculties."

III. THE MORAL FACULTIES

Let us see what are the reasons for such a view—a view that is so at variance with the scientific dogmatism of the time. The fact that human life has persisted within the scheme of things, and has persisted as human, argues that there is some inherent reason for its existence and that it has more than an accidental status in the world. The reason is that life has built itself into the structure and substance of the world, has incorporated or embodied itself in institutions that are parts of the nature of things. Life has accepted the nature of things as its body.

But the mere fact of persistence proves no more than a mere possibility of ultimate status. To show that such a status is actual and necessary requires the presentation of evidence in the way of fact, and then the demonstration of the relevancy of the facts. It may be argued that such proofs are not possible in the nature of the case; but, if so, there is a large area of what is uniformly taken to be content of human experience which has no explanation, no possible interpretation of its meaning.

A. The Faculty of Life and the Circumstantial Situation

It would be necessary here, if we were to go to the bottom of the moral life, to give a fuller account of the elementary biological principles upon which life depends than was given in the preceding chapter. But we can still indicate the most general idea of that system of principles. It is the idea of action that is the basis of the most far-reaching distinctions. The idea of action, as grounded in biological fact, where it is called "growth," involves a certain type of organization of fact, such, namely, that its movement tendencies are directed by distinctions apprehended within its environmental circumstance. This implies that no action is possible in the absence of consciousness in some degree; and it is just the anticipation of the change in the relations between the order and its environment, as effected by distinctions in the environment, that constitutes the only definition in terms of fact that can be given to consciousness. As to the origin of the fact order within which consciousness and action appear, it is to be conceived as the logical correlate of the reality which is presupposed in anything's being intelligible. That is to say, the fact order is a logical implicate of the objectivity of the judgment which asserts consciousness.

The human body is a very complicated and highly developed instance of such an active fact order. It is an individuate instance of the unity of primitive fact order with environing circumstance. As a consequence of its structure thus determined, its life is made up completely of active expressions, together with the conscious situations created by the relations which action occasions between the body and its environment. But what we want to emphasize here is that much of the environment, for the body that is conscious to the degree of the human, is itself made up of similar active bodies. The environment of life is largely life. Thus the moral life presupposes the active person acting continually within an environment which is itself active and changing at all times, since the enviroment is made up largely of beings active in the same way as itself. And since the acts of these environmental agents are determined by their anticipations of relations to their environments, no stable basis of action can be presupposed, since the body-agent must "adapt" itself to a constantly changing object. It will not, that is, ever be possible to predict what the environmental circumstance of an anticipated act will be at the time the act is finished, or even at the time it is to begin. Nor will it ever be possible to predict just how the environment will change while an act is in progress. Hence the outcome of an act is always uncertain and can never be predicted. It may be only roughly anticipated. Then the action of conscious beings is always adventure, and its outcome a matter of chance. It is forever striving to come to terms with a world which has never yet found ways or means of coming to terms with itself. But in any case it is clear that the determining factor in the direction, quality, intensity, and general nature of an act, is the external circumstance which constitutes the substance within which an act takes place, upon and into which it must issue, and in the absence of which an act is unintelligible. This external circumstance is itself therefore the "motive" of every act, is presupposed in the occurrence of the act, and is independent of all or any states of mind in the psychological individual, except in so far as states of mind merely apprehend it. But, even then, the circumstance is the "cause" of the apprehension, in so far as there is a cause involved in an active situation.

But in saying that the changes in the environment may be anticipated even roughly, or viewed as a system of probabilities depending upon the structure of the world within which the situation occurs, which structure itself is speculative and problematical, we are making several assumptions about that world. But we are not assuming anything about anybody's states of mind. Two of these assumptions about the world are important for moralists. One is to the effect that the world is in some sense orderly in spite of its instability. Otherwise an act could not be planned, so could not be as an idea. The other is that the order of its instability, which is an objective quality of the world itself, and perhaps represents the objective reality of time, may be known to the agent in the history of the order. History then, as an objective view of the time relation, constitutes the set of presuppositions upon a basis of which action and its issue are intelligently anticipated. We shall devote a paragraph to explaining what this means.

B. The Historical Continuity of Life

The first thing to note is that by history we do not mean the mere chronological account of the series of events in time. There is neither prediction nor anticipation possible with respect to these events, and prediction and anticipation are necessary to the idea of an act. Prediction or anticipation of temporal events would require time to be determinate as to both its quantity and its direction, which means that an event in time would be fixed and incapable of change, and any such determination of time is contrary to its nature. Further, the events of time, as particulars, can in no way be amalgamated into the substance of time. No unity of a concrete nature can be effected within the events of time; they can have only mathematical relations, and so their order is a geometrical contour. Hence, the account of temporal events and their succession, even their causal or any other type of determinate relations if they have such, is useless for the explanation of acts. Events can never be solidified into the permanent mass of circumstance that action implies as a basis, so the dependence of action upon historical considerations involves something more elementary than events in time. This, of course, leaves no bottom for any empirical account of action.

What is implied of time with respect to history is that the continuity of time establishes fixed tendential characters in reality. Time then as continuity or duration is not a matter of series of events but a whole of relations which has mass and breadth and hence leaves in the structure of reality traces of constitutional relations. And it is these relations that become important. They are the details of order in specific fact situations, in fact, that is, as fact is by these relations determined to a structure of constitutional relationality of such a nature as to enable fact to enter into species or kinds. These details of order, as they appear to consciousness in anticipation, at least, are the qualities of presented fact, or of fact in the concrete instance, fact as having an internal makeup, and not merely as abstract position in species. It is in this sense of abstract occupancy of position in species, where species is merely event-succession, that their science may be said to begin with a descriptive method. But the point is that these qualities indicate a character in the fact and not a mere position in the species to which the fact belongs, and it is this quality with a relational basis that becomes a specific or species-determining character, and thus becomes a fixed and permanent *characteristic* of reality. It is then time as a presupposition of order and relation and quality that makes history real. It is upon this historic reality as premise that the act previsions its end. The details of order are the capacities for action of an organized body, anticipations of changes in the body organization; and they have been implanted in the organism not by the durational aspects of time, or by the fact that time in its "lapsation" enters into the structure of life as a permanent character in the fixed psychological tendencies to act in given or characteristic ways; but by time solidified into history, which provides not fixed tendencies but ordered impulses of spontaneity established hard in the nature of things. It is in this way that a capacity to act may be objectively, even physically, real. This is probably what is meant by "instinct." But, as the theory of instinct has made the term altogether unintelligible, we cannot use it.

What appears here, however, is that this history precipitated in the structure of organized life is the principle of heredity. Only, whereas heredity is assumed to connect the capacities of an individual with empirical characters of individual forebears in their succession, which is subjective nonsense; what we want to assert is that heredity implies the substantial reality of the species itself and, in active influence at least, independent of the particular representatives of the species. That means that heredity as objectified history represents the system of the *forms of action* that the substantial species dictates to the individual. The species itself thus becomes the "motive" to individual acts and has no necessary connection with the states of mind of the individual actor or person. The moral agent acts as man. The "freedom" of the moral person is metaphysical, beyond his states of mind. He can neither assert nor deny it; he can only realize it in action. And this means that the general objective scheme into which any contemplated action may fall can be anticipated from the characters of the fact situation that constitutes its circumstance; the act, when right, is dictated by those characters, with the result that individual types of action may vary within that scheme. The anticipation of these types is known as choice, but, when we speak of choice, we beg the privilege of our own definition. The spontaneity usually attributed to the "will" in choice really lies much further back than the individual mind, within the institutional or corporate structure of culture that determines the individual's character and presents him with his circumstance. It is at this point that the objective basis of the moral judgment of acts lies; the objective reference in such judgments is to the generic scheme within which the individual agent's capacities and his opportunities are all bodied forth. Every moral judgment, that is, asserts that an act is *characteristic* of an agent, is such as faithfully to represent and express the inner constitution and structure of the agent as the constitution and structure are made by his act permanent details within the system of reality. The relational system by and in which acts and agents are characterized, or woven into the structure of reality, is what we mean by heredity. The motive of an act is thus outside the act and not a psychological fact in the agent's nature. It is a fact within the objective structure of things.

Heredity, then, is history released from time and process and succession, and with relational order made the permanent ground of continuity in reality. It is through this concept of objective history that morality, as the account of the actions of men, is given its metaphysical ground, without which no judgment about action could be true or false. But morality in this sense is purely formal and without content. It is necessary to present it so in order to lay the basis for the necessity of moral judgments. But for the concrete content of morality we shall have to await the description of the human institutions which constitute that content.

C. Character as the Unity of Mental Functions

Character, then, in its moral implication, is the system of the agent's capacities and characteristics viewed, not merely with respect to their mere descriptive relations within psychological states, but as involving a metaphysical ground in reality. The description of character, as is true of all moral discussion, is for that reason logical analysis. This metaphysical ground has been considered in two ways: It has been thought of as implicated in the system of physical or mechanical concepts as these are applied to abstract life in biology. Or, it has been conceptualized psychologically in abstract mental terms, as in the traditional ethics of "idealism." There are then two general types of ethical theory: the biological or materialistic or naturalistic, which comes to grief ultimately in a mechanical environmental system where life is excluded and the very idea of an act is contradictory, and the psychological or mentalistic, which reduces itself to the absurdity of an agent that can act in the absence of the environing circumstance which alone gives an act meaning. Empiricism in ethics is an instance of the first; idealism, particularly as modified by modern subjectivist presuppositions, is a case of the second. Ethics is therefore ready for reconstruction. It must rid itself of subjectivism and materialism and go on from Plato.

What is required on this point is a principle of unity which makes all the capacities of the agent consistent with each other, and which at the same time grounds them in the structure of things. Our principle of objective history is, we hope, such a principle. It supplies us once more with a principle of the "virtues" in the Greek sense, by which is meant simply the system of natural modes of action, the modes of action which we discover lying beneath custom and habit and tradition regarded as the structure of culture, and which are explained through their connection with nature. But we must have a philosophy of nature to take the place of natural science. The system of these modes of action, as synthesized in the natural or objective circumstance as the latter is expressed in the nature of the agent, constitutes precisely and simply what we mean by the moral character. Just how its integrity is created and maintained by and within the system of individual acts, that is, how individual acts are made personal acts, and how their direction is previsible in the system of the individual's choices expressed as judgments, is the detail of ethical "science" or moral philosophy.

D. The Corporate Nature and Function of Character

We have just noticed that the character, as the central concept of ethics in its logical phase, is quite simple in its first reference to facts in their analytical aspect. But when we undertake a final explication of the reference to metaphysical nature which character involves the problem becomes very difficult. The concept of culture, on the one hand, and that of nature, on the other, the unity and continuity of which our statement involves, are concepts of extraordinary difficulty. Also, when we undertake, as we must, to trace out the relations of the character, as agent, to other agents; the relations of the totality of agents to their synthesis in the system of culture; the nature of the objects of the environment in their personal and nonpersonal aspects; the relations of these objects to each other; the relation of their totality to the system of nature as a whole; and, finally, the nature of the relations that hold between the system of culture and the system of nature as the two constituents of metaphysical reality—all these questions become problems of extreme complexity and difficulty. Yet they cannot be avoided by any ethical theory that hopes to give a consistent account of the life of action and the nature of the moral agent, since they are all implied in the nature of an act.

All these questions condense into one in the last stretch where ethical concepts get their meaning. They all reduce to the problem of the nature of the corporate character or the corporate personality.

The ideal and relational characteristics of the corporate person, or its "virtues," are also syntheses of the individual factual virtues. Also, the corporate person is seen to have the duality of nature of the individual person, but with this duality overcome. It has the mental or psychological or cultural capacities of conscience, duty, obligation, and right and the natural or environmental capacities of order, justice, responsibility, and good. How all these ultimates of moral life are to be brought together into an objective whole of significance is just the problem of the corporate personality. It takes a number of abstract forms, but each has an essential meaning. How the "spiritual" person is realized in its ultimate body of culture; how the material person is identified with its object in nature; what peculiar functions and capacities these ultimate orders are to be found to possess—all these problems become the subject matter of the metaphysics of ethics. And all questions of ethics must be seen in their ultimate relation to metaphysics if they are to get a rational statement, to say nothing of a rational solution. And the concept which assumes the function of principle in this connection is that of the corporate person. A theory of ethics is no longer possible which has its principles all grounded in the biopsychological notion of the individual—the mere human being is no longer the center round which the universe revolves.

Chapter VIII

Social Capacities of the Person

SOCIOLOGY is the science of interpersonal relations. By this it is meant that questions of the life of persons, in any groups their culture may determine, are questions of the relations that hold between individuals. But individuals, we have learned, are, for all practical purposes, corporate persons, and this fact throws open for fresh discussion all questions involving the relations of individuals. These relations can, it is assumed in "social science," be described and classified and ordered, and their values estimated by the methods of science. They are questions of fact, and the task of research is to make these facts known as completely as possible. When they are known, the proper organization of them under a system of laws and principles derived from their own characteristics constitutes the science of society. As society is the name of the cultural milieu in which persons live and act, it is a presupposition of morality, and its peculiar moral character must be examined. These interpersonal relations may be considered as differently substantiated in (I) interest; (II) property; (III) civic or cultural groups or bodies; (IV) legal structure; and (V) corporate structure. At any rate, these distinctions furnish a convenient scheme for description and discussion. Interpersonal relations are, however, we are ultimately to see, characteristics of the corporate person and not mere bonds between human individuals.

I. INTERESTS: THEIR CONFLICT AND CONGRUENCE

By an interest we shall mean a typical relation in which an individual stands, viewed exclusively from the point of view of the individual to whom it is said to belong, and expressed in terms of his states of mind. An interest is thus the attitude which interprets the meaning or value of anything solely in terms of its relation to the interested person. Regarded as interpersonal relations, interests are generally supposed to be either exclusive or associative. They are sometimes also distinguished as individual or social, but, as we shall see, all personal interests are both individual and social at the same time. But both individual and social, in this sense and as commonly used, are mere devices of method made to fit a particular and very limited conception of the individual. They therefore have no theoretical value.

Interests have certain characteristics and can be described and their different types designated as separate classes. Interests may be (A) subjective, (B) proprietary, or material, (C) civic or cultural, (D) legal and political, (E) and possibly there is a special class called moral interests.

A. Subjective Interests

These are relations that hold between persons and have their origin in the inner structure of the mental life, are aspects, that is, of the bio-psychological individual. The good life, which is the object of morality, implies the proper functioning of all these relations as a very first condition.

x) The feelings or emotive attractions and repulsions.—By these we mean interests depending on such natural functions as sex and the biological and organic processes of life. Some of them tend to bring individuals together and thus form groups, while others tend just as strongly to drive individuals apart. The common feeling attending work and play activities and the aesthetic enjoyment of common action probably contributes more to the integration of persons into bodies than any others, while fear, hunger, and the feelings of bodily necessity tend to induce persons to live as separate units. These experiences are the common stuff of life, and, as the uniform material of life, they are the matter of moral values. Every moral good, that is, so far as personal, implies somewhere a substance made up in part of these elemental feelings, and every moral evil has a like reference to such feelings. But it is to be observed also that, as such feelings, these elements are the mere stuff of life and are simple constituents in the moral good and therefore have no status with respect to principle.

y) Common subjective tendencies to action.—That there should be uniform types of movement for all persons is determined in their common physical structure and the uniform character of the environment. But the fact is of great moral importance, because here are to be found the conditions of those common accomplishments which make up the substance of culture. Two persons can and do move together because of their identical physical constitution, and their movements have similar issues because they are all issues in a common environment and are made out of similar environmental factors. Thus is it true not only that elementary action tendencies are the materials out of which the individual constructs the larger edifice of his individual life but that they are also the materials of all the structures which men elaborate in their social and public life. These common action-forms are the solid framework into which the feeling-values are built as substance content.

The two materials which the moral life presupposes are then the elementary feeling-values which we as men all share, and the common tendencies to action which a common nature and a common environment impose upon us. Our morality can never be so lofty or exalted as to be freed of these conditions. But the tendency to neglect this fact is almost universal.

z) *Mutuality of feeling and action.*—As these common elements of feeling and action become solidified into the permanent structure of individuals, a persistent foundation is created upon which a stable life for the group is laid. So far as this common basis is constituted of states of feeling, the latter attain a certain objectivity as "mind," which tends to be regarded as in a measure overt and public, and so is often designated as a like-mindedness in which individuals all share. Too much importance has been given to this factor, and a too independent status allowed it, for it is sometimes apparently made the sole basis of the common life. But the common life is easily seen to depend for its regularity upon the rigid uniformity of the physical environment, and no stable life can be presupposed except upon the basis of a persistent unity of our "states of mind" with their corresponding objects in the external world. The mutual relevance of our states of mind and the objects and relations of nature lays down the conditions not only for action but even for the life of thought for the individual, and it also determines that the special modes or forms of thought shall be similar for all individuals. This mutuality of relevance then is the primitive ground of objectivity and becomes the basis of the life of thought, and it is thought in its uniform features that makes it possible for us as individuals to direct our emotional and active life toward such common ends as thought may determine, and so gives us a certain control over the career and destiny of life as a whole.

All these subjective interests show their incompleteness by insisting upon their relevancy to external and objective processes, as we shall see in connection with the proprietary interest.

B. THE PROPRIETARY INTEREST

This relation is, in its most general statement, that between a person and a thing. Any relation in which a person can stand to another person or to any thing can be complete or intelligible only as it implies and is meditated through an object that is specific to the relation. Every relation, that is, represents an object as an element of structure. The proprietary interest, as a psychological matter, is implied in the fact that a thing connects in some peculiar way with the life-activity of the person, the ordinary language stating that the thing is useful, interesting, valuable, etc., to the person. There are various forms of this interest, and we briefly describe them here. Each one of our classes will represent a type of moral object, and the system of these moral objects implied in the proprietary relation makes up the material basis of the world of culture.

x) *Food.*—Food and its use are too simple to require comment. The needs of the bodily life enforce it as an interest upon us as natural individuals, and it is for morality to refine that interest to the extent that it sustains and enriches our cultural life. This problem is of extreme difficulty, but it is in a peculiar way the problem of the present age to find ways whereby the things in which we have proprietary interests may, in spite of or because of that interest, contribute to the culture of the race. Thus as an interest and a utility, food, like any other property, is a necessity of our existence and is forced upon us; as a contributory factor in culture it becomes a moral obligation; we cannot ignore it or regard it as a mere necessity, for the price we pay in this case is life itself. But the price we pay for ignoring the moral obligatoriness of property is the much more serious loss of our cultural heritage. Food, then, as a moral object, becomes a requisite of the cultural life and a problem for the common thought of men in their corporate capacity. So long as each looks to his own food supply and regards it only as a necessity, we are animals on the plane of brutes; we become men only when proprietary objects are made the concern of organized common thought working through institutions of public control. The fact that for the poor food is scarce or is bad is not so serious as that it is left to their unaided efforts to provide it.

y) *Shelter.*—Similar considerations apply to shelter and, in fact, to all the proprietary things and interests. It is true, however, that the proprietary interests as we have named them form an ascending series of complexity, and this complexity increases as we go forward from the primitive requirement of food. That is, each type of interest implies a broader and more far-reaching interrelationship of persons, the object implicated by the interest becomes more vaguely determined, and the incidence of the thing upon the person becomes less and less direct or pronounced. Shelter, that is, presupposes persons living together in groups, and the various types of grouping will show differences in the various forms of the objects of shelter. The simplest of shelter objects implies the family, and corresponding to this corporate form there is its architectural counterpart. Similarly there is an appropriate shelter object for the religious, the social, the educational, the public or political, etc., relations of men. These objects have their moral significance in the fact that culture requires that they be so adapted to one another that together they constitute the material basis of culture. The technique by which the adaptation is effected involves the peculiar aesthetic form of each object-type; worship requires an aesthetic object-form different from that required by the learning process; each of them "houses" a different human relation. And none of them has any meaning when referred to the individual. It is this latter feature that concerns morality, and shelter thus becomes a problem for the common thought of men.

z) *Security*.—The proprietary interest in security likewise represents a wider motive and a further departure from the individual. The attempt on the part of the individual to provide security for himself and dependents has become the source of very serious moral difficulties in recent times, and our reactions to those difficulties within recent years have transformed the very structure of public institutions. As an individual problem it is usually described as "economic," but the failure to provide this interest with any significant degree of definition or organization has resulted in very serious injury to culture and threatens to destroy the basis of life itself. We have blindly attempted to find a *common* expression for what we ignorantly insist upon as an *individual* necessity and have failed to see the contradiction in fact which we have created. The attempts to incorporate individual interest in corporate instruments of security, as, for example, insurance associations, have uniformly ended in futility and monstrosity and often in disaster. The attempt to find a corporate body for the interest in food, as in the wholesale grocery "business," and to render that interest secure, while insisting upon the interest as an individual one, has issued in starvation to a large proportion of mankind and in the grossest form of immorality in our "business" relations. This becomes a moral problem when we discover that the interest in security is in every case a common or public interest and must be implemented and incorporated as such.

r) Ornament.—Another proprietary interest, that is, another mode of the relation of person to thing, that involving the use of things to the advantage of the individual, is the interest in ornament. As an individual impulse, at its best and rarest, it is the motive to artistic expression, and at its worst the desire for self-distinction. This urge to self-emphasis is the largest motive in ownership in the modern world, in extreme cases a form of morbid exhibitionism. The desire to control things perhaps arises out of the necessity to use them as instruments to purposes. The motive to control is therefore legitimate in that its "interest" in things is disinterested, that is, it relates to the use and not to the user, whose interest involves exclusion from use. But the only way control can be made to continue disinterested, that is, the only way to divert the interest from the private control of things to the advantage of the person exercising control, and to make the use of things moral, is to impose public conditions upon control. The primary condition entails limiting the right to control by the capacity to use, where competent assessment of capacity eliminates advantage. This prevents control from degenerating to ownership. And to do this it is necessary to place the final control in the common or public functions of society.

C. Civic and Cultural Interests

This assumes that interests, which, as we must keep in mind, are subjective phases of personal relations to things, can be directed upon objects and ends in such a way as not directly to involve the individual's advantage as a motive. It assumes, for example, that I can concern myself about the public life of my community, or about the cultivation of art, or even about affairs that are exclusively my own, with no sense of any advantage coming to me other than what comes to everybody else, or with no advantage to me except as it comes through or along with a similar advantage to other people. And this concern is objective and impersonal and nonindividual, relatively to myself, and such purposes can supposedly be made to extend to include the community of all mankind or the whole structure of human culture in the abstract. But we must notice a possible confusion in language here. We may confuse the rational inclination to, and concernment about, ends with the interest in things. And we use the word "interest" in contradictory ways. In the first place, my reasoned conviction of and inclination to an end, for example, a clean and beautiful community, is a subjective process within my mind; it is my inclination and my conviction that make me act with the purpose to realize such an end. But these functions of my consciousness all refer to and imply as their complement objects in the outside world, objects, that is, which have no peculiar reference to me, no more reference to me than to other people. Also, what I am conscious *of* is these objects; I am not conscious of my inclination to or conviction about the objects. And it is just the fact that these objects do not concern me more than anybody else that gives them their special value to me and makes them genuine ends for me.

An interest, on the other hand, is an inclination to and concern for objects which have their value precisely in the fact that they bring to the interested person some special advantage. I am interested in a business because it will make money for me. And the word may be used, and is used, interchangeably for the subjective concern, or for the sum of money or proportionate share which I have in the business. I may be pleased if it makes money for other people as well. But this is an afterthought and no part of my interest. I may be interested in a clean city because I dread typhus for myself or family, or because my interest will make me prominent or lead to my election as councilman, or merely because people will praise or like or approve of me. Whether these are all proper or worthy is not here the question. But they represent the correct use of the term. An interest is a subjective inclination toward, and concern for, objects which complement the interest with an advantage for the person who feels the interest. My interests all imply and express advantage to me. And it is unnecessary confusion to speak of common or public interests. No meaning can be made of a blunt contradiction. There are no public interests. And it is equally absurd to speak of a number of people having a "common interest" in a thing when we mean that they all expect to gain some advantage from it. Interest implies advantage, and advantage means getting something that other people do not have. A common interest is a contradiction in terms. My "interest," that is, my subjective inclination toward, and concern for, a clean city, is a public purpose and not an interest at all, if it is genuine. It is an interest if I expect advantage to myself as different and distinct in any way or degree from the advantage of anybody else. Where I expect and anticipate this advantage, I am interested; where I am not concerned about advantage, but about objects as such, I have a purpose. And all genuine purposes are public purposes; the distinction from interest being the presence in the latter of a sense of advantage.

Then any act of any person may be judged, with respect to its subjective motivation, from either of the two points of view. One judgment expresses an element of a subjective history; the other is a moral judgment. The judgment will be objectified by a reference either inwardly to the subjective motives of the individual who acts, or by reference outwardly to objective relations within the external world. But since, in order to make the subjective motivation the basis of reference for a judgment, that motivation must itself be universalized and objectified, there is properly speaking no judgment until the subjective motive is removed. And if the moral experience must be capable of expression in judgment, as it must be if it is to claim either validity or value, no moral judgment can give expression to interest. An assertion of interest is therefore not a moral judgment; it is a question if it is a judgment at all, since no objective ground of truth for it is discoverable. Here we may confuse assertions of interest with judgments about interests; the latter are of course valid, since the objective ground of their truth or falsity may always be indicated. Let us be clear on this point: if moral experience is to be real so that it may be formulated in valid judgments, this experience must not be conditioned upon what is subjective and particular but upon what is objective and sharable and common. Then there are no judgments that express interest that have validity for morals; it is true that assertions of interest are descriptively valid, are facts that exist, but empirical and descriptive considerations are ruled out of morals except as preparations of fact upon or about which judgments are made. No mere statement of fact, no mere description of events, no anthropological considerations, no mere existential judgment can be the substance of moral assertion; such propositions may only state fact about which moral judgment can be made.

There are, then, no moral interests; and there are none because there are no human concerns that have their significance in what they mean by reference to the subjectivity of the individual. The common fallacy of all our practical sciences is their assumption that their results must be justifiable to "experience," when experience means what can be particularized in the life of the individual. There are many things that are real and are constituents of the good that can never be fully brought home to the individual; and indeed most things that are real are so only as they are realized through the common efforts of thought and muscle of men.

Cultural "interests" are, then, public purposes. They are purposes or concerns that appeal to the individual *because* they do not carry any peculiar reference to his special interests, to his peculiar status of advantage. It is true, possibly, that the individual must perform acts that are subjectively motivated, that contemplate only his peculiar concern. But they are not moral acts. It will probably never be possible to eliminate the individualistic and "selfish" motives of the specifically economic act. But this act is nonmoral so long as it gives expression to a purely individual motive. That it is nonmoral is shown by its inevitable tendency to become immoral. It becomes moral only when it is brought into relation to the system of other acts which together with it express the public purpose to create, control, use, etc., goods. But then it is no longer an economic act. That I produce a potato is of no moral significance so long as I use it with sole reference to my own advantage. It is a mere fact of sustenance to my physical being; and my physical being is not an obligation in itself. It becomes such only when thought with respect to the world in which I live. It does not depend upon relations to other persons. Pluralizing a subjective relation does not make it objective, cannot give it truth. This is the fallacy of all "social" theories. These theories merely multiply the fallacies of individualism. A group of persons means no more than an individual so far as their subjective experiences are concerned, or until the relations of the individual are thought as mediated through the things of the world so that the group is constituted a corporate body. And then we are dealing with public relations and not experiences. But cultural "interests," as public, are not social but political, and morality becomes the science of the public life. It has then the same content as politics; the difference being that morality considers this public content as including the individual and his "interests," while politics disregards the incidence of purposes upon individuals and thinks of the public life as a whole and the conditions of the maintenance of the public order as a corporate structure.

D. Law and the Legal Interest

This means then that morality expresses itself fully in the formulation of the relations of individual concerns to the public whole. This does not mean the whole as a collection of persons, but the whole of life with the emphasis upon its instrumentation in the objective systems of nature and culture. When these relations are approached from the point of view of personal subjects of action with the view of interpreting them in their bearing upon the whole, we have the specific moral attitude and speak of individual duties and obligations. When they are interpreted from the point of view of their system and its incidence upon the individual, the attitude is that of civil or political law. The law is then the universalized meaning of the typical acts of men, and its moral "authority" comes from the fact that it *is* what the individual *means*. It gives expression to the integrity of the corporate moral whole, which has embodied in it every just intent of every moral agent.

E. Is There a Special Moral Interest?

We have seen that no synthesis of subjective phenomena is possible. Neither the "hearts" nor minds nor bodies of men can be effected into a unity by virtue of what meaning there is specifically and peculiarly in them. Unities that may be built up on a basis of subjective forces, such as persuasion, propaganda, "education," can be made to stand only so long as their cause is continually applied. Withdraw from them the hortatory influence that set them up, and they will collapse instantly. Democracy and Protestantism have proved this: they can exist and thrive only while they are continually supported by persuasive means. No effect or result of subjective forces can be permanent, and morality must have its ground in that which abides. Interests are subjective forces. They have no moral significance. Morality has nothing to do with interests, so there is no moral interest.

Is there, then, a peculiar character of life and action that we call "moral" and that is distinct from all other characters?

The answer to this question is "Yes" and "No." The answer is "No" if we require that morality should be a peculiar type of act or relation or characteristic that could be defined independently of other things. But the answer is "Yes" in the sense that it refers to a unique quality common to all acts or persons or things, in the sense that it may be present in any of them. The morality of an act is the meaning the act has in terms of its relations to a system of human acts, this system having objectified itself in the cultural structure of the world. The morality of a person is the quality of his relations to his world, the latter including acts, persons, and things. Every reference to the morality of the person implies this world of persons, acts, and things. So the distinctive moral quality is the reference to the whole, the cosmic reference or cosmic implication. It states the meaning of a thing and designates its place in the universe. There is no meaning to our accepted theories as to how human actions are to be made morally intelligible. We have defined morality as conduct, action, and have seen that action involves the individual as living in a world constituted of his total environment and that the most important element in that world is the class of other persons. In a peculiar way the agent's or person's relations to his world are mediated through his fellows, so that the important relations for ethics are personal relations. But any relation of persons we have seen to involve things, so that, when contemplating an act, the other person becomes a part of the thing that is the object and instrument of the act. So just as relations to our world are mediated through persons, our relations to persons are mediated through things, and person and thing become common elements of the moral object. It is this object that determines the "commonness" or "generality" of will. What this total moral object is, as integrated persons and things, now becomes our task to define; that is, we have to face the question how the person and the thing seem to identify in the superpersonal object in connection with which morality gets its meaning and universality. This ultimate object, ultimate in that it is the ground of the objectivity of all moral judgments, is the corporate person. We now undertake to describe it.

II. THE CORPORATE PERSON

The outlines of the meaning of the conception of corporate person have already been drawn in two or three places above. We are now, and have been throughout the past centuries, accustomed to look upon the human being as essentially and primarily a collection of feelings, sensations, desires, urges, etc. That is, we take, without question, the assumption that the "personality," as the essence of the person, is nothing more than his subjective states of mind, included in which are the types of bodily movement necessary in maintaining those states of mind. We forget in this that the person so described could not act in any sense; that the person who acts is primarily a body, made up of physical substances presumably exactly similar to other physical substances. We also tend to overlook the fact that our mental states depend for their existence and their form upon the body in a very important sense. We have probably come to emphasize the mental factor here because we considered it the most likely basis for the explanation of the relations among persons that seem so important to us. We can, in some sense, identify or assimilate our feelings and thought, and the relations between us seem such as can be reduced to terms of these subjective facts. On the other hand, our bodily life appears completely separate from that of our fellows, and the things upon which our various bodies depend appear to be incommensurable by any scheme we know. They are exclusive of each other in every way we can think, and, apparently so far as our bodies are concerned, we are alone in the universe.

But these assumptions of the easy communicability of our minds and the utter unassimilability of our bodies may be mistaken. At least one fact seems to indicate that they might be questioned. This is the fact that, despite the apparent incompatibility of our bodies, they do come together and, further, must come together if we are, either as individuals or as a race, to continue in existence; there is further the fact that, in spite of the apparent easy interaccess of our minds, yet our minds never or rarely do come together, and the cases where they appear to do so are as nearly unreal as may be found, and the unity as unstable as the winds. The agreement of our minds is very much overdone, being limited to rather narrow areas in science and other purely intellectual connections. The supposed common will and public opinion upon which the order of society is assumed to be based is a myth; and the "fellowship of kindred minds" which "is like to that above" is exactly like to that above—a pure imaginative abstraction which has no meaning whatever in terms of action.

The problem then is to examine the question of the permanent associability of human beings to see whether the relations among persons may have objective and indubitable reality and binding power. The question whether interpersonal relations are objective and real or are merely unstable expressions of our feelings, opinions, or other mental states, or are pure ideal aesthetic constructs of imagination, seems best approached through questioning the adequacy of the accepted concept of what the person is and implies. The traditional notion of person as a collection of mental states and characters leads, in practical life, to a great many difficulties and contradictions. We here reject it in its entirety and suggest instead of it the concept of the corporate person. Let us see what this implies.

A. The Bodied Person

The most obvious meaning of the corporate person is the physical or bodied person. In discussing the psychological possibility of a common will or mind, we saw that any real expression of mind involves a dependence upon organic process. Let us take this fact as fundamental. Let us assume further that the functions that become associated with organic structures are functions of those structures; that is, the nature of the phases of the function will correspond in definite ways to the organized interrelations of parts within the structure. This means that the movements and processes which the function contemplates will have at least their form determined by the type of inner arrangement and organization of the structure; and that the direction and issue of these movements and processes, in the sense of the nature, distance, etc., of the objects upon which they will impinge, will at least be partially determined by the same inner arrangement and structure from which the movements and processes flow. Partially, we say, for there appears to be no reason whatever to believe that a relational process dangles merely from one of its terms before it connects with its other term, since this would confine the meaning of all relations to temporal conditions and identify all relations as processes. But this would mean that no relation is real, since its becoming is never completed.

But this means, in terms of our argument, that human beings are identifiable, in their specifically appropriate object, through their bodies—that the body is the immediate ground of their association. The only argument we care to adduce here is the fact that it is the body which makes man a species, while his mind universalizes to abstract identity. As members of a species, men have something in common. What is it?

At its lowest terms it is man's common dependence upon the *things* of his environment for existence and for the continuity of existence in the species. In its highest terms it is the totality of his ends, as he is enabled through the *things* of his environment to conceive of these ends as realized. It is through his active contact with *things* that his ends are defined and planned. And it is through defining and planning ends, as imaginatively possible outcomes of the present suggestiveness of things, that his higher forms of activity are determined. But our point here, and the point commonly neglected, is that it is the *thing* that lies to hand in his immediate environment that gives the man his impulse to act toward ends, and also by the suggestiveness of its qualities it lays out before him the outlines of his plans in the possibilities that the thing discloses as to the ends action might produce from it. The thing then becomes the actualizer of all immediate active tendencies and the symbol of all ends that may appear as worthy of attainment. All my present needs, wants, desires, etc., are conditioned upon it, and it is the conditioning instrument, and the material, through which my highest aims are to be realized.

The simplest and most immediate element that is common to men is therefore property. By what is common to men we do not mean what is merely abstractly similar in their subjective qualities; we mean rather what is the basis, in their interrelations, not as minds merely but as whole men, of the possibility of their lives and actions and thought and purposes, all that is characteristic of them as men, being brought to a condition of dynamic harmony in a common objective and external world in which all subjective purposes can find realization. And this basis is property. As this common basis of life, or basis of the common life, property becomes incorporate in institutions. As such it is the instrument of all will or purpose, individual or social, the only instrument of will, and the key to every act. As such, all property is common, or public; private property is a contradiction in terms.

B. The Effective Will

Not only is it true that property, as incorporate in the social structure, is the instrument of the individual's will, even while he is following his most subjective and "personal" interests and purposes; but the same corporate property is the instrument and object of all the common motives and activities of men when those motives and activities have conditions proper and favorable to their realization. That is to say, before there can be any act of any person that has a guaranty of reaching its proper end, there must be the system of environmental things set up in institutions as the stage upon which the act is to take place. Further, the same system of things must be his instruments and his materials, the tools he uses and the stuff he works on. And this system of things alone can give reality to his ends. But this means that these things become the embodiment of his will; and, to an extent greater than we often know, the spontaneity and freedom of direction of the will-energies come to be determined by the body of things through which they work. That is to say, that to a greater extent than we are aware our action is dictated to us by the setup of fact in which we find ourselves immersed. What we are to do, how to do it, what is to be the end—all are largely predetermined in the institutional structure, which suggests the action and is thus responsible for the idea or impulse from which the action flows. We become, as agents, that is, institutionalized. What was in a hypothetical primitive condition the mere impulse and effectiveness of our conscious organism becomes, in cultural conditions, the effective agency of our larger life as it is embodied in the corporate unities of the things we use.

The real will, then, the will that is genuinely effective in getting things done, in realizing ends, is the effective power which these cultural agencies acquire from their own spontaneity and the wont and habit of men. But we must think of this wont and habit as themselves objectified and conserved in the forms of material and social objects, objects of real property. As property objects they become the ground of institutions, and as institutions they implement and condition the expression of will in all its forms. It is then these corporate property objects to which we must look not only for the fulfilment of individual aims but also for the maintenance of the interpersonal relations upon which the solidarity of culture depends. These corporate property objects are the substance of every personal or interpersonal relation. They are the effective wills, and they maintain a stable world for us even at the times when our passions and ignorance and stupidity and folly make our own wills as "personal" the instruments of a chaotic hell. The fact that a social order can survive the frenzy of war is a miracle that no individual will can even comprehend. It is the corporate will that is the basis of our hopes for the continuance of a significant form of interpersonal life.

C. THE CORPORATE PERSON

The body of property and the will that is instrumented in it, once it has become institutionalized and incorporated in human affairs, is, then, the active agent or person, the person that is the ground of all interpersonal or "social" relations. It is the ultimate moral person. The emphasis is upon institutionalization; corporate property functioning as the instrument of the private or "personal" will is the basis of all evil. No one of these interpersonal relations is in any way or degree intelligible when approached from the viewpoint of the human individual. That men ever contrive to get themselves bound up with each other in a social body is not because of any peculiar quality in them as individuals. Almost any type of very low animals could do the same. Their "association," their coming-together in the way men (and even animals) come together in fact, is due to the active relations that set themselves up among them. But these active relations alone, the mere "social" characters, cannot associate men by their mere presence. Such relations must be grounded and objectified in the things of the common world before they are a stable basis for association. The system of "social" characters, the active relations inherent in the contacts of men, the habits, customs, traditions, instincts—all these are the mere subjective content of the will and are, by themselves or all together, powerless abstractions. They come into effective rule and power and control only as they become the effective force of corporate bodies of property objects. As thus the super-individual will, empowered by its body of cultural objects, it is the corporate person, the fact upon which must rest all our theories of interpersonal or social relations.

The relation of the individual person to the corporate person is the problem of the moral person.

Chapter IX

The Moral Person—Summary Statement

WE HAVE now stated in some detail the several types of characteristics which make the agent or person what he is. It is to be noted that few of these characteristics are described as inherent qualities of the person, qualities, that is, which could be described by reference merely to his supposedly peculiar structure. Most of the characteristics refer rather to relations in which the person stands, and the different kinds of relation are determined primarily by the kinds of objects with which in each case the person is connected. All these relations are supposed, however, to center in the person, and the specifically moral nature of the person is bound up with the whole body of them. His moral *character* is what all of them imply, or, conversely, all of them are taken to constitute his moral character. Together, then, they describe the person as the substance and subject of *right* and *good*, in the sense that we discovered for these terms in chapter iii. The person who is good, or whose acts are right, will possess certain general characters and capacities which we will summarize and describe here. We shall find that five general classes of characters belong to the good or right person, the person we describe as the moral person. These five classes are physical, conscious, civil, legal, and moral, the latter being the summary synthesis of the others.

But the point of special emphasis here is that the moral person is the whole person. There is nothing in the person by nature which he should get rid of. We have said that "morality" implies a person endowed by nature and culture with *all* the capacities and capabilities which are possible to him and that these capacities and powers should be cultivated and developed to the highest point possible to them. The moral person must be the most intelligent person that it is within him to become; he should possess the most competent will that his nature will permit; he should have the most delicate, sensitive temperament that is possible. He should be able to think all things, do all things, feel all things. It is here that many of our traditional ideas are inadequate or downright false. Some of them would have morality merely in a brilliant intelligence, a capacity to know; for some, morality is an active will and a ready power to act; to still others, the moral life is a life of feeling with feeling developed in intensity or quality or both to the highest point. There is no reason to emphasize one at the expense of the others. The highest type of moral character is found in the balanced harmony of all these powers, where each is developed proportionately with the rest.

But not only are these natural capacities to be developed to the full and in perfect balance. The cultural capacities must be developed in the same way and to the same degree. Finally, the specifically moral quality will be a synthesis of these natural and cultural qualities into the most effective harmony of them that is possible. The body must have health, but it also must have grace of movement and perfection of form. And it is the unity of these that makes the body a moral instrument. The mind should be keen, but it must also be agile and sensitive and possess poise; and it is their harmony that constitutes the moral consciousness and determines the quality of the conscience. The qualities that are described below are then to be understood as including within them factors of both a natural and a cultural kind. And, in each, the one kind will be modified by the other. The person must be strong, but his strength is not the strength of the brute. It is the strength of a powerful body, balanced and directed by a wise eye and a kindly heart. And the kindly and sympathetic person will be strong, that his strength may save his sympathy and kindliness from sentimentality and folly.

I. THE PHYSICAL PERSON

Let us repeat with emphasis that the physical characteristics are moral capacities in that they are the essential instruments of all action. We enumerate some of them.

A. HEALTH

There are two aspects of the individual's health that we wish to consider. First there is the effect of health or the lack of it on the subjective life of the individual. This we ordinarily think of in terms of the feelings, but we mean also the wider influence which health has on the intelligence and the active capacity. One whose health is bad feels misery, and this is very much to be deplored; it is bad, evil, and there ought not to be such a thing. But this is not the real evil of ill-health; the unhealthy person is not, generally speaking, in full command of his capabilities. Hence he is more likely to make mistakes, to do or think things which will be obvious contradictions, or will be silly or trivial or dangerous. And he is less competent in will; his control over his acts is flabby; and he will do too much or too little, or to the wrong people or on the wrong occasion, etc. That is, health is good because it implies not only a wholeness and balance of the physical powers but a wholeness and balance of the powers of mind and will. But further it involves a wholeness and balance of all these functions of the body, of the mind, of the will, in the total person, the moral agent.

But it is equally right and good that we have good health because of the effects it has upon the social and civil whole in which we live and upon the institutions of the practical and cultural life. We are not thinking of its effects upon "others." Morality is not "social." For other people are, for morality, merely a detail within the cultural structures where the person's life is cast. They are important details, to be sure, but they have no unique significance. I must be honest with my neighbor not because he is my neighbor, or my neighbor happens to be the man he is, or because I am the man I am, but because honesty is an obligation enjoined by the system of cultural ends. I must be healthy, otherwise the home is not the competent institution in my community that it should be, and the culture of the community is lowered. My community cannot have good homes as long as there is ill-health. It is the same with the school, the church, the local government, the theater; all the institutions constituent to my community obligate me to good health. We say, if one of us suffers ill-health, all of us suffer. This is true but not the point. What is true is that, if there is illness and suffering and misery, then, by so much there is of it, or so persistent it is, these characters of illness and misery tend to become institutionalized within the community structure. Not only then are there people sick, but there are slums and ghettos and "districts" that have become incorporate in the cultural body. Not only does the individual lose his life or strength, but life and power have gone out of the culture of men, and that culture hobbles its way into the future with a rheumatic limp or a tubercular cough. We do not like to quarrel with the master, but the doctor really does give his medicine to man. The health of the person is thus not an individual quality merely but a relation of the individual to his culture. It is so, at least, when considered as a moral function.

B. Beauty

Goodness is beauty and strength and truth. The physical person not only must be strong and vigorous but his vigor must be comely and gracious. The tragedy which moral existence can be is nowhere more forcibly expressed than in the ugly child or the bent and twisted and gnarled fragment of a man that our industrial "culture" tosses by the wayside when his physical powers have been exhausted. The child distorted by tuberculosis or rickets is the ugliest thing in the world; and its promise to humanity is death, hell, and the grave, just as the broken old crone is a curse upon all that existence has ever been, however saintly her spirit, however noble the courage with which she meets her doom. The existence of such "persons," even if there were but one, refutes and condemns to futility any and every "morality" that humanity has ever held. And the fact that there is probably a majority of such "persons" in the world today, that actually there are more of such than of any saner type, makes of our "morality" an idle and pernicious dream and the life it pictures a hollow farce. And the fact that there is left in such "persons" often a suggestion of spirit and a flicker of soul leaves one to wonder if the folly and emptiness of our ethical systems are not metaphysical.

But let us inquire what are the characters of the beautiful physical person. These we may describe as (1) symmetry of figure, (2) grace of movement, and (3) harmony of form.

I. SYMMETRY OF FIGURE

Symmetry of figure, to begin negatively, is not mere mathematical proportionality. No doubt it is that, but in the case of the physical person this element is so involved with other features that its prim exactness does not intrude. But symmetry does imply certain limits, within which size and shape may not vary too much, and there may not be violation of the requirement that any one part must keep its quantitative features in some sort of statable relation with all the other parts and with the whole. The moral person may not be monstrous, and it is wrong that any moral being should in its physical structure depart so far from type that it becomes the object of ridicule. This means that it is not only a matter of relative size and shape of parts that is important but their distribution and arrangement, as a mere spatial and sensible fact, should submit to certain rules of order. What these rules are and all other rules of art is a matter for the artist

to determine; but it is a moral requirement that there be such rules
and that instances of fact should conform to them.

2. GRACE OF MOVEMENT

Grace of movement is perhaps the same fact aesthetically as symmetry of figure, the difference between them being merely one of
the different sorts of mass that is conceived as the substance or matter
of their design. As physical phenomena they differ in that, whereas
figure is, in general, an implicate of space alone, movement also involves time. But what interests us here is that this figured movement
is a part of the whole which we call good, and an essential part of it,
so much so that for the more highly sensitive moral natures the good
loses most of its significance in its absence. The phenomenon is complex, and some of the questions about it are only remotely moral
questions; but we can say that the primary meaning of right or good
action is movement that is technically perfect and competent, and so
adequate as an expression-form for the beauty which it is its peculiar
nature to express. Perhaps a secondary factor in the rightness of an
act is the ease and smoothness with which it enters into continuity
with other movements which, together with it, make a whole of fluent
harmony. Its grace is therefore the factor that not only makes the
movement individually and internally whole but which also contributes to the wholeness of the movement when expressed as a feature of another whole. Ease and facility of flow, accuracy and sure-
ness and delicacy of its contacts with its matter as both substance and
circumstance, these are the qualities that constitute grace. As a for-
bidding gesture, grace insists that there may not be excess or defect,
curves of movement may not be either fat or lean, angular or brawny,
wilful or slovenly. These are wrong primarily and essentially because
they cannot be righted with the form which they mean, it is a failure
either of intent or of skill, and they thus constitute a falsity of the
kind that is not mere error but is culpable.

In the movements of human beings, grace appears in the facility
with which they move with reference to each other. This is illustrated in its various degrees in the movements of a crowd in the
street, the minglings of a social group of cultivated people, with perhaps such movements as dancing and skating as the highest form of its
lighter and freer motives, with religious ritual and pageantry as its
more somber and heavier forms. Combined with harmonies of sound,
it appears in the opera in perhaps its most complex form, and it becomes calamity in the jazz dance. The most perfect form is probably

some one of the simpler types of work, such as digging or chopping. And grace attains extinction in modern machine-tending.

But grace of movement becomes an important moral capacity in that it is the formal perfection of the act. We have seen that the whole content of morality is to be found in action. Hence the most perfect act-content is implied in the most perfect act-form.

3. HARMONY OF FORM

The abstract rightness of an act is represented in its simplest form as symmetry of figure, and this gets a sort of active content in grace of movement. The perfect instance of their combination in an individual is harmonious form. Let us understand first that form here does not mean either shape or figure, while it implies both. Form is a purely ideal character, and "good form" can be used of any moral quality whatever. It refers to the element in acts and characters that implies the wholeness of reference as an abstract perfection, such a reference as is capable of giving expression to any content. It is thus the element of universality within which all acts are comprehended and is a concept of pure theory. But its presence as a quality in an act is immediately perceived in intuition, and it is thus a fact which must be given place in any competent description of action.

This factual element is recognized in the "good form" of etiquette and in the code of honor. It is difficult to say what exactly is meant by such expressions, but the fact is immediate to perception. It is the basis of all the honorific and deprecatory epithets we use with respect to conduct, as in the case where we pronounce an act noble or fine or where we say that an act is coarse or crass or crude. But the point is that it is there, and the difficulties we have in describing it merely point to its immediacy in fact and the universality with which it is recognized.

C. RATIONALITY OF DESIGN

One other aesthetic feature of acts remains to be described. Considered as an individual fact there is nothing left to say of an act after its form is recognized. But taken as the means of reference from the act as a form to that which it means or intends, we have to note its corporate character. In the one case the direction of the reference of an act is toward the person acting as an individual character or personality; in the other, the reference is to the objective system of culture in which the character finds place and meaning. This duplicity of reference within an individual form is the basis of design. Design thus means two things; it means perfection of static or transient form in an individual, and it means the continuity of the form of the individual with the form of the species of which the individual is an instance. These two meanings are illustrated in the case of a picture when we say it is good in design, meaning, in the lowest sense, that it is a good drawing; and in the other case we say that the design of the picture is good, meaning that it is the expression of the intent of the painter, subjectively and at its lowest, and also that it is the expression of the significance and life of the reality which it portrays, objectively and at its highest. In morality it is customary to designate this element as "purpose," but this term has become so abused and confused with interest that it is well to avoid it. It becomes in ethical theory the basis of a perfectionist and realizationist idealism, and this, it is feared, means nothing but a subjective drowsy hope which is useful only in excusing the imperfections of the reality. An act or an object cannot become more than it is when it is good, and it either has its moral perfection now or it does not have it at all. There is no eschatology in the design of a moral act. The good is now present in reality or it will never be, and a future instance of it can never be any more than it now is. The good is therefore not to be achieved or attained; it is to be done. It exists as the eternal fitness of things, and our acts should express it in the present instance. The "finite" temporal element in the good is a reference to the mode of expression as a circumstance of the act. It does not touch the good and the right. The "good" that is to be achieved or attained or realized is not the good; it represents a confusion of good with *goods*. It is this confusion that has made this a commercial age, an age quite unique in its moral insignificance.

It is at this point that the criterion of action is to be sought. That an act is designed means that it is intelligible, and the theory of ethics, as the logic of all judgments that can be made about action and conduct, has its place and center in the designed act. It is perception of this element of design which also grounds and justifies all practical and empirical judgments upon conduct, and it is this system of empirical judgments which lays the basic design of ethical institutions.

Then the person as a physical being has the two ethical capacities of strength and beauty. The obligation of the person in this direction is to make the most of them.

II. THE CONSCIOUS PERSON

The element of design, which we found to be the key to all the physical capacities of the person, becomes also the point of connec-

tion of the physical person with the person as a conscious and knowing being. Design, that is, is an identity of form and intent. Let us
briefly describe the capacities that belong to the conscious person.

A. SENSITIVITY

It is not necessary to decide whether this character is a physical or
a mental capacity. Its moral significance either ignores the distinction
between the two or implies both, and it does not seem to be important,
for morality, whether my capacity to be moved by the qualities and
objects of my world is regarded as physical or mental. The one thing
that is certain is that there is and can be no morality where sensitivity
is diseased or is lacking, and we may, for practical purposes, distinguish the physical as that which implies mere reactive irritability as
the meaning of sensitivity, while the conscious life implies what we
may call a projective responsibility.

At any rate and whatever we may call it, the person *reacts to* some
aspects of his world, and *acts* or responds *toward* others. And it is this
act that distinguishes the conscious or knowing being from the merely
living being. And as we have seen, it is the act which makes the moral
being. The act or response is distinguished from the reaction in that
it points toward the environing world and is intended to issue in that
world, that is, to have its effects take place in the external world. The
act is never "selfish," never refers to the agent out of which it issues,
and the traditional distinction of acts as selfish or benevolent fails to
comprehend the real nature of the act. Sensitivity is then the agent's
capacity to find the meaning of his act within a quality or character
of the objective world.

But sensitivity is the primitive quality out of which, as material, all
ethical ends and "values" are constructed. It is only as I *respond* to a
given situation through a disturbance or perturbation within my feeling that the situation can become an object or end to me. Responsibility is thus the primitive substance of morality. In its merely cognitive aspect it is the blank awareness of something other than myself.
When my feeling begins to distinguish the object as qualified with
characters of its own, then it "means" something or has "value," and
my attitude now is centered about the object rather than about its
own quality, that is, my attitude is active now in that it is centered
upon the external fact rather than concentrated about its own mere
inner awareness. Objects then first become objects for me as the objective or external reference point of acts, and it is within my sensi-

tivity, so far as it is within me at all, that action and morality have their origin.

Then so far as the moral life is the conscious life, or is to be determined in terms of inner or conscious states, morality is a matter of the degree and intensity of sensitivity. Then to cultivate and maintain a high type of sensitivity becomes itself an obligation, and in its higher stages this sensitivity is the content of every fine and noble act or attitude. The pity of the Christ for the sin and suffering of the world and the bleeding heart of God become the last and highest stages of evolution for the moral attitude. As this attitude becomes the content of one of the major personal virtues we may pass it here, but it should be emphasized that morality begins where the facts and circumstances of the world touch the quick of the personate living being and elevate him beyond the plane of mere reactive habit to the plane of consciously defined and designed ends.

B. DISCRIMINATION

By this we mean that the person as a moral being has not only the capacity to recognize objects as the issuing point of acts but also the capacity to distinguish classes of objects as appropriate to types of acts. That is to say, the moral appreciation of an object is the recognition of its qualities; but its qualities distinguish an object from other objects. Hence the distinction of objects as of different classes, which is the elementary act of cognition, is itself "practical" in the sense that it is perhaps first effected in situations where action is the guiding motive. Now this ability to discriminate an object and to see its peculiar fitness for the end or issue of an act is the "moral perception" that enables us to distinguish acts as some preferable to others. In this sense it is "choice," and the established attitude of making choices among objects, and determining the actions that are appropriate to them, is what we mean by "will." The person "wills" then when he makes a choice of objects with respect to action and when the fixity of his choosing attitude gives momentum to his inclination of movement thereto. Thus his established active capacity becomes the matrix or environment within which his responses are determined, and we say he has "control" of his movements.

What we wish to make clear is that the will and its volition are merely this practical expression of the intelligence and that, so far as we tend to think of will as the mere energizing of acts, what we have in mind is not will but mere muscular force. The measure of will then is not any aspect of the intensity or vehemence of its energies but the modicum of perceptive intelligence expressing itself as choice of objects and thus determining the direction of these reactive energies toward one type of object rather than another. Thus the same fact that we call "discrimination" in one connection, "choice" in another, and "preference" in still another shows the operation of the whole personality in a moral situation, and the overemphasis of the one or the other is, largely, the basis of the different types of ethical theories which have been so long and so profoundly argued by the moralists. If it is necessary to have a label before one can understand moral fact, we shall emphasize that all the active capacities have their basis in the elementary intelligence and thus accept the brand of rationalist. But we are emotionalist, or sensationalist, even, in that we insist that the content of moral experience is in every case some form of feeling and that every object or "good" of morality must somehow objectify this feeling in a form that makes the continuity of persons in social life possible and at the same time establishes the ground of the objective continuity of persons in the institutions of culture. But "voluntarism" can also be accepted in the sense that every moral attitude or idea demands, and ultimately finds, a place in the system of cultural institutions and effectuates itself there through the use of natural energies. But rationalism is ultimate in the sense that no set of moral concepts is intelligible except as forefigured on the background of thought and thus recognized as themselves aspects of the act of intelligence.

The ultimate moral act is, then, the act of intelligence, and the primary or primordial obligation of the moral person is the obligation to know. Knowledge is therefore the presupposition of all *personal* moral qualities, of all private or subjective virtues, just as wisdom, as we shall see later (chap. xxiv), is the ground of all social or cultural or public objective virtues, as also all moral institutions. But knowledge and wisdom presuppose a fulfilled emotional and volitional existence, otherwise our knowledge and wisdom are empty.

C. Working Competence—Will

But a competent will and a fulfilled feeling are the content of morality considered as a specifically personal matter, especially when we reflect that the morality of the person is simply his life of action. And it is the person as moral agent that we are concerned with throughout these chapters.

It is necessary to emphasize here then that, for moral persons, the competence of the will and the conditions of its existence are all summed up in the *work* that is appropriate to the individual person. It is the peculiarly personal nature of work that makes the problem of the social organization of persons as workers so difficult. And this seems in a peculiar way the problem of our time. The two questions that are fundamental with respect to work are then, first, what is the basis of this appropriateness and, second, how the uniqueness of the worklife can nevertheless be molded into some form of cultural order.

What then do we mean by speaking of the person's work as peculiar to him? We see this conviction in many popular phrases: "every man to his job," "each must do his own work," etc. What is meant is, stated briefly, that a man's work is defined for him by the kinds of objects his active attitudes select for him. This can be stated otherwise by saying that what a man will do in life will be determined by his objective interests, that is, the kinds of things he has already formed active attitutes toward. This is the work that is appropriate to him, since it is what corresponds to his capacities as developed through his training and experience, assuming that his training and experience were rationally directed. This is the work then that provides full outlet for all his capacities and that results in the production of the objects that satisfy his volitional and emotional requirements. He *wants* nothing more than to act as he feels his nature to require, and he *needs* nothing except objects in which this feeling can find repose. His acts and his needs and wants then appear to have a peculiarly personal meaning, to refer to himself in a way that his thoughts do not. Hence he can be free and liberal in thought and speech, which are experimental excursions into life's possibilities, but is securely bound by his work and his needs and wants to a rigid scheme which the natural-cultural system provides for him.

But his work and the objects he produces objectify his will and realize it and are the forms through which he gives outward expression to what is peculiar to himself. Likewise the performance of his work and the possession and use of its products are his happiness, since they occupy all his feeling life. They solidify each feeling in a form that will make it permanent, and they draw off and absorb the surpluses of feeling that arise out of the very abundance in which he is living. Work is therefore the basis of whatever satisfaction and happiness there may be for men; but work includes leisure as a change of work, a shifting of the form of work, so that it will leave no area of our will or feeling unexpressed.

What is peculiar about a man's work is then that it defines the meaning of right and good in their most elementary sense. A man who is not capable of thinking his way to a definition of his ends can never-theless feel the discrepancy between the urgencies of his will and feeling tendencies and the forms of objects his movements are com-pelled to result in. He can feel physically that what he is doing is not what his powers enable him to do and justify him in demanding a chance to do. And his concept of the right that is denied him is nothing more than the felt fitness between his urgent powers and their appropriate objects; and wrong for him is felt in his being com-pelled to act in ways from which this satisfying fitness is absent in his experience. A labor preacher once remarked that he could not see to read his text but could feel the patches on his clothes and the mo-notony of the grind that wore him and his clothes out together. And his intuition knew that to be the essence of wrong. And this breach between what our capacities dictate we should do and what necessity compels us to do is the ground of all wrong and frustration—frustra-tion because the dictates of our active capacities constitute the very essence of our will, and wrong because it represents the absence of all the conditions in the objective world under which we could be satisfied and happy.

D. Emotional Competence

If it were possible to furnish every competent person with an op-portunity to complete fulfilment of his active desires in types of activity which would at the same time harmonize with the acts of other persons, there would result a state of complete happiness in the sense that each individual would find satisfaction for all his demands. This is perhaps the ideal of social organization. But it seems visionary and impossible of attainment. Yet its weakness is hard to detect. It seems right in that it presupposes the regulation of feeling states through the organization of the active processes upon which these feelings depend, feelings as such not being capable of organization. Also this control of feelings through the organization of active proc-esses is rational enough, and from the point of view of thought is not easily criticized. The difficulty lies in the fact that such an abstract theoretical perfection does not seem attractive to our emotional na-ture. We may accept intellectually the perfect state and admire it as an ideal of the reason and yet not be moved thereby to any im-portant action in its behalf. It does not excite our enthusiasm, and we are left cold in spite of its perfection. But this objection seems to involve a fallacy. It overlooks the fact that a complete active life absorbs and fulfils the emotions, so that there are no excess feelings left over after action has been completely objectified. Completeness of the act is fulfilment of the feeling, both being objectified in the object which is their appropriate issue.

What is required if men are to be moved in the interest of the good appears to be an imaginative picture of the whole public order of accomplished ends whose content is made up of the types of emotional experience which persons desire. A perfect state of will, as such, will not move one; but a vivid picture of people singing at their work or images of happy firesides or family or social gatherings will appear as essentially good things and worthy of one's efforts. That is to say that a necessary and important capacity of the moral agent is the capacity to be moved by imaginative representations of a satisfying order of life for himself and his fellows. Activity in the interest of the whole good thus depends upon imaginative and emotional motivation, and the problem of supplying that motivation in proper form and degree is the most difficult of practical moral questions. But we have the key to the problem in the fact that emotion itself depends upon action, so that the inspiration of the good and aspiration toward it arise from a life spent in satisfying action. Practically, the problem of the motivation of the good life is the problem of politics; but the principles governing the use of emotional forces in the interest of the good life are to be defined in strict ethical terms. The basis, that is, of political activity is ethical principle.

E. RATIONAL COMPETENCE

This necessity to think out the principles of the whole good and the rules of method by which the good is to be attained becomes the special problem of thought and the reason. It is the question of the creation and maintenance of the objective conditions of the good life and in political and public connections is called the problem of control. But here we want to emphasize that the problem is essentially a moral problem and that politics and law and all public agencies are to get their cue from moral principles. This is especially true just now when the problem of the good life is supposed to be soluble by methods of political and industrial expediency, with the result that culture is in the ditch and the good life perhaps more remote than at any other moment in recent times. We noted above that the primary obligation of the person is the obligation to know. Here we want to add that what he must know is the meaning of the whole good conceived in terms of the whole life of mankind. Nothing short of this conception will furnish solid ground for the principles of human action, and, without principle, action can never be right. A world designed with respect to the good is the ultimate design of life for mortal beings.

III. THE CIVIL PERSON

Since the object of the individual's conscious efforts, in their highest form of reason, is the whole good of man as culturally organized, the moral agent is the civil person. This is a consequence of the fact that moral principles cannot be worked out except on a basis of the whole or universal good. Also no authoritative judgment as to the rightness of an act is possible except upon a reference of the act to a principle which the intelligence must respect. And this principle is that of the objective whole. Then the moral agent as individual is the moral agent as citizen; and the moral person will find much of his obligation to lie in activity that has distinctly civil and political bearings. This is inevitably so, as we saw, because of the closeness with which the individual's life is tied up with the various institutions within which he lives. We cannot overestimate the institutional character of these connections. Institutions are positive influences upon us in a thousand ways where our "group" relations are vague and shadowy, and when we come to realize that fact we shall see that life in all its phases is institutionalized to the highest degree. And this fact is important because most of our thought assumes the contrary, assumes, that is, that the private life of the individual is primary and that institutions are secondary and derivative factors having their proper sphere only in the accidental relations in which the individual stands with his fellows.

Civil institutions of a peculiar moral import are (A) the community, (B) the local political unit, (C) the state as co-operative order of local units, (D) the nation and the international order. Of the last two, the latter is purely ideal, and the former nearly so, when considered as obligations to individual action, and are primarily or wholly problems for solution by thought in terms of rational principle. Concerning them the individual's duty is the duty to think and to know them in their aspect of moral principle as instances of the whole good.

A. The Community

The moral significance of the community lies in the fact that it is partially institutionalized habit and custom and is merely a fact to be recognized. It has no suggestions to make with respect to principles of right conduct, merely suggesting what subjective content conduct as a matter of fact is likely to have within its bounds. It guarantees that the individual will be already supplied with a number of habitual types of action when he grows up and approaches the moral life; but it does nothing in the way of seeing that these types of action conform in any way to moral principle. For the beginning of moral recognition of principle, that is, for the first impressions of the meaning of right, we must look to established institutions. And the community is not an institution, because it has no definite objective structure as natural basis of the cultural motives it represents. The individual gets his first impressions of right from the family, the church, the school, and these differ in kind from the community. The community is therefore not a moral factor. When the community becomes organized, when there is genuine intercourse of thought and feeling among its members, and when this intercourse is appropriately instrumented, it is always because some institutional purpose is at work, and this purpose will create an institutional structure. The people of a community are a unity and have a meaning only in the interest of the church, the school, the roads, or some other institutional purpose. The community as such is a subjective abstraction and has genuine moral significance for the first time when it begins to show signs of political or religious or aesthetic organization as the instrument through which its interests are expressed.

B. The Local Political Unit

When the community begins to have purposes, and this means when it begins to be concerned about its own internal organization and about its objective structure on which depend its relations as a unit with other communities as units, it *ipso facto* becomes a political unit. These concerns are the typical political purposes; they have to do with the whole aspects of the community. Other institutions do not involve these whole relations or, if they do, they do so only as incidental to some specific purpose and have no specialized instruments through which to give themselves expression. The school, for example, is concerned with the cultural implications of community life but is not directly concerned with its industrial problems, nor has it instruments fitted to deal with the whole relations of politics. Industry is concerned with the "practical" but has no interest in the cultural. And the same is true of the other institutions. No one of them takes the whole view but politics, and it is for this reason that it alone depends directly upon moral principles.

The original, or simplest, moral unit is, therefore, something like what the Anglo-Saxon calls the township. It is a political unit in the sense that it claims ultimate (i.e., moral) authority for its dictates in and through the fact that it seeks the order of the whole life, finding its justification in the process of creation and maintaining that order and the instruments necessary to its preservation. The capacity of the person therefore for control over his relations to his fellows, and the kind of control that reduces those relations to order through the instruments which other institutions furnish it, and the rendering final and authoritative this control upon moral principles, is the highest and the ultimate of moral capacities. It presupposes all other capacities and is that which furnishes the justification for all other activity. Thus I am justified in raising corn or making shoes because an orderly life for mankind depends upon these things, just as the specific way I should do these things depends upon the requirements of that order. The political institution therefore finds its moral function in maintaining the orderly progress of life, and it finds its worst prostitution when it is not intelligent enough to know what the obligation means. A state that finds its purpose in "umpiring the game" by which men maintain a mere subsistence at each other's expense deserves the catastrophe that has come to it. The political motive must know what is meant by control.

C. THE STATE

We see then that political activity involves the relations of "communities" to each other and that this relation implies the whole to which the units belong. It is this relation of reference to the whole-good-life that lays the ground for moral principle. The state is hence the order of the co-operative relations between political communities, when we think of it as a function implying acts. It is the system of institutional agencies through which this order is maintained when we think of it in its objective form. The most important of these instruments or agencies is government, whose function is completely performed when it loses its identity in the activities of the state, when, that is, its techniques are identical with the normal processes of political life. It is to be emphasized that since the function of the township is to "keep the peace" among the various institutional and personal interests of the small area, so it is the function of the state through government to control the relations of the small groups to one another and also to "preserve order" among the institutions and activities that transcend the boundaries of the local areas. It is a concern of the state when the industrial interests of a community destroy its cultural prospects, or the interests of another institution, as when in the interest of "economy" the school system should be wrecked.

Activity within the state is the highest form of personal activity. It is the most complete form in which the person can actually *do* anything. Ordinarily the personal capacities are supposed fully to express themselves in the support of government; but it is easily seen that the mere operation of government might very well be left to habit or to social mechanism. As a matter of fact it is usually left there, and this explains why it is so easily manipulated by "interests." At present because there are societies with different histories and traditions, it seems desirable that each cultural group should determine its own political form. But each moral person has a right of access to all that culture has accomplished anywhere; and, while this is so, the interests of morality demand some sort of co-operation among states.

D. The Cultural World or International Society

This co-operation of peoples in cultural activities beyond the limits of states makes necessary some kind of world-wide political organization to give assurance that these co-operative interests are properly served. While everything is uncertain as to what form such organization should take in detail, it is yet obvious that these interests are genuinely moral, since moral relations are universal and true only as they embrace the whole range of experience. And there are many significant experiences which transcend state borders and thus call for institutions through which they may be secured expression. The maxim of the moral agent is "Nothing cosmic is foreign to me," and there must be some way in which the universal purpose may get complete expression.

IV. THE LEGAL PERSON

The legal person is the political person giving practical expression and theoretical formulation to the moral principles in accordance with which he pursues his cultural ends. Law is therefore the system of moral principles at the basis of politics. The law then, as this ideal of morality, has final authority. But its authority is still delegated. The final authority of the law in practice is its relevance to circumstances of fact in the specific case; moral principles and concepts go beyond and formulate law in terms of ideal possibilities of action for the future. The law thus has its authority by virtue of its consistency with and conformity to wisdom and knowledge; and there is, for the moral person, no other authority than that represented in his first obligation, viz., the obligation to know. As deriving its meaning and influence from the very spirit of man, the law obligates him; under it he is free; action in agreement with it is right; and the system which it imposes upon the relations of moral beings is order. From this ultimate seat of authority in the reason of men then, the law lays down the fundamental principles that govern human conduct. These are (A) freedom, (B) right, (C) obligation, and (D) order.

A. FREEDOM

Freedom, as well as all the other elementary legal concepts, is in essence a moral term. It means, at bottom and abstractly, merely the determination of action by the person who acts, and, in accordance with the principles previously laid down, conditioned by nothing except the world as it is presented to him and the knowledge of it which he ought to possess. This of course implies that the principles laid down are strict principles, that is, they are arrived at by pure processes of practical reason, reason, that is, which is free from ulterior motives and contemplates nothing but a pure act. The free man is then the rational man, the man who knows, the man who has met his obligation to understand himself and his world. Pure or formal freedom is thus limited to the act of intelligence. Real freedom refers to the extent and quality of opportunity which the world offers to the acting person.

The old question as to the "freedom of the will," however, shows that in actual practical life the problem of real freedom is somewhat more difficult to state. The difficulty arises from the fact that at the time when the decision to act is made, when the exigency of action is actually faced and the agent must choose his course, there is often time for neither thought nor reason, nor are the given conditions usually favorable to reason even if there were time. Also, each presentation of fact calling for action is a new situation in some important sense, and our ready-made solutions are only partially adequate. Generally the more important acts are performed under the influence of strong feeling, and, where feeling is tense, reason is not likely to get a fair showing. Often, also, the circumstances that demand action will change while the act is in process so as to make the action originally designed meaningless or useless. So the question arises whether there is not some other power or capacity whose business is to control action, one which works automatically without the waste of time which thought incurs. And it is notorious that the "thinker" is often not successful in action and that the man who acts successfully is frequently not profound at thought. Tradition has attempted to meet

these difficulties with the assumption that the will as a moral faculty
is a peculiar and highly specialized capacity, one which is independent
of the reason, at least at the moment of action, and possesses, along
with the peculiar property of spontaneity, the insight to apprehend
immediately what course action should follow.

The major difficulty with this assumption is that the acts of will
are in fact frequently irrational, inconsistent with each other, and
not uniform or intelligible in terms of the life of the agent. Also, they
are sometimes not consistent with what sober thought will approve
upon careful deliberation after the act has taken place, and so are
followed by regret. Thus such a faculty seems to be in conflict with
reason and good sense, and a good deal of the thought that has gone
into moral reflection has been in the effort to find some way by which
the will and the reason could agree. The famous solution by a tour
de force, the doctrine of the rational will, is perhaps as successful as
any, but it is difficult to show how such a faculty possesses the authority which morality requires. The objection of modern psychology
that it does not find such a will can be noticed; but a conviction of
a consistent philosophy of mind is more important. This insists upon
the unity of all real mental capacities, hence there can be no separate
function of will. The will is thus merely the total mind exercising
authority, meaning by this that mind as a whole and alone has the
power to determine both the ultimate question of fact and the meaning of a given situation where action is required. Willed action is, on
this view, thus rational action, the uniqueness of will has disappeared,
and action which expresses too much "spontaneity" is wilful, irrational, and so not moral.

The difficulties with respect to the will are thus removed by a
broader understanding of human nature than has usually figured in
the discussion. If reason is not capable of action on the spur of the
moment, then it should so organize the life of the agent that the total
weight of its past experience should function in whatever impulse
may set off the act. This assumes that a life that is morally significant
can be ordered with respect to principle and thus given a constitution
that will stand firm in the presence of changing circumstance. The
constant application of thoughtful effort throughout a life thus builds
a character within the moral agent, and this character has, by virtue
of its complex structure, a response ready for most of the situations
that arise. And a reference to this established character and a competent knowledge of the world is as near a definite meaning as can be
given for spontaneity. In cases where the character is not thus pre-

pared and knowledge is lacking, there is no certainty, and the moral life for the best of us remains and will remain the great adventure. There can be no advance certainty as to what act will be most appropriate to a given situation, since every situation is novel; and so far as we depend solely upon the established structure of the character as an isolated fact, at the last resort the act must proceed upon a faith that is no more blind than our knowledge is limited. But we are compelled to act where we cannot know, and this is the ground of tragedy.

This result, however, seems hardly satisfactory. In the first place it seems contradictory to attribute freedom to the agent and then be compelled to recognize a large area in which his acts must still be uncertain. And the suggestion of chance, luck, etc., which the notion of adventure implies, hardly seems consistent with the rigid demands that obligation makes upon us. There would seem to be two possible ways out of this difficulty; the one based on the assumption that we have not yet got at the real nature of will, and the other that there is something that has been overlooked in the circumstances which make up a presented situation.

The traditional theory has it that the will is a specialized and unique capacity of the person, hidden away in the depth of his personality and appearing for the most part in the case of uncertainty where the agent's rational capacity cannot make up his mind. When it appears and acts, its action has, generally speaking, no relation to the individual's established character or course of life but is an original and underived fact. This is the spontaneous will, the will that the agent "ought" to have, as the theory goes; and apparently the only question that can be asked about such a will is: Has the agent got it? He either has it or does not have it; if he has it, his act is likely to be right. If he does not have it, his act cannot be right and must be wrong. The agent's possession or not of a will is the only question. But this reduces the question to absurdity.

Now the absurdity of the argument consists in its assumption that the total meaning of "will," as the sum of all the elements that are involved in the determination of an act, lies wholly in the nature of the agent considered as isolated from the rest of the facts of the situation. And here our subjectivism comes home to us with a vengeance. This idea of will is purely subjective in the sense that it attempts to define will in terms only of its specific locus within the agent, and thus of only a part of the given facts among which will has its meaning. This "unique" and "spontaneous" will must then be contradictory when it is employed to explain the total situation to which it refers, and there will always be something left over from its explanation. And this residue, since it cannot be explained through the assumptions which are responsible for it, will bob up as chance or luck or fate or God or some other rational or irrational intruder.

Then the other possibility, viz., that there is something in the fact situation where will appears that has been overlooked, and which is necessary to a consistent theory of will, is at least plausible. The agent with his powers and capacities, his character and history, cannot explain all that is involved in an act. An act is not an act merely because its movements proceed from a human individual. There are elements in the situation where will is a fact that cannot be explained by reference merely to the individual and his powers. And these elements are parts in the structure of will. So long as we oppose the agent or person to all the rest of the fact that is involved in will, we shall have a concept of will that is meaningless and contradictory and useless except for the hortatory purposes of argument.

There are then two ways out. One is to detach the will from its exclusive inherence in its subjective and internal locus in the person or agent and describe it where it is, viz., in the total complex of fact in which the person is one, perhaps the most important, but still only one, element. The other is to redefine the concept of personality as active agent so as to get rid of the mythical powers of unique spontaneity and so as to include the other agencies that are obviously present in other elements than the "person" within the fact situation as a whole. Both these conceptions will be regarded as absurd, perhaps. But any conception may be regarded as absurd; the question is how true or consistent it may be with the facts. These two assumptions are combined, and we hope justified, in our conception of the corporate person, where the will gets a new and appropriate meaning. But it remains a significant fact that the biopsychological person, when defined in terms of will, turns out to be completely contradictory when faced with the problem of freedom.

B. RIGHT

With our new concepts of person, world, and the corporate will as the effective relation between person and world, right is the condition of intelligibility and consistency within a system of practical fact, that is, a system of fact that postulates action. Right implies action, and action implies the transcendence of the fact system within which it exists. This fact system is the "subject" of the right; it may, perhaps invariably does, include the individual, so that the meaning of right also includes the external relations of the system to other persons and systems. Thus the principle of right, which is a constitutional principle within its subject in that it determines the form and individuality of the subject, becomes a structural principle of a larger subject in that it connects its subject with others within a system. It is both the character of the individual and the substance of his relations to his world. It is his internal constitution, and the law of his continuity with his world of circumstance, and thus constitutes the moral individual or agent a corporate person. Right is thus the ground of obligation and order, as well as the basis of personal character, as we shall note below. It is in this fact that right as a principle gains complete objectivity and universality. It is a purely ideal principle of the constitution of things and, as such, serves as a pattern or model with respect to which concrete relations in experience may be judged. Thus "my" rights refer to the correctness of my position and of my relations to other "subjects of right" within the whole, when I think of them as, for example, specific decisions I could get from the courts, or as concrete values with which I might barter with another person in the interest of advantage to myself, or might match with his values in a mutual contribution to the system of values.

In the latter case I should call it an "interest," perhaps. But my rights, regarded from the traditional viewpoint as "inalienable" and "imprescriptible," refer to the private status with which nature and culture have endowed me as distinct from all other subjects. In this sense I cannot be deprived of my rights without violence to my life and existence, but the loss of my rights might leave intact the cultural structure in which my rights are constituted and guaranteed. The fallacy here consists in assuming that my rights are severable from their basis in fact. But the inevitableness with which I am bound by my nature and my culture to the structure of the whole, and from which I cannot be separated without disruption of both myself and it, constitutes the basic fact of obligation. I am bound to achieve or attain my destiny within the system of corporate personal subjects given me, and as this bond is fully rational, is, in fact, itself one of the prime conditions of rationality, I cannot reject or deny or alienate it in any way, for the penalty of denial would be the negation of the very being of any reality—the negation negates itself. I must acknowledge my obligation, and this means that whether I look at the fact from the viewpoint of my private self, or from that of the fact itself, only one interpretation is possible. As long as I am I, I must acknowledge my obligation; and as long as the constitution of things is what it is, or as long as there is a constitution of things, then I have rights, and I must acknowledge my obligation.

C. OBLIGATION

It is the tragedy of contemporary thought to have wasted its efforts in the attempt to find the basis of obligation either in the psychological facts of individual consciousness or in the "social."

The motive of the psychological approach to the question is easily apprehended. It is the assumption of the absolute subjectivity of the real which underlies all modern thought since Descartes; the assumption that reality is a state of mind. The seat of obligation cannot be found within the personality or agent as the theories have all conceived the person. But obligation cannot be found in the individual person, because it is not there. The seat of obligation can only be discovered to lie within the total "impersonal" or superpersonal complex, of which the agent is only one factor among many, and where the whole body of the many other factors often outweighs the personal factor by large odds. The seat of the fact of obligation, its locus in existence, lies, that is, within the complex structure of the fact system; but it is not the sort of thing that can have a specifically designated place and be "found"; its essence is relational, and it does not exist there but *holds* there. But this is true of all ethical concepts; they do not directly refer to existences but hold within the system where alone existence has meaning. The psychological method involves what is called the fallacy of the simple, the mistake of looking for a thing as an element which has no elementary existence. The psychologist assumes that obligation must be some very rare fact within the consciousness of the individual, and it has been a mystery merely because he has so far, as he thinks, overlooked it. He can then ask whether the ethical concepts may be identifiable with any of the typical states of mind. These questions can be argued indefinitely, for they have no meaning. Obligation is not a state of mind.

It is of course true that obligation instances itself as a state of mind, appears in consciousness; but in the case of obligation we take the appearance for the fact and reality only at our peril. We cannot depend upon the "feeling" or "sense" or "conviction" of obligation.

When this psychological quest is reduced to absurdity, the "empiricist" embraces his only alternative. The seat and essence of obligation is in the "social." What cannot be found as fact within the confines of individual subjectivity must be found as "fact" within abstract or general subjectivity: for only what is subjective can be fact, can be real. This is the axiom. But empiricists approach the problem with the same psychological method which, as we have noticed, goes to pieces on simplicity. They conceive a universe of unique, that is, distinct persons, with relations between them which are practically infinite and describable in every case in mental or psychological terms. True, the individual psychologist was wrong in searching for the tie that binds within the subjectivity of the individuals; but as social psychologists we shall find it between the individuals. For, only the individual is real, and, if what we want is not in the individual, we shall find it outside of him externally referring to him. The individual's subjectivity slops over; and the hazy and tenuous connection which we seek has its proper lair in the slippery and nebulous viscosity which fills the interstices between the individuals.

But sociology, so far, has failed to construct out of this *Urschleim* anything resembling a principle. It therefore knows nothing of the principle that binds the moral agent to his fellows and his world. What it has ignored is the world of obvious objects which is the basis even of the reality of mental states. The constitution of these objects is the reality to which the principle of obligation refers. Concretely, obligation has its material existence in the family, in property, and the entities, *persons* they are, which human beings create by their simplest actions. These objects constitute the texture of the cultural world, and it is this world and our continuity with it in both nature and culture that we have in mind when we say obligation is real—when we acknowledge our obligation.

D. ORDER

The person is then both creature and creator of law. Principle has meaning, that is, only in relation to person, and the essence of the personality is the law which it promulgates and by which it binds itself, through its own objective other self (property, etc.), to its fellows and, by thus binding, creates the substance of its other-self in institutions. It is trivial, of course, to try to state the principle of personality in terms merely of individual human beings. Individuals are, since they alone are essentially real, of all possible types. And no one type can fully express the meaning of the principle of all. The principle of all individuals or persons is the law of their continuity in nature and culture. The real, as individual, can only be defined in and as this principle of continuity. And we have seen that this principle is obligation. But obligation also constitutes the world. There were no world if individuals had not owed it, if it had not been the substance of their obligation. As then the multiplicity of its objects represents merely separate crystallizations of obligation, that obligation itself requires to be elevated to the principle in which the substance and constitution of the world will itself appear as individual. This principle is order. It is nothing less than the universality and continuity of the objects which the practical act has created under the limitations of time and choice, these objects effected into the corporate whole which each of them implies.

V. THE MORAL PERSON

The four topics enumerated have indicated the major characteristics of the moral person. Morality comprehends (1) the character of the particular in the physical being. This is the substratum of life with all its variety of details of fact and process and of all the rules of habit and growth that make up the natural world. In the distinctly human sphere it is the physical body and all its possibilities. But there is implied in morality also, as complementary to the particular, (2) the being as conscious. It is through *consciousness* that life becomes *universal*, in all forms which we have noted. It is in this form of the universal that life creates itself into a world, postulates itself as other than itself, that is, acknowledges its capacity for progress, recognizes its possibilities, and is thus the basis of (3) social existence. This is the third form of its being and the basis of civil society, the ground and presupposition of culture. Just as consciousness and the sphere of life awaited the ordering of matter into the physical world of nature, so culture presupposes society and the development of social ends. Then the natural person and the cultural person unite in (4), the moral being proper, the being that can act, and the result is the individual. The individual multiplies within the moral realm, embodies himself in its substance, and becomes the person corporate, the presupposition of the realm of values.

There are four types of acts which correspond more or less roughly to the four characteristics mentioned above. These are the virtues of individuality, the forms of action that are proper to the person regarded as subjective, unique, and in so far as his action can be interpreted in terms of his inner nature. The following chapter will examine them in their general characters.

Part III

The Subjective or Partial Virtues

Chapter X

The Personal Virtues

SINCE we have defined morality in terms of the active life, that which is good in the person must be some form or quality of his acts. The problem is then how to describe and distinguish the types of acts of the person so as to exhibit what there is in them that is good and to point out the various forms that the goodness of concrete action may take. In the previous chapter we noted the various active capacities that belong to the person, the capacities and abilities that he has been endowed with by nature and culture. It is to these capacities that we refer when we speak of the virtues; but we imply, of course, that the great number of capacities may be generalized into a small number of typical forms of action.

We noted also in the preceding chapter that certain of the personal capacities refer in a unique way to the person himself as agent or originator of acts. These are the physical capacities and the conscious capacities. Since they refer backward and inward to the agent for their meaning, we shall refer to them here and in the four following chapters as the subjective virtues. But we noted also that certain other types of capacities more directly involve the person in relations with his fellows and with the external world. These we call the "cultural capacities," and, when in later chapters we regard them as virtues, we shall call them the "objective virtues." These latter are the activities which constitute civil society as legally and politically organized.

All these subjective virtues and objective virtues considered as synthesized in the life of the rational being are the act-forms of the moral person, that is, the person in his peculiar ethical capacity. This moral person and his acts, together with the objective circumstances which action implies, constitute the subject matter of ethical theory.

I. THE MEANING OF SUBJECTIVE VIRTUE

It was suggested above that by calling certain activities "subjective virtues" we mean that these activities are thought of as deriving their meaning solely from reference to the active agent from which they proceed. They are thus self-referent and "personal," where personal carries the suggestion of what is unique and private, what belongs, that is, to the agent considered as standing alone and without relations to other persons or things. This self-reference is easily seen to be the chief character of the natural capacities, the physical and conscious processes upon which life most directly depends. We shall see how in each of these cases the tendency of action is to direct itself by reference to something within the agent. And while this may seem to contradict what we have said earlier about action always involving an end or object outside and beyond the agent, yet we shall find the discrepancy merely apparent.

Let us take physical activity first. We have said that by moral capacity or virtue we refer to the type or form of a characteristic act. Now the agent, as source, and the object, as issue, in any act, or the "motive" on the one side and the "result" on the other, get their meaning from the relations in which they stand to this form. The mistake of ethical theory on this point has been either to attempt to interpret the agent or actor (in his aspect of "character") in terms of the objective results of the act or to interpret the results of the act in terms of and by reference to the agent (character, intention, etc.) as standard. As against this we see that both the character of the agent and the nature of the objective results get their ethical significance from their reference to a typical act considered as standard. The agent is "good" when he measures up consistently to a typical action-form or to the form of an act regarded as ideal. The man is good when, and in so far as, he *acts* thus and so, the thus and so describing the form of an act that reason or moral intuition accepts as standard. The result is good or bad by the same standard. It is a standard however because it is a type that has consistently been intuitively discerned in acts of a given sort and not because it is set up as a standard by some motivated choice.

Then the typical or formal character of the act determines the moral quality of both the agent of the act and the object of the act. In the case of physical activities, for example, work, play, recreation, and, in part, of aesthetic activity, this type or form is often some generalized aspect of need, want, desire, considered as necessities of existence. That is to say, the form of the act is often necessity, and in such cases the moral quality of the act is almost identical, or approaches identity, with the technical quality of correctness. This gives a general appearance of truth to utilitarianism. Also it is the reason why the "morality" of work and play and artistic activity is so

hard to make conform to "moral" principles. We do not see that such
activities have their own principles in the very form of the act, that
they are "free" acts in the sense that their form discloses immediately
the principle to which they conform. The usual language states this
fact in the proposition that "need," "want," are the grounds of physical
activity; work is grounded upon the necessity for food, play upon the
necessity of development and growth in the body, and art upon the
necessity to establish order in the feeling life. And, having thus recognized the type or form of these acts in necessity, we have proceeded
to exclude them from the moral life on the ground that they are not
expressions of will and freedom. We forget here that it is the act that
makes us free, not freedom that determines the act, that only because
of, and in and through action, freedom is realized. And we mistakenly
assume that it is out of our freedom and our "spontaneity" of will
that acts originate, that freedom and spontaneity pre-exist in some
mysterious way and have the capacity to originate acts. But the *act* is
the original fact, and all the qualities, including freedom, and whatever necessity there may be, of our will and character are derived
from it. It does not proceed from them.

The form or principle of physical action is then necessity. Let us
see what this necessity means. It is usually taken to mean that such
acts are mechanically determined, that they result from a fixed setup
in the facts of nature just as a triangle results from the intersection of
three straight lines. This illustration will enable us to see the mistake in
this notion of necessity. The triangle does not "result" from the intersection of lines. The triangle is the act in which three lines intersect,
and its being is contemporaneous with the intersection. Triangularity
is the reference of lines to the form of the act by which they constitute themselves with certain characters. That is, triangularity, in its
aspect of necessity, is the quality or aspect of self-reference of lines.
Thus mathematics defines its objects in terms of the operations by
which they are formed. So the necessity of physical acts is the fact
that these acts get their total meaning from, and justification in, their
reference inward and backward to themselves as the objects which
they constitute. Work "arises out of" the "need" for food; but, upon
this ground, food means the need and capacity for work; and so in all
cases of necessity. As an act, then, work is an instance of the infinite
process, and its principle of necessity is that work shall always mean
work. Work is then principled in necessity in that it is always a reference to itself and nothing more, an infinite turning and return of an
act to itself. It is thus subjective, and its principle is self-reference.

But necessity as the law of repetitive fixity is part, at least, of the ground of freedom, since it is the plane upon which acts are always possible, and upon which the plan of every act must be drawn if it is to be realized. I know that I can always act because necessity has prepared the ground of circumstance upon and within which the conditions for action will always be present. Necessity thus prepares an open field and the freedom from restraint and the positive access to the tools I shall need to accomplish ends. And in this sense necessity is a positive implicate of the freedom that is characteristic of acts that are determined within natural conditions.

Thus the virtue of the physical life is subjective; it refers action backward to the need of the subject or agent from which its processes begin. But this necessity is capable of a broader interpretation.

A similar result is attained by consideration of the conscious activities. When an act that is performed is consciously mine, the principle of its performance, as and in so far as conscious, is its conformity with my mental state. This conformity becomes thus the type or form of the act in a way similar to that in which necessity becomes the type or form of physical acts. And, just as the necessity of physical acts may be considered as an element of the ground of objective freedom, so the conformity of an act to the state of mind that motivates it is the ground of subjective freedom, the sense of spontaneity and autonomy out of which acts as intentions appear to issue. And as this intentionality *is* the form of the act of consciousness, that is, the characteristic mode of its expression, the act of consciousness conforms to itself, and this self-reference is what we mean by saying that the virtue of all conscious acts is subjective virtue. Whatever thus I intend or "will" to do, or whatever I feel as the proper form of my sentiency, is what it is by virtue of its reference to the principle or form of the act in which it is defined. It is thus a reference to itself, and the act in which this self-reference is expressed is a virtue in the subjective and limited sense which we have defined above.

Since the conscious aspect of acts, or acts considered as conscious, will concern us again later in this chapter as the content of virtue, we can here leave off the discussion. But we want to insist that the virtue of acts when interpreted in terms of consciousness is a subjective virtue and that the attempt to locate the full moral quality of an act in the fact that the act is conscious leads to many of the historical contradictions, "problems," of ethical theory. And, what is worse, it leaves behind it a long train of acts and forms of acts which human beings will persist in doing and regarding as good and valuable but which have no justification in the morality which the subjective method prescribes. It thus involves a continuous break between the system of convictions of men and their modes of conduct, and this is a continuing source of moral skepticism and cynicism. This subjective viewpoint ignores the fact that an act has whatever value it has in itself and of its own nature only as an element within the system of acts and does not derive its value either from the conscious "purpose" out of which it is supposed to issue or from the object or person in or upon which it issues. The fact that an act is done and exists or occurs imposes upon moral theory the task of finding a place for it in the objective moral scheme; it is substantial in its own nature, and the system of ethical concepts, agent, character, end, good, right, etc., all derive their import from their being some aspect of the form or principle of the act.

II. SUBJECTIVE VIRTUES ARE PARTIAL

The end of the moral life is the perfect act—"Life is an act"—and its critical instants are means to the perfect act if not the perfect act itself. It is so because, as itself the system of acts, its principle involves a reference beyond itself. Hence an act performed on the subjective principle of self-reference will be *partial*, *potential*, and *incomplete*. Let us see how this is true.

An act whose form is subjective, whose principle is self-reference, as, for example, acts which express needs and wants and those which express conscious motives, is an act that is partial. When I act out of need to produce an ear of corn, the act will always be partial, since the ear of corn requires, to complete its own nature, many elements which lie outside it and which are not represented in my need. Thus the fertility of the soil, the heat and moisture of the sunshine and air, in fact, all the elements of nature, enter into its substance. An act directed merely at the production of the ear of corn will neglect many of the elements that enter into it, and the consequences are fatal to the ear itself. If I neglect the soil, I will soon exhaust it so that it will not produce corn; so, if I want corn, I must act so that not only corn but all the conditions upon which corn depends will be sustained. But to produce corn from "need" means that all these other factors are ignored, so the act defeats its own end, perverts itself. This is true of all physical, that is, economic, industrial, play, recreative, activity; all these forms of action contemplate an act as isolated from its conditions in its circumstance, and thus all involve that their act shall be ultimately self-destructive. Such acts lack full moral character in that they imply action under conditions in which the act may not be continued to its end; it is continually broken off from its environing conditions and appears in the form of eternal repetition. If we think of this failure of the act to embrace its end in terms of consciousness as its motive, then we express the failure as dissatisfaction or unsatisfaction. Satisfaction thus implies, in conscious terms, the success of an act in accomplishing a genuine reference beyond the subjective state from which its motive comes. It implies, that is, that an act is partial until it reaches wholeness in its end. But this, so long as the act is principled by self-reference, it can never do. There is thus no end or satisfaction, either for activities that are based on necessity in the economic or industrial world or for actions based upon the whimsicality of consciousness or mental states in the world of "experience." We shall see under what conditions such acts can attain full moral quality and worth when we come to discuss the objective virtues and shall get hints of it all along as we prepare for that discussion.

The "good" of a subjective act is postponed; that is, it must wait until some way is found to go beyond the subjective limitations. So far, then, its virtue is *potential* merely; it refers us simply to what can be done. But it refers to what can be done merely in the abstract; it could not tell us, as we saw, how the ear of corn could be raised without at the same time creating the conditions that prevent corn being raised at all. Hence it is the source of the "idealism" which can find satisfaction and virtue in the good heart and the right intention, states of subjectivity and self-reference in which the obligation to act cannot arise at all. There is no call for action in the real sense where all that is required of action already exists in the mind ready-made. There is, of course, a sense in which the subjective or potential virtues are important. When we speak of the future possibilities of a healthy and intelligent child, we endow the child with great worth, the worth, namely, of the acts and ends that it is hoped the child will one day fulfil. But it remains true that such virtue is now merely possible, and the failure of it by death or wrong training and development appears to us as the worst of evils. The virtue of the child is therefore a mere abstract hope, the idea of significant action to come, and its goodness consists merely in that it presages future accomplishments; it is goodness in the sense of innocence, the not having as yet performed unworthy acts.

This partial or potential virtue is *incomplete*. Virtue may exist as mere promise or as partial performance. Such an act may indeed be complete in the sense that overt expression of energy has ceased, and in the further sense that an object that is complete in itself is achieved. I may produce the board from the log, and the actual work on it will stop. Also the board may be perfect after its kind. Thus the work is good work, and the board is good as a product, both in the potential sense that each has further important consequences. It is upon the basis of these further consequences that I may pronounce both good; that is, the goodness in both cases lies outside and beyond the act or the object, is completed in what is to be further done with them. They have a "pragmatic sanction," and in the limited circle of values where these further consequences are ignored the act of sawing out the board is perfect after its kind if it conforms to the principle of such acts, viz., the principle of the technical competence of the act in its response to a subjective need. But this conformity is itself subjective and partial in the larger sense that more than mere technical correctness is to be demanded of any act. I must act so as to produce, given appropriate conditions, a technically perfect board; but, in addition to this, I must further perform the act in such a way as will further and be consistent with the competent performance of other acts by myself and others and consistent also with the production of other objects. My act must not deny freedom of action to another person, must not reduce people to poverty, must not keep boys and girls out of school; in fact, it should contribute, directly or remotely, to all these and other ends. My act must, as Aristotle says, be done to the right persons, at the right time, in the right amount, with right motives, with right ends in view, etc.

In short, my act must be complete and whole, not merely in the local and isolated sense that it must represent its technical kind but in the sense that it must articulate with the system of my values and through that with the system of the world regarded as the locus of all acts and all values. To be right and good, my act must not be wrong in any sense, and this requirement is what justifies the claim that acts by themselves may possess absolute and objective worth. It is true, of course, that this absolute worth may be exhibited in any specific case as concrete, and the portrayal of objective rightness in concrete cases is what constitutes descriptive ethics. This is not, however, mere empiricism, not mere description of the factual circumstances in which right is imbedded.

Subjective virtue is thus partial, potential, and incomplete; and it is so because no consistent account of it can be given without going beyond it to the whole which gives it its character.

III. SUBJECTIVE VIRTUE IS PARTICULAR

The limitations of subjective virtue shown above all sum up in the observation that such virtue is specific, particular, relative. To connect the virtue of an act with its own technical perfection is to deny it any meaning, since meaning always involves the reference to that which serves as standard of valuation. The making a situation specific, therefore, consists precisely in severing this reference, and the only basis left for attributing worth to the situation is to say that its worth lies in itself. The moral life then becomes an infinite succession of groundless choices. This is what comes of making action depend on the spontaneity of will. Every act comes as a consequence of a mere preference for which no reason can be given, and this is the same as to say that the will is essentially irrational. Either choices submit to reason, in which case there is nothing unique in them as different from ordinary acts of decision, or they do not submit to rational direction, in which case they are preferences without ground or basis other than the whims of present consciousness.

This is why in the history of ethics there has been the dual tendency—on the one side to the rational or volitional determination of every act by the agent who performs it, with an ultimate negative issue; and on the other side the subordination of every act to the fiat of an external authority, thus separating the act from its ground and posing the old question of freedom. What is not seen in recent ethical thinking is that psychological particularism leads inevitably to one or the other of these positions. We cannot say that each act has its principle in its concreteness as present to consciousness without sooner or later explaining its presence. And as mere presence has no explanation, one must be jumped up for it, and authority, or the rational will, is the easiest way out.

Subjective virtue as particular is a form of self-reference that contradicts itself. There is, however, a positive content of subjective virtue, and we must exhibit its form.

IV. THE POSITIVE MEANING OF SUBJECTIVE VIRTUE

This question of the content of the good life, of the stuff the good life is made of, is one as to the nature and quality of that content. And this is a matter of the meaning of the term "good," considered solely with respect to the kinds of experience which, with other things, enter into the good.

As the term has been used in ethical discussion for centuries, there are two major aspects of its meaning that have appeared, and the theories have divided with respect to these aspects. One type of theory, the one which has perhaps had most advocates, is to the effect that the good is some form of mental state. And these have differed widely on the question of which mental state it is that identifies with the good. But all agree that the good is some form of experience, feeling, sense, will, reason, or some combination of part or all of these. It is with this experience theory of the good that we shall be concerned in this chapter. The other type of theory assumes that the good is some kind of extra-experiential object, and the purpose of life is to attain or acquire this object. We shall be engaged with this point of view in Part IV, and the types of action engendered in the struggle to attain this objective good, what we shall call the "objective virtues," will be discussed in Part V.

But while we have these distinctions in mind it is worth remarking that most ethical systems have been mixtures of both in varying degrees. Some of the prominent theories of the latter type have conceived the good as objective but as somehow coalescing with experience when attained, the elements of experience in the result being transformed into something beyond experience as ordinarily known. Some of the former have also, while insisting that the good must be an experience in the form ordinarily known, tended to think of this experience in terms of the objects that are necessary to create and maintain the experience. We may begin this question with the reflection that there probably is some sense in which each of them is true. We shall in any case accept what appears to us to be a necessary synthesis of the two underlying ideas, viz., that whatever is good must be of the form of experience but must also transcend or lie beyond experience in the sense that it persists in a way such that it may itself be a criterion for judgments made about experience. That this objective fact, which we shall in general call "culture," is itself in large part a product of experience, nevertheless does not prevent its being described as a fact over which experience has no final control but is itself the basis of whatever control may be exercised over experience in determining its direction, its content, and its issue.

But here we are dealing with the proposition that the good, which as a type of action that we call "virtue," is experience. And our first question is: Which experience? Each of the major types has had its advocates, with opinion divided between feeling as including sense and reason, with will in the general sense of action getting a share of emphasis.

A. The Good as Feeling

In this viewpoint whatever is to be called "good" is a state of feeling which can be described in psychological terms and can be distinguished from everything that is not of the nature of feeling. The theory generally supplements the description by connecting feeling causally or otherwise with objects, but uniformly regards the objects as distinct from the feeling once the experience is had. The feeling is immediately known when experienced, and there is nothing in terms of which its essence may be stated except itself. In whatever way the outer world of objects may be conceived as related to experience as feeling, these objects are yet of different and foreign stuff. The task of this theory is therefore mainly descriptive, for the most part one of enumerating the qualities of the feeling by which it is known and by which its uniqueness is established. There are two types of feeling theory. One identifies the elementary experience with pleasure-pain, and the other with the vague experience of striving or aspiring or realizing, states of mind that are variously named and characterized. The latter is frequently confused with will-theories in intricate ways, and the best example of this is found in the religious forms of ethical thought.

It is not necessary to go at great length into the discussion of the proposition that the good is experience of pleasure or avoidance of pain. There is a very limited sense in which it is just obviously true; but it is one thing to argue that pleasure is good and pain evil, and another to say that the good is nothing but pleasure or the avoidance of pain. That pleasure is *a* good is clear, but it is by no means clear that it is *the* good. And it is not at all certain that there are not many things besides pleasure that are good. It is common to connect pleasure, regarded as the good, with desire, on the assumption that pleasure is the object of desire. But it is quite obvious that, while the desire that ends in pleasure may be good, there are many instances in which desire would be approved in spite of the fact that it issues in what is not pleasure. The relations of the good to pleasure and desire are somewhat subtle, and the theories have held almost every possible conception of those relations. It is enough for our purposes to remark that, for perhaps the very great majority of mankind, pleasure is, of one kind or another, whether experienced immediately or in contemplation, either consciously or unconsciously held to be the proper and appropriate issue of desire, and, as the issue or fulfilment of desire, is the good. This, we may be sure, is the ethical creed of the great mass of men, even of those who because of some religious tradition would vehemently reject it when clearly stated.

But the great mass of men do not think very deeply, and their ethical convictions are very good evidence of the fact. When we examine the conduct of men objectively and without asking for their opinions of it or their motives for it, we find that the facts do not fit the theory. It is not true that men act always or even generally at the dictate of desire, nor is it self-evident that desire is any large element in the basic reason or ground of action. Of course every act would follow from desire if we should agree to call desire that which precedes the act in every case; but even then we should find our word "desire" being used for a great variety of very different sorts of facts. It does not seem evident that desire, if we are to hold strictly to the meanings of terms, is an especially important factor in action. It is so, it is to be admitted, in some highly emotionalized and spectacular situations, such as the theorists like to borrow as examples from literary people; and it is so in many critical junctures in life. But for the most part life is emotionally colorless and drab, rather matter-of-fact and plain featured, and it is this humdrum of existence that is basic in the moral life and development of mankind. And in this main current of the moral life desire, especially if it is to mean any pronounced longing of feeling or any clear inclination toward ends, is not predominant by any means. In the morally more stable instances of life men are likely to be characterized as stolid, and this stolidity would have to be counted as a moral asset. It is the dependableness of the unthinking and readily satisfied mass of men that constitutes the foundation and solid structure of society, and with them desire is not an important matter. Of course, desire is elemental for the class of romanticists and aesthetic adventurers who desire to "live dangerously," but any competent intellectual or aesthetic comprehension of the facts of life will arrive at a conclusion which nearly approaches that attained by the plodding mass. It may be admitted that in a world turned topsy-turvy by a complete reversal of all natural values through economic and industrial imbecility, desire is a dominating force; but it is so only as a symptom of disease; it certainly is not the normal condition of the good life.

A simple analysis of the facts of life will show that men under ordinary natural and cultural conditions are in pursuit of concrete objects and that these objects so determine their action that they are not consciously dominated by any qualities of mental states at all. When I am doing something that is morally good or right, I do not consciously have any mental states; my mind moves among the objects of the environment as if it were one of them, and I am not conscious of being urged or driven or drawn by anything. It cannot even be said that I am interested; my mind is not active at all with respect to its own states. I am "absorbed" or "lost" among a group of objects, and I am not conscious in any obvious way of my difference from other objects. The mental "states" that are important are the good sense and sound perception that tell me that these objects are worthy of my engagement with them, and the occasional glimpse I get of their consistency with other objects I have had in mind. These are characteristically cognitive states and get their form and significance from objects. But I do not hunger or thirst after them; the next moment after my absorption with them I may dash them to pieces. As a matter of fact the most important types of moral experience are those which we do not take too seriously while engaged in them, and they are so primarily because the realization of the emotional or other importance of what we are doing interferes with the technical processes by which the important thing is done.

On the whole, then, it seems best to be wary of the proposition that the content of the good is feeling. If it were so, then all virtue would be subjective, and all ethical concepts would be psychological categories. But morality is action, and action implies objects with their stable characters; it does not depend upon the instability of feeling or upon the passive immobility of mental states which feeling seems to imply. And yet it is true and important that states of feeling may legitimately become the objects of action consistently with moral principles. But in that case they lose their content as feelings and become objects in the ordinary sense. I have the same right to demand satisfaction of my feeling life as of other things; the error consists in assuming that anything I demand, and because I demand it, thereby becomes a state of mind which I may characterize as feeling and which gets its worth because I conceive it as an object of desire.

We may note incidentally what we may call the aesthetic interpretation of the good. This seems to be the mere abandonment of the consciousness to the enjoyment of the experience of sense. It raises important questions about the relations of feeling and sense by apparently ignoring any distinction between them. I may enjoy eating a good dinner; this implies that the mere gratification of taste with the variety of delicacies in succession and its continuance to the point of surfeit is what is good. After I have eaten I will take coffee or wine and smoke a good cigar. This will be followed by good conversation

—the whole picture illustrating the idea of good as satisfaction of sense.

The only comment this calls for is this: that certainly it is true that sense enjoyment is good. It may be made the object of specific acts. But it is not necessarily the "highest" good and is surely not the whole good. It is also not of the type of the good, since it is not true that all good must be of the same kind as pleasure or sense enjoyment. There is a fallacy here about the highest good that it is worth while to note. The highest good is generally supposed to indicate a graded scale of goods, a scale in which the successive stages upward represent more goodness or a more valued or worthy good, where "more" seems to refer to intenser or richer attributes of mental states. The famous "refutation of hedonism," that goods differ in kind and that some kinds are intrinsically more good than others, proves nothing except perhaps the proposition it is supposed to disprove. That is, you must accept different goods as merely different kinds of mental states before the distinction of more or less or higher or lower good can apply, which means that the calculus must be accepted in the effort to disprove it—the method by which it is disproved presupposes it. What this means is that the quantitative interpretation is false whether it involves different degrees or kinds or stages or whatever. But it is false only because it is being applied to a substance which it cannot qualify, that is, as quantity it can characterize mental states but cannot characterize the objects that give mental states their moral significance. The only way to avoid this is to see that the "more" good implies a more inclusive and more intricate or highly organized objective system. It is the objective reference that makes anything good, whether that be a mental state or whatever else. The good is not an intrinsic quality; it is an extrinsic relational system in which the qualities of things are involved as moments.

The conclusion is thus that the good is not feeling. The good is not feeling because it is not a state of mind of any kind. This means that the virtues of states of mind, the subjective virtues, do not represent the whole meaning of virtue.

B. The Good as Will

The good then is not identical with feeling experience. Is it identical with those feelings of energy or striving which appear to underlie the active life? It does not appear that any such voluntaristic theory is tenable, for, if the energies and strivings are to be understood as merely states of mind, they fall under the same criticisms as do feelings. They would, as states of mind, appear to fall within either the class of feelings or the class of cognitions, the only other alternative being the possibility of identifying them with actions proper, when actions are taken to be unique types of mental states. But if they are actions, then they are the *factual* content of morality and not states of mind in any sense at all. There seems to be nothing that can be made of the doctrine of will as a subjective force which exercises its energies through states of mind. Either will will turn out to be a rational act of choice or decision, or it will become impulse or motive or some other aspect of feeling. There seem to be no states of mind to which the moral will should conform or with which it should identify, and the psychological theory of will ends by destroying its object.

But this means that will is an aspect of the objective element in action. It is not a phase or character of the states of mind involved in action. The direction and force and impact and issue of an act are determined by the structure and the relational system of the objects among which it takes place. In so far then as an act gets its character from the agent which enacts it, it is the physical body and its organization that determine it. But the act, any act, does not get its *specific* character from the bodily organization; from that it merely gets its point of origin and the initial motive of its direction. It may also be said that it gets the physical forces concentrated from the point of the bodily organism, that the organism forms for the act a stable background as a fulcrum for its leverage. But with respect to its nature, form, and effects, these are largely determined in the relational and qualitative character of the objects which form the environing circumstance of the body. In any case the analysis of an act does not refer us directly to mental states. Thus the will, when looked at as the ground of explanation of action, appears to refer us to the total objective situation within which the act occurs. It is the effective force of this organization of objects which explains all the distinctive features of will. And this force appears to observation in the momentum which any organization acquires by virtue of its relational perfection and completeness of structure. This objective view of will is more readily explained in terms of "social" relations, where will, whenever found as a real force or agency, has always the corporate structure and is adequately described only in the corporate theory of will. In any case, since it does not belong in a discussion of the subjective features of virtue, we shall postpone it until we reach the discussion of the objective theory of virtue.

But enough has been said to show that the good is not a state of mind which we can call will and identify with action, and thus blow both hot and cold on the question of its being objectively real. The good is not mere striving or energizing. The truth which this voluntarist theory misapprehends is this—that the relations among the objects within which action takes place are the basis of the energies and impulses which determine the direction and issue of the action. But this has nothing directly to do with mental states.

C. The Good as Reason

Then is the good the state of reflective thought or the act of thinking of the agent? We shall approach this point of view in the same way as we did the other theories, and our discussion may be brief. The good, we may say, is never the thinking or the thought of the agent who contemplates it, nor is the good the action in which the good is realized. The good is not a state of experience for anybody. The good will always imply and involve, directly or indirectly, experience as part of its content; but there is no case where the good and an experience can simply be identified. And this is true however exalted we may conceive the experience; no experience is good enough to be the whole good, or to be altogether good. The good is then not reason, for reasons similar to those given in the cases of feeling and will. There is, however, this difference: reason, thought, is an activity, is action, and the good is in every case an aspect or phase of action. But in so far as we can identify reason with action it becomes identical with the organic relationality of an object system, becomes, that is, the rationality of an ordered whole of objects. And in this sense we can say the good is reason or reason is the good; but it involves a distinct change in the meaning of reason; reason here certainly is not a state of mind; it is in any case the rational order of a fact system, and judgments that have validity can be made about it. And in this case we may question whether our "good" is the central concept of ethics or is rather a norm of logic.

The good then is related to states of mind in so far as those states logically imply a world of objects in which action can be real and ends can be realized. But the good identifies with no state of mind or experience. No states in their content imply this world of objects, and, as feeling and subjective striving are content of mind and never its form, they lack the objective reference which constitutes the good as real. The good then is this world made rational, or the world as rationalized, and the logical and factual necessity that it be and become rational is the *raison d'être* of action and the ground of all that actions means. It is in this sense that the good is to be accomplished through action. And it is in the sense that it is in the rational world that the feelings have their place that we can say they are good; but there is nothing that we can say is good because it is or contains feeling which has not also elements of the objective world.

The reason that is good, or the good that is reason, the world of objects which is the ground of all that action can mean, its rationality —this is the good. But it is not good because it is, as it on occasion can be, represented in and as a state of mind.

D. The Good as Happiness

In so far as we can conceive of all experiences, and the objects which they imply, being incorporated together in a total harmony through action, we can say that the good is happiness. This whole of experience will have feeling as its peculiar element of content, the stuff or material that gives it weight and substance. It will also have reason as the order of the relations that constitute the structure of the whole and maintain its integrity and guarantee its stability and permanence. As a feeling content objectified thus in rational harmony, the whole will have momentous energy, force and power and actualizing capacity which give to action its constructive power to realize ends within the system of objects. This is the good as will—the corporate will. In this sense of the wholeness of experience, grounded in and upon the wholeness and integrity of its world, happiness is the good. But happiness as thus conceived is not any peculiar kind or sort of experience, it *is* not an experience at all. It is an object, independently real. It certainly is not feeling, and more certainly not pleasure, neither of which possesses any of the essential features of happiness. Nor is the good as happiness sheer exercise of the reason or thought as a subjective process or as mental states. Only as the reason itself is objectified as wisdom in the world of objects does it enter in as an ingredient of the happiness that is the good. And the happiness that is the good is not a series of spasms of impulse such as is commonly called "will." Happiness, the good, is will as the weight and power of the corporate reason there is in the order of objects—it is will when it becomes, that is, realizes, the world.

E. The Good Is Not a Mental State

Then the forms of action that we call the virtues are not conditioned upon our states of mind but upon a solider ground. We have seen that we have to recognize a substantial share in virtuous action for mental states. But because it is only a share, and at best a smallish part of the meaning of action that connects it with mental states, the principles of action derived from the mental states of the agent are subjective. The virtues that are derived from our states of mind are subjective virtues, and this means that they are partial, merely potential, incomplete, in fact they lack most of the characteristics of genuine virtue.

Let us be clear that we do not mean to deny that these subjective and personal qualities and capacities are virtues. They represent the best in the life of action that can come from the individual or person considered as their source. They are the total goodness of the person when taken by himself, or when he is considered in connection merely with other persons. That one's states of mind and "heart" and "will" are good states of mind when of a certain quality is obvious. It will always be right to feel charity, benevolence, mercy, etc., and the person who feels them will always be *so far* a good person. These qualities are good as far as they go. But as states of mind they are never all of what we mean by good; they never express all the meaning that we attribute to the good. Charity, for example, can never represent the total good that is possible in any situation where it is appropriate, nor can any action proceeding from charity be the whole of what such a situation demands.

The following four chapters will describe the more important subjective virtues as exemplifying the conclusions reached in this chapter.

Chapter XI

Sympathy—Virtue as Pure Subjectivity

WE HAVE seen in the preceding chapter that virtue cannot be regarded as full-bodied and complete so long as it is identified with any state of mind. Sympathy, as the assumption that virtue may be expressed in its full degree in terms of some form of inner consciousness, is the pure instance of this subjectivity, a pure instance of inward reference to the inner state of feeling; and its significance lies only in the fact that it is an index to the quality and intensity of feeling. It tells nothing about any object in the world that is substant to my feeling. The mere feeling of sympathy does not give the slightest hint as to what sort of object there may be, the action I might or should initiate toward the object, or the degree of energy with which I should act, or with what purpose. The tendency is to regard virtue as completed in the mere feeling, and no *overt* or real action is required.

This is to say that my goodness is demonstrated when I have given evidence of a right heart, and the good intention pays all the obligation I can have. I make a public expression of sympathy for the poor, symbolize its sincerity by a donation, and proceed to assume that my duty is done. I may now, with a clear conscience, proceed to business as usual and profit by methods that create poverty and misery faster than any alleviatory scheme can cope with them, but I am not responsible; the poor you have always with you; they are either degenerate or inefficient, or they are the hapless products of a progress for whose unfortunate consequences nobody is at fault, although I may claim a share in its benefits. Thus virtue and goodness are strictly and wholly conditions of the inner man, and the only real action that obligation or duty requires is just enough to symbolize the presence of the state of mind. Plainly, this sort of effort to make a full virtue of sympathy turns into a practical contradiction.

And yet sympathy is, in its own way, a genuine virtue, its limitation being in the fact that it has no definite relation to objects. Its function is solely to maintain such a condition of the inner life as is

192

favorable—in so far as mere states of mind may be so—to significant action. It is personal virtue in its lowest terms. It reveals the agent's character to himself, and its expression exhibits that character to other persons for approval or criticism. And, while it may stimulate the agent to act, it suggests none of the qualities that make action moral, qualities referring to the direction, intensity, purpose, etc., of the act. Sympathy has nothing to do with these; hence, while it is a virtue, it is limited, imperfect, and incomplete. And as we shall see later, it is better to call the goodness which sympathy represents by another name.

In the sense of pure inward self-reference, sympathy has a number of forms of expression which we shall proceed to describe. There is first the religious form, which, interpreted as a pure spiritual function, is (A) desire, or sympathy as the feeling of need, with the idea of action based on the conception of common need, helpfulness, charity, etc.; (B) pity, in addition to which there is also the feeling of contempt or hatred, together with the idea of action based on the conception of common contempt of its object, the idea being to act in order to remove the cause and condition of action; (C) love, which ignores real activity and finds fulfilment in the mere inwardness of the feeling. This fulfilment may be either individual, as in the case of the saints, martyrs, etc., or collective, as in the fellowship of other persons.

In the religious experience sympathy is interpreted as a pure spiritual function, and this seems to mean that it has and should have no connection with the cruder conditions of the world. Sympathy appears to be the supreme virtue because, through its experience, the individual or agent is lifted beyond and out of the petty and coarse and crude relations of physical existence. Where physical existence is hard and the outward conditions of life are intolerable, sympathy still guarantees a significant experience in spite of such conditions. Consequently, the inward sphere, the realm of feeling, becomes the real, and the outward and "material" the unreal or evil. The life of physical action and the effort to make out of external conditions the substance of a significant life will be looked upon either as mistaken and wasted effort or, at the worst, as downright wrong and wicked. For in struggling with the "world," one is misspending time in which he might be "realizing" his being in the fulness of inward assurance; or, in compromising with the "world," in manifesting a preoccupation with the "worldly" affairs of ordinary life, he may lose his inner substantial soul and character itself. The ultimate of moral experience is then, in the extreme religious view, this feeling of pure sympathy. It is the assurance of full realization of all that virtue can mean. There are three forms of this inward virtue which may be variously named, and each may be interpreted in an individualist or a collectivist sense. We shall use their most common and popular names.

A. DESIRE

This is the feeling of sympathy in the sense of absence of internal harmony, the feeling that the inwardness of the person is incomplete and unsatisfactory. It is the feeling of need and longing which may be either individual or shared, and, in so far as it implies action, it assumes that the action is complete when the need is satisfied. The objects involved in action, if any, disappear within the substance of the satisfied desire. This feeling does not, therefore, contemplate the creation or maintenance of an objective world as the instrument through which needs might be permanently satisfied or satisfied progressively as they arise. The object becomes absorbed in the satisfaction, and the result of any action on the basis of desire is to leave the actor merely with a changed content of mind; whereas he was once in desire he is now filled, and the fulness is the complete realization which he seeks. It is a condition of his own inner being, and the world is left where it was, except that it may lack the object wherewith the desire was satisfied.

In its collectivist sense desire implies the possibility of needs being mutual and sharable and communicable; it implies that numbers of individuals share or participate in a common need that is present in the inner selves of all at the same time. This common need leads to overt action—if at all—similar in kind to the individual's action in the same case. The acts that it contemplates have to do with real objects only in so far as they are absorbed and become the new mental content taking the place of the original state of want. Desire and need contribute nothing to the support of an objective world, and the virtues they imply are simple references to the subjectivity of the agents in whom they exist; they involve an agent only in his capacity to be acted upon. The agent is passive recipient of whatever changes may occur; he is the receiver of the results of action that is dominated by chance and accident. Desire, need, and their supposed object are all equally subjective, and the virtues they contemplate are pure states of mind and are hence incomplete and imperfect.

B. Pity

This virtue is closely related to contempt, hatred, etc., and so far
as it involves objects its relation to them is the reverse of that of desire. In its individual form it is the revulsion of feeling which the agent
experiences in the presence of a negative stimulus, one suggesting to
the agent loss or detraction from the completeness of his mental state.
It also implies that the stimulating object is a sentient being in its
present state miserable. Being essentially negative in character, it
neither intends nor strives to do anything positive or constructive
with respect to the outer order of life. On the contrary, all its meaning lies in the suggestion it makes to the effect that there is something
present in experience which ought not to be there, and so far as any
overt action is implied the action would be intended to remove from
the world whatever object might be a stimulus to the feeling. Its
characteristic direction is in the way of reform, and its significance
lies in the fact that it recognizes that life as it is is not as full and rich
as it might be. The action it implies, however, is negative, since it
involves the removal of objects and conditions which it adjudges
unreal and unfavorable to the continued existence of satisfactory
mental states. Essentially, then, it is the same as contempt and hatred;
is contempt, perhaps, with its tendency to violence subdued, and
hatred with its permanently destructive tendency submerged in the
realization that the present stimulus is probably ineffective as regards
our present state of mind.

Pity, in its collective or mutual form, is ordinarily described as the
merging or fusion of the feeling attitudes of a number of individuals.
But it must be kept in mind that no real fusion of feelings of different
individuals is possible. What is meant perhaps is that the individual
who feels pity will have his feelings stimulated to a higher intensity
by the fact that he is surrounded by a crowd of persons behaving as if
they felt pity. But there is no fusion from one person to another. The
same feeling that will lead the individual to kill a wounded and suffering dog will, when suffused through a large mass of persons by
mutual stimulation, lead them to make war on a neighboring state on
the ground that their neighbors are "low" and "base" in culture and
presumably miserable. Pity thus leads to united action in the direction
of reform, and its obliteration of slum districts and "social" sources
of diseases, etc., is so far admirable. Thus, it is a sort of negative base
of advancement. But it remains subjective. The action it contemplates is supposed to issue in a state of mind, one in which satisfaction

is indicated by the absence of certain disturbing factors. It has no meaning and no force where the problem calls for the positive replacement of the disturbing factors. "Movements" in social life motivated by pity are notorious for the incongruous sillinesss with which they sometimes express themselves. Thus pity will lead to the erection of a hospital for cats, or refuges for birds, while hospital facilities for children are notoriously inadequate. Sympathy as pity is a virtue, and it is important in the moral life; but it is limited by incompleteness and subjectivity. There is no appropriate object for it.

C. Love

The moral characteristics of inner states of feeling all converge in the virtue of love. In this experience abortive efforts at external expression such as we saw in pity and desire are transcended, and the feeling finds its perfection in the fact that no overt act, no external expression is required of it. The virtue of the individual is fulfilled simply in his being what he is. All the attractive and repulsive tendencies of feeling are gathered up into one ultimate inwardness in which their variety and diversity are lost. They emanate from the agent in a grace and beneficence which require no outward means or instruments—the fulfilment of all they mean is already contained in the original impulse. Hence love ignores all forms of activity and finds fulfilment in its own inwardness of feeling. It represents what the agent is, the completeness and totality of his feeling life. It is subjectivity in its pure form, the virtue that is complete in the mere intention. No overt act is thus required, and the height of moral formalism is attained. The most exalted of the historical ethical systems— Spinoza, Kant, even Aristotle in his distinction of a pure intellectual virtue, and in some respects Plato—all reach this absolute ideal of perfect quiescence, the ideal of a life that is perfect in its passivity. But they reach it by ignoring facts they set out to explain, the facts of the life of action that it is the function of ethics to explain.

Naturally this explanation involves an interpretation of the facts in terms of the mind and consciousness through which the facts are apprehended; it does not mean that the facts shall disappear and be lost in being apprehended or in being felt. The ultimate explanation of the facts of action must be the definition and delineation of the perfect act, and the perfect act is embodied in the relation of the mind to the world that constitutes the circumstance and environment of the mind. The demand for real action is the demand for the perfection of this relation, the demand that the relation between the world as it is and the world as known be made rational. Action is thus the rationalization of the world, the transformation of the world into a form consistent with the demands of knowledge. And this cannot be accomplished within the mere subjective states through which mind symbolizes its objects to itself. It is effected and achieved only when these states are considered as realized in objects that are not subjective in any sense. It is only through these objects that mind can find and demonstrate its reality.

Sympathy, then, in all these religious forms, is a virtue. It represents the fineness and nobility of the personal spirit. But as such it is merely potential; the realization of it as virtue in the full sense requires other factors which we shall examine as we proceed.

There is a political sense of sympathy, in which the order of the external life is based on some sort of a common inner state. In this political view there are (A) socialism, based on the concept of a common welfare or happiness as the synthesis of all types of subjective experience, (B) democracy, based on the concept of a common conviction or public opinion, and (C) absolutism, based on mutual respect and reverence as a form of mental compulsion.

Political experience assumes that the values and goods of life can be given permanent and tangible form in the world. It also assumes that, as permanent tangible forms, values become external standards by which the experiences of individuals may be tested as to their worth or worthlessness. It assumes, that is, that experiences as well as objects may be evaluated. It appears, however, that in order that experiences may thus be equated to standards, they must somehow enter into the structure and substance of the standards to which they are equated. This is the demand that political forms be grounded in experience considered as the universal of which the separate experiences of individuals are instances. Since the experiences are the separate values or worths, the political standard itself must be the ground of values. Political reality is thus a unit or synthesis of existence and worth, assuming existence as the universal (abstract) in which all fact in its plurality is represented, and worth the concrete universal of which experiences are the individual instances. Ethical theory therefore which undertakes to find a bottom in politics for its conceptions is seeking the ultimate beyond experience as a principle which can be made to account for the unity which, as matter of fact, is characteristic of the experiences of men, for it is recognized that there can be no unity or unification of experiences as such, that is, regarded as subjective states. There can be unity only in terms of objects, and this we have made clear in the theory of objective will. This unity, considered as a principle of experiences in the form in which it is discoverable in fact, is variously named "mutual interest," "commonwealth," or "common or general welfare." But, in any case, it is interpreted in terms of objective fact. We shall use these terms to avoid the more metaphysical implications of the concept of the objective will, which cannot be made intelligible on the ground of either political or ethical explanation so long as that explanation is limited to experience. Obviously, it is not a question of psychology.

Sympathy as a subjective ethical principle, when referred to politics for its ground, appears in the three forms of welfare, conviction, and respect. Each of these is assumed to symbolize a mental state that is common to all individuals that have experiences or who are the bearers of values. Together they refer to their universal in the realm of worth. We shall discuss these in order.

A. WELFARE

What is required here by subjective theory is an experience common to all individuals and one which can be regarded as the basis of the unity of life. For the theory, what is required must be experience, for it rests upon subjective assumptions. And it must be common, since it must explain the fact that life is uniform, that individuals are obviously constituent elements in the species of political-social order.

How, then, does welfare or happiness serve as this principle? And why have so many competent moralists held to the principle of happiness? The explanation is simple. The principle, in assuming a basis in the elemental stuff of feeling primary to all experience, satisfies the requirement of universality. The principle also assumes that, since feeling is the beginning, it is also the end of all experience, the goal toward which all experience strives.

But what is common to all experience cannot be the principle of distinction among experiences. And, of course, there can legitimately be brought up against feeling the charge of instability and subjectivity —a charge which strikes hard at a claim of universality.

It is not mere uniform presence that is meant by universality. What is meant is that the separate experiences of feeling, if they are to be connected universally, must be shown to bear to each other stable relations. And, to do this, some element other than feeling must be appealed to—an element through which feelings are given continuity in experience.

This element the more philosophical moralists have always identified as reason. It is supplied by the advocates of feeling in their more or less unconscious assumption that natural or cultural objects may be substituted for individual instances of feeling. For each feeling, tending ordinarily to be conceived in terms primarily of organic feeling, there may be assumed to be a corresponding object, ordinarily thought of as some economic or practical good. So the hedonist becomes a utilitarian by assuming that for each feeling or recognizable unity of feelings, a concrete object may be substituted. But this is openly acknowledging that, to get the universality necessary as a basis of valuation, we must convert experiences into objects. And this abandons the theory of welfare.

So the welfare or happiness doctrine gets its plausibility from its trick of noiselessly gliding back and forth between feeling and an object supposed to be the equivalent of feeling. And with this easy reference to objects, the utilitarian takes advantage of the tremendous pragmatic proof: the theory succeeds. As a consequence, utilitarianism has done more practical good in the world than ten theories that could render a reason. And in emphasizing the significance of natural and cultural objects in the explanation of action, the theory has come very near to a satisfactory ethical theory. What must be corrected is the rather naïve assumption that for an object to be ethically real it must abstractly correspond to some designatable feeling, the assumption that an object gets its value from its particular relation of correspondence to a feeling.

The peculiar relation to objects is not, as welfare theorists tend to assume, an external correspondence. It is the essential *moral* relation and is explained through the analysis of the act. From the analysis the object and the feeling emerge as form and content of the real. It is the superficial relation of correspondence or "association," as we shall see, that is in error. Objects have values in themselves; they are values, that is, or principles of worth. And it would be nearer the truth, though not quite true, to say that the feeling gets its significance from the object. Both have their value from the relation which they constitute by their mutual reference.

Now this utilitarianism and hedonism, the prominent "welfare" theories, are instances of the subjective interpretation of virtue and are built on the assumption of common feeling. Their "equalitarianism" is a veiled interpretation and a stretched application of the older religious doctrine of sympathy, and their democracy is an attempt to give objective meaning to the traditional religious "fellowship," which is always of "kindred minds" and not of objects.

What has given the welfare theory its very great hold upon modern thought is the profound truth to which it gives eloquent utterance: The ultimate *good* is to be created out of natural and cultural *goods*. Its error lies in the childish assumption that these goods have a one-to-one correspondence to distinguishable feelings in individuals.

B. COMMON CONVICTION (PUBLIC OPINION)

We have seen how the theory of the common welfare was driven to abandon its doctrine that the good is feeling and how it then adopted the semirationalistic doctrine that the good is economic or other goods (property) supposedly corresponding to organic desires. We now have to examine a further change and development of the viewpoint in the direction of a pure rationalism. In this case the good is still subjective, hence the doctrine is incomplete, and its account of virtuous action partial and inadequate.

But in this new point of view, as its advocates believe, virtuous action is not dependent upon or peculiarly related to any feeling. Feeling is rather uniformly ignored, even to the extent of omitting or refusing to allow it any claim at all. What takes its place, however, is still a variation of the attitude of sympathy and thus a characteristic form of feeling.

It asserts that the good is a common conviction in the minds of individuals—a familiar and simple doctrine, since it forms the basis of the ethical and political thought of recent times. It states that the good becomes ultimate in the common convictions of men, that when men *agree* and form *covenants* and *contracts* with each other, the good is already accomplished. Or, when faced with the charge of subjectivism, the doctrine is extended so as to explain that it is only through the common convictions of men that the good—here conceived either in terms of abstract freedom of speech, person, or activity, etc., or the right to unlimited possession of property—is created and maintained. The doctrine, while denying that the good is feeling, still asserts that it is a state of mind.

And when facing this charge of subjectivity, it seeks objective validity either in the abstract universality of the state of mind—freedom, right, etc.—that is assumed to be identified with the good; or in a social order abstractly and theoretically objectified in property rights, insisting that the right of property will guarantee the community of good through practical property relations.

The good, then, for democracy or the theory that men's activities can be objectified through a feeling of conviction common to all men is either an abstract state of mind or an equally abstract socioeconomic or political scheme of property relations regarded as the object and objective of that state of mind. The state of mind may and will vary from context to context, but at bottom its meaning is derived from the assumed fact that there is a state of mind in which all men share, a state of mind that finds its content indifferently in the mentality of different individuals. As this doctrine is more distinctly political than ethical, or is assumed so by the theorists, we may state its ethical bearings briefly, insisting, however, that as long as experience content is to be made or recognized as the criterion of men's actions, there can be no essential difference between ethics and politics. In fact, on any ground it involves fallacy to separate them. This, however, is not the problem here.

The one point that commits democracy to the theory that the good is a state of mind is its insistence that this state of mind is a form of the reason. The common conviction in the minds of men is a fact of their reason or intelligence, arrived at by the logical technique with which the reason invariably works. This conviction may be and generally is attended by and supported, even made effective, by characteristic types of feelings; but the feelings are merely "added unto" the conviction, as it were, and not necessary to it. Its essence lies in its being derived from and through the logical operations of intelligence; hence men are enjoined to think, since thinking is of the very stuff of the good. The theory is thus confused, the term "conviction" being ambiguous in both its psychological and its objective implications. It may thus imply either a strong determination of the will (as the effectiveness of its feeling concomitants) or the mere consequence of trains of logical thinking which carry no references to action. And moral and political theory both make effective and frequent use of this ambiguity.

Briefly, then, what we have to lay down is that this state of mind is not relieved of subjectivity merely because it is arrived at by thought. The fact that objective truth is obtained only by thought does not imply that all that is attained by thought must be objective truth. A conviction may be false; and, as we have already seen, its validity is not affected one way or another by the fact that it involves feelings. The practical contradiction of the theory of a common conviction is an interesting fact: While all men have a uniform conviction against war, for example, war nevertheless occurs with unremittent fury. And under the conviction of equality, shared by all men, the greatest inequalities have been realized. All believe in freedom—it is a common conviction—but a significant freedom was never perhaps so rare in the world as now. All believe in human rights, but rights are more generally and ruthlessly disregarded than ever before. The fact is, simply, that the doctrine that the good is a rational state of mind, the theory of democracy, has become a practical contradiction in every one of its special meanings; it is not true when interpreted as freedom, or as rights, or as respect for law, nor is it true in any sense.

Now the doctrine attempts to save itself, as we saw, by explaining that it is not abstract rational right, freedom, etc., that it means, but right, freedom, etc., as objectified in the actual relations of men. And the symbols of this realization are the existence of property, order, society. This we can accept, as we accepted the corresponding point in the theory of feeling; but we must also make the same reservation here. The good is nature, property, order, society, but not because they are correlatives in some way with states of mind. They are good, elements of *the* good, by virtue of their being what they are; and action tending to create and maintain them is virtuous action. But this is altogether to abandon the principle that the good is a state of mind.

The most plausible form of this theory is that which finds the rational function of man identical with the structure and constitution of nature, as in the Stoic ethics and the doctrine of "natural right" in modern politics. But these must be corrected to show that the identity of "mind with nature," though real in every concrete case of action, is not demonstrated so by a mere correspondence of objects with states of mind.

The good, therefore, does involve a rational state of mind. This is the true insight of democracy and its principles of freedom, right, etc. But it is the object, natural or cultural, and in the concrete, that objectifies the state of mind and also dictates the form of the logical process by which the state of mind is proved rational. The state of mind is not objectified by its "commonness" or by its appearing in the minds of all men.

C. Mutual Respect

The good is often described as the state of mind in which men respect each other, not as one individual to another, but through the common respect of all for the whole. This point of view is illustrated in one phase of the utilitarian philosophy, in which the "good of all" is apotheosized as the basis of the law governing the relations among men. It is also observed again in most rationalisms, which tend to set up some form of the whole as the ground of authority which regulates the actions of individuals. Right, duty, obligation, are thus determined by reference to this abstract symbol of the whole, and the varying ways in which the whole is conceived determine the different types of this theory. The strong point of this view lies in the fact that it includes most of the obvious truth of the other views and can also present the most consistent metaphysics that it is possible perhaps to lay down as a basis of ethical distinctions. If it is true, as we have all along assumed, that behind all our actions and judgments about actions there lies the objective system of nature and culture as the ground and the basis of their truth, then this system, in so far as the doctrine of the whole refers to it, makes of this whole-concept the most complete and consistent theory that it is possible to devise.

But there are difficulties nevertheless. There seem to be two ways in which the concept of the whole may fail. In the one case the whole is thought of as a "whole of experience" and the total structure is thus open to the charge of subjectivism. In the other, the whole is safely guarded against subjectivism by carefully depriving it of all experience qualities, the result being so "objective" as to be completely abstract and without the semblance of recognizable content.

What is the moral significance of sympathy? The assumption behind the doctrine is sound. It is to the effect that there is no morality where the agent is not affected in character by his relations to the facts in the midst of which he lives and by the way in which he responds to those facts. The moral quality begins with the nature of the agent, and except for the presence within the agent of certain characters his reactions would not differ from those of any other object. And there is a sense in which it is true that all the activities in which the agent engages exist for the purpose of maintaining his character. What we mean when we regard sympathy as the basis of all virtue is that there is the primordial quality of sensitivity in the moral being and that all variations of the moral life have their ground in it. And it is true that all moral activity has for its purpose the maintenance of beings whose sensitivity makes them ever ready to respond to the circumstances which surround their lives. It is the presence of this character that ultimately marks the distinction between movement and action, and which draws the line between a dead mechanical world and a world of cultural possibilities. With sympathy morality is possible to man; but the development of other capacities is necessary if morality is to be fully realized.

The following three chapters describe three other virtues that represent various aspects of the sensitivity that is the ground of all forms of subjective virtue.

Chapter XII

Generosity—Virtue as Other Reference

WE HAVE seen that subjectivity in the form of sheer self-reference cannot be regarded as a complete virtue, that is, there is
no form of action intended by it that can be shown to be consistent
with the simplest idea of an act. We noted, however, that the presence
of sympathy indicates something good in the character or moral constitution of the person. This we called the "quality of sensitiveness,"
meaning by that the delicacy of organization and nicety of balance
of the personality which makes it quick to respond to situations presented to it. The supreme test of the depth and quality of the culture
a person represents is the promptness and proportion with which he
responds to certain types of circumstances; at the bottom of the personal character is a quiveringly delicate aesthetic form, an equilibrium
in constant imminence of reorganization.

This sensitiveness is the highest degree of moral perfection the person can attain as an isolated being, that is, it is the most important
capacity of the person that can be explained by backward reference
to the person. It seems to be the product of two conditions. There is
evident in it a history of delicate nervous organization running perhaps through a select heredity of some duration, such as has been
attained in certain types of cultural nobility, or in a long line of pure
country breeding. Contact with the soil, or the clean heredity which
such contact affords, is the most refining of influences. There is also
evident in any fine instance of sensitivity the clear indication of a
continuing stable and peaceful outer world as the environing circumstance in which the sensitive person grows up. Balance of character
cannot be maintained in conditions of chaos and confusion, and periods of war or economic aggressiveness will miss sensitivity in both
directions. On the one side it will be missed in the direction of excessive crudity and brutality in a military age and on the other by
defective coarseness and stodgy flabbiness in an economic age. Between these two extremes of elemental evil all the grades and qualities of moral sensitivity are to be attained. And the degree of moral

204

evolution attained by a person or a people is correctly measured by the readiness with which the quick is touched.

Sensitiveness is the common moral quality therefore in all the subjective virtues: sympathy, generosity, friendship, integrity, with all their many variations and subvirtues. We now take up for analysis the virtue of generosity.

Generosity seems a natural complement to sympathy. Just as sympathy in all its forms contemplates the interest or place of the self in virtue or the part in virtue played by the agent, so in generosity we have the opposite character, that in which the reference of the agent's feeling is away from the agent and toward the person or object upon which action is supposed to issue. We must keep in mind that all the subjective virtues are defined in terms of their reference to the character of the agent. Generosity is then the other-referent aspect of the subjective factor in action, the factor in which the act is designed with respect to the inner states of the actor, but with reference to some effect intended for another agent considered as recipient of the consequences of the action. Thus a major defect of generosity, as of all the subjective virtues, is that the act contemplated is designed to issue in an agent regarded as an object or end, whereas an agent is never properly the object or end of an act.

This fact emphasizes another common characteristic of all the subjective virtues. Their ultimate objective is always to modify the inner feeling of a person or persons, even where their proximate object may not involve a person. They are all personal virtues—all, that is, get their meaning from some reference which they make to the unique subjectivity of the individual. In generosity, therefore, we are dealing with the same fact that we were concerned with in sympathy, only we are looking at the fact from a different angle, the view, namely, of the person toward whom the feeling is directed by the impact of the act. But it would be wrong to say that the act is directed upon the other person by the feeling; the feeling merely passively designates the person as a proper recipient of the act. But this implies a clear misunderstanding of the nature of the object or end of an act.

We now proceed to note the various forms of generosity.

I. ALTRUISM

Altruism is that form of generosity or other-reference in which sympathetic feeling is directed by action toward another person considered in isolation. That is, altruism concerns the other, not as part within a relational whole, but as a person alone and by himself. The action it contemplates then is intended to do something to the other person, to change some condition in his inner constitution as an isolated individual. Characteristically it aims at effecting his inner states of mind, so that the agent's sympathy will somehow counteract or modify a present condition within the inner life of his "other" and change it into what to the other is a more satisfying condition. The inner state of the agent and that of the person toward whom the action is directed are thus supposed to be brought to a common equilibrium, so that they share the same feelings and merge their inner experiences into a mutual whole. Since the situation is pictured as altogether mental, as a condition brought about within their mental states alone, the tendency is toward mysticism and an intuitive form of explanation when description of the situation is attempted, and any reference to overt action tends to be ignored. In the case where this mystical interpretation is appealed to, there is no ethical question involved, since there is no action which can be conceived as the medium through which the fusion of mental life is achieved. Sympathy is assumed to make its way into the life of the other not through action but by some undesignated direct means, and these means are not proper subjects of discussion, since to question the meaning of the direct relation is a call for the facts, and a reference to crude facts is supposed to represent a misunderstanding of the nature of sympathy. Sympathy itself as the fact, therefore, with all the convenient qualities we may want to endow it with, and lacking all inconvenient qualities, is to be accepted without explanation. But this attitude has no ethical meaning, since no definiteness of relation can be established between the sympathetic states of mind and an act by which these states might be objectified. The meaninglessness of this "spiritual" interpretation of sympathy is generally recognized in ethics, where sympathy is taken not to represent mere states of mind but in some way to involve overt action.

The ethical meaning of altruism is thus through criticism seen to be a question of a form of action and not a matter of a supposedly independent state of mind, for the latter is recognized as by itself unintelligible. This form is that in which the action of the agent is supposed to issue in or upon the other person as an isolated object, an object whose relations to other objects may be ignored. Further, the act must be overt and expressed in external fact and not a mere attitudinizing of the agent's mind with respect to the object.

In short, altruistic action as regarded in ethics is supposed to do something *to* somebody. It cannot be a mere feeling or other mental modification with reference to somebody, since this is not an act in the sense in which ethics conceives of action. Now, as every act is supposed to have some bearing on the good, the altruistic act is that act in which the feeling of the agent *does good to the individual* upon whom the energies of the act fall. And as from this point of view of ethical altruism my moral world is made up of a vast collectivity of individuals, my moral life will consist of an infinite series of single acts, each directed upon some one of these individuals, where the assumption is again that the end of an act may be a person or agent. Naturally, most of my acts will have to do with the limited group of persons with whom my relations are more direct and intimate, and this fact defines my major duties as those which concern my neighbors. And this limited circle of my neighborhood becomes, equally for the ethical, the political, the legal, and the religious development of these simple ideas, the central concept in the practical thought of modern times. Democracy, Protestantism, individualism, in all its forms, are merely developments (extreme and extravagant, as many would say) of the simple concept of the agent in an active relation to his neighbor. These viewpoints all rest on the assumption that doing good to one person automatically does good to everybody, at least to everybody within the neighborhood of our interest, and that the total of good is merely the sum of all these goods. But the discovery of the extended significance of an act, and the suggestion that the end of an act is never properly a person or agent, involve other aspects of altruism, such as liberality, benevolence, etc., which we describe below.

Now the subjectivity and consequent weakness of altruism appear here, that is, at its very heart. Its fallacy is the assumption that doing good is necessarily doing good *to somebody*. It assumes that the object and the objective of the act are always another person and that the meaning of the act lies in the simple fact that it is "done to" the other person. The morality of the act lies, it is supposed, in the special or particular character of the act and can be judged without involving in the judgment any references to objects other than that in which the act issues and that from which it originates. This is of course easily proved false by a mere reference to the logical nature of the judgment; and its fallacy is not in that its description of facts or its choice of facts is wrong but in that its attempted explanation of the facts violates the essential rules to which any judgment must conform if it is to be true. No aspect of a judgment can be understood by merely being referred to the narrow situation presupposed in an altruistic act; the act is not therefore an instance of a complete moral relation, for the reason, mainly, that as thus limited it is unintelligible. And this reflection disposes of all empiricisms, including the aborted form of empiricism which undertakes to base ethical judgments upon "specific situations."

A virtuous act is never done *to* somebody or *to* anybody; it is only the energies of the physical movements involved in the act that may impinge on a particular person. This person may be perhaps the "object" of the act in the physical sense, but it is not the objective of the act in the sense that is necessary to ethics. Altruism is thus an imperfect virtue, right and good in its subjective intent, but lacking the objectivity which the full meaning of morality demands.

But this conclusion does not imply the acceptance of egoism. The weakness pointed out above as the moral breakdown of altruism disposes of egoism also and for identical reasons. Egoism assumes that the ground of explanation of an ethical act lies in a supposed reference to the actor. And it becomes contradictory in the attempt to make the agent both subject and object or end of the act, to identify agent and end. But all such backward reference, as we saw in discussing sympathy, is fallacious, and this includes the reference to the "ego." It is not, of course, implied that the actor and the person with respect to whom action is performed are of no consequence to ethics. The contrary is emphatically true. There is, that is to say, an element of profound truth in what both altruism and egoism really mean. But this truth is not stated in the formula that action, to be virtuous, must be done in the interest of, or with special reference to, the inner feeling or experience of some individual; or when stated in the formula that action is all intended to the good of the actor. A good act is not done *to* anybody, although a person will always be involved in the object. What is true is that the agent and the object or the objective of an act determine a relation which is the basis of all judgments which express the qualitative significance of either. In simpler language this involves that no completely adequate judgment of an act is possible which does not include within its ground the idea or concept of both agent and objective end. The falsity of both egoism and altruism lies in their insistence that this ground includes nothing else but these two ideas, and the two theories differ only in the distribution of emphasis between them. They are alike in the assumptions upon which they rest and in the common falsity of these assumptions. They have the possibilities of truth in them in that they imperfectly grasp the essential points of meaning in an act.

Generosity is a partial and subjective virtue in that it fails to interpret as broadly as it should the objective of an act upon which it insists. It tends to see the objective merely in terms of certain subjective states of the agent, and no act can be complete in these terms. The "other," also, when regarded as merely another person, is too narrow. There are many acts that are obviously virtuous with which another person, in the sense of altruism, is only remotely concerned. The awareness of this defect has led to the attempt to generalize the "other" and thus to broaden the scope of the application of the concept.

II. LIBERALITY

Liberality is a doctrine which attempts to generalize the interest in the "other." It attempts to cure the exclusiveness of the "other" theory by showing that *the* "other" should be *any* "other." Liberality is thus primarily a political attitude. But at this stage of the ethical problem, viz., the problem as to what constitutes the moral ground of an act, there is little point in emphasizing the difference between ethics and politics. The problem of the nature of the relations among persons is the common quest of all the phases of practical philosophy. But, as an ethical theory, liberality refers to the objective of action as only vaguely and indefinitely determined. It still holds that the essence of an act is a question of the persons who are influenced by the act but still puts the major emphasis upon the attitude of the actor. But it emphasizes merely the indefinite plurality of persons, without raising any questions as to whether the act has any tendency to impose an organization of them into higher personal bodies. The liberal act refers to persons, but only in a vague and indefinite way, and the subjective element appears in it when it is observed that these indefinite unspecified persons have meaning only as the hypothetical terminus of a certain feeling which the agent is experiencing. The liberality of my act is, after all, my liberality, and the act when performed may leave those to whom it was directed just where they were before. The act in its essence is not modified by increasing the number of objects to which it refers; it still refers to a feeling in the actor whether the other persons involved are one or many.

Liberality has a number of forms which we proceed to examine.

A. LIBERALITY IN EMOTIONAL ATTITUDES

As an attitude of emotion the reference to the plurality of persons is closely akin to sympathy in its more indefinite meaning. What liberality means in this sense is the indefinite well-wishing which every cultivated human being experiences for everybody else and which everybody perhaps fails or omits to connect with his active life at all. There is no impulse to action inherent in this attitude, and it appears rather to have the reverse effect upon the one who feels it. I am likely to regard my duty as done, or at least as not pressing, when I am engaged in wishing everybody well; in fact, in so far as I think at all, I shall probably take my well-wishing itself for the act. I am experiencing a quiescent state and merely glow with warmth in my liberal moods, and this fact is perhaps what explains the utter incompetence, except for voluminousness of expression of conviction, of political liberalism. I can easily accept my feeling for other people as the equivalent of doing them a good turn. Liberalism easily degenerates into a mere "point of view" and is of little ethical consequence. But it is good in so far as it indicates a sensitiveness to the meaning of human problems.

B. Cosmopolitanism or Humanitarianism

But liberality is capable of becoming much more than a mere state of mind or empty attitude. It has become, in more than one ethical system, the very significant conviction that one's moral obligation extends as far as humanity. It is thus the means of completely universalizing the concept of human good and of making the abstract good of mankind a possible object with respect to which action might be determined. But it is clear that by the time one's ideas are extended and expanded in meaning to the point where they embrace such universality, the mere attitudes of well-wishing are far surpassed. Also, their objects have become so abstract as to negate any act which might be supposed to involve them. And the primary value of such a broadened liberality of outlook lies for the most part in just familiarizing ourselves with larger ideas and in helping us to escape the provincialism of mere feeling. The generosity that develops through liberalism to an intelligent cosmopolitanism is perhaps as lofty an ethical attitude as men are capable of; but it is a mere attitude still, and we must keep in mind that as such it faces serious practical difficulties. One of these is that the mere finality of the idea is likely to deceive us; the whole good must be a good for each as an individual, and there is grave danger of losing the individual in such a far-flung conception. The good must be experienced if it is to be the whole good, and there is difficulty in making the welfare of humanity significant to me. The comprehension of the interests of mankind as a whole may be with me a mere feat of the intellect, to which I may not respond with any warmth or enthusiasm. Hence, it is difficult to connect such an abstract notion as the whole of humanity with my active attitudes, and still harder to connect it with my action techniques. Just how should I respond to the call of humanity? The idea is hardly concrete enough to suggest any specific form of act; I know, for example, what I should do if there were poverty in my community, but what should or could I do to relieve or eliminate poverty in general. Liberality thus seems a virtue for philosophers and prophets but out of the reach of ordinary people.

But in so far as liberality in this larger sense of humanitarianism shows the necessity of making over our mere attitudes into clear ideas, it represents one of the more important personal virtues. It at least states the problem of how we are to put substance into our moral feelings and indicates clearly the necessity of a more comprehensive virtue than is represented by our personal viewpoints.

C. LIBERALITY AND THE MEANS TO THE GOOD LIFE

We have seen that liberality as a mere state of feeling takes on a moral significance when it clarifies itself as an idea, and this it does through assuming certain types of relations with objects. We saw that, when humanity was made the object of our liberal feeling, the latter was ennobled; but in being thus transformed it became an idea. It is clear then that it is the object with which an idea connects that determines its nature rather than the type of subjective motive it arises out of. This is peculiarly true when the motive of liberality comes to embody itself as an idea in those objects upon which we depend as means to the good. These are of various sorts, the most elementary one being property. This is for the most part a natural object transformed into a special instrument for the working-out of purposes, but there are property objects that are not mere transformed natural things; some are cultural objects adapted to use in attaining ends. But objects as means are not all property; cultural objects generally that have become incorporated in the tissue of social life as permanently available means to the good are practically identical with the good and are not property in any accepted sense.

The point is that these objects, property objects and established cultural forms, represent the meaning of liberality when it expresses the universal and genuinely human meaning of objects that are designed as means. Property, under the influence of liberality, becomes the system of material tools to which all moral agents are guaranteed access for use. It means that as a moral function there should always be available to the agent the instruments he may need to reach his ends. Of course it is implied that intelligence will limit his access to just use and will determine when there is a real use and not an abuse of the tools. The human or liberal motive establishes public libraries so that there may be always available to every agent certain objects as means; but it also specifies, not always intelligently, the conditions of their use and the ends toward which they may be used.

It is from the same motive of liberality that there are established many other objects as means. The legal and political bodies of rights are such objects. Opportunities to educational training are such objects. The various "liberties" assured to us in political organization, privileges provided by religious and social institutions, all these come into existence and are maintained by the universal human interest in the whole of humanity. They represent in many ways the highest accomplishment of morality.

But we must observe once more that none of these important results are products of the individual and certainly not of his subjective feeling. Except in so far as the individual's "interests" in "others" are purged of their narrow individualistic reference to specific persons, and perhaps also away from any reference to persons but rather to objects, they remain empty and without consequence. Any genuinely moral interest must look beyond and over the heads of individuals if it is to become a genuine virtue. This means that, even in the interest of individuals, the individual's interests must be overstepped. We must look beyond the individual if we are to find the meaning of the individual. Liberality leads us to these issues only when it ignores mental states for the objects through which those mental states or purposes may be realized.

D. LIBERALITY AND THE ENJOYMENT OF THE GOOD LIFE

Another instance where liberality is important is in the notion of the most widely extended enjoyment of the good life. What another person merely feels may be an object to me, even if not to him, and the object may be universalized by me so as to represent a permanent state of satisfying feeling for all men. But, when the feeling is made an object, it becomes an idea. It must be noted that we are not here arguing that this idea of a universal state of feeling is necessarily good; what we do mean is that it may be good for me to hold it as an object. And in contemplating the experience of all men everywhere as satisfactory, in spite of its obvious practical impossibility of realization and in spite of the fact that I now know that it is impossible, I have chosen as an end for myself one aspect of the total good, and my act has the universal character of the good. Such an end is not the less significant because it is unattainable. Its significance lies in that it maintains in me a persistent conviction that men's experiences are important; it sustains my sensitivity and keeps me ready to respond as occasion arises. But I am sensitive to, and respond to, objects only and not to my own or anybody's feelings.

But for this reason also this expression of liberality is only partially and potentially good and does not rise to the status of a complete virtue. There is no guaranty, in the absence of other and more objective influences, that my interest in the happiness of mankind will lead me to important acts or to any acts at all. And the tendency for such a virtue to regard itself as complete when the state of mind is maintained, as instanced in periods of inactivity of religion, shows the contradictoriness of the attitude.

The other-reference of generosity comes near to fulfilment as a virtue in the case of liberality. But it has within it the weakness of subjectivity, and most of its moral energies are lost in combating the ever present tendency to confuse the real objects of action with the subjective motives out of which the action arises.

III. BENEVOLENCE

Benevolence is extrovert sympathy. It is supposed to be an obligation to establish in human nature, as a fixed trait of character, a permanent tendency to take the viewpoint of the "other." It is an instance of other-reference and so a species of generosity. One may be liberal with respect to money, property, etc.; and we noted the extension of the attitude to political relations and institutions, where there is a significant but incomplete realization in the object. But benevolence seems restricted to relations among human agents, and its point of reference is always humanity. It seems to contemplate humanity as a whole as if it were merely an enormous mass of inner experience, and it is toward this mass that its well-wishing is directed. It is thus a purely subjective attitude, both in its initial motive and in what it contemplates as object. In spite of its attempt to objectify itself and thus to take on full morality, the term still refers characteristically backward to the character of the person who feels it; and it is a virtue, as is supposed, because it represents a fixed state of mind in the person who gives it expression. Its goodness is a reference to the type of character it issues from, and it would remain what it is if the world of other persons and things existed merely in the benevolent person's imagination.

The subjectivity of benevolence is the explanation of the futility of its attempts really to do something worthy. It explains why there are so many futile and senseless foundations, and the absurdity which large contributions usually succeed in setting up in "benevolences." The really objectionable feature about it is the assumption that because somebody has given liberally, or established some spectacular nuisance, these results must be good. The "benevolence" of the donor explains and excuses, and finally blesses and sanctifies, whatever monstrosity it may be his whim to endow. For this reason it is really dangerous, since it tends to institutionalize and solidify the whims and caprices of rich and well-meaning but ignorant persons within the structure of culture, where it is very hard to get rid of them. An iron dragon fountain may disgrace the public square for generations merely because the donor's benevolence has become hallowed. Again it tends to put the control of public functions in the hands of the least desirable type of persons; their competence to amass wealth, and the complacency that goes with it, are no assurance that their power will not be abused or expressed ignorantly and dangerously. There is no consistent or rational meaning that can be given to benevolence when we undertake to treat it as a virtue; it contradicts itself at every point.

The importance of benevolence and the other forms of generosity will appear when we come to study the objective virtues. Here we shall see that, in so far as endowments, foundations, etc., can be institutionalized in public forms, their moral significance is great.

IV. CHARITY

Charity as generally practiced is commercialized benevolence. It is little to the point that we make it mean "love," since that is nothing but a confession of complete subjectivity, and, so far as morality goes, it makes little difference what affective quality our mere states of mind possess. The mere existence of love or any other interesting state of mind will not guarantee it rational expression, and morality is a matter of expression or realization of objective ends through overt action. In the purely subjective form its only meaning is in the sensitiveness of perception which it indicates; but this sensitiveness has of itself no effect on the direction its own expression will tend to take. Men kill each other for love, and love may be and often is the force behind the most immoral of acts. There is no moral value to love as such, and the moral quality which may come to be attached to it has an origin elsewhere. It is pure subjectivity.

There is no need to discuss charity in the sense of almsgiving, either as organized or as unorganized, nor as public or private. It stands proved to have no positive moral significance whatever and is on the contrary the ground of many of the worst of evils. At most it can signify an unfortunate and evil condition, but it contributes nothing to the solution of evils or the removal of bad conditions.

V. PHILANTHROPY

Philanthropy is charity on the grand scale and is, as we saw, the form that benevolence tends to take when its subjectivity is pointed out. Its worst feature is that it transfers to the hands of individuals what is essentially the special function of men in moral bodies, that is to say, what ought to be institutionalized as the expression of the moral will and sentiment of men in their corporate political capacity. The idea that we shall have libraries only when it may please some individual to build them is fortunately passing, and nearly every community in the civilized world now has such facilities furnished through the co-operative effort of the whole body of people. Philanthropy has no moral significance; at best it testifies to the sentiment and sensitivity of the one person who does it.

The argument for charity and benevolence which states that we shall have to put up with them until some better method is known unwittingly gives itself away, for already better methods are known and are in actual operation under nearly all possible types of conditions. Also, the newer methods work. There are many large communities in the world where charity is next to unknown and where philanthropy is impossible, and it happens also that in such communities culture is at a high level.

We see that generosity, or the attitude of interest in other persons, is an imperfect moral principle, and the imperfection is equally great in both the aspects of its meaning. As a mere attitude of mind it has no clear design as to what sorts of action should follow from it, and as a consequence the acts that do follow are uncertain in purpose and indefinite in effect. Likewise the attempt to adopt generosity as a principle of cultural progress leads to contradictions. The theory of generosity rests on the assumption that our states of mind are inherently good and that their presence is the only justification that can be required of them. This overlooks the fact that states of mind are, as such, indifferent as to moral quality and have moral characteristics only through relations that connect them with acts and through acts with objective ends. Generosity is a subjective, partial and incomplete, virtue; it is only that part of virtue which exists in the inclination of mind or intention toward other people in trying circumstances. It does not become a complete virtue when it adopts a plan of action, since, so far as it is our generous impulse that adopts the action, there is no warrant that the act will be approved by moral principles of wider scope. As we sometimes say, generosity becomes profligacy unless controlled by intelligence. But this is to acknowledge that it is not generosity but intelligence that is at the basis of an act and determines its character when it is right.

The real motive behind the attempt to make a virtue of generosity probably is, when stated negatively, the consciousness that there is something wrong with action that is governed by reference to the self or actor. Also, and positively, there is the instinct that action should be free of any special connection with persons at all or with any special type of objects. In short, action should not be "selfish"; it should be free of all interest. In this sense, and in so far as generosity approaches such a meaning, it comes very near to the very heart of moral virtue in the idea that an act can be judged rightly only by its "form," that is, it can be judged truly only when its character is seen not to depend upon the specific quality of either that out of which it issues or that upon which it issues. The act of rescuing a drowning man is right in itself and does not depend in any sense upon the nature of the actor or of his states of mind or the nature or character of the man who is rescued. It is right for any man to rescue any other man under any circumstances, so far as the act itself is concerned; and questions as to the rightness of rescue can arise only when matters other than the persons concerned are introduced. The presence of conditions which, as far as can be known in advance, will make the attempted rescue fail condemns the rescue attempt as folly, however "noble" may be the will or "intention" of the agent. Rescue, that is, is always right, so far as anybody's states of mind are concerned, and what is wrong where rescue is involved is something in the circumstances that makes it impracticable.

But this means that the act of rescue is a virtue when it is *disinterested*, not determined with reference either to the person who acts or to the person acted upon. In so far as generosity implies acts in this objective form, acts, that is, which have a form of their own not dependent upon the individuals concerned, then generosity is a full-fledged virtue. But it is then called something else and described properly as a form of objective virtue, since its subjective reference is lost. An act can be right only when it can be performed, with adaptation, by anybody and with respect to anybody. This of course does not mean that acts are independent of persons; it means that, along with persons, other than personal circumstances are concerned in the determination of the virtue of an act. Generosity means that the one thing that must not be concerned in the determination of the virtue of an act is the interest either of the actor or of the person acted upon. The virtue of an act lies in its cosmic implications.

Chapter XIII

Friendship—Objectified Feeling

THE study of the subjective virtues has already suggested to us that the one indispensable condition of the moral life is the association of persons in the cultural body of society; that the important fact about men is their relations to the cultural system; and that the morally important quality of the person taken singly is that quality which is most conducive to the highest type of cultural relations with his fellows. We have noticed already such qualities as sympathy and generosity in their various forms and have pointed out some of the important cultural relations that these virtues make possible. We saw that sympathy means that such relations will be cultivated among human beings as will finally modify their nature in the direction of a higher sensitivity to the meaning of life.

It appeared also that, with an expanding and intelligent generosity cultivated in men as individuals, the selves and personalities of men, while losing none of their worth or value, will tend to recede into the background as conscious subjects or objects of action, and the acts by which men are related to each other will become the important factor in the cultural world. This shift of center of meaning from the inner substance and quality of persons, and from their environing circumstance, interpreted merely as the ground of opportunity for acts, to the acts themselves and the circumstances constituting the structure of acts, is what we mean, so far, by moral objectivity. It does not mean that persons or agents will mean less and circumstances more; it means that persons will mean all the more in proportion as we realize that the quality of their inner being has precisely this objective structure realized in the cultural system by their acts. Hence the ground of all the relations that are possible between persons is this common ideal and actual circumstance through which acts are realized in fact. The term by which we indicate this objective ground of interpersonal relations is the "cultural structure," and the process by which such relations are established is "friendship."

Friendship, that is, is objectified feeling—feeling expressed in com-

mon objects and made a sharable good, so far and to such extent as it
is capable of objectification. What friendship intends is to establish
feeling relations among human beings and to institutionalize the relations there as the substance of culture, to harden feelings down into
the objects by and upon which the stability and continuity of values
may be assured. It is the task of this chapter to try to see how far this
purpose may be realized.

There are a number of elements entering into friendship, which we
may now consider.

I. LIKE-MINDEDNESS

It is often assumed that persons, in order to be friends, must have
mental characters that are alike. Precisely what are the characters of
mind that the likeness is based upon is rarely explained, so this likeness means little more than that minds are such by nature that they
can enter into relations with each other. Since like-mindedness is
generally regarded as a thing that may be cultivated or developed, it
is capable of change, and upon this the adaptations of friends are
effected.

Now the most likely real character that like-mindedness can mean
is the common emotional bent of individuals, which appears to be due
to the fact that common external circumstances occasion that their
minds should respond in pretty much the same ways. And common
modes of expression give at once a firm basis for the continuity of the
life of the individual with that of his fellows, and fellowship thus
attains conclusiveness and finality. Assuming all this enables us to connect interpersonal relations with the feelings, and the readiness with
which feelings change seems to give full credence to the connection.
Men come together, then, according to the theory, because they feel
alike, because their feelings vary in uniform ways, and because their
feelings are conditioned upon the same objective situations. All these
features apparently are known immediately in the quality of the
feeling.

Moreover, it is the common enjoyment of this shared feeling that
is supposed to give to such bodies whatever stability they have. Fellowship of kindred minds is thus one of the important factors in the
structure and stability of society, is a sort of blind motive force and
the cause and basis of the formation of nuclei of persons within the
mass of humanity.

But the stability of these formations is merely apparent. As was
noted above, feeling has the capacity for change as one of its essential

characters. While it is an attractive force within a small area, it is still a divisive agency so far as the organization of life on the whole is concerned. This is obvious when we reflect that any organization which is held together by feeling tends to dissolve as soon as the feeling cools or wanes and that the method generally adopted for keeping together such bodies is exhortation and the continuous creation of the exciting stimulus that feeds the change of feeling and keeps it going.

II. COMPATIBILITY

The solid stuff of friendship is sometimes said to be instinct. The constancy of friendship is a fact which we must acknowledge, one whose significance in the cultural world would be hard to overestimate. We must find then the roots of friendship in the very substance of life itself, and this substance is said to be instinct. Men's feeling attitudes vary from moment to moment, flit from one context to another. The instincts, however, it is supposed, have none of these characters; they are permanent fixtures in the life of the race, and thus the basis of its continued existence as a race.

But there is a difficulty here. If instincts are racial characteristics, then all members of a given race will or should have approximately the same instincts, and if friendship rests upon common instinct, then all persons of the same race ought to be friends. But the fact is that friendship presupposes differences among friends. Consequently, instincts must be individual rather than racial traits if they are the basis of friendship. Then the difference between a friendship based on feeling and one based on instinct is this: feeling is capable of no uniformity; it varies not only from person to person but from moment to moment in the individual; whereas instinct varies from person to person, giving the basis for complementariness, but is constant within the individual. The individual's "constancy" is therefore a matter of the fixity and rigidity of his instincts; he may thus be depended upon, and his action may be predicted. And it is this mutual predictability or dependability of friends that indicates the basis of friendship, and this is premised on the permanency of the instincts of the individual and the variation of the instincts of one individual from those of another.

But the fact remains that friendships are valued for their emotional possibilities and not esteemed for their instinctive basis. Even the dependableness which we attribute to friendship because of instinct would be meaningless if value were not attached to it in terms of feeling or some other sort of experience content. And instinct is unconscious, of itself, at least. It is not, that is, aware of itself as a content and is hence not an experience in the sense that feeling is.

Friendship, which is a high type of value in terms of experience content, cannot be made out of a stuff that of itself has no experience content. Friendship then seems not be explained in terms of either feeling or instinct. Friendship is thus a limited virtue, an instance of a partial, incomplete, and imperfect moral relation. It is then a personal virtue, that is, it implies characteristics of persons which may become the basis of genuine acts when and if the proper objective conditions are present.

III. MUTUAL INTEREST

Such objective conditions, it is sometimes supposed, are present in the case of mutual interest. An interest implies, it is also supposed, the direction of the personal capacities toward or upon objects which are elements of the common environment, natural or cultural, of persons. But whether the interest of a person is directed upon a natural object or a cultural object, or upon no real object at all, is not always easy to say. If, for example, I am interested in a plot of ground, the object of the interest may be crudely economical, or even miserly when I wish merely to hold it for an advance in price. But, on the other hand, the object of the interest may be purely aesthetic or sentimental or religious; it may be that I want to dedicate the plot to the uses of humanity at large. Or, what is frequently true, my interest may be a mixture of all or several of these, the proportions of which I do not even myself know. But these questions, while fundamental for certain connections in ethical theory, are important for the problem of the definition of interest, which is the concern here.

An interest is that direction of personal intent upon an object which is assumed to have its sole meaning, for the person whose interest it is, in the bearing it has upon the interested person alone and exclusive of other relations. The exclusiveness of the object of interest to the interested person is the gist of the meaning of interest. Hence a "mutual" interest is contradictory. Of course two persons may be interested in the same thing; but the interests are exclusive. The difficulty of the problem of interest lies in the ambiguity of the term that is due to this contradictoriness and in the extraordinary pains that have been taken to justify it as a ground of personal relations in spite of its contradictoriness.

But we need not go into these complexities of theory. What we want to see is whether interest in any sense represents a genuine moral relation. To state our result at the beginning, we shall find that it has a genuine and real bearing on moral relations considered as strictly personal, but that it is subjective and incomplete in the same way as are other personal characters. This we can perhaps best show by means of examples of the various types of interest relation. These will be largely matters of definition. And it may be remarked that interest can be defined so as to mean many different things and has not usually been clearly defined at all.

There are four fundamentally different phases of interest. These we may designate as (1) psychological, (2) organic, (3) logical, and (4) cultural.

1. PSYCHOLOGICAL INTEREST

As a psychological fact an interest is the act of mind engaged in attending to anything. It is thus the same thing as attention. And what is to be noted especially is that it is, on this view, the mental operation of attending that is the interest and not the thing attended to. A thing is an interest then only because we are conscious of it. From the point of view of psychology anything may be the object of an interest, since mind can attend to anything or nothing. But this means that the term loses all distinctive meaning so far as kinds of objects or even kinds of experience are concerned, since it is a factor in anything that can be a process of mind and is present in every experience of whatever kind. It is therefore the factor present in all aspects of the equation and may, so far as description or definition is concerned, be canceled out and ignored. From the psychological viewpoint interest is merely another word for attention and has no descriptive meaning.

2. ORGANIC INTEREST

Organic interest is, as we define it, that attitude of mind which regards an object as having its sole significance in the relation it bears to the organism. It is more properly called "organismic." The relation to the organism may be direct or may represent any degree of indirectness. But a reference to the organism, explicit or implicit, and in some degree, is the sole meaning of an object as an interest in this case. This type of interest embraces the economic and all the ordinary practical interests, such as the interest in property, comfort, status. It also includes what are popularly called "social" interests, in which the meaning is constituted by a thinly disguised or rhetorical reference to the organism. Many of the formal relations in religious or aesthetic activity are of the same sort, as is shown in their affinity for property. It is to be noted that this reference to the organism constitutes a real distinction of one kind of interest from others, and this fact gives to the organismic interest a moral value. For organismic interests, and whatever other kinds of interests there may be, have to be ordered into the life as a whole, and this reference to the whole involves moral considerations. Organismic interests are not "low" merely because they are simpler than some others; there probably is no way by which a graded scheme of values can be justified so long as we are within the realm of interest, since interests are always specific and particularized references in which objects stand.

It is to be noted that both psychological and organic interests are subjective, since they have their whole meaning in their reference to a particular and exclusive individual.

3. LOGICAL INTEREST

The logical interest is that attitude of mind in which things have their significance in their relations to the objective world. This objective world may be, in a given case, the world of mind, but it does not mean the particular mind through which the reference is made. It means the system of such references together with the background in which the order or system of reference is conceived. Or the objective world may be the system of objects abstracted from any reference relations to mind and conceived to be self-subsistent. The logical interest is thus an objective relation. Such logical interests are fundamental not only in ethics but in the entire sphere of knowledge, since they constitute the ground and instrument of all distinctions and thus of all experience. But they have no peculiar moral quality—they imply no specific moral relations. And they of course are not interests in the sense defined or perhaps in any sense.

4. CULTURAL INTEREST

By cultural interest we refer to that attitude of mind in which things have their significance in their reference to the system of institutions. Institutions are defined as the objectification of the values of men, accomplished through action of men individually and in groups, toward ideally defined ends. Man's interest in knowledge has been transformed into objects, and these objects have been built into the school, which becomes a permanent institution. The definition states that a cultural interest is the attitude of mind in which things have their significance in their relation to the historic system of these objectified values or institutions. But in this case the interest itself is an act, since it expresses itself in an object. And this means that interest connotes spontaneity for actions, and our conception of interest has developed to the point where it means almost exactly the opposite of that with which we began. At first it meant a passive inclination of the mind toward an object; now it means a tendency toward action with reference to the object, like that involved, for example, in possession, control, etc. This is the ambiguity inherent in the idea of interest, and we must somehow overcome it. But our definition of cultural interests as the general interest in institutional life has been stated in purely abstract terms and requires illustration.

You have, say, an interest in mathematics. There is a question of mathematical theory or method which appeals to you, intrigues you. It is this specialized direction of the appeal to you that constitutes the interest. We may call this a "special interest." The fact that this problem appeals to you, that is, that it exists or is present in *your* mind, is meaningless so far as the problem is concerned. You say that the problem ought to be solved, not that *you* ought to solve it. In another connection, when you are talking about yourself, then there is a different problem, and the solution ought to be found by you. But this reference to you is no quality or attribute or relation of the problem as a mathematical problem. You now conceive the problem purely in terms of its relational status in the system of mathematical truth, and *you* do not appear in the situation in any way. There is no sense in which the relations of this problem to the system of mathematics could possibly exclusively concern you. You, so far as this problem is concerned, *are* the relation of the problem to its solution, or the reference which it demands to the system of mathematics. But, when you *as you* appear in the situation, your thought is "interested" and ceases to apply to the problem under any form of truth. So the genuine interest in the problem is a consciousness of the purely objective relation between the terms of the problem and the system of mathematical truth that is implicit in it and to which it refers; it is a relation which cannot be stated in terms of existence and "consciousness" and subjective personality. So, when an interest becomes real, it is no longer an interest; interests are necessarily subjective. As real it is a relation of a present, that is, specific, instance of a relational situation to the system of all such relations that have become historic or have objectified themselves in the system of mathematical truth, the institution of mathematics. Cultural relations are all such references to institutions; a type of relation objectifies after its kind, and the kind becomes fact and lives. But they are not interests.

Now to return to the ambiguity of interests. All the differences in
the world lie between the interests we described in (1) and (2), the
psychological and organic, and those described in (3) and (4), the
logical and cultural. The essence of the first pair is their specific reference. A state of attention (1) has no meaning except in so far as it
refers to the consciousness where it occurs. Its reference is inward
and exclusive. But no objective meaning can be given to it under these
conditions; all that can be said of it is that it exists where it is. It has
no quality, no attribute which does not refer merely to itself, and it
has only the relation backward to the point of its origin which, as a
relation, excludes the possibility of other relations. True, it may have
other relations in other contexts; but in other contexts it is not the
same, for it *is* here just this context and nothing else. And this as such
has no meaning. Any definition of meaning includes other relations;
what a thing means must be something other than itself, even if it
be only itself in some further relation or stage of development. The
same is true of (2). An object as property is purely private, has no
meaning whatever, has only the existential reference to the organism,
is a genuine "interest" only in the sense that it is a self-referent thing
which need not even have status in consciousness. True, the same
object as the condition of a cultural relation has meaning, *is* a meaning; an object, for example, a hoe, has meaning when used in the production of food, but none when not so used. But this is clear; (1)
and (2) constitute a type of relations that are unique in that they
have no objective meaning. They are existences upon which meanings
supervene.

Relations, "interests," of the types described in (3) and (4) are
characterized by the fact that they refer to objects. Their meaning
lies outside them, within that to which they refer. These objects constitute the institutions of life. But these institutions objectify the relations of experience in every way that can be stated, and this fact
becomes the ground of all judgments—of all scientific or truth judgments in the sphere of logic and knowledge and of all value judgments
in the sphere of culture. It is the system of institutions which makes
all the relations of life and experience available to all persons, makes
them mutual "interests" of all men. But as such they are universal,
are values, and are not interests in any sense.

The doctrine of mutuality of interests thus formulates the problem
of values. The doctrine or theory of values is necessary because there
are facts that are not mere interests, not mere instances of self-identical givenness or self-reference. There are facts, that is, which tran-

scend the meaning of interest and lead into a new and distinct field, a field where objects "possess" worth, or substantially are, worth. Friendship is such a fact. As a ground of relations between persons, then, the friendship that is ethically real is that grounded in the historic systems of institutions of culture, and the "persons" who may be real friends are the institutions whose order of friendship constitutes social or public reality. Thus "interests" must become impersonal, disinterested, cease to be interests if they are to be real and have ethical meaning. Mutuality of interests is a contradiction unless interests can be transcended, and friendship as a moral fact must have a firmer basis than interest.

IV. COMMON INTELLIGENCE OR PURPOSE

In the last topic we say that interest is contradictory and meaningless in the sense that it suggests meanings for which we can find no basis. What interest fails to get expressed in its blind groping for meaning is usually termed "purpose." But this term has become the object of so much abuse that it is well to avoid it. What it means is that intelligence is capable of breaking through the limitations of self-reference and thus of ignoring the distinctness of one "self" from another. It permits, that is, a universal implied in and for selves, which interest precludes. Purpose in this latter sense is the basis of community life and common action and a system of ends, and constitutes the cultural environment in which the individual lives.

When therefore we speak of friendship as depending on a common intelligent comprehension of ends, we have gone far beyond any form of interest. But we have also gone beyond any ordinary meaning of friendship, for friendship is usually thought of as having a basis in instinct or in feeling. In the interpretation in terms of intelligence, feeling is one of the conditions of friendship, one of the materials which, together with others, may be woven together into the whole which constitutes the foundation of any permanent relationships among men. But neither the mere feeling for other people, nor the whole of experience relative to other people, constitutes friendship. Experience, whether as whole or part, considered as a genuine and adequate basis for order in the relations of life, simply will not do. It must be transcended by some such concept as that of a whole of order in which natural persons and their feelings and experiences are mere details. These wholes of order are persons; but they are not individuals, if the latter term must be limited to human beings. The relations among human beings are in reality mediated by other things than feelings or other experiences; feelings are totally incompetent to establish order in the relations of men. The important moral relations in life are institutional relations, and these are personal, and can be called experiences only in the sense of experiences which have become incorporate and thus objectified in concrete forms and matters.

Let us take a few examples to see more clearly what this all means.

One of the chief relations of friendship to be perpetually created and maintained in human life is that of peace and order as the condition of welfare. It is the most important and the most universal relation in life. As a practical problem it is the task of politics. And the successful solutions of the moral problem that history records have been accomplished by political methods. The method of politics consists in building institutions into the tissue of life as the instruments through which human purposes may get expression. One of the major functions of such institutions is to embody and give form to feeling, which as it stands in its natural state is a mere abstract material or stuff, but which under appropriate conditions of action may take the forms of characteristic values. The doctrine of friendship makes the mistake of assuming that the feeling which constitutes the material of value may itself be the active agency which shapes human relations into values. But feeling has no such active capacity; it possesses command of forces, as is illustrated in impulse, but it cannot direct them to the production of any definite form. It can move, but it cannot act. You may get results from the force of feeling; but you will never get a formed object or any shape that expresses design, and the result will have no intelligible relation to the feeling which it follows. Its force is, like all forces, irrational. Feeling and its forces are the material out of which intelligence may shape ends for conscious and sentient beings; but it is not such an end.

Or, concretely, and by way of example, intelligence sets up a system of schools. Ostensibly, the school is a means of preparing the young to meet the battles of life. And this function is usually thought of as consisting in the mere training of the intelligence and the softening and adapting of the feelings. These things the school no doubt does, and it is possible that in doing them something is done in the way of adapting individuals to a common life. But the major effect of the school, so far as individual characters are concerned, is to sharpen interest and exaggerate private and individual motives. It makes people more "individual," so far as their ordinary relations are concerned. But these effects, in spite of the fact that they are directly intended,

are not so important as other effects which are not intended and are
not yet even recognized. Let us see how this is true.

In training individuals to "think straight," the school discovers that
there are uniform rules which thinking must follow if it is to be
"straight." These rules prescribe uniform modes of procedure for all
who care to think at all. They also determine where and at what point
the thinking shall "come out," that is, they determine the objects
which are at the same time the objectives to which thought shall tend.
And these objects will be common objects in their general design and
contour, at least, since all persons are endowed with the same type of
thinking capacity and under similar circumstances will be presented
with similar materials. And in so far as action is intelligent, the acts
of individuals will harmonize for the simple reason that they prefigure
the same objects, the design of which is a model or pattern which the
movements involved in the various acts will tend to follow. It is not
necessary that these processes be conscious. Much of our thought is
unconscious in the sense that we are not aware of its detail and process. But this detail and process are nevertheless determined by the design of the object which we have in mind while they are being carried
through. This means that our relations to each other are for the most
part determined by the types of objects which we intend; if we move
toward common objects, our acts will harmonize; if we have different
objects, or conceive them differently, our acts will tend to clash
where our objects do not agree. By objects is not meant here "ideals"
or ultimate objectives; these have little enough influence upon our
lives, mainly because we do not have clear ideas as to their form and
design or meaning. By objects is meant then the ordinary things and
conditions and circumstances with which our acts are immediately
concerned. It is about these and in terms of these that we think, and it
is with respect to these that we act; for this reason our "ideals" and
ultimate "goals" are of no great consequence until we can translate
their abstractness into the common objects and situations of everyday
experience.

But we have here the basic principle in accordance with which the
relations of men, and especially their active or moral relations, are
determined. What we have perceived and felt as objects and conditions and circumstances of ordinary experience are in reality the
substance of institutions, and this substance is shaped into an orderly
system by the characteristic acts which the specific design of these
objects and conditions and circumstances impose upon men. In these
objects friendship has a real basis. This is the principle of institution,

which is the ultimate premise of all moral and practical thought.

But this may sound like fatalism, as if men are caught in the vast "machine." The answer is that caught they are. They have no choice, so far as larger purposes are concerned, but to act in and through these systems, which constitute the structure of culture. But, it is not a machine, and this determinism is merely bondage to law and the universal; to realize his freedom, the agent must recognize this law, must choose his institutional tools with which to accomplish his ends. But he is free within the institutional structure, and it is only within that structure that his freedom has any meaning.

The important institutions are the practical, that is, the political (including the religious, economic, governmental, social, educational) and the theoretical, or those specialized with respect to knowledge (including the professions and their organizations). We are here, of course, a long way from friendship as conceived in terms of personal feeling. But let us follow to the end.

Political institutions are our ultimate agencies of moral friendship because their function is to maintain the general conditions under which mutual life and action are possible. The original stuff of life, as raw stuff, is made up mostly of religious and industrial activity. These stuffs tend to be irrational when left to themselves, and it is only under the guidance of the political purpose that they can be brought to form and headed in a consistent direction. The forms of activity through which politics acts to guide and direct this inert stuff of religion and industry are the social and educational activities as institutionalized in the governmental system. The political motive operating through government to direct the mere momentum which life is, is the highest type of specifically moral function. But there is one prerequisite to the good or moral life which politics cannot meet. The political motive is subject to law, and it cannot make law for itself. It enacts law, promulgates and enforces it, but does not create it. This function of making law belongs by nature to the speculative or knowledge motive.

Theoretical institutions (institutions in which the speculative knowledge function incorporates itself) determine the laws by which politics directs the movements of life in so far as those movements are to have moral quality. They represent the control by intelligence of the creative genius of human life. Of course it is not intended to say that the knowledge function controls to any appreciable extent in actual political activity, or what is usually called such. What we mean here, and what satisfies our purpose, is to point out that, in so far as politi-

cal activity is moral, as it is when it is genuine, it is guided by laws
and principles that are gained from the activities of life and formulated through and in the activity of knowledge as represented in the
professions. But the professions are themselves now corrupt, and the
consequence is that politics is feeble and society is lawless. But the
law that is right, that is, the law of rightness or justice, is worked out
in its formal character in the studies and libraries by men who make
it a business to know, and it is not their fault if it is not put into operation as it should be. It is pathetic, of course, that the professions have
fallen to the low state; the fate of life in this world depends upon
knowledge, and whether its direction is to be upward or downward
depends upon those who know and whose only function it is to know.
It is within these institutional activities that friendship becomes a
strictly moral function.

But we have apparently strayed far away from our original topic
of friendship. We have been showing how and why the concept of
friendship is morally inadequate and how and to what extent it will
have to be modified and developed before it takes the full significance of virtue. We saw that it *intends* to be a principle of human
relations and human unity; but it makes the mistake of assuming that
those relations can be consummated through and in experiences of
feeling. But the objective tendency toward institutions is there, present in friendship; only, friendship, as grounded on feeling, has not the
means by which the objective tendency can be realized. Its failure
when it comes to express itself in universal and objective forms it is
now our duty to portray.

V. COSMOPOLITANISM

Completely objectified friendship implies the world of persons in
its entirety as organized and incorporated in a moral whole. It also
implies that the world of impersonate circumstance should be ordered
and adapted to the requirements of furnishing a body for the universal moral purpose. In short, friendship in its moral implications
involves that the world be a single community of friends. There can
be no moral action or moral living in the full sense until the conditions of universal "brotherhood" are provided. And friendship has
the element of universal truth in it in its suggestion that to be a person
at all means to unite with all other persons in the task of realizing the
Great Person. And as the common experience of men it has set the
bounds within which morality must find its meaning. There is no
mystery, therefore, in the Greeks' regarding friendship as the highest

of personal virtues and the ground of the justice in which virtue is complete.

But what we want to emphasize here is that friendship, as commonly understood, is a "personal" virtue and, as such, is subjective and partial, inadequate and incomplete. Its failure to qualify as virtue is demonstrated when it undertakes to universalize itself. Let us show then the two cases where it has failed, in political internationalism and religious universalism. Also we may show the field of its greatest success, that of nonnational or world scholarship.

Internationalism in the political sphere fails because it has no adequate law. Its attempts to formulate such a law have failed because it has sought to construct an international law on the model of national legal systems. But these fail because of their subjectivity, their bondage to interest, their attempt to give rule and form to the private and internal and personal motives of men. It looks for principles in feeling, where there are none. A genuine international or, better, world law, will have to differ in principle from existing national codes. And this means, since the principle of law is dictated by its content, that world law will have to ground itself in a content different from that which forms the basis of national systems and, as a consequence, will have to create a unique system of instrumentalities through which its purposes are to be implemented. It is not our task to describe here in detail what this content is or these instruments must be; but we may indicate some conditions that both must fulfil. National systems, we say, "private" law, fails because it rests on a content of subjective experience, interests; it attempts to give form to the inherently formless. Then the law that is supported and sustained by its content, as all real law must be, must adopt a content in which there are by nature elements of form through which the design of the law can get permanent expression. This element of content is the inherent intelligibility of life, the tendency of life at every point to embody itself in an object that designs an end or a perfect form, which object is at the same time the condition of the truth of the knowledge by which it is recognized. If this language sounds Platonic to the average mind, then objective law is not a problem for the average mind. It is not the occasion to go into the details of meaning of objective law. What we see is that the "friendship of the peoples," which we think to be created and maintained by "education" and propaganda and which invariably involves mutual deception, is no basis upon which to attempt the order of the moral world. No moral world as an internationally organized system is possible on a subjective basis, and the essence of friendship is its subectivity in that it attempts to perpetuate itself on a basis of common or shared feeling. Feeling does not become a ground by being multiplied in its instances; it cannot become a ground at all because it has not the elements of legal objectivity in it. The ground of the real is this objective law.

But the universal church is in the same case, and there is no need to go into detail. While religion rests on a basis of feeling in any form, it cannot be objectified—in fact, the institutional weakness of religion lies exactly in its eternal striving to do the impossible, viz., to give a permanent form to a content of feeling. The success of the church, as well as that of political organization, has always depended upon its concessions to the "worldly." I mean its spiritual accomplishments have all been attained through abandoning its subjective purpose; by making contacts with, and content of, elements of the world as the solid body in which spiritual accomplishments can be perpetuated, its spiritual purposes have been realized.

Friendship is the highest point of perfection reached in the experience of the moral individual, considered as an isolated person. It is the chief of all the personal virtues and the capacity in which all other personal capacities, as such, are summed up. But it still rests on subjective bases, and there is no principle by which it can be universalized without modifying its intent and meaning. The life of friends is incomplete until it is grounded upon objective and "impersonal" factors within the real world. The Epicurean gardens presuppose a field tilled in sweat and anguish with the rude instruments of nature. We have seen that in none of its meanings is friendship complete, neither as like-mindedness, compatibility, mutual interests, or any or all of these as expressions of the attempt to attain universality. There is a last chance that there is a synthesis of all personal capacities that will lead us to the conception of perfect virtue, and we proceed to this question in the next chapter on integrity.

Chapter XIV

Integrity or Personal Wholeness

IN PART II we described the natural functions of the person and found it necessary to consider them as moral capacities. We were concerned with the person as a physical system and a product of nature, with such elementary cultural characteristics as develop from the relations that hold among such natural beings. In Part III we have discussed the cultural phases of the personal life, the capacities and capabilities that are possible on a basis of the life of the natural person as that life functions within the system of human institutions. Through the operation of these institutions the natural environment is transformed into a cultural environment and thus given a form of existence within which, as environing circumstance, the person has his moral being. We have now the task to bring together the two types of qualities and to show their relations to each other and to describe how all these capacities of both types are unified in the moral person. We shall see that all the capacities attain a harmony through the activity of intelligence, the highest form of act as personal; that the act of intelligence objectifies itself in the system of knowledge, which is the one and only permanent contribution to culture made by the individual as personal agent; and that the active relating of the person as intelligent to the whole body of knowledge, considered as the historic accumulation of all personal acts, constitutes the highest function for the moral life as personal. This bond of connection of the individual agent with the system of culture is obligation. We shall see in Parts IV and V that obligation itself is objectified and built into the system of culture in wisdom and that wisdom becomes a part of the structure of the world. We shall see also that obligation, as the wisdom of institutionalized life, transpersonalizes the natural-cultural person into a moral being of higher order, viz., the corporate person, and that this superperson acts morally through justice or the contemplation of the whole as ideal. This ideal of a world ordered in wisdom is the objective content of the good.

We here summarize the capacities of the person.

I. HEALTH

Naturally we do not mean by health merely the proper functioning of the organism. We do certainly mean that, but we refer more especially to the general soundness of the whole person. "Sanity" would be a better word if it had not been already used to indicate soundness of mind. The characters of the body that constitute its health have been discussed in chapter vi and need not be repeated here. It must be emphasized, however, that by health in the general sense we refer to the organism and its functions operating in a complete working harmony with all the mental functions of the individual. And we think of this organic and mental competency and harmony of the person as being in close and steady balance with the movements, objects, and processes of the world. A healthy person then means not only a vigorous and sturdy body but an active and competent mind, with the two effectively adapted and attuned to each other, and the whole articulated with the processes of nature and culture in such a way that the harmony of body and mind is maintained and the processes of nature and life are furthered.

From the point of view of the body considered by itself, moral health is a matter of maintaining a proper balance among the bodily functions. If the mind and the nervous mechanisms are to work properly, they must be supplied with the materials they need. This means that the circulation, for example, should be adequate, and that the blood stream should carry a sufficiency of the substances that the tissues need. And this in turn requires that the digestive and respiratory systems perform their functions rightly. In these processes the moral quality is concerned for the most part with deficiency and excess. Excess of food, excess of work, excess of sleep—all these throw the organic life off its balance and disturb the mental functions. In the same way too little food, not enough sleep, and less work than is necessary for exercise of body and occupation for the mind—all these have their serious consequences. But it is not all a matter of excess and defect. We should eat, sleep, work, play, think, and dream in accordance with Aristotle's rule: At the right times and in the right places and under the right circumstances and with respect to the right persons and ends, etc. An amount of food perfectly proper for me on a workday may be too much for a rest day or when I have a fever or when I have a difficult mental task to perform. The rule that we should have to adopt would be extremely complicated if we attempted to provide for all circumstances, so we abbreviate it and say that in all these things we should be reasonable, or perform activities in accordance with the principle of right reason, or as a prudent man would do them. In objective terms the rule states that an act should be appropriate or proportioned to its end. The rule therefore states nothing more than that intelligence governs the moral functioning of the organism, and in any given case of physical activity all that can be said in advance is that we should act according to reason. What reason prescribes in a given case can be known only by deliberately facing the issue when it arises. And the only preparation that is possible for the emergencies of life is to cultivate the habit of resorting to the intelligence as cases arise and applying intelligence in the ways suggested by our past experience.

A similar account is appropriate for the health of the mind. The mind is an organic synthesis of a variety of functions and capacities. The moral health of these is the problem of keeping each of them at its normal stage of proficiency and all of them working together in such a way that their total effectiveness in the general intelligence or "common sense" is the greatest possible. Unsoundness of mind is in most instances perhaps just this lack of co-operation among the various mental functions, owing to a variety of causes which are not well understood. But cases of actual "insanity" are not so important as the imperfect and partial balance of mental functions which occurs so often among "intelligent" people. The case of a man who could remember all the numbers of the cars of a long freight train as it runs rapidly past would indicate an extraordinary mental power if he could also think accurately in a delicate experiment or arrive at valid results in very complicated arguments, or act, on occasion, with ordinary good sense. Such a memory is useless if not a handicap if its possessor does not know any significant use to put it to or if he does not possess enough intelligence to distinguish the meanings of things remembered. The rule here is, negatively, any specific or particular act of mind is likely to be exaggerated if it develops unusual power. Or, positively, the healthy mind always acts as a whole. This means that the act that represents the moral integrity of the person contains in it contributions from all spheres of the personality, and an act that is fragmentary indicates a breach, momentary, at least, within the unity of mind-body which we designate a moral person.

If there is any one aspect of life more important than others for morality it is what we may call "moral probity" or integrity. By this we mean the whole unity of character exemplified in the faithfulness of the act to its object, its appropriateness to it, and its consistency with the whole character. And it is implied that the control of the mental processes, so far as they are concerned in action at least, is to be effected through the control of the objects to which mental processes refer. The quality of a mental process will depend greatly upon the nature of the object that is involved in it, and this quality, since it is the basis of the mental function, is a condition upon which the morality of the act depends. So it is generally true, not only for morality but elsewhere, that the makeup and constitution of the mind are determined by the nature and character of the objects which are its content. So it is literally true that a man *is*, mentally, what he thinks, feels, dreams, eats, makes, loves, etc., so far as all these states have their status in appropriate objects. But, if this is true, the best and perhaps only way of determining or modifying the quality or intent of the mind is by controlling the objects that make up the mind's content. If I want my mind to be strong in its mathematical and mechanical functions, I will see that mathematical objects and machines make up my environment and thus determine my mental content. If I want my mind to become delicately responsive to beauty, I will surround myself with beautiful things, and these things will make up my mind. So, if my mind is to be morally clean, I must live in a world of wholesome objects, and it is in the interest of maintaining such a world that action has its meaning. There would be no explanation of an act as distinct from a movement if it were not implied that the world of objects can be altered by action.

Thus a sound mind in a sound body expresses the moral requirement of health, if it be properly understood that the basic relation of mind and body is one of functional or analogical identity or complete active unity. The moral person is, as a natural being, a perfect synthesis of physical and mental powers, and the moral quality of the person relates to the type and degree of that synthesis.

II. STRENGTH

It should not be necessary to explain that by strength is not meant mere physical power. Physical power is nonetheless a necessary ingredient of the good life. The physically weak man cannot be a good man in the fullest sense, for there are many things that he cannot do, and morality we have seen to involve all the capacities for action that a man can have. It is, of course, true that a man without legs can be "good" in the sense that his feelings and inclinations and instincts are sensitive and quick, but he is not a good runner, hence, not a good man. So the crippled man, the sick man, the insane man, the ignorant man, the passionate man, the wilful man, the limited in capability in any way, is not a good man. There are, that is, many things involved in being a good man that the person limited in any way can never partake in or understand; the ideal, that is the right, is that every man should be all that a man as man can be. Strength refers us then to the fulness and plenitude of capacity in the moral agent. And while it includes all the powers, there is a class of capacities to which it specifically refers. Many of these powers are connoted by the term "courage" when courage is not connected with mere brainlessness or brutality, that is, when "moral" courage is meant. Such terms as "sturdiness," "ruggedness," "uprightness," "forthrightness," all indicate what we mean by moral strength. They all signify persistence against obstacles, but they all also imply that the strength displayed will be tempered and guided by intelligence. It would not be the sign of a strong man to oppose the thunderstorm or the earthquake; it would indicate rather a lack of judgment which makes his exhibition of strength ludicrous. When you are compelled to go a mile, it is sometimes good sense to go two miles; it is all a question of what kind of force it is that you are compelled to meet. Many people get along with some of their acquaintances on the principle that it is a matter of courage and good sense to say "Nice doggie." Strength manifests itself often in the effort to avoid too much vigor, and the ideal of strength has admirably been expressed as imperturbability, the power to hold the personality together under the shock of many and varied onslaughts from nature or fortune.

What is meant by strength may best be described as the causal efficacy which the moral personality attains through the perfect and orderly unity of all his mental and bodily capacities. This unity is a sort of storage battery in which all the powers are potential and are allowed to become active only at the suggestion of the whole good as the good is pictured to the intelligence. It is perhaps the most difficult of requirements to restrain action in the presence, for example, of extreme suffering, even when you know that the good of the sufferer is furthered by it. The "self-control" that is necessary in such cases is probably the best possible test of the integrity of the agent. The man who can face and dissuade a violent mob has often been thought a most perfect type of human character. But this is too near a negative interpretation of moral integrity. A better case is that of a man who has accepted a task, after employing the utmost of his intelligence in settling upon its rightness, and then "sticking it out" or "seeing it through" to the point just short of stubbornness and blind obstinacy, in the performance of the actions necessary to accomplish this task. The strong man would give up the task, regretfully, perhaps, but cheerfully, if he became convinced that its completion would cost him too much of his strength or if it should mean too much loss in any other way. And here once more we see that the element of moderation that keeps the balance of character is a matter of intelligence and knowledge, and while this intelligence manifests itself in many cases in a rather simple form of common sense, which looks almost generically different from intelligence, yet at bottom they are the same; and Simple Simon is as wise and consecrated in the acts he can understand as seven men who can render a complicated reason.

Moral strength, then, means a competent and broadly trained intelligence working through the physical and mental capacities to create and maintain a world appropriate as an object, an objective, an instrument, and an environment to the active person. The emphasis is upon the intelligence because we are here at the point of origin of causal efficacy, and the ultimate cause is, in the moral person, intelligence. It is ultimate in the sense that all other causes have their meaning in their relation to it. In the concept of moral strength, we are face to face also with the basis of order, order being unintelligible except when thought in terms of the proportionate disposition of realities which it is the function of intelligence to effect. But all this implies in intelligence the function of control, even the control of other mental functions. And in presenting the claims of other functions, as feeling, for example, which it is well to do, it is also well to remember that no mental capacity except intelligence possesses the capacity for guidance and that in the absence of intelligence any other capacity will ultimately lead to shipwreck and ruin. Strength comes from the pure heart, perhaps, but the pure heart falters without the guidance of the competent mind.

III. SENSITIVITY

We have seen that some form of sensitivity is the distinctively moral quality in all the personal or subjective virtues. It is equally basic to sympathy, generosity, and friendship and to all the various forms of each. This raises the question whether sensitivity is the active element in perception, whether it is itself a phase of that quickness of apprehension that distinguishes the competent intellect. We shall incline to think so; but here our question is as to whether and in what way sensitivity is a quality of the whole person, a feature of the integrity of the moral being, and thus one of the fundamentals upon which morality rests. The test of the person's morality is the promptness and adequacy with which he recognizes a situation as one that should appeal to his moral nature and then responds to the situation with appropriate forms of action. This does not mean to emphasize situations which have a predominantly emotional appeal. It probably takes the same mental power, and a prescience of the same kind, to appreciate the quality of color in a rose, or the consistency or truth of a complicated mathematical demonstration, that it does to respond to the appeal of a suffering child. That is, there is probably no essential difference in kind between the perfectly simple and true case of intellectual apprehension, or the true instance of keenness and nicety of perception, and the genuine case of moral sensitivity. The act of mind is probably the same in all three cases, and the ultimate thing or capacity or power I "see" with is the same as the thing or capacity or power I know with or feel with; what I "see" and what I "feel" and what I "know" are at bottom the same experience. This does not mean the intellectualizing of the emotions; it is identifying the ultimate thought with the ultimate feeling as a perfect instance of the unity of form and content in which neither is reduced to the other, but in which either in the true instance is recognized as what is at the bottom of any experience.

Sensitivity, then, is the proper name for the response of the whole or integral person to its appropriate object; if we prefer, it is, with respect to action at least, the *quid proprium* of the personality, the quality or capacity of the person that identifies with the personal substance. A man *is* then what affects him, when the affection is regarded as the basis of the fuller developments that we call "intelligence" and "feeling." As the response of the whole person, there are in the primitive sensitivity features of both the organic and the mind-life; but, while the organic and mental are distinguishable phases of any sensitive experience, they cannot be separated out as factors that can exist or operate by themselves. Sensitivity has the form of an instinct, which, while observably complex, defies complete analysis or identification of any one feature. As an instinct its operation is unconditioned, or, if we prefer scientific language for nonscientific realities, internally conditioned. But its action is immediate and depends upon nothing but the presence of some object appearing in the form of some one of its essential qualities. It is therefore not feeling, for feeling as such does not require any objective counterpart, that is, is purely subjective, or pure subjectivity. And it is not intelligence in the phase of either sense or thought, for intelligence in either phase is mediate in its operation, even when it is mediated through its own forms.

Sensitivity has thus a certain specific value. By this is meant that if we regard it as attributive in nature, and not itself a substance, it is the species or universal that it directly qualifies. Its specific function appears to be to provide the ground of continuity, not only between nature as life and culture as value, but also of continuity within both nature as a system and culture as a system. It provides, that is, for the continuity of culture *with* life, but also for the continuity *of* culture and *of* life, considered from the viewpoint of their internal structure. It is sensitivity then which makes the animal a man, and a man Man. It is thus the element of universality in life which makes life capable of culture and morality.

IV. INTELLIGENCE

Our use of intelligence up to this point has been for the most part to refer to the simple cognitive function, the one function among others that make up the mind: the function, viz., of identifying objects. At this juncture we shall use the term as the capacity of comprehension, and we mean by this, not merely its power to identify objects or its power of synthesis over objects, but also, as a variation of the latter, its power to integrate the personal capacities and to express in full the whole meaning of personality. It is the intelligence alone, or what is better called the intellect, that enables the person to see himself in terms of all his capacities, his self. It is the same intellect that enables the person to *see himself whole*, to make himself whole through and by means of the intelligence itself. Personality in this connection is nothing more than the organic unity of all the physical and the mental functions, as effected and maintained by intelligence. We shall see later that this personality is objectified and integrated in a still broader unity in the corporate person, where subjective and objective functions are unified, where mental and bodily faculties are bound together in real or objective structures.

A moral situation, then, for the moral comprehension, or intelligence, is a situation in which all the capacities of the person are fused and concentrated upon an object with respect to the good. This pulling myself together and directing myself to some end is my *act*, by which I mean to alter not only the world but also myself and to state the altered world and the altered self as a new synthesis. An act points in two directions, and a perfect act is a relation of analogical identity between two objects that are both ends. That is, the "subject," or person in terms of mental capacities, and the world manifesting itself as quality, are superseded and transformed into the objective or corporate person; this corporate person has the same moral status as any natural person, except that it possesses more powers and capacities and is hence able to attain ends that are beyond the reach of the "natural" person. These ends are moral objects, and are the proper content of politics.

The intelligent act is, then, the process of objectification of mind, the process in which mind comes to terms with the structures of nature and takes them over as the instruments in which it embodies itself. Henceforward the mind as corporate agent works *through* these objects to accomplish other ends, and retains them organized in the institutions of culture, and consciousness in the ordinary sense is left behind. Comprehension, in the normal and literal sense, is the proper act of mind; for this reason all its pronouncements are universals, all its judgments are "authoritative," which means that they have transformative power over fact. This act is the meaning of the verb "to will." This does not mean to distinguish the "rational will." All will is rational, and all reason is volition in the sense that it intends ultimately to impress its form upon the face of things. As a consequence all thought is moral, and logical error is evil; it is wrong to be wrong. This gives to intelligence or comprehension its own sort of universal significance and enables us to explain many things in ethics which are otherwise inexplicable.

Thus it appears that it may enable us to deal with the "historic problems" of freedom, God, immortality, etc., which as strictly ethical problems are plainly irrational to ordinary cognition, since no objects that are real can be formulated in cognition as expressing what these problems imply and suggest. That is, we can never say what they mean. I can never say objectively what I mean by an infinite and absolute good; its existential and its value characters are contradictory and mutually exclusive, so that I cannot conceive it as existent and at the same time objective and real. I cannot conceive of the existence of an object that is such that I must respect it, for the values that determine respect are repugnant to existence as we know it. This is the ultimate *reason* why an act is necessary; existence is compatible with elementary values only after it has been transformed by the moral urge, and the act which transforms it is an expression of this urgency. These problems cannot even be stated in terms of the ordinary cognition, for they all have behind them a ground in the assumption of mind as limited to the psychological sense, that is, consciousness, and are thus limited by the conditions of existence upon which consciousness depends. So none of these problems is intelligible to consciousness. Then so long as we are dealing with the person as the *human* individual we cannot deal with them, since the cognition of the individual is limited to what can be comprehended in consciousness.

Ultimate problems must, then, be stated, not in terms of consciousness, but through intellectual interpretation of what on moral grounds and by moral cognition we know to lie beyond consciousness in the institutional structure of culture. Moral cognition, or comprehension, *in the degree in which it functions in the human individual*, has its basis in the elementary sensitivity which is behind all our experiences. But while the moral comprehension of the individual agent enables us to state the problems of God, freedom, and immortality, that is, to conceive them under terms in which a solution is possible and intelligible, it does not by any necessity find the solution. Whether a solution is to be actual depends upon the kinds of capacities we find the corporate mind to possess. So long as we are dealing with the subjective personality and in terms of consciousness, no adequate formulation, so no solution, of such problems is possible.

Now this corporate mind, which is here postulated by the demands of morality for the solution of certain problems, has been discussed so far as its discussion can be carried on in strictly ethical terms. But the *conditions* of the problems which are set by morality also suggest the sort of approach that is necessary in order to attain to an adequate statement of the corporate mind. The conditions, we say, are headed by the discrepancy between the ultimate characters of existence and those of value. Morality, by its postulate of the act as ultimate, leaves the attainment of full corporate reality postponed, and action forever remains adventure. We therefore must go beyond the act and morality, if morality is to be limited to the human individual, for the concept of the corporate mind through which the problems of God, freedom, and immortality are made intelligible. This transcendence of morality is suggested in religion and aesthetics, and we cannot discuss it here. But its conditions are set by morality, so that religion and aesthetics are but the higher morality of institutional life.

Intelligence, comprehension, the act in which thought integrates itself, knowing in its universal form, is therefore the highest active function of the individual. But an active function or capacity is what is meant by virtue. Intelligence is then, as knowledge, the summation of all virtue and the totality of his obligation for the human individual. The first and highest, and at the last, the only, obligation of the individual is the obligation to know. How this knowledge of the individual is related to the wisdom in which objective virtue transcends it we shall see in Part V.

V. SUMMARY OF THE PERSONAL VIRTUES

We have seen that sympathy, when it means the elementary sensitivity described above, is the beginning of all morality, since it marks the specific point of beginning of intelligence, at which point a movement becomes an act. It is thus the basis of all the personal or subjective virtues, that is, all the capacities by which persons assume transformative power, or control, over objects. The primary ethical question from this point onward is as to the different types of objects that action involves, the different modifications of the actor, and the different techniques of control, that correspond to these object types. Generosity, for example, seems to consider the act as directed upon an object which is an agent at the same time, that is, an object of the same kind as the actor. This is an isolated object, since an act in any case implies unity in the agent from which it flows, so an object that is an agent must be single.

Now a virtue which permits of pluralizing the object, friendship, will represent an attempt to make the active relation hold generally; it represents a higher form of personal virtue. The final virtue for the person is then that in which the plurality of "others" is brought to unity with the agent, giving the conception of the agent as the center of meaning of all the virtues, that is, of all morality. This, we saw, limits virtue and morality to subjective persons. But this very limitation makes it necessary to go on beyond the subjective or individual person to the corporate person. Integrity, wholeness of person, which is the final demand made by the nature and constitution of the person, compels us to go beyond the person to the *order of persons*, and to investigate whether and in what sense personality may be attributed to the order of persons. The demand for a clear conception of the order of persons can be met only by the concept of the corporate person, and to find and describe the characters of the corporate person will be our task from now on to the end.

Part IV

The Nature of the Moral World

Chapter XV

The World as a Moral Object

WE SAW in Part I how the facts of experience determine our problems for us when we raise questions as to the nature of life and action, duty and obligation, etc. Also the facts of experience determine for us the essential meaning of the terms which we must use if we are to make questions of life intelligible. They indicate what terms and conceptions will be central to our discussion, and they show how the relations of these terms and concepts formulate the laws and principles which govern our thought. It was from analysis of the facts that we derived the law of morality and determined the two central concepts within its meaning, viz., person and world. In Part II we took up the question as to the nature of the person and, by examining the characteristic capacities of the person, found his moral excellence to lie in the power to act. In Part III we examined this power to act and found that, with respect to the person as ordinarily defined, there are a limited number of characteristic forms of the power or capacity to act. These forms or types of activity are the virtues, and we discussed and examined some of the more important of them.

Throughout our analysis of the person in Parts II and III we found that it is best understood when we define the person in terms of his relations to the act. That is, what the person is is determined from his acts, which are given as facts; we do not determine the nature or moral quality of the act from the hypothetical nature of the person who acts, since his nature is not directly known. This person which is known only by inference from his acts is the person as agent. But the person as agent is also the being that knows his object or objective or end, since an act is not possible except as governed by an end, and this capacity of knowing is an essential feature of the agent. Our analysis of this knowing capacity involved a discussion of all the subjective powers of the agent and resulted in the discovery that the agent cannot be fully understood merely from his relations to his act and that all discussion of the person and his capacities or virtues is fragmentary and incomplete until we know something of the relations of the act to other things than the person. That is to say, the act implies something more than the person. This limitation of the personal capacities which comes from their dependence upon the acts of the agent considered as an isolated fact we called the "subjectivity" of the personal capacities. And we found numerous places where, in order to overcome this subjectivity and to get a more adequate notion of the person, we had to look outside and beyond the mind and experience of the individual in the direction of the object which every act implies.

Now, if we generalize this idea of the "object which every act implies," we come back again to the concept of the world, which we found necessary to the formulation of the moral law, but discussion of which we postponed for the time while we were coming to an understanding about the nature and meaning of the moral person. This means then that we cannot go on to a final statement of the nature of the act or of the person until we investigate the moral world, and this becomes our task in Part IV.

I. THE WORLD AS OBJECT

The world in which persons act is made up of natural objects and cultural objects, and these objects will be of many different types, since we mean by object in this connection anything that may be considered as condition or circumstance to the act, or anything *implied by* the act when we think of the act as directed to an end. The world of objects is then a premise upon which the act depends for its full meaning and must be presupposed to exist as background of every act as its vague matter or substance. But there is another aspect of externality which the word "object" connotes. This is the sense in which object means objective, or that which is external to the act in anticipation, or as that which the act becomes or in which or upon which it issues. In this sense the object is a sort of practical conclusion drawn from premises by the act and also exhibits itself as a premise upon which other conclusions can be based. From this relation of objectives we get the idea of a continuity of objects, and this idea is the abstract notion of a world. In both these senses the object is the presupposition of a world and is the subject matter of logic and metaphysics and, taken as such, has only indirect moral implications. But it is of first-rate importance in determining the basis of the validity of moral judgments, and any adequate discussion of ethical theory must take this question of the objective implications of action very seriously. The factual aspects of the question we shall treat of below in Section III. We must, however, hint at the logical and metaphysical aspects of the object here, for the world of nature, as an existent system of fact, is unintelligible otherwise; and this makes the world of culture, and the synthesis of the natural and the cultural in the moral world, also objective problems which we must face. Let us look for a moment at each of these, keeping in mind that it is the object of acts that we are interested in.

A. THE WORLD OF NATURE

Nature appears to us in action in the various phases of it which the natural sciences attempt to explain. That is to say, nature is matter, force, cause, inertia, impenetrability, etc., when considered in its static condition; and it is life, impulse, growth, process, etc., when thought of in its various capacities of movement. These are generalized in theoretical discussions and become the concepts of *substance, matter, cause, life,* etc. We shall briefly state the character of each of these which gives it moral significance, it being understood that it is only in metaphysics that they can be given adequate treatment.

1. SUBSTANCE

Our law of morality speaks of the world of nature as the place, or locus, or arena, or forum, or general scheme or frame of things that is necessary before an act can be conceived to exist as real. To try to think of an act that does not take place anywhere, does not imply a world, is merely to muddle our thinking. But with the question as to what are, or must be, the qualities and characters of this world, we have to think of them as the basis of the qualities of sense which make up the material basis of our experience. The difficulty here comes when we assume that, if sense qualities have such a basis, it ought to be discoverable by a descriptive analysis of these qualities as facts. But no such basis can be found in this way. The only way out of this is perhaps to reflect that things that are real are real either because they are syntheses of sense qualities or because they are syntheses of logical qualities. In the one case we can tell concretely and directly what an object is; in the other we can only say abstractly what it is, or rather must be, and then indicate the "what" or the "that which" in a given case by a long description. It is only by this latter, or logical, method of description that we can say anything about the meaning of substance.

In a given case, an orange *is* a synthesis of sensible qualities, round, sweet, yellow, etc. That is to say "orange" is what underlies these qualities and makes their mutual references all point in the same direction. These qualities tell us what the object is in the sense that we shall know with what experienced qualities it will be appropriate to associate the name. But if we ask what the orange is independently of these qualities, for example, what there is in the system of nature that guarantees that there shall be oranges or objects with these qualities, if we ask, that is, what is meant by orange in general or the species orange, we have a quite different question on our hands. For there are no qualities *of orange* in general; all qualities of the kind in question belong to this, that, or the other orange. Then I can, in answer to the question of what an orange is in this general sense, only point out the relational aspects of my experience and thought about oranges and show that these relations necessitate the concept of orange in order to make themselves intelligible. The substance of orange is then connected with this logical necessity, and we can say that orange is that which explains the coexistence of certain qualities in certain relations. And it is only because of this substructure of relations, and the laws by which they constitute a system, that we can think at all.

What this means in connection with my action is this: I must know or believe that the qualities which appear in my experience indicate a permanent condition which I can always take for granted when I wish to act. If I wish to go out of the room, I must be able to assume that there is, as there appears to be, a floor or other structure under my feet which makes it possible for me to walk. And unless I could take for granted a number of things of the same or similar kinds, neither action nor thought would be possible at all. This is what we meant in chapter iii by the "implications" of the facts of action. If the facts are what they are for our experience, then certain other things are true that go beyond experience, and the certainty that something beyond experience can be modified so as to become a factor in experience is the only justification for action in the highest sense. For instance, I want a house, let us say. This house does not exist, is beyond experience. But it is an implicate of many things that do exist: There are timber, brick, and other materials; a lot can be obtained, and carpenters are willing to work. All these facts are in existence, and they all mean "house." But I have no money, which is all that is lacking. This situation constitutes the conditions of action for me, and the act is intelligible only in terms of such conditions. The concept of substance tells us then that the meaning of any fact is a reference, immediate or remote, to a system of realities or objects that make it intelligible. Or, in other words, substance is the ground of the intelligibility of anything and everything in experience. It must be thought of as external to thought, in *rerum natura*, since it must be presupposed if there is to be such a thing as thought. Of course it is true that all this is unconscious in ordinary practical activity. But here our problem is not practical but one of showing what sorts of things are involved when we say that the world of objects must be taken into consideration when we discuss action.

2. MATTER

Substance, we saw, is, as a practical conception, the presupposition of a world of real objects, actual and ideal, with respect to which action takes place. Action presupposes actual objects as its material ground; it presupposes ideal objects as the form of the end in which it is realized. Matter is the presupposition of a world of actual objects *through* which, or with which as media, action may take place. It is the stuff or material instrument which action requires if desired or ideal objects are to be brought into existence. For my house I require timber, bricks, ground, work, and money; these are the materials that are actual or already in existence out of which my house must be built if it is to be built at all. The world of nature is therefore from this point of view a great storehouse of materials awaiting action to give them the form of value objects, and it is the presence of this world of materials as "resources" that constitutes the strongest stimulus to action. This aspect of nature is simple and need not be emphasized.

Matter, however, has another meaning which is almost equally important. If I am to have a house after the ground is bought and timber, bricks, etc., are placed on it, I must still have some way to bring these materials together in precisely the way that is necessary to make a house out of them. Some of the materials must be shaped in special ways so as to be able to establish effective relations among the rest of the materials. These specially designed objects we commonly call tools, and it is from the world of nature that all of them are derived. In the larger extension of the term "tools," so as to include the general idea of means, this conception is especially important, in that one of its uses is to mediate the connection between nature and culture. But what we wish to say here is that at bottom all tools are objects of nature either directly or as modified to suit purposes which are more complex than nature, by herself, presupposes.

3. CAUSE

The two ideas of substance and matter are presuppositions of action in the sense that they are the static or fixed conditions upon which action depends for its meaning and realization. But substances and matters might conceivably be in existence eternally without there ever coming into existence any new object; they might constitute a world that is fixed and dead and which could exist throughout all eternity just as it has eternally been. In this case of a merely material and substantial world there would be no reason for action even though its conditions were present. In order that action may get a foothold in such a world, there must be some way to overcome the fixity of substance and matter, that is, there must be some ground of change in it, some way to think of the facts of the world as being real and corresponding to what they appear to be. This requirement that the world be something other than it appears, and yet consistent with what it appears, is met in the concept of cause.

Cause, then, is the assumption that the world of fact may change and still mean something. Change, that is, need not involve the disappearance or passing-away of that which changes: The boy changes to a man and yet remains the same individual. Cause implies that things may change as much as they may be required and yet the change will be orderly in such fashion that it can be treated as a permanent character of things. In this way we are able to think the world in terms of its changes just as effectively as in terms of its fixity, and change really becomes necessary to the orderliness of the world. It is the moral function of action to see that changes among the phenomena of the world are such as contribute to the order of the whole, and this fact is perhaps the only answer that can be given to the question of why men should act at all. Cause then refers to that character in the phenomena of nature by means of which they can be thought of as capable of order and form and is at least the original and elementary suggestion out of which a particular act arises. When we speak of one fact as being the cause of another, we think of the two as being so related through change as to modify the character of the whole situation in which the two facts lie, so that the two facts, while remaining what they were before, yet enter differently into their objective environment in such a way as to change their bearing upon the whole. Cause is therefore that character in nature that makes an act possible and meaningful, that is to say, the character which gives body and reality to the mere subjective determination which appears as the intent of a purpose. Cause is the instrument or process through which intentions become real and is presupposed in every act.

4. LIFE

It is this connection of cause, as meaning orderly change in nature, with intention, as the free indifference of subjectivity, that we mean by life. Life then means growth, for orderly change as modified in direction by free indifference is what is meant by growth. The "indifference," of course, makes the conception difficult. What is meant is that a system of orderly change may proceed in a variety of different directions while its internal structure remains the same; but what kinds of combinations it as a whole makes with other things will vary widely and will depend upon the nature of those elements of its environment which have been determined upon by the direction in which the change system is proceeding. The elements thus hit upon will then determine the nature of the growth. What these elements are to be in a given case is a pure matter of chance, and this fact is frequently emphasized when we say that life is governed by will or purpose rather than by cause. But there is no real difference in the two conceptions. Both have in them an element of chance, and their assumed difference is due largely to the fact that the element of chance is recognized in will but is supposed to be absent from cause. In what direction a causal process will effect its energies is determined largely by what happens to lie before it, a fact which is sometimes given a volitional interpretation in the term "selection." It is also given a physical interpretation when it is described as following the course of least resistance. But as the environing fact itself is under a degree of order, the forms determined by a causal process that is directed by freedom will themselves show a certain regularity, a fact of "permanence" which we indicate in such terms as type, kind, species, etc.

It is in this sense that we can say that life has "ends" and "purposes" and that its ends and purposes may be made to vary because of some factor within life itself. So we may think of "freedom," or this possibility of variation of ends, as determined by the impulse of life from behind, and as consistent with and dependent upon causation in the life-process. In any case the factor of freedom or spontaneity, which we tend to make the *quid proprium* of an act, has a basis in fact in this element of chance or indeterminateness or uncertainty which is due to the infinity of possibilities from which any causal process may "select" the elements in which its order and substance are to be completed. This infinity of possibilities is just the objective world that is implied in any act. The objective fact of freedom we are to recognize as the real opportunity given in the objective world implied by an act, and it is upon the presence of this world of objects in the agent's environment that his moral destiny will depend.

The world as a moral object, in its simplest and most immediate form, is the world of natural fact within which, through action, the life of the moral agent is determined and his freedom realized. The knowledge of it that is relevant to the good life is just the content of the natural and the biological sciences, and the "control" of which these sciences sometimes speak is itself a moral or practical concept.

B. The World of Culture

The world, for morality, is, as we saw, the environing opportunity to action and the instrument of action. It is the total of environing circumstance in which an act can be realized. We have seen that nature is the basis of the whole and that the more primitive conditions of action are already laid down in the material world. The same concepts therefore that make the world intelligible for the cognitive or knowledge function explain, so far as they go, this world in terms of its practical meaning.

By the world of culture we mean the structure that has resulted from man's efforts, throughout his entire historic career, to control nature in the interests of his own purposes. It is the system of nature as modified by human purpose. This structure is called "culture" or "civilization" to distinguish it, as the work of man, from the original nature which we described in the last section. It is the work of man as a type, of men in their corporate capacity and of men as individuals only as they function as elements of agency within the corporate body. It is usual to describe the whole of the cultural system as constituted of parts called "institutions," and the characteristic institutions of the moral world we describe in the following chapters of Part IV.

Here, however, we want to notice the nature of the general relation between the person or agent and the institutions that make up his environment, for it is in the form of institutions that the environment comes into direct relations with persons. The individual as a natural being is a system of causes connected at every point with the whole causal system of nature. Hence his career is already determined to be one of continuous movement of a more or less orderly type. That is to say, man could conceivably live in the world as a mere animal, and as a matter of fact perhaps much of his career has been that of an ordinary animal. The difference lies in the fact that, for reasons originating in the type of chance or accident described above, that is, from the "chance selection" from his environment of those of its factors which should become the ends of his important movement-forms, he developed faster in adaptability to the environment than others, and this adaptibility, first a product of chance, becomes the basis of intelligence. His adaptation to the environment thus became, through the intelligence which it itself created, an adaptation *of* the environment *to* his own purposes. Man, that is, became man and ceased to be an animal when he created artificial systems between himself and nature through which to express his mental and physical reactions to nature. These systems constitute the basis of his culture, and they are, for the most part, the objects toward which his energies of thought and action are directed.

Action is, thus, the form of mediation between the person and his world, and it objectifies itself in institutional forms. The direct contact of action with nature has itself been highly institutionalized, for example, in industry; so that for the most part action is directed *toward* these institutional or cultural objects rather than *upon* the objects of nature. Institutions thus become both the object-world within which we act and the instrument by which our action is expressed. In this latter capacity the culture-world lies immediately present to the hand of the moral agent and constitutes his opportunity as a moral being in all its significance. If, for example, he is to give expression to his purpose to develop his intelligence, the educational system lies ready to his hand as the occasion, the material, and the instrument through which the purpose may be carried out. And the most distressing weakness of our moral world at the present moment lies not, as is sometimes said, in the essential weakness of that instrument, but in the fact that it is effectively available only to very small numbers of people. We have industrial instruments enough to make a competent living for every person, but they are unfortunately not within reach of most of us. And the same is true of most of the other aspects of culture; they exist and are reasonably competent, but they are not available to most people. And the greatest, perhaps, of the moral problems that face the peoples of the world at the present time is just this question of how to make the opportunities, which already exist potentially in institutions, available to all who could effectively use them; and its solution will involve some very fundamental changes

in our modes of thought and also in some of the institutions which
have become adapted to obsolete modes of thought.

C. The World as Moral

The problem just mentioned is, in one of its important phases, just
one as to how to readapt some of our existing institutions to the world
of nature the better to serve certain of our new purposes which have
come into existence since the present adaptation was made. Or, in
general terms, the distinctively moral "world" is the world in which
all factors and parts of the systems of nature and culture are integrated into a whole which gives adequate expression to every purpose. That is to say, morality, in this general sense, is simply the complete and adequate integration of nature and culture, the synthesis
having been effected by and in accordance with the purposes of our
active life. Morality is then a matter of the ultimate order within a
system of life-culture as thought effectuates it in the interest of higher
values. And the moral world is the world that is made an adequate
instrument for the expression of the purposes of men. It is thus not
distinguished *from* the political, economic, industrial, etc., worlds;
these latter are distinguished *within* the moral world as its constituent
parts, and it itself is primarily the system of laws and institutions, regarded as the objectified action-forms of men, by which their order
is created and maintained.

At this point one of the worst of delusions exists as to the meaning
of morality. It is the assumption that morality is a quality of specific
acts. Of course it is true that specific acts have the moral quality; but
the problem lies just there as to what is the nature of this quality. The
morality of an act, taken as an isolated phenomenon, cannot be determined. It is only as an act can be interpreted in terms of a whole of
life and culture that it can be said to have a moral quality, for it is
this whole that is good, and it is the relation of the specific case to the
whole as principle that constitutes the meaning of goodness. The
moral *quality* is therefore a relation, the quality of standing in a certain position of reference to something. Hence some of the famous
moral problems—whether you may lie when under compulsion; kill
in self-defense; divide the one biscuit with your fellow in shipwreck
—all such questions are irrational and have no meaning, since they
assume conditions that make a moral act impossible. It is absurd to
ask if it is right to let myself be killed when I could defend myself.
If those are the alternatives, there is no moral question, since the con-

ditions assumed make any rational relation of my act to the system of cultural purposes out of the question. Such questions can be given a meaning only on the false assumption that the moral quality is a character of the mental states of the persons concerned in action. Of course "it" is wrong if I kill in self-defense. But what is it that is wrong? When I say that it is wrong to kill in self-defense, I mean that *something somewhere* is wrong. But the wrongness is not directly a character of my act. The wrong is in the situation that imposes the necessity upon me and leaves me no rational alternative. The "right" and the "wrong" are therefore matters of the relation of agents to objective circumstance. If I and my companions are shipwrecked, any act we may perform will be wrong, that is, it is wrong that we are limited to that act. If I steal because my children are starving, it raises no question as to whether stealing is wrong. Stealing is always wrong; it always means that something somewhere is wrong, and its challenge to the moral agent is to find out what and where the wrong is. His first obligation is the obligation to know. As an isolated act theft has no moral quality, and the tragedy of much ethical discussion is that it wastes itself on problems that are irrational in their statement. And the moral agent can look upon the systems of criminal law only with the consciousness of unutterable humiliation.

The moral world is, then, the total world in which acts have meaning; and the essence of meaning in every act and in every moral judgment lies in their expressing some relation between the natural world and the cultural world as that relation formulates itself in a personalized situation. The standard of principle for every specific act and every specific judgment is contained in the objective and external situation, and this objective situation also defines the personal attitude out of which the energies of the act flow, and the objective situation is determined in any specific case as that upon or within which these energies issue. But what is presented as specific, as the condition of an act and as the criterion of a judgment, that is to say, all the details and facts, either subjective or objective, in the active situation, are merely symbols signifying the total human world, which stands there as the ultimate seat of all the meanings an act can have, and which constitutes a persistent challenge to us to know it, with the alternative that we shall continue to act blindly and perhaps wrongly.

The moral world as an object of knowledge now becomes a problem for us. We must make an effort to find out, first, in what sorts and forms the object appears to us in "experience," that is, how the object appears in its ideal personalized aspects, and, second, how it appears as the real issue or completion of an act.

II. OBJECT AS IDEA

The question for us here is: What is the core of meaning involved in an act as that meaning, which actually is objective fact, is formulated in the experience of the agent? What is the form in which the objective world (the world of nature and culture) appears as particular fact in the experience out of which the act proceeds? We shall find that it takes a good many different forms, that there are relations of order among these forms, that some of them, which are quite generally overlooked, transcend the limits of mere "experience" and make connections with the real or objective world. We shall find also, or should, if we were to look to historical accounts, that it is at this point of "psychological" analysis that recent periods of ethical speculation have been most successful and have also made some of the most inexcusable of blunders.

A. THE OBJECT AS IMPULSE

One of the simplest forms in which the objective world appears as an element of action in experience is impulse.

Psychological and biological investigation of recent years has increased and clarified our knowledge of the impulsive life, at least in its mechanical details. Impulse is the point of beginning, in organized matter, or matter organized to the point where it has functions, of movement. It is thus a fact that is largely speculative in nature, since all questions of origins are for the most part speculative. The impulse is then the elementary outburst of energy arising in organic tissues when these tissues are the terminal points of a nervous stimulus. As such and as the mere beginning of movement the impulse has no intrinsic moral meaning, for movements are not facts of the moral world when taken by themselves. As a consequence, and since movements do have some relation to moral facts (in mere fact the basis of every act is a movement), ethical theory has attributed to impulse the double character of being the impetus to movement and the point of origin of the meaning through which a movement becomes an act. But this makes the conception of the impulse extremely complicated and possibly contradictory. Yet it enabled theorists to endow the impulse with potential moral quality, and the question then became the famous one as to whether the impulse, as the psychical beginning of an act, or the facts that come as consequences of the act, are to be regarded as the criterion of the moral quality of the act. For it seemed that either the one or the other must be the ground of the morality of the act, since there was nothing else it could be after the act is accepted as an isolated phenomenon. If impulse and result are, respectively, origin and end of the act, and thus limits to and not parts or phases of the act, nothing tangible is left of the act itself to which the moral quality could attach. Consequently, the search for and description of the "original impulses" upon which acts are supposed to depend came to be the major issue in the explanation of morality, and many of its results had a good deal of significance for our knowledge of the psychological and biological facts of life. But this knowledge is only preliminary to moral explanation; it has of itself no direct ethical significance, since the act itself is left out of the picture. What was not observed here is that "motive" and "consequence" are vague and inadequate psychological symbols of the "person" and "world," the synthesis of which constitutes the act. They are therefore psychological abstractions and are of little importance for ethics.

B. Motive-Intention

The ambiguity of this conception, which arises from the fact that it places too large an emphasis upon the conscious aspect of experiences, gives rise to a much more complicated problem. The extension of the connotation of impulse now makes it a "motive," and motive is contrasted with "intention," which term is used apparently to counteract the psychological emphasis which had been placed upon impulse and to emphasize the overt and external aspects of fact involved in action. Both motive and intention exemplify and exaggerate the ambiguity of impulse. A motive now means that which stimulates the external or motor or movement phases of an act into existence. But it also means that which turns or veers our attitudes in a given direction, that is, it shows a direction-tendency of our minds with respect to the facts involved in the presented situation. So either of these terms becomes a toy to play fast and loose with, and they by turns are useful as devices of analysis and as description of the facts. But they have no direct ethical significance of the type they were assumed to have. They both assume that an isolated fact can be found and exhibited which, as a substantial factor of an act, is the bearer of the attribute that constitutes the moral quality of the act. They both represent the atomism which believes that anything, to be real, must be simple, self-identical, isolable, definable in terms of itself. With this entity discovered, the theory assumes, the moral quality follows as one of its attributes. It is hence a mere question of finding and identifying a fact of which morality is a simple quality, and ethical science is a pure empirical procedure. The morality of an act is then a question of the quality of its "motive" or "intention," and this is determined by mere observation.

Thus the terms "motive" and "intention" become unintelligible. Let us try our hand at definition, remembering that definition rests upon quite different grounds from those assumed by empiricism. One of these grounds is the idea of development, and a definition of motive will show how it comes into being.

The experience which comes to be a "motive," considered as that which represents the inception of an act, arises as a presentation before the consciousness of some external or some internal sensation. That is, it comes from some externally perceived fact, some object seen, heard, etc., or from some perception within the mind itself, or perhaps from a sensation arising within the organism. This gets an affective quality from some context or other, since all quality has a relational "origin," and, if the experience persists, it grows and develops by connection with other experiences and the development within itself of new elements of feeling. As its sensory complexity and the intensity of feeling increase, it attains the status of an idea, at which point its relations with other experiences, present or represented, become matters to which attention may be directed. That is to say, there begin to be defined within the experience objects upon which thought and conscious effort may be directed. Around some of these objects collect desires or feelings intense enough to serve as foci for attention. The object which has been merely represented now becomes an object of desire, a desideratum, an objective, one, that is, which is pictured as worthy of action directed toward bringing it into being. This objective is now the center of the whole experience, in that all other elements present get their meaning from it. It persists, and as a stable idea, begins to connect itself with activities designed within imagination to suggest actions, overt processes, by which it could be realized. Into the idea, which, as persistent and clear enough to define an object, may now be called the "motive," there enter factors from the total field of consciousness. But, as parts of the idea are representative in nature, factors from previous experiences also enter in. When the idea is considered with respect to its subjective aspects of feeling and desire and their corollary tendencies to overt expression, it may properly be called a motive in the sense of that which moves or causes motion. When looked at as the representative prefiguration of an object which may be created, it is an intention. But motive and intention are the same fact; and their essential features include the idea prefiguring an object surrounded with feelings intense enough to suggest modes of overt action designed to bring the object into existence.

It is now possible to say, quite properly, that the motive causes us to act and that it determines the character of the act. The same may be said of the intention, for they are the same. But there is a further distinction to be observed. The motive-intention determines the character of the act so far as only the form of the object by itself is concerned, together with the abstract methods and processes necessary to produce that form. The object intended is thus conceived to stand alone, supported only by vague notions of technical processes that would be involved in producing it. The object is then characterizable by neither quality nor relation, a pure formal abstraction. The object has form, but as yet no meaning, and until meaning supervenes there will be no *directed* action, no action determined in advance by the results and consequences in which it is supposed to issue, until, that is, it is determined by objects not yet in existence. And, to attain this qualitative and relational meaning, the object must be represented in the further system of relations which connect it as a detail within a future whole, the nature of which whole retrospectively confers upon the object the meaning it is to carry. This whole will have qualities and characters of the personal sort, characters, that is, which individuate it, and also characteristic features of the external world. These latter relations are various in nature, and the specific one of them that corresponds most closely to the design of the object will determine the kind of meaning the object is to have. If, for example, the object is a physical thing, the use to which it is to be put by its creator, the purpose it is to fulfil, will appear in its design, and will classify it among things that are practically useful; and it becomes an object of utility.

But this means that the motive-intention has now become a purpose, an idea that designs an object as a member within a system of meaning. This may be briefly described.

C. Purpose

Purpose is thus a developed intention. It differs from intention in emphasizing the external relations of an object as the essence of the meaning of the object and in referring the object to an external system of objects rather than to the subjective system of experiences. It is for this reason that purpose is a peculiarly important ethical concept, since it represents the mode of connection between the world of inner experience and the objective world beyond experience. It is the "principle of objectivity of thought," at least for practical connections. Another important feature of purpose is that it becomes a permanent factor in the character of the individual, since it represents a fixed type of meaning in his relation to the external world and thus becomes the instrument of his adaptation thereto. Its peculiar function is to refer to the external world and to formulate in experience elements that symbolize the permanent characters of the world. In this function it begins by initiating definite images of the structural relations of the world. These are preserved, since they do not, for the individual experience, change their form. The purpose is then a pattern, a universal form symbolizing a type of thing, that form, namely, with respect to which all instances of the type are designed. As operating in the mind of the individual it is a plan, and this presents a connected scheme of the series of activities necessary to give full expression to the individual life. As permanent elements of the individual's character these plans are his "ideals," the type-objects which, if and when realized, make his life complete.

D. Ideals

But the ideal has another purpose or function which has not appeared in the earlier stages of development from impulse through motive, intention, and purpose. We have said that the essence of the individual's obligation is to know. And none of the above stages have been characteristically cognitive functions. The world they present therefore has existence only in possibility, and none of them is capable of giving reality to its objects prior to their execution in action. None of the objects could be known to be realizable in advance of actual experimentation, and action in accordance with them must remain the eternal adventure. There ought to be, indeed there must be, some cases, at least, where action can be known to be objectively significant in advance of its performance. It is with the ideals, or, to avoid the popular meaning of that term, it is with the ideas that this knowledge becomes possible, and objects can be designed in idea which must in the nature of the case exist. Otherwise an act is meaningless, since on no other ground can a faith in the worthiness of a contemplated act be determined. And the existence of these objects can be known in idea previously to the discovery of the fact by the ordinary modes of experience. These are a priori objects, and their main function is to direct the thought upon genuine practical matters and save it from the vagaries of utility and other empirical considerations. It would be nonsense to try to *produce* by ordinary empirical methods a triangle, yet such an object must exist. And there is no reason to try to demonstrate the good, and yet the good must be. It is the function of the ideas to provide the eternal patterns by which all experiences are proved and corrected. They represent the ultimate knowledge that is at the bottom of obligation, and a full account of them would carry our argument over into the field of metaphysics. These ideas are also significant in that they identify with objects when objects have been completely realized. And they are the anticipations of reality which in the experience of the individual convince and assure him that his obligation is real and authoritative. They are thus the ends of experience in that they are that into which experience is completed when made fully adequate to its own nature. They are thus ends, being objects that are universal.

E. Ends

As an end, each of these ideal forms embodies a synthesis of the act which creates it with the thought that is its design. The life of action and the life of thought here converge, giving the idea of an ultimate from the point of view of which all things and all thoughts have their meaning. Such statements must not be misunderstood. They necessarily have the form of pure abstractions. But such objects appear as realities in every experience that is fully intelligible, in which we know there is a reality that completes and fulfils our thought and our act. It is for this reason that perhaps the highest form of experience is that which embodies the skill of the workman in forms of the ideas, such, for example, as may be observed in the creations of a competent cabinetmaker or mechanic or sculptor, or in the "makings" of the poet. There is in such an experience all there can be anywhere within the whole scheme of reality, for within the experience there is no requirement of anything beyond. All the thought of life has been or is being incorporated in the substance of reality by the adequate performance of the activities which that thought adumbrates in advance. Thought and act are one. It is the end because there is nothing beyond. It is thus perfect satisfaction, complete fulness, life as thought made real in itself as act, as end.

But the end as experienced, which is experience as end, is the criterion or standard for all possible practical acts. We will indicate in the next section the forms which these practical acts may take.

III. OBJECT AS END OF ACTS

We have so far been dealing with objects as psychobiological processes and as ideas. Objects are realized in these processes, but they are
realized out of the stuffs of the processes themselves, with independent objects appearing only in anticipation. An object as a purpose or
an ideal or an end comes to its fullest expression within the experience
in which it is defined. It exists, but its existence is limited to the environing circumstance of ideas and ideal relations. A triangle, or the
house which I hope to build some day, is as real as any object in the
universe, but the scope of its reality is limited to the region which its
definition circumscribes. Such an object has as much influence in the
world as any object can have, and its connections within the world
are more far-reaching than those of most other types of objects. Any
act can be directed toward it and designed by it, but no act can be
effectuated through it. In order to maintain a stable environment in
which persons may execute their plans, a system of objects upon a
physical basis must be continually created. An act not only must realize itself in an ideal object but must materialize and exemplify itself
as a factor of the stability of the external world in order that action
may always have a solid ground on which to proceed. We have now
to inquire what the objects are that make up the substance of that
stable world. We shall approach its description from the points of view
of the object as (A) result, as (B) thing, as (C) tool, as (D) body, and
as (E) end.

A. OBJECT AS RESULT

Acts always issue or come out somewhere. And the place where,
and the things with which they come out, are of varying degrees and
kinds of importance. If we think of the cessation merely in terms of
its stopping, with no regard to the place where, or kinds of things with
which it stops, we may think of the act as having reached a result.
Results will mean nothing except that they symbolize the cessation of
the act and remind us that the act in question is of no further consequence to us. If I am interested merely to know how long a clock will
run or how far a pendulum will swing in a given case, I have the
results I want when the movements have stopped and I have made
appropriate measurements. I may desire to walk to the top of the hill
just to see what can be seen from it as vantage point. When I reach the
hilltop, I have my results. The object of the action may again be the
performance of the action itself; all I wanted was a walk, and the act
was completed when it ceased. Such acts are often regarded as not

possessing moral value, but we must remember that every genuine act possesses moral value. What we mean is that no important consequences of certain kinds follow upon the completion of the act. I am not paid for walking to the top of the hill, and I may miss my dinner by going. But it is nevertheless by such activities as these that my capacities were developed to the point where they were adequate to their special purposes; to say nothing of the aesthetic meaning which such acts may have. And an aesthetic ingredient is an element within a moral experience in probably every case. There is probably no way other than by reference to this aesthetic element by which we could determine the relative importance of these various kinds of objects; the question is rather meaningless in any case, since such distinctions do no apply to the parts within a system where the nature of the system makes all the parts equally necessary to the maintenance of the whole. Pushpin, in its place, *is* as good as poetry, and the trivial has its importance in its triviality.

What is meant, then, by the result's being unimportant is merely the fact that, for our more usual purposes, the place where, or the mere thing with which, an act stops is unimportant. But there are plenty of cases where all the importance in the world depends upon nothing else than the fact that an act stops at a given point.

B. Object as Thing

An act frequently issues with the appearance of a number of distinct qualities which have a body of relations apparently supporting them. This is what is usually termed a thing. Its definition is, essentially, that which supports a more or less uniform collection of qualities. "Thing" is for the most part a term used in discussing the knowledge function and is not generally considered as having moral bearings. But we have noted that an act of knowledge is at the bottom of every moral situation. The place therefore of the thing as the possessor of qualities or attributes must be inquired into.

There are two fundamental connections in which the thing is of elementary moral significance. It is the basis of the distinction of means from each other and of the distinction of means from ends. Or, it settles the question as to what in a given case is to be a tool and what not, the question as to what is a tool or instrument and what is a mere stuff or material.

It is the qualities of the characteristic thing in a situation that tell me what I can do with it, and, for the most part, what I can do about it, although this latter depends somewhat upon relations. But it is obvious that it is upon the qualities that I depend when I have to determine how a thing will fit into the purpose with which I am concerned. It would be folly to make a handle for a heavy hammer out of willow wood, just as it would be to make a penstock out of hickory. I know this because of the qualities of the two kinds of wood. The qualities of one make it tough and strong; of the other, light and fragile. And when we reflect upon the importance of things as tools, and remember that their quality as tools depends upon their qualities as things, we can appreciate the importance which the thing has as the issue of an act. It means that I must strive to make some things hard, others soft; some lithe and some rigid; some heavy, some light, etc. The quality of a thing may itself become an end; the hardness of steel has been an important practical problem and perhaps will remain so.

The qualities of things also determine the elementary stuffs upon which action must depend if it is to issue in significant ends. This is obvious and does not require discussion. The thing, then, as that issue of acts which is determined by mere quality, is the basis of some of the most elementary moral distinctions and, as a problem of knowledge, shows how far morality depends upon the development of knowledge and intelligence. The thing as an individuate substance is the ground of all quality, and quality is the essence of all value.

C. Object as Tool

We have just seen that the tool is determined, from its point of origin at least, by the thing and is a matter of specific quality. What we want to see now is that, from the point of view of its function or its place in an act, the tool is determined by the end it serves rather than by the stuff or material from which it is derived by distinctions of its quality. Whether, then, a tool is to be made of hickory or willow wood will depend upon what I want to do with it, that is, upon what type of object I want to produce by its use. Of course this is a reference once more to the qualities of a thing, but it is the quality of the thing into which the act issues, as depending on that out of which or that from which the act issues. This means that the object as tool represents a halfway point in the act and that as an object it is lacking, in some degree, the full meaning which characterizes ends. But it also means that the distinction between tool and means, or end, is one which cannot be drawn in sharp lines and suggests that it may have been overemphasized in most ethical discussion. There is therefore no such thing as a mere means; every means, to be a means, must also be an end, and there are no abstract ends, no ends that are nothing more than ends. It is not a good hammer to drive nails with if it is not a good hammer as such and even though it never drives a nail, and its goodness can be determined before it has driven a nail. If I am a mechanic, I can tell the quality of the steel; and if I am a carpenter and a man, the hang of the hammer in my hand will tell me its history and its destiny. Its being a means consists in its being an end, the distinction between them is an abstraction of both based on a neglect of their quality; and, when their quality is ignored, they are nothing.

Then what I want to be able to do with means and end, if I am a moral being, is to handle them so that I can see the one in the other. I see that this board lying neglected on the ground will make a pair of bookends; that is, the board, not I, makes the bookends. This hickory tree will make good ax handles. This boy will make a good scholar. This space and soil and sunshine will make a rose. This insult will make trouble. This anger will make murder. This lust will make tragedy. The whole process of life and the meaning of existence lie in the experience that can thus connect a present existence with a future value and that knows the nature and quality of the objects and thoughts that enter into the formation of the connection. Man has become a being of culture because he could conceive an ax, and he could conceive an ax because he could conceive of a tree to be cut down. He could see the means in the end and the end in the means, and he learned to interpret the identity between them through the other objects of his environment. The quality therefore of a thing is the key to its moral significance, and it is because things have qualities that they can become valuable. The end is the value of a tool or means, and the means or tool is the value of the end. What we have now to observe is their unity in the concrete.

D. OBJECT AS BODY

The identity of the means with the end gives to the combination the character which we call "form." Possession of form by an object gives it body, by which it has structure. By its structure it has a constitution, and the constitution designs it an individuality, by which it is the end. And by its being end we mean that it contains its kind in itself; there is nothing further for it to become; the act which produced it is not only ceased, that is, ended, but bodied or incorporated. It is this incorporation of the act that gives the object structure and a constitution, and so a design, so that the act has become realized in the form of the body and has created the permanent kind or type, to which other bodies may be made to correspond by reproduction. The formed body is thus the immortalization of an act, and the persistence of the act in the body, without being mediated through energies and movement, is design. Design is thus the latent power out of which all energies flow. Design is the act that creates without moving and without means; it "wills," and it can do this because both movement or process and means have been taken up and incorporated in the form by which alone design expresses itself. At this point moral theory identifies with aesthetic theory or expresses itself through aesthetic concepts.

The ultimate object of an act is thus to give itself form in a body, to incorporate itself so that its form may be made a permanent design and its continuity with the world guaranteed. And this is the meaning of the entire discussion of the object—to show that an act is meaningless except as it presupposes a world of mere body in which its reality may be demonstrated and proved. The difficulty that has vitiated all ethical theory since Plato and Aristotle is the vicious assumption that an act is or may be an immaterial phenomenon. An act that does not create an object, an act of "will," one that ends in itself, is a meaningless abstraction; and it is inconceivable that Aristotle could have seriously considered it otherwise. The thought which has itself for object creates itself a world; the world is inherent in the thought just as the end is inherent in the means or the means in the end. Then the morality of our states of mind, or our good intentions and our right heart, and of the corresponding results and consequences, is trivial and absurd. The right heart and the good intention are morally barren in any case, and even where they are followed by acceptable consequences it is not true that the consequences are attributable to them in any sense. If it were true that the "right heart" is transformed into an act, which of the necessity of its nature produces an object, it would still not be the basis of a moral quality, for the morality of the situation could not be derived from the rightness of heart, which has no objective quality. This question is not worth discussing. The problem of the same nature that is important now is the assumption that moral or "spiritual" or "cultural" values are of a different sort from material values and can subsist without them or in the face of the presence of contrary material forces. Our problem is not that we are absorbed with "material" goods but that we assume that we attain to spiritual goods by withdrawing from material connections. There can be no good of any kind in the world so long as physical objects are not adjusted to the necessities which the good enjoins. And the shallowness of the religion and art and morality that are present with the chaos of industry proves the point. There is no spirit until there is its adequate body; and the meaning of this just now is that the content of the good life, the body by which it survives, the economic and industrial activities of men, constitute the stuff of which morality is made. So that what ethics should be doing now is trying to find some way to put design into the distressed industrial body of our civilization and thus give to it the order by which it might incorporate into reality.

E. Object as End

All there is to say on this topic has been said, and this occasion will be made the opportunity to stress the objective reality and individuality of ends. All ends are corporate; they have a body through which they express design. These corporate bodies, or selected specimens of them, are made the subject of detailed study in the succeeding chapters of this part. These represent ultimate forms of the good, or the good in its concrete manifestation. Together they constitute the ultimate or absolute good, which is the whole meaning of reality. The good is therefore the institution of life, or life instituted or set up and incorporated by an act. But as the act is the act of the institution itself, which comes into being by its own design, the object identifies with the act, and we can say either that the act creates the body or that the body acts. The two statements have the same meaning, and there is nothing more to do about it than to try to understand its instances. The world, the object of morality, is the instituted act and is presented to us as fact in order that we may understand.

We shall begin with the family.

Chapter XVI

The Family as Organized Instinct

WE HAVE seen that the world in which the moral person lives and acts is a system of institutions, that these institutions are corporate embodiments of both natural and cultural factors, and that it is these institutions which afford to the person the materials, the instruments, and the opportunities that a life of significant action requires. These institutions constitute what we have called the individual's total circumstance; they are not a mere environment in the sense that they happen to be there in his vicinity and passively await the action of the person. They are of the same active nature as the agent; they respond to the acts of the person with acts of the same nature as his own; they share in his life in perhaps every phase of it, because they are the incorporation of countless agents' lives in the historic process; and in their own life-activities they stimulate and provoke and evoke from the person the acts that make him what he is.

The school, the church, the industrial, the political, the social institutions not only are there but beckon and call upon the individual to share their life. But they go even further; some of the more intimate of the institutions simply compel us to become factors in their activities, the refusal to respond on our part having fatal consequences even to our natural existence. Others obligate us; they give us a Hobson's choice of entering actively into their lives and fortunes or paying the penalty of surrendering all claims to culture. They are moral persons and have life and a destiny which can be clearly distinguished from the life and career of individuals. They exercise power, both ideal and physical, over the individual; they constitute the essence of meaning for some of the most essential ethical forces, such as authority, conscience, obligation; and they thus give to morality the basis in reality for the uniformity and universality which ethics claims for its laws. The ground of conscience, authority, and obligation is the same set of facts: it lies in the tie which binds the individual, by bonds of nature and of culture, to the institutionalized world in which he lives and moves and has his being. And conscience, authority, and obligation all have the basis of their power in the consciousness of the individual that he must conform to the dictates of the common life in which he shares.

It is probably not quite correct to describe this basis as a form of consciousness, if we mean by that term that mental elements are clearly perceived. It is nearer the truth to say that conscience, "respect" for authority, and the "sense" of obligation operate in us more as instincts whose activities are unconscious until our response to them has taken overt form and thus called our attention to them. In any case the relation of the person to the institution is fixed and imbedded in the substance of both nature and culture, and the fixity operates upon the individual as an overpowering force which he can disregard only at the peril of his natural and cultural destiny.

For good or ill, then, the moral person shares a common life with the circumstance that constitutes his world. He will prosper with it or perish with it; it is a person of the same flesh and blood and life as himself, and it is the immortal parent of the infinite succession of his brothers. To it, in the last resort, attach the roots of all the moral forces and factors that life may permit him to develop. And back to it will return in the end the reward or the failure and loss which happens to tell the tale of the individual's career within its ambit.

I. THE FAMILY AS HISTORY

Such a world in miniature is the family. In its historic early stages the family constituted the total world of the individual during the formative period of his life. However we may think of its organization, so long as it is essentially the group of elders and their descendants living together in close contact, it was in the family group that the child got his habits and his thoughts, his hopes and his faiths and ideals, his mental equipment, as he does his bodily features and capacities. The "spontaneity" of the individual will consists in a certain uniqueness in the way these characteristics get worked together into his personality. But, even here, the mode of organization of the individual's character is pretty thoroughly determined by the traditions and customs that grow up and become permanent common characters in which all share. As the family comes to be and remains the permanent fact through the course of history, it naturally becomes the parent of other institutions, for other institutions are institutions in a little fuller sense than is the family. They represent distinctions between functions of life, which have each come to specialize a body of its own. Thus the education process which was originally a function of the family develops to the point where it specializes organs of its own which it sets up as the body through and in which it is to function. It is in this sense that it is true that the family is the mother of all institutions; the church, the school, industry, all are specialized functions of the family, embodied and instrumented in organs that are appropriate to their peculiar types of activity.

But the point here is that the family is the total world for the individual through the period in which he acquires his elementary capacities and characteristics. It is the sum and synthesis of all his activities, and it is only later that some of the forms of action will specialize themselves as separate institutions. Within the family the child learns all his fundamental techniques and develops all his peculiar capacities and abilities. He develops his capacity for knowledge, for faith, for work, for play, for comradeship—all of these became possessions of the individual under the influence of and through the instrumentality of the family. The family is thus at bottom a conservative institution; and as its limits are narrow, the horizon it will give to the individual is limited. But it is deep and concentrated and serves to hold the individual to his tasks and to the realization of his possibilities when a more expansive and far-seeing influence would fail. The depth of its power and influence has made it an object of worship, and many people look upon any changes in its form as necessarily destructive, as the "breakdown" of the family. But the specialization of the functions which the family once performed, and their separate institutionalization in different functional organizations, makes the breaking-up of the old or traditional family inevitable; in fact, that event has already happened. There is no possibility of preserving the sanctity of the traditional family while both parents work and are away from home most of the day. Nor can it survive the taking of children into the school at very early ages; certainly not the placing of young children in industry. Nor can it survive the miseries imposed upon it by an industry dominated by exploitation. Where parents begin to murder their children to save them the misery of slow starvation, or the worse fate of growing up diseased in body and deformed in character, there will hardly prosper the ancient family and the "home sweet home" of our tradition. Nor will sensible youth undertake the burdens and responsibilities involved in family life with these possibilities staring them in the face.

But the "breakdown" of the family merely means that human beings are being introduced to a larger world, and it is to be hoped that they are endowed with the abilities to meet that larger world's

THE FAMILY AS ORGANIZED INSTINCT

demands by highly specialized institutional agencies. The individual still learns the old injunction "honor thy father and thy mother," but he also learns, or should learn, to adapt his emotional nature to larger and larger human groups and more comprehensive institutional structures, with the ideal at the end of realizing the quondam Christian injunction to love all men and accept them in a realized brotherhood. This he may do without losing anything of the depth or intensity or significance of his attachment to the smaller group; indeed, the depth and meaning of his "family" relations should be increased by his learning that they may become universal in their scope. This is true of work and play and government and the forms of order and all the relations in which men live. Each characteristic relation originally established in the family has founded for itself an institutional body through which its proficiency and effectiveness and the extent of its operation have been increased a thousand fold. As a consequence we have today the "world" of the moral agent made up of a large number of more or less distinct agencies to all of which he must make some sort of adaptation; rather, he is adapted automatically and more or less fully to each of them separately in the course of his growing up to maturity.

This "breakdown" of the family has defined for men in recent years their greatest problem, perhaps the biggest and hardest problem they ever have been or will be called upon to solve. The specialization of human functions and their incorporation into distinct "technical" instruments has imposed, or is now imposing, upon men the task of making all these special agencies harmonize and co-operate to the end of the whole good. It is distinctly and painfully obvious that they are not co-operating now. In what way or detail is the church contributing to or modifying the process of industry? What do we do through educational agencies to make the processes of government more effective or right? As a matter of fact we have been so busy during the past few hundred years in developing and perfecting these separate institutional agencies as *technical* organs that we have not even become aware that they are actually operating at cross-purposes with one another. Education perfects its machinery at the expense of government; industry thrives by exploiting religion and morality; religion becomes efficient by encroaching upon industry; all of them sabotage the state. In fact, the *relations* among our technical institutions are interfering with one another to the extent that none is competent or adequate to give full effect to its purpose, and the whole of our practical life is left in confusion.

What the sacredness of the family means, then, and it is the worthy object of our profoundest reverence, is this: The family has kept before man throughout his career the ideal that all his purposes may be made harmonious and that he could realize all his ends not only without interfering with the purposes and ends of his fellows but while actually furthering and contributing to them. This is man's noblest ideal and his profoundest conviction, and the family has immortalized it in his "heart." But it is more than an ideal and a conviction. The family has kept it continuously and constantly demonstrated throughout history that the way and the only way for man to reach his ends is through co-operation with his fellows. And the family has proved that no halfhearted method will work; co-operation, mutuality, brotherhood, is the one ultimate and absolute law, and it may not be ignored in any detail.

The family is the demonstration and the proof that there is a significant way of life; and it has promulgated the law of that life.

II. THE FAMILY AS BODY

This is the account of the family as the organization of nature. The family is nature organized in physical and material form. This is its essential meaning, and all other meanings are derived from it. All the other meanings represent ways in which aspects of the bodily existence are to be developed or realized. Just what this natural basis is we shall want to see, and we shall ask also how the distinctly moral features of the family have this same basis in nature.

The aspect of nature whose order and organization it is the function of the family to create and maintain is instinct. The family is organized instinct; or, rather, the family is the organization of the natural instincts.

It is perhaps natural to think first of the sex instinct. But the sex instinct is only one, and perhaps not the most important one, of the instincts that are given orderly expression in the family. It is sometimes forgotten that the sex instinct by itself does not necessarily lead to the family and that there are other ways by which it can find expression. What has given to sex the enormous and rather morbid emphasis in contemporary life is perhaps the fact that other forms of instinctive expression have so developed as to interfere with sex relations. It is a diseased and irrational industry that is now forcing the sex instinct into morbid and irrational expression. But it is no more fundamental in life than a number of other instincts. The fact that it is the means of preservation of the species does not give the family its importance: the species could be "preserved" with better results if nine-tenths of the human species refrained altogether from breeding. This could be accomplished by the specialization of peculiarly competent individuals to that function, as is done in the case of domestic animals. The significance of a thing never depends upon its necessity.

There are many instincts more important than sex that get organization in the family and thus become the foundation of important cultural development and high degrees of institutionalization of life. Play is such. It may be that play is a product originally of the individual's surplus energies. But other origins are equally plausible. The family could very easily get its original impulse from dancing, in which certain elements of grace of movement appear to be inherent in the human form; the presence together of the male and the female in such a pleasurable activity might very well suggest the more permanent union of the two. In any case the dance has always been connected closely with the marriage ceremony, and it would be absurd to attribute all its influence to sex.

Similar complementariness is to be observed in work, conversation, singing, etc., between the male and female, and this fitness may lead to permanent association. This often happens now: people find themselves married before the possibilities of sex exploitation have been thought of, merely from habitual association or some other type of stimulus than that of sex. The importance of sex in the life of men and women is overemphasized, and the excessive emphasis of the present has come from the degenerative influence of commercialism, through its exploitation of sex as a means of advertising.

The family, then, is the institution in which instinct is reduced to order, and, since the orderly expression of our natural capacities is the first condition of the moral life, the family relation becomes the most elementary stuff out of which the good is made. The family is the total world for the organization of the human instincts during the first few and most important of the moral person's years.

III. THE FAMILY AS SPIRIT

When we speak of the family as a spiritual order in the instinctive relations of life, we do not use these words in the sense in which they are used in the older tradition. This old tradition hardly succeeded in spiritualizing the family but fell short at the point of a rather imaginative idealization of it. It pictured the family as it could be under what were supposed to be ideal conditions and tended to ignore the fact that most of the conditions it stipulated for the family could not exist within the region where the family is real and important. And the fact that it ignored the real physiological, economic, and industrial conditions upon which the family must rest if it is to mean anything, and the fact that the real family tended to develop in a way that ignored the tradition, led to the fallacy of assuming that the family was breaking down, when as a matter of fact it was merely changing in some of its external characters while holding strictly to the fundamentals upon which it has always rested. The main point of this change is in the control of the development of children. This function, in the tradition, was a prerogative of the parents, and generally this meant the father. The organization of the family in the matter of control was a pure absolutism, and the directions of development in the lives of the children depended upon the whim of the parental will. The parent could, until quite recently, refuse to send his children to school if he did not "believe in education," as parents frequently did not, or if he objected to the sort of thing the child was being taught, as he often did. At any rate, the control of the child's development has, for the most part and for better or worse, passed from the family to the social agencies and is now recognized as a public problem. The family at the present time, especially in cities, exercises a very small fraction of the total of influences that determine the child's development; many of these influences are due to public or semipublic organizations, and many others, some of the most important, are left to accident. The boy is in school six hours in the day, sells papers on the street two or three hours, plays marbles in the alley an hour, and in the evening is the Lord knows where, so he gets his "training" from a variety of sources, some of which are of doubtful value. In selling papers he assumes obligations and responsibilities in the way of his relations to others which men have not yet learned to discharge in strict agreement with moral principle, and he is well on the way to become that rather sorry specimen we have come to call the self-made man—the man whose universe, especially his morality, centers in his petty selfish and private self, and who is, as a product, just about the sort of thing he would be likely to produce. The family has lost the function of control over the child, and in this sense, viz., the highly idealized "mother's knee" type of family, the family which was a purely spiritual arrangement that could ignore the facts of the world outside, this family has "broken down." And we perhaps do well to lament it, for it will never return.

The old family rested on the assumption that it furnished within its own confines all that would ever be necessary for the child to learn or acquire and that the child could, at a certain age, be allowed to enter into a world he perhaps did not understand but over which he would nevertheless have mastery because of what he learned in the family. It was the assumption that our values in and for life may be determined independently of their relations to the facts of existence, so it was a religious rather than a moral attitude. But the facts of existence keep asserting themselves, refuse to be ignored, and thus constantly disturb the neat systems which our abstract assumptions build up. Assumptions are, however, stubborn things, especially if they express our convictions, and we refuse to give them up. So there was nothing to do but to charge the fact situation with perversity, and the "breakdown of the family" was charged up to sin and immorality and license, abstractions that are as ideal as the supposed spiritual basis of the family.

What we must see is that the family as a spiritual or cultural agency is such just in proportion as it succeeds in achieving and establishing a rational order within the facts of existence. Existence in the forms of matter and power is the very stuff of life, and, if morality is to contribute anything to life and its values, its contribution will have to come from transformations it can effect within existence.

It ought to be remarked here also that the family is not, when it is performing its natural and cultural functions, a subjective arrangement, not a group consisting of persons held together merely by subjective ties. The notion that a family can be maintained in the face of unfortunate physical conditions if only its members "love" one another is disproved by the facts in almost every detail. The basis of love itself is for the most part physical, and, where these physical conditions are not favorable, there is no possibility of spiritual unity. It is of course true that imperfect conditions in the facts can to some extent be overcome by mental adjustments, reorganization of habits, etc., but there is a limit beyond which this is not possible. The basis of spiritual values is physical nature. In the two following topics we will illustrate what this should mean for a more rational and positive interpretation of the meaning of the moral life.

IV. THE FAMILY AS ORGANIZED WORK

Morality assumes that a harmony of existence with value, nature with culture, is possible. This assumption is implicit in every genuine act as the principle which constitutes the act, and it is the only final justification or meaning that can be given for any act. An act would be unintelligible if I could not exert force or power upon physical existence and transform that existence through an act into a pure spiritual value. This means that the existence is modified in such a way that an element of value can share its place with it, that the two can coexist where before there was only existence. We shall here illustrate this in the case of work.

The problem of work is of course the problem of industrial life generally and is difficult. From almost the beginning of time work has been regarded as a "curse," and the conviction persists that it is and must be unpleasant drudgery and torture to which nobody will submit except under some form of compulsion of necessity. And perhaps it is true that throughout most of history the life of man has been made meaningless and miserable through toil forced upon him by some human master and that life characteristically is a choice between doing some disagreeable task or starving. This is true of a huge majority of men today, and perhaps it has been true throughout the course of civilization. The extent to which it is true is the most damaging argument against the significance of that civilization. There is a tragic sense in which it is true that where one man works *for* another there is a slave, and, what is worse, a master, and "man's inhumanity to man" is the fact of which he should be most ashamed.

Of course it is true that work is necessary if we are to exist. But it becomes more and more true that work is a corporate and not an individual function and that therefore the control of the process of work is no longer an individual function. It is suggested here that the principle of the new control may be discovered in the necessary structure of the family, in its principle of spontaneous self-organization. The question is whether work may be organized so as to assure an existence that is compatible with an acceptable scheme of values. The working life must be transformed into a cultural power, and the facts of work must be hallowed with values. There are, of course, persons who argue that work will always be mere drudgery; but if it is to be so, then either life itself is a failure or intelligence a sham and a delusion. And the fact that it is not so is proved in at least one very interesting and momentous case; for the artist work is not drudgery, however exacting it may be of the attention and however painful the fatigue. Thus, so far as ordinary work approaches the condition of art, its drudgery and disagreeableness tend to disappear. The farmer drives his team home in the evening whistling in an exalted fatigue and rejoicing in his oppressive weariness; he approaches a plain table with relish and delight and mocks at the fears and cares of a troubled world. But he does this only so far as he is free, both from the oppression of a master and of debt and from the ever present uncertainty of nature which may destroy his crops at any instant.

The problem, then, is one of fitting work into a scheme of things of such a nature that the unpleasant features of work may be eliminated. The expenditure of energy is not unpleasant; in fact, for a healthy being, one, that is, who can be moral, activity and the putting-out of power is decidedly agreeable. What is objectionable about work is its excess, either of effort or of duration, or the disproportion between it and other activities, say, recreation; or the lack of balance between it and other interests, music, reading; or the failure of the proper relation between work and the control, use, or disposal of the objects which it produces. All these objectionable features are consequences of the fact that it is not the worker's own intelligence that controls the work process, and it is this that suggests the principle of self-directed activity which is found in its elementary form in the self-organization of the family. What makes work disagreeable is then that it is too hard, or lasts too long, or is so light as to be trivial, or prevents my fishing trip or the attending to my roses, or it prevents me from reading the new book the library has recently bought, or from going to the theater, or it does not permit me to send my daughter to college but sends the employer's daughter to Europe on a sightseeing expedition. It is this latter fact that is making most of the trouble in recent years. The vast majority of people are denied the privileges of education and the good life, while the minority are squandering in idleness or vicious display or brutality the resources upon which these privileges depend and which were created by the majority of workers. When these conditions are rationalized, there will be the cure for the unpleasantness of work, and the unpleasantness will never disappear until they are changed and their more negative effects eliminated.

How are they to be changed, and especially what is the part which the family will play in their modification?

Considered as the institution which we have assumed it to be, the family will contribute little to the determining of proper conditions of work. The functions of the family are primarily two. The first is the breeding and nursing of children through the first few years of life. This function should organize the instinctive life of the parents, in its most elementary biological features, and this will be the basis of the more important emotional components of their "happiness." The work-activities which organize the instinct life are the self-controlled activities by which instinct creates for itself an appropriate structure.

The second function of the family is to provide a refuge and resting place, including recreation and physical sustenance, when the work of the parents is not in process. In fact, the functions of the family show what they should be in what they are in their best instances now. The "home" is a place to eat and sleep, a basis of operations of children's play and school activities, a place where the woman can sit down to the piano or receive her friends after the work is done, and where the man can sit in a huge chair with a cigar and a newspaper after supper. Now many of the conditions that make such a family possible are not part of the family's duty to provide. They should be provided for the family in a rational industrial organization controlled in its last details by public or political authority.

As individuals in the family, we have the duty to think out the methods whereby such conditions may be created and maintained as a background of family life, and to vote into existence the political authority to maintain them. Here our duty as individuals appears— our first obligation is the obligation to know.

It is assumed that every person is a member of a family and will have the interests of the family. Then the family is a problem for his reflective thought, since the conditions upon which the family depends are beyond the reach of his unaided action to provide. Hence he should approach the problem as one to be thought through and should determine the relative degree of dependence of the family upon each type of condition. He should ask what kind of industrial system is demanded so that each individual would have full and free access to everything necessary to the full development of his powers. We cannot here discuss needed changes in the industrial system; but it is clear that some form of freer access to the means of a full life must be provided. The tragedy of a young person fully capable by native and acquired capacity and of willing temperament to reach the highest stages of culture, but denied the opportunity to the provisions necessary therefor by poverty, is the one circumstance that condemns unequivocally the system in which we at present live. The person, as the only instrument of thought, has to face the problem of devising ways and means, after the end has been clearly perceived. It is his problem as an individual, the problem of every individual, and there is no moral life possible except so far as individuals will consent to think. And to think is all the agent can do as an individual.

Assuming that all individuals will think in so far as they are capable, how are the results of their thinking to be made effective in the way of setting up the instruments and preparing the arrangements by which a full life is to be guaranteed to everyone? The answer is: through the organization of individuals in institutions. It is only as we approach the problems of life as a corporate unit adequately implemented in institutional machinery that anything affecting the whole good is to be done. If young men and women are not able to continue their school training, ways must be found to enable them, provided they are adjudged capable. It is now known that they are no longer needed to work to provide the moral world with its necessities. In fact, just now, or any time, numbers of youth are out of school and at work while their able-bodied fathers are unemployed. As individuals they never can get the means to educate the youth. But the facilities for education exist. Only, the goods of life are not rightly distributed, or since the very word "distribution" has come to suggest perversion, we had better say, the goods of life are not properly allocated to their function. Huge stores of goods are hoarded while human beings starve and perish of cold. A dissolute rich man will waste on a silly hobby or a depraving vice enough money in one night to educate a young man or woman. Such conditions can be dealt with only through political agencies, through the corporate strength and intelligence of the whole people. It is suggested that it is not a question of distribution of wealth; there is a serious question if the institution of wealth is not an anachronism. It is a question of adjustment of moral functions to the conditions of their proper performance, or a question of the distribution of opportunities. But distribution is not the word, since it suggests privilege. What is required is a reorganization of the processes of life in such a way as will afford free access to the objects of significant action for every person. It will probably involve the substitution of some other means of estimating value and implementing its transfer than the age-old and for ages condemned system of exchange, money, and finance. But the question as to how all this is to be done is a political problem; that it be done is a moral imperative. It is a moral imperative in that its necessity as principle is demonstrated in the fact of the family. Let us turn to a brief discussion of the moral function as politically implemented and institutionalized.

V. THE FAMILY AS ORGANIZED CULTURE—AS POLITICAL BODY

The family is a political state in miniature. It embraces many of the factors and most of the functions of political life. Let us see how this is true.

In considering the family as a political unit, we do not imply that it is or need be the close-knit group of parents and children the passing of which is so much deplored. This group, in which children are to live in a family to maturity and spend most of their time in close association, is gone, and it will not return. It is therefore not in this sense that we shall speak of the family of the present as representing a genuine political unity. Such a theory of political unity in the state, that is, the old notion that a state is held together by the common experiences, traditions, interest, etc., of its people, is now seen to be false. No state maintains itself or attains its destiny because of any subjective experiences of its people; the life-force of a state is grounded in things more substantial than states of mind. Consequently, it is not patriotism or love of country or loyalty to or respect for law that gives to the state its power to live and prosper. So also we do not find in the most successful family that its existence and meaning depend primarily upon love or affection or any other mental tie between its members. That these mental bonds are normally present and have their appropriate types of meaning is recognized. But it is not upon them alone that the success of the family as a cultural institution depends. However strong and clean the emotional and mental relations among individuals, they will not cause the family to survive the failure of the industrial means and requirements upon which its mere physical existence depends. Nor will any amount of affection stand against the instinctive divergences of character and habit caused by traditional religious differences. If the family is to survive, it will be because of forces more fundamental and objective than those which arise out of mere states of mind. It will—in fact, it does often—survive the divisive tendencies of mental, temperamental, and emotional forces. And it does so because in the family there meet and coalesce agencies which are of more substantial character than any mental forces. The family, therefore, often persists in spite of the absence of strong emotional ties, and it often perishes in spite of the presence of the strongest of these ties.

The ties that bind the family into close unity are the institutional connections which the family maintains. The family is the point where the educational, social, political, legal, industrial, and religious institutional relations and connections of life all meet. Not only do they meet in the family but the family is the point where what there may be of difference of direction, etc., among these institutions and their trends must be brought to some degree of unity. The motives of education and industry, which frequently run at cross-purposes to each other, must somehow be composed if either of them is to reach any important conclusion. And the family is the place where the most immediate conflicts among such institutional tendencies must be resolved. But the function of finding harmonious ways in which the multiplicity of institutions may express their several geniuses is the political function. Thus the family is the model in miniature of what the state ought to be. Its peculiar function is not to provide satisfaction for the instincts of the original parties to it, however low or high we may consider these instincts, whether the mere animal sex desire or the more idealized emotion of love. Neither of these is an end. Both are means, endlessly. They are, finally, subjective states and cannot be substantiated. The function of the family is, on the other hand, to provide that there shall always be moral agents, and this is, in the end, also the function of the state. And both are destined to see to it that these moral agents are properly endowed by nature and by culture with all their possible capacities and that these capacities be adapted to each other in their most elementary forms of expression.

Let us see what this means in the form of example. An instance hinted above is just at present one of the most distressing difficulties of the family. This is the conflict between the requirements of education and those of industry. Now the conflict between these two is having a very pronounced influence on the family and is turning the family organization away from the purpose to provide competent moral agents. Young people at present see clearly, if they are intelligent (and moral questions are involved only where intelligence is assumed), that to provide a child with the food, clothes, etc., which nature requires, and with developed abilities, as culture requires, is impossible under the limitations imposed upon them by industry. They must both work to maintain themselves; so the enforced withdrawal of the wife from her job by the appearance of a child would endanger the material safety of the home. But a degree of security is essential if the parent is to be able to plan for the future development of the child. In the absence of these conditions young people marry in the hope that their combined efforts may in some remote future provide the home in which the family is to be reared, or they marry with the understanding that there are to be no children and that the arrangement is to be merely for the mutual convenience of themselves.

The conflict of legal institutions with economic and social institutions comes into clear view in cases of divorce. All the major "evils" which beset our family life are due to the blind conflict between such institutional forces. There is no need to illustrate the point further.

But it is to be insisted that the understanding of these evils, and of the issues their presence gives rise to, depends altogether upon seeing them as institutional conflicts which manifest their evil consequence in the family and which are to be met by adjusting the divergent institutional trends by methods determined in the interest of the whole of the social structure. Since politics has this function of oversight of the whole, such evils as beset the family and such developments as the family requires are questions for politics, and our morality in the narrow technical sense consists in no more and no less than the determination of right political methods. Since this determination of right political methods is a purely intellectual problem, our primary obligation to the family is the obligation to know.

It is clear, then, that the evils which now appear in family life are not all due to the weaknesses and faults of the individual. Or, in cases where the individual has traits that unfit him for family life, the strong probability is that such individual traits have their origin in the institutional conflicts mentioned above. The family in which the individual grew up was distorted by these institutional forces. In families where industrial oppression is severe there appear many of the traits which prevent the development of that degree of compatibility between persons that is necessary to the first organization of the family. In our present society, the weightiest factor operating against the family is the conflict between the institution that is supposed to furnish us with our material existence and that whose function is to provide us with our cultural capacities. These are industry and the school. The older view therefore that evil is all personal, or "individual," and that all the moral categories get their meaning from their reference to the individual and his qualities seems to be wrong. Or, if we are to continue to hold to the individual or personal view of good and evil and obligation, then the person or individual must be regarded as of the higher or corporate type. We appear to be obliged to look to the relations among persons, as these relations are institutionalized within the public structures of social life, for the ground and point of reference of all moral categories.

The family is historically perhaps the oldest, in any case the most elementary, of these institutionalized systems of interpersonal relations. It is within the family that we see the entire structure of life and culture writ small. Hence we may be prepared for changes in the form of the family as life and culture advance to new levels of value. But it will remain the symbol of that ultimate unity of moral facts and functions which constitutes the principle from which moral categories derive their meaning. It is in this sense that the family is the laboratory in which the moral agent gets his first and most important lessons in the adjustment of practical instruments and agencies. This means that the acquisition of moral capacities is effected in the political process, the process by which the institutions of life are adjusted and adapted to each other so as to construct the world within which moral action occurs.

VI. THE FAMILY OF THE FUTURE

There is to be no effort here at prediction of the form the family is to take in remote years. Indeed, within a few years from today the family may appear in a form that will seem to us strangely new. So prediction in the literal sense is out of the question. But the fact is that just *now* the family is a quite different thing from that which is represented in either our theory of what it is or the image that most people accept of it. What it is now is a rather indefinite set of relations which correspond only loosely with our notions of it. These relations also show the dependence of the family upon agencies with which, only a few years ago, it would not have occurred to us to connect it, and of which many people are not aware today. The main feature of the family just now appears to be what we may call its corporate tendency. This means that it finds the center and point of reference for its relations and values outside the *home*, if by home we mean the traditional group of persons domiciled as a unit in a specific location. In the traditional view the family is a self-referent unity of which the characters are defined by their reference to each other, these references consisting of the states of mind of the persons who compose it. Love is the major relation and function of the family in this view. But in the present family the organization seems centered in and determined by factors outside the group of persons involved. It has, that is, an eccentric organization, where the order of the old family was incentric. What the family is, as we have noted above, is controlled largely by the institutional facts and forces that environ or circumstance it. Its content of relations lies outside the persons and the immediate group which they form, within the complex of institutions which constitute the substance of culture. Hence we understand the family better by looking into it from the viewpoint of its outside connections and not by attempting to stand within it and looking out. We are attempting, that is to say, an objective interpretation of the family. What the family is now seems better understood by observing it through or from the point of view of the school, the church, the community, the industry or industries in which its members are employed—in fact, all the connections in which it stands to the objective world of culture. And the family is the sort of body or fact it is, because its determining content is made up of the relations among these institutions. But as a center of meaning for all of them it is rather the effect of their combined trends than some metaphysical entity out of which these trends and their institutions flow. It has, that is, so far as its origin is concerned, an empirical rather than a metaphysical basis, and it is from its empirical character that its structure is to be understood. The family is explained in terms of its outside institutional connections.

The family has its significance therefore in the fact that it is the laboratory in which the individual learns how to adapt conflicting interests to each other and thus gets his first training in order and discipline. But the order and discipline that he learns refer only incidentally to his own subjective faculties; his training is not self-training or self-regulation or self-discipline. The problem of order and discipline for the individual is the problem of how to adapt the forces and circumstances of his environment to each other in such a way as will offer greater promise of, and opportunity for, action. The arrangement of his own internal faculties by sheer force of will is impossible in any case and never happens in fact. The moral problem, the condition that makes action obligatory, is some situation within the person's circumstance which calls for rearrangement or adjustment, *not to himself*, but to some other situation, ideal or actual, which it suggests. Or, we may say that it is *within* the situation that the problem lies, and not between the person and the situation. Nor is it, except in rare cases, and these approach the pathological, an adjustment to be made within the individual's mind or character or among his mental processes or capabilities. In short, the *object* of moral action is not, except in abnormal cases, the character or mentality of the person who acts; and the *objective* of moral action is such only partially and incidentally and vicariously. Moral action strives to make some difference in the world, in the objective *order* of things and persons, and not within the internal economy and structure of the person. Or, again, if we must regard the end of action as within the person, it is once more the objective or corporate person that we mean. No other person can be the object of an act under the conditions of moral principle. The significance of the family lies in its being the laboratory for making these objective changes in which the person gets his first training; and his first training is important because he gets it during the period before his imagination has become hardened by custom and prejudice and before habit has stiffened his organism and character into immobility. He can yet make mistakes, be wrong; hence he will at least be willing to try something that has not been proved by wont to be hopelessly obsolete and inapplicable to conditions as they are because it was adapted to conditions of an earlier day which no longer exist. He can still learn because he will consent to try and can risk being wrong.

The family gives us our first training in the control of the world. This training is not self-control; there are few cases, and they are pathological, in the life of the moral agent where the object of his act is himself. And none where the object of the act is not the corporate person; the object can be the natural individual only as a detail within the corporate personality.

It will thus be the problem of the future family to maintain an organization of persons united by the common task of controlling the objective world in the interest of action, and maintained by the systems of cultural objects which come into existence as a consequence of their action. These cultural objects are essentially ideal, and the largest constituent in their makeup is the mass of value-substance compounded from the feeling life of the persons who act. The two traditional purposes of the family, the internal organization of the personal group based on feeling, and the propagation of the species, will both become incidental and not a part of the end which thought holds out as a goal of family life. Both purposes will therefore be better served vicariously and as an incident of the larger purpose. Family love will thus become objectified as a permanent ingredient in the world because it rests upon a real foundation and not upon the instability of mental states. And the function of procreation will become incidental to the creation of a persistent object and thus be given substance in aesthetic value. Both will then be freed from the sentimental slush and coarse morbidity which have befallen them from their traditional subjective interpretation.

Chapter XVII

Industry as Organized Work

IF WE mean by work the direction of energy by the individual upon the material conditions of existence to the ends of self-preservation, which is as near as anything intelligible could be to the accepted idea of work, then work has no moral significance. For morality, as we have seen, implies that the acts of men inevitably involve the relations of persons to each other and that they never refer to the actor considered as an isolated being. Nor does an act ever refer to a person as the object upon which it issues as end. The person "to" whom an act is done is only a part of a larger whole which is the object in every case. Self-preservation is thus not a moral motive; nor is the "preservation" of an "other" a moral motive; it is neither right nor wrong. For the modes of motion that can have a unique and singular thing for end-term are movements, and we have seen (chapter ii) that movements and actions are generically different. Hence when we speak of work in connection with persons, if we speak of it as a moral term, we necessarily mean to refer to interpersonal relations, actual or ideal, along with the relations in which the person may stand to his world. The simple conception of a workman addressing his energies to the world as presented in his immediate circumstance, his relation to which is mediated by his individual tools and capacities, is an abstract ideal of individualism, and can be true of fact only when fact is selected in accordance with the economic or quantitative principle of wage as a measure of all human relations. No such simplified situation has of course ever existed, nor could in the nature of things ever possibly exist. But we have nevertheless a social and a political and a legal theory based upon the noble blacksmith at his forge, the farmer binding his sheaf, the shepherd feeding his lamb. But as some implication of order is inherent in any real act, or in any act that can be conceived to take place within the realm of fact, morality will have to ignore such isolationist assumptions. All such assumptions rest on the "principle" that work is a primitive necessity, that the world presents to the person the alternative to work or starve, the necessity in the situation absolutely precluding choice or intelligence. Of course no such alternative can be presented to a being that can think. Work, on the contrary, is an expression of a power that is inherent in the internal constitution of the person as integrated with his world; its "necessity" is internal and rational. The agent must work if he is to become and remain a competent moral being; if he is to be all that his capacities imply that he can and should be.

I. WORK AS PRIMITIVE NECESSITY

This theory tells us that work is the response to a stimulus from within us, viz., hunger. It states that "everybody is as lazy as he dare be," that the actor will remain inactive until set in motion by some stimulus of hunger, sex, etc. But there is no need of further stating the viewpoint and less point in criticizing it. It simply has nothing to do with the facts of the active life and ignores the essential distinction between action and movement. Of course I will *move* toward food when I am hungry. But we are assuming that work is an *act*, and an act implies a movement or a series of movements that are directed toward an end by intelligence. Hence it implies a definite type of relationship holding among the various things which the act involves. And the nature of this relationship is precisely what we want to understand in connection with work, since it is upon this relation that the organizability of the processes of work depends and upon the organizability of work that its implications of ends can be justified and explained. The history of work then is an account of the stages through which it passes from the primitive, impulsive movement to the ultimate form of action which it assumes in the moral life. And this historical transition is realized in a progressively developing order among the facts of personal or moral relations. Work is thus the instrument by which man becomes moral; and, considered as action ordered with respect to the objects of its circumstance, it involves intelligence at every stage and degree. And it is the relation to intelligence that gives to work its meaning. We may note the various stages in the development of the relation of work to intelligence. This relation appears in the fact of control.

II. WORK AS SLAVERY

By slavery we mean to refer to that condition of the active agent in which his acts are controlled from without. Intelligence is there, but not within the acts of the agent himself. It means primarily that the acts of the person are directed by another person, that the acts of one person become the private possession of another. The principle by which such a condition is established and maintained is force, which means that the relations among persons are to be maintained without intelligence. But without intelligence the slave cannot act, cannot adapt his movements to prevised ends; nor can the controlling force employ intelligence, since to control the situation the force would have to be addressed to the actor, who by the hypothesis has no intelligence with which to receive the command. The situation in slavery is of course contradictory throughout, since it does not present the conditions of an act, and slavery itself could be maintained even temporarily only by gradually relinquishing the principle upon which it depends and by granting wider and wider fields of freedom and opportunity to the slave. Since force cannot be directed or imposed upon intelligence, it is made effective by controlling the instruments with which men work. But this in itself is a denial of freedom. Two persons cannot be related to each other merely through the machine or tool which they may use in common; and two persons can never be conceived as related in terms of force. The presence of force in a personal relation means the elimination of one or both persons. Hence the slave situation is contradictory throughout, and no place can be found for it in the discussion of morality. The use of force in the relations of persons now is consciously accepted nowhere except in "industry" and in military connections, and neither is recognized as having positive moral significance.

III. WORK AS SERFDOM

The slave is the product of that stage in the development of human relations in which control falls into the hands of the strong individual. It is a product therefore of the private motive, just as the use of force in any case is due to private and specialized motives. The presence of war and "free enterprise" industry in the world means that public purposes are poorly developed or inadequately instrumented and that the dominant force is private advantage somewhere. Force particularizes itself and is appropriate to a private situation only. The beginning of development of the public purpose recognizes this with respect to slavery, and as a consequence the condition of the slave is somewhat mitigated. The more nearly the control of action approaches the public form, the more widely will be extended the person's freedom, at the same time that his acts will be endowed with the public purpose. This is achieved by placing at the disposal of the person the tools that are necessary if he is to give adequate expression to his acts. This means that political organization has progressed beyond individual domination and that ideas of the order of the whole begin to be operative in determining conduct. Work therefore begins to be intelligent in proportion to the degree that order is established in the relations of persons, thus establishing what is called the public life or the public will; and the ends of the moral life begin to appear in objective forms in the products of artisanry, which develop into the genuine works of art later, the models of objectified perfect acts. All this takes place through the growth of intelligence toward a position of control in the relations of persons, and intelligently organized relationships constitute the public body. With the appearance of *wrought* objects, that is, objects that are pure products of work expressing intelligence, there comes into being an objective standard as the basis of the perfection of acts, and this fact is the basis upon which develops the concept of moral principle. But the important thing to note is that authority outside the worker has given way to intelligence within the worker, and with this change there goes the objective condition that gives to moral principle its validity. This condition is the objectified perfect act, the act adequate to its object.

IV. WORK AS INTELLIGENT ORDER

Perhaps the best instance of intelligently organized work is the case of the medieval craft guilds which developed under the influence of the primitive active impulse. Here the work activity of the person came to be free from the external authority of the master, and the activity passed from the state of servility, in which every move must wait upon an external stimulus or permission from the "boss," to the state of service in which the movement was directed by the worker's intelligence upon an object which, as end, was to be the medium of a relation among persons. This object thus becomes, by virtue of its free creation, both the symbol and the means of an exchange of values among persons, which exchange is itself determined as to its limits by the principle of the object's perfection. That is to say, the law is that the object produced must be the perfect embodiment of an act, and all the relations of persons to the object, or of persons to persons as mediated by the object, are controlled in the interest of maintaining the adequacy of the object to the act. The object is then the standard principle of all judgments relating to the act and, as such, the basic law of morality. Work thus is dignified and ennobled, since it has become the very principle of morality and the standard by which the adequacy and competence of acts are to be judged in all fields. And morality implies in this case that the processes of exchange and commerce, and the purposes and uses to which objects are to be put, shall be governed by this principle that objects must remain full and complete embodiments of the acts that create them. Goods, that is to say, are to be valued by reference to the principle of the good, and the principle of the good is that an act models an object which as instrument appropriates or adapts a person to his world. Work thus, as the expression of intelligence in the activities of men with respect to the objects of their common environment, becomes the criterion of the moral worth of acts in general and thus suggests the principle upon which a moral order of persons is possible.

As such, then, work becomes the specifically moral function in that it is a synthesis of all the various personal capacities. It is thus responsible for the internal order of the personal character as well as for the organization of the world of persons in society.

V. WORK AND INDIVIDUALISM

We saw the significance of the principle of freedom from external control in the passing from slavery to a guild organization. It symbolized the process by which a movement becomes a voluntary act, an act whose point of origin is within the actor and not outside, and whose issue is foreseen by the actor and functions as part of the determining cause of the act. With the development of this freedom we see the acts of men acquiring for the first time genuine moral quality, and we are likely to deduce from this that freedom is the only or essential condition of a moral act. In fact, this assumption of freedom has become the basis of many important ethical systems, and no one would doubt its validity if he did not feel fairly certain of extraordinary reasons against it. We have no desire to undervalue the significance of freedom as a moral condition; yet we must observe that the effort to make freedom the sole principle of morality has thrown the entire system of moral concepts into contradiction and that there are very good reasons for regarding the doctrine of freedom with skepticism.

This assumption that freedom is the basis of the personal character, and at the same time the principle of the organization of persons in the active world, is the foundation tenet of individualism. It would not be possible to trace here the development of work through the period of the growth of individualism up to the present time in which it holds exclusive sway in all the affairs of men. We shall have to content ourselves with an analysis of its major concepts and with pointing out the importance which these concepts have had in the moral order of the modern world as well as in the theory of morals.

With respect to work freedom means, in its literal sense, the capacity of the individual to determine for himself and without external hindrance the conditions under which his activities are carried on. That is, he is to decide when, how, how much, where, for what, etc., he is to work, the absoluteness of his decision being limited only by the necessity to adapt the conditions to the equal freedom of another person. It is the consideration of the existence of this *other person,* and the types of relations that are possible between persons, that begin to throw suspicion about the absoluteness of the idea of freedom. This adaptation through the adjustment of the "stipulation of equal freedom" is the phenomenon of *contract,* in which, as a practical concept, freedom takes form in the specific case involving other persons. The "stipulations" are the whole set of contending claims of the two persons and represent the necessity of stating freedom in terms no longer of subjective motives but in terms of objective fact. But the necessity of adapting these objective conditions *to each other,* as a limit to the absoluteness of the person's freedom, as we shall see, throws the doctrine of individual or subjective freedom into confusion at every point. But despite its contradictoriness the doctrine has had enormous positive importance in the development of the modern processes of work and equal importance in the organization of objective life in the political order. Modern industry is a product of this doctrine of contractual freedom, as is also the corresponding form of politics which we call "democracy" and the religious system of Protestantism. But the contradictoriness of contractual freedom has been uniformly overlooked. The contradictoriness lies in the fact that the spontaneity of the subjective agent is all used up in matching the "stipulations" or objective conditions. By the time the terms of the contract are agreed upon the contracting *parties* have become unimportant, and the contract is an ordered relation within and among objective facts. This contradiction lies in the two opposite assumptions that the term connotes, viz., that freedom is merely the impulsive character of the individual's mental states, his "spontaneity," and that freedom is the sum of objective circumstances which as opportunities determine what shall be the content of his acts.

This ambiguous concept of contractual freedom has been the most potent influence in creating the peculiar form of institutionalization that the processes of work have taken on in modern times. That is, it has created industrialism, with its mass production, its collectivizing of persons, its concentration of power and authority and of life and effort in small areas. It has thus organized the objective conditions of freedom in a way that separates those conditions from any necessary connection with the personal motive to action. This has meant that these objective conditions have been independently organized, as have also the personal or subjective conditions, the two becoming contending forces. And as a conflict between forces means that one must give way if there is to be movement at all, the "control" or "free" motive has come to be expressed through the objective and external things of the work process as these things have come to be organized in the institution of property. The material of work, and its tool or instrument, the machine, have taken full control of the process and the purpose, with the consequence that "organized industry," completely devoid of purposive foresight and sensuously blind, has fallen into the ditch.

VI. WORK AND THE UNION: THE COMBINATION OF PERSONS

This concentration of the material conditions of freedom in the institution of industry modified profoundly the traditional institution of property and made it necessary for some similar combination to be effected among the persons who work. Property, which traditionally was the system of personal means to action, now is organized in the corporate impersonal form as a means of control. It was with the purpose to match the power of property with an equal power that the persons of industry were organized in the union. The important result of this development was that the worker was separated from his tools, which now have a purpose different from his own. It is in this way that the severance of personal "rights" from property "rights" became complete. The labor union is the response to the demand to balance once more the personal with the property right. And the two now discordant elements of the full freedom which work implies find themselves each organized into a body whose main purpose is opposition to the other. Thus we have the "capital-labor problem," in which the relations between the two are all conceived in terms of force as objectified in the "right" of property, where "right" is subjectively interpreted to mean ownership or, in symbols of force, possession. Both sides have exactly the same policy and proceed in accordance with the same theories and by the same methods toward the same ends; both are seeking domination, so their ends are inherently contradictory. Since they accept force as principle, they assume that the purpose of any good is to be used *up*, to be exhausted in the use, and its substance transformed into the symbols of power. Power then rests upon the destruction of goods; and waste, both of power and goods, is the characteristic "product" of industry. Power as authority to command is thus the object of force, it is merely force objectified and reserved as the instrument for further transforming of goods into power. This process of transforming goods into the symbols and instruments of power is known as exploitation. It is to be noted that it is essentially destructive, that it assumes that what it exploits is already a good, that the purpose of the good is nothing more than to be the instrument to power, and that the purpose of work is either to create goods or to transform goods into power. The good thus exists to be used up, destroyed, and the highest purpose of power is to control the process of work by which the good is destroyed, thus increasing power without limit. The "collapse" of industry is thus not an accident but is inherent in its very nature. Naturally industry does not consciously accept such assumptions. But as we saw above it does not consciously accept anything; what intelligence there is in it is exhausted in the struggle for control, so as a whole it is essentially purposeless and blind. This prostitution of the work function is called "business"; the perversity of intellect which writes its apology is called "economic science."

In the development of industry as organized work under these negative and destructive conditions the stages through which it passes are interesting and instructive. In the first of these stages the good to be transformed into power was nature. Nature spread before man what seemed to him inexhaustible supplies of goods which were merely to be taken and used up. Resources of metals, timber, soils, etc., were there waiting to be used. These resources were transformed into the first significant power over nature that had ever been accomplished, and the possession of this power stimulated the desire for more. Also the organization and implementing of this power in the instruments through which it was acquired and in which it was stored increased its efficacy by many times its original force. But the principle that the good is to be used up soon led to the point where natural goods were relatively exhausted, that is, the portion of them remaining was not sufficient to absorb the enormous power which the exploited part had created. Hence new sources of good had to be discovered. It is to be kept in mind that, in the view of "industry," the good is that which is capable of being exploited or transformed into power. The next available type of good, the one most easily, that is, cheaply, available, and one which is in nature already partially transformed into power, is human energy, the physical strength and capacities of human beings. Industry then set about the exploitation of human energy, set out to use up and transform human energy into institutionalized power. The result shortly reached was that man's physical resources were absorbed in the industrial machine, and the remnant of the human body was left with its characters measurable only in terms of fatigue and the power to consume, that is, in terms of what it lacks, wants, and what would maintain it in a minimum of existence. Even the wants become a property convertible into power. This is the ground and cause of the universal poverty and suffering that have attended the "development" of industry.

With man prostrate, his energies, that is, the goods which are his by nature, transformed into abstract power, the industrial motive had to look for further worlds to conquer. Nature and man are now transformed. There remains therefore but one existing source of goods that are not already destroyed to make way for power. This is the sphere of culture, whose substance has lately been discovered to possess rich possibilities for destruction. There exist ready to be transformed into property and power vast resources in religion and the church, in education and the school, in the state and government, in aesthetic activity and in art, in spiritual goodness and morality. These are rapidly being exhausted, that is, used up as the materials of power, and there shortly will be left nothing for power to do except to expend its energies upon itself, in which the final "good" will be accomplished in universal confusion. This self-destructive use of power, the exploitive force exploiting itself, is now well under way in universal war.

These consequences are inevitable so long as work is viewed under the ambiguous concept of freedom—so long, that is, as freedom is confused as to whether its content lies within the sphere of mere states of mind, on the one hand, or, on the other hand, in the objective conditions of and to action. This is conceived on the one side as the abstract absence of hindrances to a state of mind being felt, the freedom *from* an unsatisfactory inner state; and on the other the concrete presence of external things which are appropriate to the task of giving form and body to the state of mind through action, the freedom *through* access to property objects. Freedom in the one sense is the vacuum in which a state of mind can be conceived. This is "political freedom." In the other it is a concrete structure made up of the physical and cultural means to action. This is moral freedom. One is subjective freedom; the other, objective freedom. An adequate economic theory would state the conditions appropriate to each case and demonstrate the necessity of the latter.

VII. INDUSTRY POLITICALLY ORGANIZED

But this alternative of subjective or objective freedom does not exhaust the possibilities, if we care to go beyond the economic considerations to their grounds in ethical principle. There is still the possibility of ordered freedom, in which the subjective factor—purpose—and the obective factor—property—may be brought to some degree and kind of harmony. We have seen that industry, or the system of organized work, when organized on a basis of its own technical processes and principles, is self-contradictory. Is there another possible type of organization in which the technical competence of its instruments and processes may be saved while ridding them of their pretense to the status of principle, with their consequence in the vicious predatory motive? We are facing a condition where work, the very instrument through which we hope to accomplish our moral ends, has turned upon us and threatens to destroy us. Yet there can be no doubt that work is the characteristic activity of moralized man. An "industrial society" seems doomed; is a "socialized industry" possible? If so, what is the proper instrument through which it may be accomplished?

Individualism finds the unit of reality on which the order of life depends in what is unique, exclusive, peculiar to the individual. Socialism finds it in the group of individuals. We suggest that both are false to the facts and false in principle. Both neglect the objective condition of order; they depend upon the pseudo-principle of privacy. Let us consider the possibility of order as based on the concept of the public embodiment of purpose in the objects that are the appropriate instruments to the expression of purpose. Purpose, the substance of subjective freedom, and property, the substance of objective freedom, may possibly be brought together in the good.

How in detail this objective good is to be accomplished in practice is the problem of practical politics and is beyond our province. But what is to be done and why, and what are the principles and guiding rules to be followed, are questions of theoretical politics, that is, morals. Ethics will therefore tell us the logical formulations of concepts which will be adequate to embody this content of the objective good consistently with principle; how, that is, we must think if there are to be any purposes realized at all.

An act, let us recall, is the expenditure of energy by a person to the end of transforming a thing into an object or end by the use of means or tools. Tools are generally end-objects that have resulted from previous acts. Their peculiar importance comes from the fact that they, being end-objects of previous acts, are permanent means to ends, so that the use of a tool is continuous in the production of many objects. The plow, for example, may be used by many different persons for many seasons and turn the soil to produce a crop for each. And all the time it is a model for the making of plows. So also a book may be read by many persons and kept as a permanent tool for the use of many generations of men. It can also be reproduced or copied. It is this fact that makes their importance: they, being usable by all, are independent of any subjective or personal reference. And the principle that controls their use is obvious: they should be of free access to all who are competent to use them, ready to produce any object consistent with their design that any person may find to be involved in his purposes. But with the peculiar development of our legal notions of the appropriation of objects, we have these objects under the control of persons who use them to produce still more objects which they may control or who may not use them at all. But their control over them is such that they prevent their use by anyone else or allow them to be used only on terms that restrict the user's freedom and increase the owner's power. Also, those who control objects of use can, by withdrawing them from use, acquire control of the objects that are produced, so that the stimulus to the production of any object may be stultified at any time. Thus this peculiar type of control of objects results in the denial of them to the use of those whose purposes depend upon them, and the object as a means defeats the very purpose for which it is intended.

All these results follow from our peculiar notions about the control of objects of use. These notions are to the effect that control is the special privilege of the person who happens to have come upon the object first; to have had the privilege given him by someone, for example, his ancestor; or to have been able by ruse or trick to acquire it from the producer. Control, that is, is in every case personal and private, and its incidence is shifted from objects to persons, and is to be exerted by one person over the actions of other persons. But this we saw to be a violation of the principle of freedom, so it cannot be what control should mean. The most important problem with which we

have to deal, in the political organization of society, is how to im-
personalize and objectify the principle of control. The industrialization of society has brought it about that control is essentially a function of property. This is in opposition to traditional theory, for which
control is a function of subjective purpose. The change in viewpoint
may give us a new clue—the suggestion that control is a public function exercised through the relations of persons to property, with a
view to the order of the whole.

This is the question of how to make property public in the relation
of control so as to guarantee access to its use to any person whose
moral ends demand it. It is the question, that is, as to the *free object*,
how to free the object from the restrictive control of power so as
to be accessible to persons. This is once more a question of practical
politics, and we need not speculate on the types of answers that have
been suggested. Suffice it to say that the method employed in the past
has been to guarantee that persons may *not* have free opportunity to
objects; it has been that of the suppression of public right in the interest of private power and authority. Whether this method will work
in reverse, that is, whether private power and authority may be controlled in the interest of public right, remains to be seen. But it is the
one condition of a moralized society, and a first ground of the continued existence of society.

VIII. WORK AS AESTHETIC ACTIVITY AND THE OBJECT OF ART

The object of work is, ideally, this free object. It is called the object
of art. But the aesthetic object and the aesthetic act are but special
instances of the moral object and act. Or, if we prefer not to raise the
question of the relation of the moral to the aesthetic object, we may
say that they are of the same kind; both have this character of freedom. They are neither of them qualified or limited in any way by
forces outside the active situation in which they are created. Both
have their meaning as the fulfilment of acts that are characteristic of
the person. They are then ends, both in the sense that they represent
the completion of the act, that they bring the act to issue, and in the
sense that there is nothing beyond the object toward which the subjective freedom of the act can aspire. The object produced by work
then is a typical good; is good in itself in the sense that it is of the
kind to which all ideas of good refer for their meaning. Its good is in
itself in that it is the objectified, realized relation of the person to his
world. If its goodness were made dependent upon something else to

which it is the instrument, it as object could never be complete but would remain forever the occasion for further action, and it is the appearance of "never getting anywhere" that gives to the practical life too often the sense of futility. Action must find an object in which it may be whole, and if this object is never found outside or external to the act, then it must embody or objectify itself in the act. And the perfect instance of the good act is that which achieves for itself a beautiful and competent body, an object in which it is perfected as its own end.

But in order that the subjective freedom of the person may be thus realized in the creation of perfect objects, there must be present the external conditions which make it possible. These conditions are found in the system of circumstances which furnish the materials and occasion for action. The creation of the good implies this system as the substance of objective freedom.

IX. THE MORAL STATE

This system of objective freedom is the moral state. It is the organization of existing natural and cultural goods within the scheme of freedom in such a way that persons shall always have the occasion and the opportunity and the means to significant action. Both this occasion and this opportunity are provided by the control of existing goods without regard to the acts or purposes of specific persons. Occasion and opportunity to action depend upon the control of goods on and by principle, that is, by law and not subjective caprice. This is control through public purpose in the interest of ends and the types of acts that produce ends. It is within this system of public objects that all the types of cultural objects are brought to appropriateness or fitness to each other and through this appropriateness of objects that the harmony of purposes is achieved. This condition is called "peace" and represents the order of life in which the relations of persons are harmonized through the objects in which they are mediated. This is the moral polity, the corporate organization of life in the state of culture.

Chapter XVIII

Education and the Organization
of Intelligence

IN THE chapters on the subjective virtues we saw that the good
life presupposes intelligence at every point and in every relation
in the life of the person. It was necessary also to assume that the individual's first and most fundamental obligation is the obligation to
know. This implies that he is to be endowed by nature and culture
with a competent intelligence. And the control of natural and cultural forces in the interest of assuring competent individuals seemed
to be a function of institutional organization. The organization for
the production of persons intellectually competent is the school. We
have here the task of showing that education is a moral function and
that, as such, it is instrumented and objectified in the public school.
We wish to inquire also what sort of institution the school must be
if it is to produce persons of the highest degree of intellectual competence, for, if our first obligation is the obligation to know, then the
development and cultivation of intelligence is our most important
moral function.

What we want to ask in this chapter is, therefore, what the nature
of the educative process is, what the basic ideas or concepts that
govern that process are, and what type of organization will best embody the process consistently with its moral purpose.

What, then, is the nature of the educative process when considered as a moral function? We can state the answer briefly by saying
(1) that education is the act of inquiring into the nature and value of
things and takes the form of communication among persons; (2) that
its basic concepts are the principles and laws by respect to which the
process of communication carries a content of truth; and (3) that the
process requires an organization that is appropriate to express the
ideas and embody the symbols of truth communication in their most
adequate form.

Before entering upon the discussion of these topics let us make as clear as we may be able just what we mean by the intelligent person and by the obligation that is involved in knowledge. We ordinarily think of a person as possessing capacities that are peculiar and unique, qualities of himself independently of any of his relations to his fellows or his world. We say that a certain man has great capacities but that he never uses them. But, as we have seen, capacities are negligible and practically nonexistent, certainly meaningless, apart from their use. It is only in the fact that man sustains perceptible relations to his outer world that we can know that he has capacities, even if such relations are no more than those involved in speech, etc. That is to say that in discussing the capacities of the individual we have to keep in mind the typical forms of objects and situations in his world and to judge of his capacities on a basis of the characters of these objects and situations in so far as we observe them to be modified by his presence among them. If my being present in a given situation makes no difference to the qualities of objects or to the organization of the situation, then whether I possess a given capacity or not cannot be determined. Then, so far as a man's active nature is concerned, the man must be considered as one fact within the totality of facts and relations that constitute his world if his capacities are to be described objectively and in terms of action. All qualities and characters and capacities must be describable in terms of action if they are to be considered moral.

All this applies literally to the capacity of knowing. But the distinctive thing about knowing is that its objects, and its objective world, are for the most part ideal. This is especially true with respect to situations involving action; these must be set up and organized in ideal terms *before* they can be materialized in action. Even the position and movements of the actor have to be represented ideally, in the imagination of the actor, before they are expressed. The capacity to know, then, is the capacity ideally, and antecedently to their existence, to set up orders and systems of fact in the expectation that action will realize them in perceptible form. Knowledge, that is, is essentially imaginative and projective; and, while its images are representations of existing fact, yet it disregards presented limitations of existence and projects its objects into the future and the ideal. The ideas in which my knowing is expressed are always of objects as they are, it is true, but also as they can or may be. In knowing a stone, I perceive or image it as it is, but also as the object I could chisel out of it or the object I could build it into; it presents itself to me as a bit of sculpture or as an element in an arch. Its qualities are symbolic expressions of the forms and orders I can fit it into, the objects I could make it into or make it a part of.

Now, it is just these objective relations, both ideal and perceptual, of the person and their possibilities of control, that are the tangible data of education, the facts within which the education process moves. The assumption that education makes is that there is an organic relation between these facts and the inner processes and functions of the individual mind, so that, if you control the relations among objective facts, you not only determine their qualities but you also modify the inner makeup and arrangement of the mind to which the facts are present and thus determine the qualitative form of the mind. The capacity for knowledge in the abstract is, then, the capacity of the mind to adapt itself to objects; to make itself up after the plan and structure of presented objects; its "presence" among these objective facts is merely the fact that it has been assumed or observed in terms of relations of the facts. Concretely, the capacity for knowledge is the power of mind, through the instrument of the body and its movements, to change or adapt objects to each other and to itself, after its own makeup has represented the qualitative and other relations of presented objects. As education is conceived to be concerned with the development of these inner or mental functions, the educative process will be the process in which we undertake the control of the external facts and their relations, which are the mental functions in the form in which they have existence in perception. The assumption of education is thus that, if you can shape the organic or outward movements of the individual with respect to his environing object system, you thereby determine the quality and organization of his mind and that the "capacities" of the individual are nothing but abstract symbolic representations of this quality and organization.

The intelligent person which we seek through education is the person conceived as complete in himself but as being so through the fact that he is, when we think of him in terms of mind and capacity, the synthesis of his objective circumstance, which his own inner unity represents. This inner unity, which is the type of all order and organization in the external world of fact, is expressed in language, and language becomes the medium of communication, which, we have seen, is the substance of the educative process. Of course we are taking language in the broad sense, but as a technical process education takes the form of language in the narrower sense. It is the expression of the inner unity of mind in symbols of the world of fact. The effort to divide the educative process into education of the intelligence, of the will, of "character," and of the emotions is misleading, therefore; the "mental function" to be educated is the intelligence as the unity of mind or the common cognitive thread which runs through all manifestations of mind. And the degree of its educational perfection is the degree of order and unity observable in its fact world. The first obligation, therefore, of the moral individual, is the obligation to know, to maintain the cognitive unity of his being within the changing features of his circumstance.

A. The Educational Function

The educational function is the control and direction of the process of communication in the interest of producing intelligent persons. Communication is effected through the common environment of persons and things, and this common environment expresses the cognitive interest of persons as the unity of their individual lives and at the same time the condition of unity for their common life. The substance of morality, then, educationally speaking, is the system of these objective relations which constitute at the same time the "character" of the person and the matter of social life.

The description of these matters may therefore be made rather brief. The education process will be a manipulation and control of the objective relations of persons, under as highly favorable specialized conditions as possible, as these relations are being expressed through things common to persons. It is a process of bringing experience into the laboratory and of testing and recording its qualities and characters. The laboratory is the school, and the apparatus are the various symbolic forms of language in which experience is embodied. The persons involved are the teacher and the student; and the relations between teacher and student, and among students, that are offered us for description are represented in the qualities free, public, universal, and objective, which characterize personal relations under the special conditions of the school.

The teacher and the pupil are distinguished mainly by the fact that, with respect to experience of the subject matter of the learning in a given case, the one is mature and the other relatively immature. The technique of the relation is a matter for the education expert to describe, and, unfortunately, one which he has yet to describe with any degree of accuracy. But the question of the general conditions under which the education process can be made most effective is a matter for ethics to determine, and for politics to provide, in the sense that the conditions imply a reference to the whole structure of life. That is, the standard or rule by which these conditions are to be determined is the principle of the whole good. If it be a matter of the time or place, or extent or quality of instruction, or the general method to be followed, or any such matter of procedure, the answer to the question is found by observing what effect the procedure will have or is likely to have on the whole life. If it be argued that this makes the question difficult, and perhaps uncertain, the reply is that questions of educational procedure are much more profound and obscure than has as yet been recognized, it may be because of the element of chance which we have found must be recognized as constituent to experience in any case.

I. FREEDOM

One of the conditions presupposed in the teaching-learning process is that of freedom. This is known and recognized and has been for a long time. But what has not been so fully recognized is that freedom means a number of things that are very different. The most obvious of these is that the education function cannot be made subject to the external control of authority. Nobody can tell another how or what to teach or, in the last analysis, how or what to learn. The relation between teacher and learner should have as its end-terms the free spontaneity or curiosity of both. Anything short of that will deaden the whole process. This means two important things. One is that the theory that learning depends upon the "interest" of the learner is true only when interest means free curiosity, which it perhaps never properly does. It is not true when the word means some specialized reference to the learner's private concerns, and this is what it almost invariably does mean. This disposes of "vocational" education, which is not education but training; not an appeal to spontaneous curiosity but an attempt to deaden this curiosity in the interest of routine.

The other meaning of the rule of free spontaneity is that it disposes of "supervision" of the teaching or learning of individuals. What supervision therefore is possible is a control over the machinery of the process, and this can rarely be advantageous. Neither the teaching nor the learning can ever be vicarious; no one can ever do it for another. And while it may be possible for an experienced teacher to suggest useful elements of technique to a less mature teacher, the use of them or rejection of them cannot be enjoined.

But the largest point of meaning of freedom in connection with education is what is called freedom of mind from the annoyances which hinder concentration. The worst enemy of education is the distraction of mind caused by poverty, insecurity, disease, etc., and by athletics and other irrational "social" functions. No one who is hungry or in fear of losing his job, or sick, or on the team, is in condition to do intellectual work.

2. PUBLIC PURPOSE

Another condition of the learning-teaching relation is that it must be public. This means that it must be motivated from first to last and at every point by the public purpose. It can never become the instrument of private interests. Private influence upon education reduces it to propaganda. Of course it is true that the "public" school under the authority of government is not necessarily dominated by the public motive. The public motive is not necessarily that represented in governmental agencies. It is the motive of the whole good which we have seen is the heart of the meaning of morality. It is true that education might, for a time, at least, effectively express the public motive while yet under private influence. This would be true and possible if the private influence were identical with the public purpose, or it could be true in so far as the private or personal influence should become genuinely moral. This however implies the possibility of the identity of the private with the public motive, which has proved a doubtful maxim when applied in practice.

If it is argued that, as a matter of fact, privately motivated schools are sometimes freer than public schools, the reply is that this is true. But it is an accident; the private motive cannot be reduced to rule, and there is no rational control or direction that can be given it. The public motive can be directed—its direction can be known and its course predicted and anticipated. If it be argued that free inquiry is dangerous, the reply is that it is—to that which does not have truth enough to defend itself. But freedom is irresponsible; yes, but its results are irresponsible only so long as they have not materialized, and until then they are ineffective. Freedom is never effective until it is real and true, until it has become rationalized and made effective in institutional form. But then it is not dangerous. The freedom that is dangerous is the lawless caprice of the individual.

3. UNIVERSALITY

Education should be universal. By this it is not meant that there shall be a schoolhouse in every so much territory, or a teacher for every so many children. It means that every person shall have full and free access to all the conditions that make for a developed character. And the mere presence of a schoolhouse and a teacher, however externally adequate and attractive they may be, are only slight parts of the total conditions required. There must be present to every child, as the medium within which he grows up, an atmosphere of culture that will stimulate his curiosity about significant things and tax his intelligence to its last ounce of energy. The world must be peopled with good persons whose every suggestion is toward the cultivation of the inquiring mind. This cultural medium must be there and sustained within a system of permanent institutions. It is these institutions that are at present most sadly lacking.

The worst defect of our moral world at present is the lack of access to the material means to a developed mind and character. This is due to irrational cultural institutions. It is not true that, as we have become economically prosperous and politically and legally free and religiously enlightened and aesthetically refined, more and more persons have increased access to cultural conditions. The reverse is nearer true. It is even charged that, as our wealth increases, the smaller the proportion of persons that have access to its cultural possibilities. As our freedom broadens, fewer and fewer persons know what to do with it. As our spiritual outlook grows, we are tempted by more and more insidious follies. But educational opportunities should be free to everyone to make of himself all that he has it in him to be. And when we give positive meaning to our opportunities, we see that they are in all cases realized only in these economic, political, legal, and religious conditions. Among these the most important condition is that the moral agent should not be forced to exhaust his youth and his capacities in the mere necessity to keep alive or to support persons who should never be dependent upon him. The worst moral tragedy in the world at present is the spectacle of an immature person working to make a living or to support himself or dependents. Education is not universal so long as the cultural structure of life denies to him the means, which includes the leisure, whereby he may develop his mind.

B. The Educational Method

The method of education consists of two rather simple systems of principles. These are (1) a general method, consisting of a few elementary propositions respecting the nature of the mental life as it

operates in teacher and learner, and (2) a special method, or a set of
maxims representing modifications of the operations of mind to adapt
them to the peculiarities of specific subject matters.

<h3 align="center">1. GENERAL METHOD</h3>

The general method consists of the principles which embody the
results of psychology in so far as these relate to the dynamics of mind
or treat of mind as an active agent. They are not immediately usable
as rules or maxims governing the details of teaching or learning but
are rather ideals or standards which maintain the proper attitude of
the teacher and the learner to the problems which the active mind
must face with respect to its own procedures.

In many ways the most important of these principles of general
method is this: *Mind always acts through its body and is known only
in and through its actions.* This principle means that mind never acts
directly upon its object but can act only through the movements of
the organism and the objects with which the organism comes in contact. All we can know of the mind must come through a knowledge
of the objects and instruments of the mind within the environment,
the most important of which is the human body itself. This is an important principle and is frequently misunderstood. It does not involve
ethical pragmatism, or behaviorism, or even utilitarianism. What it
means is that the "idea" or mental factor involved in action is continuous and identical with the movements of the object which action
equally implies. The *act* is itself the expression of this continuity and
identity. So the "idea" or "motive," and the organic processes and
the object, are all aspects of the one self-identical act, and the argument as to which of them is the key to the character of the act misses
the point of their relations. But practically the principle means that
we can deal with the mind only as manifest through objects and
processes in the act, so that the unity of idea and object in the act
becomes the subject matter for ethics and education alike.

The second principle states that *mind always acts as a whole or as
a unity and is known only as such.* This means essentially that all the
"mental" phases of the active situation are involved where any one of
them is present. When the mind acts, it is the whole mind that acts
and never a part of it. Every object which I know is, in the com-
pletest case, a point around which all the activity of my whole mind
centers. It is this fact of the reference of all aspects of the mind to an
object whenever any one aspect refers to the object, that is the secret
of the organization of the mind. Naturally it must be kept in mind

that by object as the center of the mind's organization we do not mean the physical object in every case, although it is likely that the physical object is the origin and archetype of all objects. But the unity of mind as conditioned upon objects suggests to us, as a corollary of this second principle, the definition of the mind as the active unity which exhibits itself in and comprehends the organization of objects in our world. Thus the very definition of mind is most effectively put in terms of objects, and this makes unnecessary and superfluous the question as to the peculiar relation between mind and its object and relieves ethics of the burdens of epistemology. It also makes unnecessary the question as to which aspect of mind it is that determines the moral quality of the act, since the act and its quality are not determined by any mental process. There seems thus no point to the search for motives and springs to action; ethics is not empirical psychology.

The third principle states that *mind, as essentially active, completes itself or makes itself up in the objects of the external or practical world and is controlled only through the manipulation of the objects of the practical world.* This principle shows that the object is definable in terms of mind as well as mind in terms of the object. An object is the terminus and corporate embodiment of an idea or act of mind; it is the idea realized. This is the feature of the mind-life that furnishes the basis for educational theory so far as that theory involves special method. It includes two great truths. (*a*) The first is that mind is complete and fully developed only when it embodies itself in corporate form, that is, when it creates for itself a body which is the appropriate instrument or organ of its action through which alone it can act completely. Of course there are many auxiliary instruments to action which may be regarded as extensions of the body functions, that is, the physical tools which the moral agent uses. The sum of all these tools constitutes the material of the work life and in this special connection is called the "system of property." The same objects in another relation constitute the aesthetic world, etc. But all show how the moral person is, through the act, made continuous with his world: the world is the ultimate object which the person means. (*b*) The second truth embodied in the law is that the control of men and of human affairs generally is effected through the manipulation of these property-objects. Control is then the practical act of mind as corporately individuated. It is upon the layout of these objects that the organization of human life is effected, since they constitute the substantial element in institutions. This is the principle therefore from which we should approach all questions of order and organization of men in society, and this question involves, for its full comprehension, the whole list of what are called the "social sciences." Thus history, politics, law, economics, even religion and ethics, all find their ultimate practical principle in this statement. In all researches where the interrelations of human beings are the subject matter, the principle through which that subject matter can be best approached is this simple proposition that the external world is the object involved in the act of man. This makes all the "social" or human disciplines dependent upon ethics. It will accordingly be found that any imperfection in these disciplines will be ethical—they all fail where they are not squarely planted upon their ethical foundation.

2. SPECIAL METHOD

Special method involves the adaptation of these ideas of general method to the subject matters of specialized subjects. In a highly abstract subject such as logic the fact that the mind acts only through its body is a little hard to see, but it is probably agreed that even the most abstract of ideas are mediated through some form of image, and an image is for the mind a direct transcript of the object it represents. It is also probable that in the formation of the idea the nervous structures operate very definitely, even if no expression in the muscular system appears. The only point we need to make here is to observe that the principle of special method has already been suggested, viz., that the approach to any special field of study is a matter of acquaintance of the student with the object-system peculiar to that field. But the working-out of these matters is the task of education theory.

C. The Organization of the Educational Process

What is required for the organization of education is simply to find and furnish to the process as above described the proper and appropriate material instruments and means. And the principle is that the materials shall be adapted to the requirements of the process and not the process to the materials. It is this latter condition—that the process of education is compelled to accommodate itself to the artificial and accidental conditions of the means supplied—that constitutes the basis of much criticism of the education system of today. It is this same condition which creates the autocratic "administrator" and furnishes him a fertile field in which to sow the seeds of confusion. The school system is top-heavy with a horde of superintendents and supervisors and principals, so much so that it is a rare teacher that can instil an element of life into the work under the burden of deadening authority. This is the explanation also of the continuous weakening of the curriculum with triviality and horseplay, from the kindergarten to the college. The learner gets no notion from his school career as to what work means, and the intellectual effort and the self-control required to make that effort effective are unknown to him. Consequently, fraud and chicanery are often resorted to in order to achieve the results that should come from work, and the moral basis of the child's intellectual life is broken down in the very process through which his intelligence is supposed to be developed and trained.

But the school in these matters is merely taking over for itself the methods and attitudes which it finds ready-made in the social structure within which it exists. Instead of dictating to the social structure the methods and procedures and principles and norms on a basis of which the social structure could maintain a healthy existence, the school accepts for its own the blundering catch-as-catch-can scheme that it finds about it. It should be continuously examining the grounds upon which the organization of life rests and suggesting new principles as the changed conditions of life demand them.

It is not our business here to suggest a system of organization for the school. But it is our duty to insist that if the school is to give life and expression to the moral purpose to furnish to the world of action a sufficiency of intelligent persons, then its organization must embody the principles of work and freedom and publicity and universality which we described above.

D. Specialization and Technique

It is this influence of an irrational practical life-system within which the educational function must operate that is responsible for the peculiar and objectionable forms which the educational motive takes. A social "system" which robs life of all its essential values leaves the individual no choice but to try to find, by hook or crook, a place within the system where he can secure for himself the necessities of mere existence. And he must accept and adopt the methods which the "system" prescribes. He has no choice. Hence he must "specialize" his activities, which, if we would honestly face the issues involved, means that he strips his activities of all their moral quality. For the moral quality of an act is just its reference to the whole which the act wills to create, and this element of wholeness is precisely what his action lacks in so far as it is specialized. Instead therefore of developing his whole capacity, or all his capacities, he is obliged to neglect most of them in the interest of the exaggeration of the capacity by which he finds the scrap upon which he may exist. The college student must "major" in some subject from which he is to derive his living, the idea being, apparently, that he should get the materials of his culture from fragments that he picks up on the side as he pursues a livelihood. But his "major" and his "specialty" mean that he has got certain fragments of capacity which he is to offer for sale; they are not to be used as creative cultural functions. His "education" becomes commercialized, which means that it loses its moral function. In education we do not aim at producing moral persons but human machines; not agents capable of complete acts but "agents" who sell themselves as implements which repeat a movement indefinitely. We do not produce a man whose whole act creates a house but a salesman who puts together building material for sale. Morality requires that education produce men who can build houses that can take their place in a beautiful and happy city, not that will stand up until they can be sold. The act is whole and morally right only when its object is capable of becoming a part of the end. This is the principle by which we judge every act.

E. Practice

This specialized and exaggerated, one-sided and unbalanced, "capacity" is the ideal of technique. Its meaning is the polar opposite of what is meant by morality. That is to say, technique, instead of being a basic moral function or a moral function at all, is a nonmoral instrument designed to be used by the moral purpose, and is therefore a contradiction. But as so used its meaning lies in the fact that it intervenes between a purpose and an end, it becomes a perfect specimen of an instrument or tool where the word "tool" is used in the invidious sense.

It is this commitment to specialization and technique, made necessary by an economic system that came into existence by the accidents of history, that has been responsible for our false conceptions of practice and the practical life. The real practical life is the moral life, the life of action brought to harmony and order by intelligence, in which each of the various special interests, economic, biological, religious, etc., finds its appropriate relation to the others and its place in the whole. But our prevailing conception of the practical is the precise opposite of this. It assumes that a practical motive reaches its perfection when it detaches itself from other motives and, with conscious and purposive disregard of any genuine end, attains the specific result for which it strives. But this is to neglect the fact that a *result* is an *end* only and precisely when it is the bearer of values whose substance lies within the relations which the abstract result stands in to other facts. The value of a result is not a property of the result. It is an aspect of the relations in which the result stands to other facts. In the absence of the other facts and relations the result is empty of meaning and can never be satisfying. Consequently, a "society" which is essentially "practical" will be dominated by wants and needs, its life lies in what it lacks and what in the possession can never satisfy, since it creates to infinity a series of false desires and a series of monstrosities to satisfy the desires.

But a real practice, morality, sees its end in the whole of life, the good, from which each result derives the qualities which give it its character as end. It is of course true that this "whole" is not itself *an* end, not a particular goal among others and differing from them in remoteness and abstract greatness. It is *the* end. And this means that it is the principle by which all action is guided and by which the values of all specific ends find their proper relation to each other.

F. Summary

Thus is education culturally perhaps the most important of the "worlds" into which the person is born and in which he lives his life. It is important because it is from it that the person obtains the capacities upon which the direction of his life depends. The moral function of education lies then in the fact that the educative process is the instrument to moral accomplishment. It is the very essence of education that it should open up to us the abundant life, and this life consists primarily in the wisdom by which we see things in their proper relativity of value. Its purpose is then to prepare us for life; but life is not the biological and economic process only. The life for which it should prepare is that which adds to the natural existence the abundance of the cultural, which enables us to see in the good person the good world. The latter is nothing more or less than the orderly whole of all the activities and objects necessary to sustain the act by which it is created. It is this act which is the end, the ultimate object, the good which morality contemplates.

Chapter XIX

Religion and the Organization of Faith

ANOTHER important "world" in which the person lives and through which he finds some of his rarer forms of expression is religion and its institution, the church. It is therefore a moral world, and the peculiar quality with which it endows life must be described and its place discovered within the good.

Religion derives its moral status from the fact that it deals with ends and the capacities by which those ends are achieved. In its peculiar approach to ends it also brings into prominence certain capacities which would otherwise perhaps remain dormant in life or tend to disappear. It is these ends and capacities which we have to describe here, and we must point out their place within the whole. We saw that education is concerned with the intellectual capacities, as industry with the physical and the family with the biological. In a similar way religion deals with the emotional or feeling capacities of men. These it rationalizes, in so far as their peculiar content will permit, and thus subjects them to moral direction. Also, it provides certain means and instruments through which the feeling capacities are to be expressed, and in the system of which means the feelings are made objective and real elements of the world of fixed values.

I. FEELING AS AN END FUNCTION

Feeling is the capacity to determine by anticipation the experience *content* of ends. It is thus a companion function with the imagination, by which the *form* of the experience of ends is anticipated. What, exactly, in terms of immediate experience, is to be the meaning of an end that is set up by the intellect cannot be determined by intellect in advance of the end's being accomplished. To know precisely what an end is to mean before it has been realized is beyond the capacity of intelligence in its ordinary discursive form. Yet what the end is to be after action has realized it constitutes the only standard by which action may be adapted to, and guided toward, the realization of the end. In order to select forms of action, and in order to choose means and instruments appropriate to a projected end, the meaning of the end, in terms of its future empirical content, must somehow be known in advance of its existence. It is feeling that gives us this insight into the meaning of ends before they are accomplished. This insight we must have in order intelligently to determine the types of acts and the kinds of means necessary to achieve the end desired.

Thus our ordinary intelligence, in the form of imagination, can disclose to us in advance of existence the abstract form and design of an end. But it cannot tell us what in terms of immediate experience shall be the content of that end. It can never say, in advance of realization, whether an end, when realized, will be desirable and satisfactory. It may be known in advance as acceptable, but never as satisfying, since assent is an act of the intellect, while valuing is not. It is through feeling that ends, which are abstract forms or designs of real objects for the intellect, become meanings, or have value.

But this means that feeling is a variant aspect of the cognitive function, just as all mental processes are forms of the noetic act, and that its immediate insight into the nature of nonpresent objects is a primitive form of knowledge. It is a form of knowledge similar and corresponding to the scientist's prediction. It is also akin to the leap by which intellect sees a type in a mass of particulars in induction, or to the flight by which intelligence passes from one idea or judgment to another in inference. In a similar way feeling reaches into the future and the nonexistent to determine what a sentient being shall experience when it has passed the hazards of time and circumstance involved in futurity. It retrieves the stuff of an experience out of the void and fits it into the imaginative frame which the present circumstance of mind provides. Feeling is thus a nonactive form of knowing, or a cognitive determination of mind which "acts" by permitting itself to be fitted into an imaginative frame; and it implies a function of cognizing certain peculiar types of objects by allowing itself as passive matter to be fitted into the intellectual scheme or design of those objects.

Feeling, then, is a complex experience. It is both active and passive, in somewhat different senses, in the sense namely that it can enter as an element in either an active or a passive situation, and mediates both the active and the static elements of the world. It is thus the substantial link between the material and the sentient, the physical and the organic, the inert and the living. It has within it the element of cognition as a constituent of its substance. It has also within it, with the same status as the cognitive, the blind incognitive nescience as the physical or nonbeing constituent of its substance. But both the cognitive and the incognitive are real in feeling, and their presence together there is the explanation of two of the most significant features of life. In metaphysics we should find one of these given in the *experience* aspects of the principle of individuation and the other in the formal aspects of the principle of corporeity. In practical philosophy this distinction between substantial *noesis* and substantial nescience draws the line between religion and art, as two of the chief aspects of the moral world.

The cognitive function of feeling is the basis of the intuitive knowledge of the mystic and of the aesthete; the blind incognitive nescience of feeling is the basis of instinct as the knowledge function appropriate to mere life. In religion both intuition and instinct are operative, hence religion is actively concerned with the world and is practical. Intuitive cognition is belief. This is distinguished from scientific or philosophical knowledge by the degree to which it can exhibit the grounds upon which it rests. It is that degree in which some positive but indefinite measure of cogency quite obviously attaches to its purported grounds, but which never attains the definitiveness and clearness necessary to genuine knowledge.

Instinctive cognition is blind and is called "faith." This cannot state its grounds and is an expression of the pure active cogency of feeling, without any reference to the scheme or design of objects in existence, which latter is the basis of "proof" implied in the requirement that judgments have grounds. The problem of religion, morally speaking, is to advance from faith to belief, while at the same time stopping short of intellectual conviction, which would remove the distinction between religion and philosophy and deprive religion of the insights it derives from the nature of feeling as the prophetic function—the function, that is, of anticipating the experience content of those objects which lie in the future oblivion of the world.

When the cognitive function of feeling approaches the clearness of intellect and yet remains feeling, when, that is, feeling and intellect coalesce in the supreme effort of mind to identify with its object, it (feeling) is the content of aesthetic design. Here feeling has its peculiar system of concepts, just as it has its own peculiar system of concepts for religion.

The moral function of religion lies in the fact that both its constituents, intuition and instinct, are determinative of ends. Both capacities find their meaning in the relation they sustain to ends, both, that is, are elements within the active life. It is necessary to analyze intuition and instinct as moral aspects of religion.

II. RELIGIOUS INTUITION AS DEFINITIVE OF ENDS

By this expression we mean that the objects of religion are given their form and their meaning content by and through the knowing function in the act of designing them within the raw matter of experience. The act of knowing religious objects carves them out of the indefinite possibilities of experience, gives them form and design, and endows them with the color of meaning. They are then intuitive objects, ideals, essences. They, with other varieties of objects of the same type, like the aesthetic, political, etc., constitute the substance or stuff of culture, the medium within which all acts are performed, and the material of both the means and the end of every act. Religious objects are thus essentially practical objects—objects that have their existence and meaning within the world of action. They are, however, not capable of the kind of independent existence ascribed to reality by logic.

But these objects have logical implications nevertheless. Any competent discussion of them will treat their practical implications as their meaning content, regarding their logical implications as the ground of their order. And this includes both their order as constituting an important element in a system of knowledge along with their order considered as the basis of being, through control, realized in the active life. They constitute, that is, an aspect of the content of the good when thought of as real and realizable in experience. But they constitute also the good considered as the principle or norm which operates in the guidance and governance of action, and as the law of the good as the instrument by which thought about them is kept true to its own standards. These latter aspects of law are what we mean here when we speak of these cultural objects of religion as having logical implications.

When we therefore say that practical and cultural objects *have* logical implications, we mean that they *are* essentially constituted of logical implications, and they are intuitive objects in that they have not only their origin but their very form and content from intuition but are yet susceptible of intellectual formulation. This means that they may be cognized in terms of pure logical concepts only *after* they are intuitively defined. But they are not objects of "knowledge" until after they have been designed in intuition, and in this act of

design their relation to anything of strictly logical character is symbolic. It is the attempt to know these intuitive objects, that is, the
attempt to cognize them discursively, that is responsible for the symbolisms of religion, so that the symbolisms of religion are formal systems standing halfway between the abstract constructs of theology
and the system of moral action-forms that get expression in the ritual.
But knowledge cannot cognize them until after they have been created in intuition. Knowledge, that is, cannot anticipate them; they are
"known" only in prophecy, they are prophetic objects, and it should
be said rather that they subsist for the insights of intuition and the
attitudes of the will, than that they exist for the intellect.

Knowledge, that is, cannot anticipate them, cannot make these cultural or practical objects intelligible antecedently to their definition
or previsionment by intuition. They are not ideas, certainly not Ideas.
But they are nevertheless "matter of fact," intrusively and blindly
stubborn and possibly irrational, but *there* on their own grounds
which logic can only accept. They are not aspects or relations of
truth, and it is idle to argue about them. It is possible and useful to
argue about their order, but their being and their quality of meaning
are constituents of the world, and thought can only accept them.
They are "ideals," rather idols, images, symbols, graven on the scheme
of the world by the sheer impulse of life. But being *there*, they are
incentives in the active life, and it is in this fact that their moral significance lies. They are practical objects, realizable only in anticipation, have no concrete meaning, vague, indefinite, undefinable goals
of active instinct.

These characteristic qualities of practical objects make their scientific and theoretical treatment exceedingly difficult. That is to say,
if we are to think of them in their order and in their relations, by which
they become elements within the deliberate scheme of things which
we hope to control, we must see how they at the same time are moral
concepts, or may become such, by methods about which we shall also
have to inquire. We must show then how the intuitive ends of religion
are moral concepts.

III. INTUITIVE ENDS AS MORAL CONCEPTS

This is the task of showing how the practical ideals of religion have
to be reshaped by intellectual effort in order that they may become
the basis of law, for we cannot think without law. But we cannot
have ends without freedom, although we can anticipate and define
them and *hold* them; and freedom questions the concrete applica-

bility of law. Hence religion has either to accept a pure or indifferent freedom in the pursuit of the good or to limit its freedom, in which case it faces the difficulty of external limitations in authority. But in the case of pure freedom it must surrender its appeal to law or to any form of rational control over the pursuit of ends or accept a conditioned control which lays the process open to a modified chance. In the other case the pursuit of the good will depend upon the arbitrary will of some external source, in which case the pursuit becomes pure chance, that is, irrational. There can thus be no law for religion, since law implies clearly defined concepts free from all taint of uncertainty. Yet ends can be certain in their attainment only when the progress toward them is subject to the rules which determine certainty. And these rules are law. Morality, then, requires law, since it involves the function of control; while religion is a matter of the freedom that implies chance and "will" and the indirection of caprice.

Hence religion is creative, but it is not in itself capable of order. Its assertion of caprice admits of no limitation. Once limit its capricious freedom, and it makes peace with art and becomes idolatry. It is the moral religions that reject art and graven images. The instinct of religion perceives that art is not morality, that there is a distinction between the two. The one then cannot be the other. Its freedom must therefore be unlimited, caprice; there can be no reason why it should pursue one end rather than another, although it may by free choice enjoin conformity to moral law in the process of pursuit. It escapes authority by accepting indifferentism.

It is true, of course, that morality involves chance. But its chance is not the unlimited indifference of caprice. Morality knows or can calculate with approximation its chance, its chances, and in knowing them can, in a measure, take charge of their incidence upon its acts and purposes. Its chance then becomes accident, adventure, speculation, where ends may be known not immediately but mediately and within the scheme of law under which their design becomes intelligible. The purpose of morality is thus capable of continuity with design in nature and law in the world, and the control of the direction of the hitch-up becomes the meaning of an act. The essence of a moral act is then this character of adventure, in which it can be only partially known what the meaning and issue of the act is to be. The meaning of an act cannot be fully determined even after its movements have issued in tangible results. Part of its meaning remains really nonexistent, ideal, and, from the point of view of the act, by remaining ideal, gives significant content to future time. The ends attained by an act are not results; they are not objects defined and finished by time as past but objects designed in future time; they are ends, and ends can never be made fully intelligible for the reason that their total meaning cannot all be given in any experience. Indeed, it is equally true that the total meaning of a real end, as the completion and fulfilment of an act, cannot be known in any sense or to any intelligence for the reason that there is no time in which its elements are "all in." Some meaning will always lie beyond in the possibilities which the act which created the end laid out in the form of further action.

It is the system of these further possibilities of action that constitutes, for the moral intuition, the real world of nature and culture. For religion also the real world is always beyond; not a further world that connects its ends with the data of action and feeling, but one in which action and feeling can themselves only be symbolized. Its symbols then are not moral objects, not even patterns of such or of any objects, but replicas of its eschatological hopes. Then reality as represented to religion involves the denial of the actual world. To be real, its symbols must negate the moral conditions of reality as known; and these conditions become religious objectives of faith. They are symbols of acts not yet performed, and the attempt to realize the symbol congeals the act it represents into an eternal and pure and abstract form. But these are the forms of art.

IV. RELIGION AND ART

Religion thus inevitably institutionalizes itself in art forms wherever it adopts the moral motive to realize ends. Truth for it recommends itself as speculatively designed beauty, and the real becomes that ideal object through which the fragile beauty of pure design may be made accessible to the intuition. Hence its expression is always symbolic, allegorical. Religion has no direct way of giving itself expression. It must express itself through and in symbols. But such a representation of religious expression is external and does not state the fact as experienced by the religionist. For him the symbolic form and the transsubjective symbolic object somehow are the reality and the truth, although they have no being except in his experience, and he refuses the correction of his intelligence that they are mere symbols. His feeling transubstantiates the form through which, and the object in which, it gives itself expression. Hence he is in immediate contact with his reality, and the objects of religion become identical with his own inner experience. But, if he is intelligent, he will not make the Protestant blunder of assuming that his experience makes the reality; it is the objects that are real, and his experience partakes. The good for him thus is not an end and not a problem; it is what he realizes now as now realized within his own soul. Nor is there mystery about conscience, duty, or obligation; all these are immediately experienced, and there is no occasion or utility in the attempt to state their meaning in terms of the intellect.

The object of religion represents therefore a contradiction. What it is to the religionist's feeling is not what it is to his sense and his intelligence. This necessitates the reference of religious objects either away to that which is not experienced at all, but which may be experienced in some imaginative future, or inward to the immediacy of intuitive realization of objects as now containing their past and their future careers in something ineffable. But this means that religion is likely to accept action as the expression of an indefinite and recognizably unsatisfiable desire, or action will be looked upon as the essence of unreality, to be negated in an experience that is passively whole and without relation to anything either in the world or beyond it. In its attempt to define objects, then, because of its negation of action, religion is likely to issue in a vague eschatologism or an equally obscure mysticism.

But the moral significance of religion lies in the conviction that somehow there must be a reality and a substance for what the religionist feels. Religion involves conviction, and this is an important moral fact.

The point of fundamental import for morality in this connection is that there is no rational connection between the symbolic art form through which the religionist expresses his feeling and the ends contemplated by his feeling as they appear to intelligence. The ceremony, ritual, music, architecture, and sculpture in which he expresses his feeling have no intelligible relation to what they are supposed to represent. No ceremony, ritual, can be right or wrong, yet all such forms are supposed to represent perfect probity. No music, sculpture, etc., can be good, yet all such forms are supposed to represent supreme goodness. Such symbolisms can be only correct or incorrect, that is, for experience they are judged as consistent with the custom which founded them. Here we see the tendency always present in religion to make a principle out of abstract wont, and the reason why its motives become essentially conservative. It is interested in salvation, and the saving of souls becomes the process whereby souls remain forever what they are.

V. RELIGION AND THE FORMS OF THE ACT

Religion institutionalizes itself in the church. This fact is of profound significance for morality, since the church becomes one of the "worlds" within which the individual's powers get their meaning and direction. What particular qualities are developed in the individual by the acts and ministrations of the church we need not inquire. But the characteristic corporate *act* of religion is ritual, and its relation to morality is then the question as to whether there is any specifically moral quality attaching to ritual.

The main difficulty here is to try to find an element of the universal in ritual. There seems to be no such element from any consideration of the facts, and there is equal difficulty from the point of view of interpretation, for ritual is essentially custom, and custom cannot be universal. Yet the form of ritual is an *act*, and the significance of the ritual depends upon the perfection of this form in the act of worship. Hence it grounds the individual in the ideal of formal perfection of movement, and the sense of form is perhaps the basis of all intellectual activity, certainly of all morality. The sense of form is the ground of art and aesthetic activity obviously; but it seems to be equally the basic impulse in logic, and it may also be regarded as the ground of scientific method. Form is the empirical ground of all action.

As this principle of form, ritual becomes the basis of order—it is thus at least one of the sources of the motive of organization of life, which is a primary purpose of morality. Therefore religion, which is essentially ritual, gives us the ideal form of the perfect act, and the perfect act is the ultimate end of morality. Religion also, as expressed in and through primitive feeling, gives us the experience content of acts, at least in so far as that content can be anticipated. It is its representation of the form of the act and its anticipative presentation of the content of the end of the act that brings religion so close to morality and that explains why religion and morality should so often be taken to be the same thing. But religion can claim no truth because it accepts no law; morality can claim truth because it submits to law; whether either attains truth may be doubted: but both attain significance in adventure. The assertion of freedom puts truth in jeopardy. It is the form of action that also gives grounds for the claim of some religions to be moral as against those whose acts are supposed to be pure forms without content. It also explains, even if it does not justify, the claim of religion that it can accomplish the good with other means than those of knowledge, or by means of peculiarly specialized types of knowledge which differ essentially from logical knowledge.

The moral significance of religion is, then, that in worship it furnishes an instance of a formally perfect act and gives suggestions with respect to the empirical content of acts while acts are as yet non-existent but subsist only in the design of the agent's will. The act of worship is the supreme instance of an act whose essence lies in its metaphysical implications, for worship would have no meaning at all, unless as an instance of formal art, if it did not imply and refer in every detail to the whole of reality as its end. And this implication to the whole is the essence of the moral act. Worship is thus the morally perfect act. And by a perfect act we mean one that is totally identified within its object. The act disappears in the design of the object.

Chapter XX

Art as Organized Beauty

I. ART AS A MORAL PHENOMENON

IT IS perhaps generally recognized that art and morality are different things, and the argument as to their relations may be extended indefinitely. They nevertheless have important relations to each other. Our problem here is to inquire what are their relations, and this to us means, with our conception of morality as the whole of the good life, the question of the place of art and beauty within the system of the whole. Art and beauty are in any case a part of the moral agent's world.

It is obvious that there is a sense in which art and beauty, which are objects on their own account, are also aspects of the aesthetic experience and thus phases of the active life. And whatever is of the nature of action is a phenomenon of morality. It will not be our purpose to write a theory of art or of aesthetics but merely to describe art and beauty in that aspect in which they are related to action and thus have a place in the whole of life. Our assumption is that any form of activity is essentially moral and that whatever stands in certain relations to action is on that account to be regarded as a moral fact. Again, action implies and involves the world of persons and objects, and art is meaningless apart from these persons and objects. We may distinguish three types of activity connected with the experience of art: (A) art as beauty creation; (B) art as beauty appreciation; and (C) art as beauty comprehension. We proceed to describe these in the order given.

A. ART AS CREATION OF BEAUTY

By beauty creation we mean the production, in physical or ideal form, of objects of beauty. It is implied that beauty is never real in the absence of these objects and that such objects come into existence through the agency of some form of action. It is as a form of action that the creation of art is a moral fact. The high degree of moral quality attaching to art production is due to the fact that it is a perfect type of act, as to both form and content. It is however not the question, so far as morality is concerned, as to what technical forms of action are necessary to produce beautiful objects, or whether one form of action is better than another in a given case. This, we assume, would be the function of a theory of aesthetics in the sense that the theory of the subject is the sum of all the principles and practical maxims by which a given material may be converted into an art object. Morality is not concerned with such a question but with the larger question of the nature of the aesthetic act and its appropriate object, to try to show how that nature determines a place for such activities within the life-whole, for it is this life-whole that is the ground of all moral determination.

Our assumption on this point would, then, be that all acts that are calculated to produce, and normally do produce, objects of genuine beauty are moral acts in that they contribute to the good life; and this will be true whatever theory we may have as to the specific nature of beauty. So far as beauty is an element in the good life, it and the activities its creation involves will be moral phenomena. This does not reduce beauty to a mere moral phenomenon. Beauty can be a moral fact and, in addition, be all that it is aesthetically. In fact, it is a moral fact precisely for the reason that it is an aesthetic fact, since its being an aesthetic fact is what gives it its place in the whole good. Every aesthetic fact is thus a moral fact; it is good that there is beauty.

B. Art and the Appreciation of Beauty

Not only is every genuine aesthetic object a good but every appreciation of such an object is a good. Appreciation of beauty is thus the instance in which experience as such is real. Although beauty in this sense is a "state of mind," it is such in a different sense from mere psychological presence. We do not say that no states of mind are good; what we do argue is that the good is not always, and never merely, a state of mind. A state of mind that is a good has a quality or character that it does not have by virtue of its mere presence, and this character gives it a certain objectivity through which it can be represented and communicated. We can then say that it is good to appreciate beauty, while it would not be true to say that every good is appreciation or that every appreciation is good.

The appreciation of beauty is good on two different grounds, both of which may be present in any given case. In the first place, the mere presence or existence of the feelings connected with appreciation of beauty is good in itself, since it contributes positively to the whole of life. And this is true regardless of the transcience or permanence of the feeling or of perhaps any other specific quality of the feeling. That the good should be whole does not require that every element in it should be continuously present or that any element, as such, should be a good. The wholeness of the good is not a mathematical quantity but is a system of quality with a structure that is independent of existential determination. This avoids the static fixity and all-thereness which a too literal interpretation of wholeness demands. But, in the second place, the appreciation may not be in the form of feeling, but may be either of the form of pure sense or of the pure intellect. I may appreciate an object through the pure sensuous feel of its form, where the experience is as nearly purely sensory as possible. Also I may appreciate by direct intuition a mathematical construction. In cases like these "feeling" in the ordinary sense is at almost an absolute minimum and in any case is not involved in the act of cognition which appreciation implies. The object appreciated may present itself as an instance of pure sensuous form in which the form (in the intellectual sense of design) is not distinguished either from the content of the object regarded as independently external or from the content of the object regarded as contained in the intimacies of the feeling of the subject who appreciates it. That is to say, the feeling substance of an aesthetic object can be experienced through other characters than its pure quality.

It appears thus clear that appreciation is an activity that is distinct from creation or from comprehension, and it is on a basis of this distinction that comprehension of beauty in aesthetic theory is to be distinguished from ordinary cognition of objects, which may be present with it; that is, an object may be recognized both as to its existence (cognized) and as to its aesthetic value (contemplated) within the same act of intelligence.

C. Art as Beauty Comprehension

A study of the forms of the contemplation of beauty, and the discovery of the logic by which the system of these forms makes the beauty object intelligible, constitute aesthetic theory. This study is a moral object in that it is one of the elementary types of the good. But its discussion belongs to aesthetic theory.

II. THE MORAL FUNCTION OF ART

Not only is it true that art and beauty have a place within the system of what is good. They have a peculiar function there, and their contribution to the good is unique in the sense that they furnish features and elements of the good which could come from no other source. In the case of any particular moral act or object there is one character that determines its nature as moral, and we have seen that, in its abstractest form, that character is the reference the act or object makes to the whole good. We have now to see that such a reference to the good must have its ground in the nature of the act or object, and we must find what character of the act or object it is that furnishes the ground of reference. That is to say we have to find why it is that some objects refer quite unambiguously to the good, while others do not so refer in any way at all.

To state the case shortly, such a reference relation is not a function of any particular quality or character. Perhaps it is never true, outside the abstractions of pure mathematics, that a character of an object can be cited as the basis and reason for a relation in which the object stands. But it certainly is not true of the beauty object. There is no particular quality of a picture or a melody that unmistakably refers us to the whole, none that we can point to as that which makes the picture or melody good. Goodness is thus not a quality of an object or act that can be perceived, for there is no specific point from which the experience can be said to arise. We do as a matter of fact often say that a picture is good because of its color, etc., but something else with identical color might not be regarded as good at all. In fact, a quality of an object cannot in reality be abstracted from the complex mass of qualities and relations which make up the object as experienced, and yet retain its meaning as that quality. The quality *is* a function in some way of all that the object is and means, and it is in this aspect by which it represents the whole object that we find it capable of representing the goodness of the object.

Then the basis of the reference to the good that an object makes is the wholeness or integrity of the object, and in the case of the aesthetic object this character of wholeness or integrity is called "form." By this term we do not mean mere shape; form does mean shape, but shape is the least that it means. Form in this use includes with shape such characters as structure and organization, arrangement of parts and distribution of qualities. It is form in this sense as belonging to an object that enables the object to suggest a relation to a whole as a system of objects which includes it along with others as constituting the whole. Form thus is the common character of both the object and the whole which it implies, and the reference to wholeness is carried in this logical relation of identity. This relation is represented and expressed, in and by the artist's technique, as if it were a specific quality of sense, or as some unique harmony of sense qualities. In its mere descriptive or existential aspects this relation is the basis of the relation of an individual to its species. We have here tried to state it in its value or meaning phase and have seen that, whereas in its descriptive or existential sense it implies organization, in its value sense it implies order. And as the content in this case is one of sensuous or imaginative objectivity, the form of an object or an act, what we have just now called its order will be the harmony of its organization. Harmony in this sense implies feeling; but it also has a cognitive implication in the mutual appropriateness of the parts, that is, it implies structure as the ground of objectivity. But we have seen also that the same character which constitutes the object also constitutes the whole to which the object belongs by constituting and grounding the relation between objects, and as a consequence the internal harmony or order of an object is also the harmony or order of the system to which the object belongs.

Then the function of art and beauty, considered as moral, is the aesthetic organization of all the sensory and imaginative aspects of activity under forms supplied by the aesthetic contemplation. It is in this process, and this process only, that the issuing of an act in an object is intelligible; and it is this process that makes the cognition of an object possible in pure intellect; so that at this point we are driven into the sphere of metaphysics. What the forms of contemplation are is the central problem of the logic of aesthetics. Art and beauty thus function morally in a peculiar way in giving to life, in both its particular and its whole aspects, the character of the harmony which is the basis of all meanings of the good. And as the form of life is carried in the structure of the institutions of culture, we shall want to see how beauty lays the basis of goodness in the family, in industry, in religion, in education, and in politics as the fundamental institutions of life.

III. BEAUTY AND THE FAMILY

We have now the principle that beauty is the basis of the form and harmony and inner appropriateness of the objects and acts of which the good life is made up. With respect to the family, the principle is responsible for the organization of the sensory and imaginative factors of the family life. These sensory and imaginative factors are for the most part those objects and acts which have to do with sex and property, the two foundations upon which the family as an institution rests. At its simplest, then, the family is either a scheme calculated to give form to the exercise of sex or to a property arrangement or to both. But this is to make the least of the family; in actual fact the beauty motive has imaginatively reconstructed the system of sensuous objects and activities and has re-created them with respect to a new form. In nearly all cases and almost universally, beauty has transformed the sex-property motives into the home, and the home is one of the highest achievements of our human culture. We may repeat that in its lowest phase it is an arrangement of life based on sex and property, or rather it is this fundamentally, since sex and property will always be the existential basis of any family. But it is as the home that the family has special moral significance.

It will not be necessary for us here to go at length into the meaning and significance of the family. What we are interested to see is that it is an essentially cultural institution and to point out that it is the motive to beauty that makes it so. The family is essentially a system of symbols by which the natural crudity of sex and property, which are the crude feeling-material of the family as an object, are glossed over; and it is by means of these symbols that the sensitive individual is enabled to put from his mind the irritating urges that come from the functioning of his body. It is to be emphasized that art does not transform its object in the sense of changing its existential nature; it deals with external qualities and relations, and the object remains in substance what it was. Mere sex contact is a foul thing; it and the processes of nutrition and excretion are things we like to forget. Hence in the effort to put these natural necessities out of our sight we have hidden them behind the most beautiful and significant of human creations and have distracted our attention from them by creating values whose sole function is to allure us away from the crudity of mere existence. Out of these natural necessities thus have come, perhaps by revulsion of elementary feelings, all the fine arts, as well as the more important institutionalizations of the coarser forms of activity, such as the church, the school, the state. And the significance of the home is in the fact that as the beautification of sex and property it has been the parent of all other cultural institutions. The home itself is the objectification and incorporation of the impulse to beauty.

IV. BEAUTY AND WORK

As a form of creative activity work is an aesthetic phenomenon by nature. The organization of activity for the creation of goods is what is meant by work considered as a system. Work is the organization of

330 THE GOOD LIFE

activity, whether individual or "social," for the creation of the goods ordinarily called "necessities," as food, shelter, clothing. As creative activity it is essentially aesthetic in form, and the perfect instance is farm work under conditions that approach the natural, that is, where the work is not mediated by too complicated machinery. This approaches genuine artwork such as is employed in painting, sculpture, etc., and it is most emphatically absent where too many of the necessary processes are mediated by machinery. The painter cannot paint a picture by guiding his brush with a complicated drawing mechanism, nor can a farmer cut his wheat with a combine.

The difference between real work and machine work is distinguishable in every phase of the activities involved but is perhaps stated best as the difference between creation and production. Creation implies activity by a free agent, while production implies that the agent (there may be none, as where the "work" is done by automatic machinery) is limited and restricted in action by the form and intensity of the process to which he is held and by the plan of the type of object which is to result from action. In a genuinely free act the object that results is never predictable, so no accurate plan or scheme of its form can be set up in advance of the action that creates it. A genuine act of freedom has an extension into the future, and the future itself is determined by the order and process of the act from moment to moment as the free act proceeds. Another fundamental difference between creative activity and production is that the object of creation can never be repeated, while the object of production can be repeated indefinitely. The product of creation is an individual, the result of production is the particular, and has within it no suggestion of universality. The principle of creation is law and implies freedom; there is no principle of production, for objects (things) are produced by rule. The principle or law of creation is intrinsic within the process which creates and only becomes realizable to experience as the plan or design of the object created. The act which creates an object also creates the principle by which it creates the object; the principle has no existence until the object is finished. The process of production is dominated by a force or power external and antecedent to the process, and what in creation is genuine activity is in production reduced to movement.

From this point of view of the relation of acts to their object the principle governing work is deduced. The principle is that all real activities are *organized into* their instruments, structured within the objects through which they come to expression. In the perfect case the object through which the act gets expression and the object into which as end the act incorporates itself are the same object. From the point of view of my active life, an object is strictly real only when I can see in it the completion of my characteristic acts; and this is so even of objects of nature which appear to me to be complete and whole. They are objects of my ideal acts, and I accept them and recognize that the activity which creates them is the activity which I find in my own life. I will them thus.

When we recognize the truth of the principle laid down above, the most perplexing problem both of work and of art appears clear to us. It is the problem of machine control and the tragedy of factory work and monotonous production. The organization of factory work appears to be impossible on any lines that would be satisfactory to either morality or art. It is impossible and will always remain so while the principle just stated is ignored. So long as the activities of men are controlled as to their motive and form and intent by extraneous and ulterior forces, or by agencies other than the free purpose which they recognize within themselves, there is no possibility that work can be right or good or beautiful or satisfying in any way to anybody. In factory work as organized at present the motives and intent of workers are dominated by the purposes of somebody not connected in any way with the processes of the work, and their activities are controlled by no purpose but by the inexorable grind of the machinery to which their acts are attached as mere fragments of movement. The principle that activities should be organized into their instruments is violated when the instrument commands the act as to both its energy and its form, as is the case with acts under machine control. The instrument in this case remains an instrument, always a mere tool, which can never come to the status of a real object.

The case of hand tools which themselves may be works of art, and the skilful use of them, is the perfect illustration of the principle that an act incorporates in the object that is the synthesis of its means with its end. It illustrates what should be true of all work, viz., the completion of the activity should transform and objectify the instrument into the perfect object, the means into the end, the object, that is, which *is* just the incorporation of the acts by which it is created. The act and its appropriate tool thus become soul and body for the object they create; then it is *good;* it is artistic work, and the object is beautiful and complete in that its design is an implication to the whole good. Even the ideal plan of a right act is nothing but the intuited corpus of characters which the object of the act possesses, and the fact that this body of characters exists as yet only in the imagination merely means that the plan is an early stage in the career of the object. Between it and the stage of fulfilment there are only acts as ordered moments of movement, and there is nothing implied here which was not in the earlier state except the publicity to which the enacted plan is brought out, that is, the act becomes overt.

V. THE PRINCIPLE OF PUBLICITY

The practical maxim of action, then, the principle formulated for application to specific cases, is that all action must be overt, above-board, public, and its motive must be immediately evident. No good act can be secret, clandestine, private, for the attempt to perform an act under the conditions that limit it to one person, or a specific place, or a specific purpose necessarily limits the freedom which is the one and only condition under which an act may come to completion in a valid object. And no thing can be good, as we have seen, which does not have this reference to the wholeness which completes it. It is obvious that this implication of wholeness of meaning for an object is absent where there are any restrictions upon its expression. This is shown in the fact that most, perhaps all, really great art, as the expression of perfect activity, has, historically, a religious motive, that is to say, a metaphysical implication. This does not imply that the presence of a religious motive always insures greatness. But it does imply and necessitate publicity in action; it always involves the formulation of acts with respect to the wholeness of the act as carried out in an end that is whole which at the same time is the object of an indefinite number of other acts, as in the example of religious ritual or a unitary scene in a dramatic performance. These cases are not instances of "co-operation" but of the individuation of a number of persons and instruments into a new superperson in which the act lives. It is cases like this that explain how corporate persons can act.

An act, then, that is serious, real, valid, candid, honest, generous—in short, an act that is good in any way—is always public. A secret act is a contradiction; a private act a perfidy. An act that cannot be proclaimed is a confession of guilt, and an act that withdraws into darkness is the will to evil and unrighteousness.

If we now come back to the problem of factory work and "large-scale production," we may see that the usual diagnosis of the moral disease is faulty. The factory organization and its management perhaps satisfy none of the aesthetic conditions which we have laid down as governing moral action. The activity involved is not work but drudgery. There is no need to point out the particular phases of the processes which fail to come up to the standard. The whole situation is wrong in principle. And what is wrong as to principle cannot be right in detail. The motive and purpose of an industrial act, as at present "organized," lies outside the act and so can never take its place as the principle of ordered structure of the object into which the act issues. The act can never be realized, never be given permanence within the public order of life. While the motive is private, there can be no realization of objects, no accomplishment of ends, nothing can ever be done. As a consequence there will ensue the eternal repetitive process of turning out things that will always be less than objects, the infinite factory process which will always be a process of progressive disintegration of the object which it never quite completes, with continuous deterioration of the qualities which endow objects with their values. Nothing can therefore be valuable or possess worth where the act is not free, where the will which commands is not the will which executes. And where the purpose that controls the processes of action is the purpose which withdraws into the darkness of privacy, there is and can be no work which accomplishes an end. Such processes are endless because they are end-less. They must go on forever spawning a brood of fragments which cannot become whole individuals, with each "product" a little worse than the last. And the contradiction that is inherent in such private activity is what infects each product with falsity, makes of the whole a huge mendacious prevarication which must resort to pretense and sham and advertising.

And what is false is ugly. And what is ugly cannot take place within the good. In order that work may be a significant moral function in life, it will have to be organized in accordance with the fundamental requirements we have laid down. This calls for a new motive, new types of process, and new standards for gauging the value characters of the objects that are its ends. It calls for a reinterpretation of the concept of person, in which it is demonstrated that the real or genuine person is always the corporate person as instanced in the unity of participants in a beautiful rite or in a drama. The motive, we said, may not be private but must come clean with a purpose that all may view. The process must be rescued from mere movement and restored as a valid act. And the end must possess that wholeness and completeness and harmony the perfect forms and instances of which are only to be found in works of art.

VI. BEAUTY AND RELIGION

We may remind ourselves that we are dealing with both beauty and religion here as factors in and of the good life. They have therefore for us a moral significance, and it is this moral value that we wish to portray.

We may be brief here, since the matter of our principle is already settled. We have noted that the moral function of art is to organize and endow with value the sensory and imaginative phases of action under forms supplied by a rational feeling. As dealing here especially with objective forms, our question will relate to the institution of religion, since the institution is the aesthetic organization of religious values. Reminding ourselves also of the principle discovered in the discussion of work, we note that this principle, as the urge to public expression, the instinct that all action must be overt, public, is the institutionalizing motive in religion; and we shall accordingly be dealing with objects within which religious values are expressed. These are the cathedrals and rituals and forms and ceremonies as objectified expressions of what in the nature of the case cannot be reduced completely to consistency with *material* substance, and which therefore become a class of ideal objects. As ideal objects they are peculiarly adapted to the expression of sensuous and imaginative values, since the element of materiality in them is utilized as the medium through which symbols of values may be expressed. Through symbolization then a mere thing becomes a perfect object, not because its thingness is lost, but because it is transformed and identified with and transmuted into the value it represents. It is thus that, while religion undertakes to express itself in terms of pure value, it at the same time succeeds in expressing its values through the most perfect symbolic forms, and the most perfect art is also produced.

It is thus that the pure spiritual values of religion are represented to the consciousness in aesthetic form and become thus high types of moral good.

VII. BEAUTY AND EDUCATION

It is not the purpose here to discuss the organization of the educational system. It is agreed that the system, even in its most material aspects of buildings, etc., could and might be organized so as to satisfy the demands of sense and imagination. And it is equally agreed that such organization is taken for granted, whenever we think of education as the growth process of the system of culture, as the system of means and instruments by which culture extends its domain over nature. But we are in despair when we come to observe the actual organization of education and the general tendency for the organization and management to fall into incompetent hands. The reason for this lies in the fact that persons who are competent and realize the significance of the cultural values involved do not care to be bothered with the routine which organization entails. As a consequence, only those who are capable of developing a competency for routine will accept such tasks, and this limitation to routine cuts them off from perceiving the values in the interest of which the organization exists. As a consequence, the school system is organized in accordance with standards set by culturally mediocre minds, and such minds are peculiarly limited in the perception of beauty and the realization of its significance for the whole life of the individual.

There is a similar criticism to be passed on the method and process of education in their bearing upon art and beauty. The assumption is that everybody should be taught art, and therefore the teacher is always able to teach it. There is no necessity that art and beauty be taught directly at all. And, where it is taught, it should be only to persons capable of developing some capacity, and the teaching limited to the technique of expression. Beauty and the experience of beauty are beyond the reach of the teacher's methods, so far as they are aimed at directly. They come, so far as they are not parts of the natural endowment of the individual, from the general effect of his contacts with nature and culture that are provided through the established subject matters. Contacts with nature in botany, physics, zoölogy, and with culture in economics, history, languages, ethics, etc., provide the substance of beauty. And the intellectual capacity developed in the mastery of these subjects furnishes the competence for the expression of beauty. The only thing requiring to be directly taught is the technique of expression. He who has no beauty to express will never practice art, the beauty must come to him from nature and culture, and it is always some aspect of the nature-culture system whose expression constitutes art. The greatest contribution to art and beauty that education can make is in endowing the student with a competent knowledge of these fundamental subjects of nature and culture, and it will contribute only a little less significantly if it will realize that it should leave art and beauty and their destiny to those who understand them.

VIII. BEAUTY AND POLITICS

We remind ourselves once more that the moral function of art lies in the fact that it organizes the sensuous and imaginative elements of life into forms of the good. The function of politics is to organize the total or whole life in accordance with the principle of the good. The aesthetic principle of the good we have seen to be publicty; the principle that the good is always a part of the public whole of reality, that it always appears and is available to all in proportion to the capacity to make use of it under conditions set up by the nature of the good. The relation of art to politics is then simply stated: Art furnishes the organization of certain elements of reality, the sensuous and the imaginative, and prepares them for organization and incorporation with the whole good. Politics then adapts art and beauty to its place within the system of the whole and binds the whole together as one organic whole of good by the principle of publicity. Politics is then the organ of morality, the instrument by which actuality and existence are given to the forms which abstract morality pronounces good. The political power incorporates the principle of publicity itself into the system of law, and law thus becomes the active instrument through which the good is given concrete and objective forms. For example, morality can only say, "Do justice," but cannot enforce its decree through its own devices. Politics has the task of seeing that justice is done and has conspired with morality in the invention of the law as the instrument through which justice is done. Morality tells us that we should be just; politics tells us that we must be just and shows the way through the law.

The specific function of art and beauty is, as we saw, expressed in the organization of the sensuous and imaginative elements of life. But it has a more generalized function which it acquires through its relations with politics and law, and this general function is, from the point of view of principle, at least, of still greater importance. It is through the aesthetic capacity in this general sense, the capacity for beauty as such, that we are enabled to know the good when it is done and to apprehend the truth when it is achieved. It is beyond any of our intellectual or moral capacities to apprehend the good as the good or the true as the true; they can be known only in the form of beauty. There is ultimately no *reason* we can give that the good is good or that it should be good; or that the true is true or should be true; and there is no moral end that justifies itself to us merely by being a moral end. The good and the true must appeal to me by virtue merely of their sensuous and imaginative perfection in an object, and it is from this latter that we derive both the notions of true and good. Then the aesthetic object is the ultimate whole and is pictured to us as the political state, to which our obligatory attachment must be established through an aesthetic tie. It is the objectification of the good life itself in its wholeness and completeness, the good externalized and eternalized and substantiated in the structure of the world. We can never realize this good by knowledge alone, or by action guided by imaginative standards of sensuous perfection. It is beauty that is the creative artist, the maker of the world out of chaos, and it is only beauty that can say at the end, "It is good," or can say of her judgment that it is good, "It is true."

Politics, then, is morality universalized and objectified and thus realized as art.

IX. BEAUTY AND MORALITY

There remains only to summarize the conclusions already arrived at. Beauty gives to morality the insight that the mere order that politics and law impose is also a harmony. The principles we have enunciated above then all are synthesized in one great norm, and, whatever peculiar name we may adopt for this norm, its character is proportionality. By this we mean the universal of what is just and fair and true and comely and wholesome and proper. The content to which the norm applies may be anything, absolutely. And this means that goodness is infinite, that the possibilities of the good are boundless; and they are infinite and boundless by the law laid upon them that they must be such as fit into a harmonic whole. It is this concept of harmony that lies back of all our forms of thought in the principle of consistency, and it underlies all the forms and schemes and plans of our wills in the idea of a pictured perfect world. But it is the harmony of beauty that is basic to all forms, to all realities.

Chapter XXI

Politics and the Unity of Life

WE HAVE seen that the good is a whole life. And life has been taken in two senses; one embracing all the inherent powers and capacities that belong by nature and culture to the actor or agent or person, and the other involving all the external conditions in nature and culture necessary to the performance of the complete act. We have also seen that these factors, regarded as personal capacities, and taken in their specialized forms, constitute the virtues. Considered as referring backward to a point of origin in the person, the powers and capacities involved in action constitute the system of the subjective virtues. When we think of life and action in terms of their external and historic conditions, especially in the positive way that contemplates the presence of the necessary materials and instruments to useful action, we are thinking in terms of objective virtue. The various forms in which objective virtue manifests itself will be described in Part V.

In Part IV we have been concerned with the more important specialized forms of the external conditions of life or with what we have called the "moral world." It is now our task to show how this world, as made up of the various natural conditions and cultural institutions, acquires the character of wholeness by which it assumes the moral quality and becomes the condition upon which moral quality may be attributed to other things, including persons. The institution through which the wholeness of life, both in its subjective and in its objective form, is created and maintained, is politics, or the political state. As the political state is thus a moral institution, we have here the duty of giving an account of its essential form and structure. It is the function of the state to create and maintain the order and balance of the total system of life, to give to life, that is, its moral significance. The state is therefore the generalized instrument of morality, the implement or tool through which the larger aims of morality are accomplished. It is also the final object or end of morality, both in the sense of the ultimate goal to be reached and in the sense of the perfect body

338

or organ through which moral action is most effectively embodied. It is here our task to inquire into the content that enters into the state and to inquire into the form that morality demands for that content.

I. THE CONTENT OF POLITICS

It is first necessary to remark that, as we have defined the state and its relation to morality, politics has no peculiar content, no content that is exclusively its own. There is no specialized type of action or form of life or kind of object that is purely political. Any type of action or form of life or kind of object becomes a phenomenon of politics by virtue of its relation, or possibilities of relation, to the whole; and it is this relation to the whole, when interpreted as the instrument by which the whole is constituted, that determines the political character of any fact. Hence the facts that become important in political discussion or political practice are the facts of personal life in the family, the church, the educational system, and industry. And so far as any fact is to be considered with respect to its immediate qualities and attributes, it is a fact of one or more of these institutions. When its relations to other facts, especially to facts of institutions other than the one to which it belongs, are involved, then we have the possibility of the political relation, and the relation becomes an actual political relation when considered as forming a part of the total institutional structure of life. But in its peculiar quality or character, and in its more immediate relations, every fact is a fact of one or more of the major institutions of life.

Every fact and every relation are, then, features of the family, the school, the church, or industry, and there is no fact or relation that can be described as peculiarly political in nature. Doing a day's work is a fact of industry, and all its specific characters and the technique of its processes are to be determined from the viewpoint of industry alone. But when there is a question of the quality of the product, or its price, or of the effect of the product upon the worker or his relations to his fellows, or upon the general conditions of order and the peace of the community, the day's work is a political fact. It is such because, in such relations, its very meaning is a reference to the whole and not a specialized reference to the local situation and circumstances within which it occurs.

But this means that political facts are public facts. They are not the peculiar concern of anybody but the general concern of all. They are also not mere aspects of somebody's mind but fixed conditions in existence. And in this reference to the whole of the good life the facts that we term "political" are also moral facts. They are thus objective in the sense that their interpretation involves, not a reference to the narrow situation in which they occur, certainly not to the mind of the agent by which they are experienced, but a reference beyond to something as an end. They have thus frequently been described as purposive facts, or facts of purpose, but this description has itself become a form of reference to the specialized situation in individual experiences. But this special form of reference, especially as it refers to the will of the agent, has nothing to do with morality and can have nothing so long as the fact depends upon special or technical connections. The important relation for politics in its moral aspects is that in which fact refers to the objective system, thus giving it the public character. It is this public character of the moral relation that explains the peculiar meaning of ethical concepts and gives to them their universality. Thus an act or an "intention" is *right* not because of any specific quality it possesses, or of any reference to the situation in which it occurs, but because it fits into the total scheme of things, and its qualities are important only so far as they help to determine the fitness.

An object or an instrument is *good*, then, not because it possesses a certain quality, or is adapted to a particular place or individual, but because it, by virtue of its quality and adaptability, is such as fits into the scheme of things as a whole. Its quality and its particular relation have the character of goodness to the extent that they contribute to this fitness. When we say a thing is good, we do not mean that it is good for Jones or Smith but that it is good to eat, or wear, or enjoy, or to play or work with, and these imply objective relations within the whole of life. And it is because of this public character of appropriateness or adaptation to the whole that the object can be said to be good for anybody or for anything. That is, what makes a handsaw a good handsaw is the fact that it fits perfectly into the system of human culture. That it is useful to me or to anybody is part of its fitness, but it is not of itself the ground of its goodness. That it does fit is determined by its peculiar qualities and the nature of the special situation as measured by the technical processes of specific and local use. But its character as a moral object, its goodness, is determined by its place and function in the whole; and it is a good object for any special case because of this universal relation. The handsaw is a good handsaw not because it serves the purposes of the individual agent but because it is such as makes it capable of effective use by any competent agent. "It hangs well in the hand," we say, and not, "It hangs well in my hand." From the point of view of the using, the handsaw's goodness refers to the whole of persons, and from the point of view of its product its goodness is a question of its relation to the whole of objects.

It is the public character, then, of the act or object or agent that constitutes its moral quality, and it is this fact that makes morality the basis of the state and that makes the final form of every moral phenomenon its political form. There is then little point to the attempt to draw fine distinctions between morality and politics or between ethics and political philosophy. There are in any case two aspects of the good life, whether we regard it as essentially moral or political, that are fundamental. These are indicated in the two problems: the question of the nature of the content of the good life and that of the types or kinds of order this content is capable of taking on. Since the problem of the nature of the order of the life-content depends very largely upon the nature of the content, the two problems may be taken up together.

II. TYPES OF POLITICAL ORDER

As to the question of the content of politics with respect to the relation of the function of political organization to the good life as lived by citizens, there are three possible attitudes: (1) that there is no content; (2) that the content of political activity is confined merely to functions of control; and (3) that political activity should furnish furtherance and guidance to citizens.

As to the problem of types of order there are four theories: order may be based (1) on *power;* (2) on *freedom;* (3) on *intelligence;* or (4) on *speculative activity*. We shall discuss briefly each of these.

A. The Content of Politics

The nature of political content may be viewed in three ways: that there is no content; that there is a content; and that this content may be either positive or negative in nature.

I. NO SUCH CONTENT

The most widely held view as to the content of politics at present is that there is no such content. This is shown in the universal distrust of government and of public activity out of which grew the modern democratic states. The essential conviction behind modern democracy is that "the people" is motivated by some inherent natural or metaphysical force which determines the people's destiny, so far as its natural genius is left free and unhindered. Governmental activity, or concrete activity on behalf of the state, is in the nature of the case a hindrance and opposition to the operation of this force and is thus a priori wrong. But the confusion of the point of view does not prevent its seeing that some state activity is necessary, so that any form of public or governmental activity becomes in this view a necessary evil. This conviction has been formulated in maxims of political wisdom, which change their form as the various aspects of public activity are negated. In an age of general oppression democracy is formulated in the maxim "that government is best which governs least" or which interferes least with the activities of its citizens and which leaves them most severely alone with the destiny that shapes their ends. As oppression gives way to vigorous activity of citizens, they begin to feel that "the less government the better"; and, as activity becomes vigorous enough to direct government to its own purposes, the maxim becomes "less government in business and more business in government."

This viewpoint is, as we have seen, right in its assertion that politics has no content peculiar to itself. But it is wrong in failing to see that the very possibility of meaning of all experience content lies in its becoming the vicarious content of politics. Individualism would say that politics should give way to industry and business, that this is the stuff of life. But it fails to see that industry and business are made rational only by becoming the matter out of which politics molds the good and that, of themselves and left to their own resources, business and industry destroy themselves and the culture they are intended to support. That is to say, the insight that politics has no peculiar content leads to anarchy when all content is denied, and the very principles of individualist democracy lead to chaos. The doctrine that government is a necessary evil can thus provide for no ultimate good, and this means that on this doctrine ultimately nothing is good.

2. CONTENT CONFINED TO FUNCTION OF CONTROL

The doctrine that the state should have a positive function but should be restricted in operation to mere control is a result of the realization that pure or unlimited democracy is anarchy. Hence the state is now limited to the police power and is to umpire the game by limiting the acts of persons so that there may not be so much conflict as to interfere with the game. The citizen has the right to do all that he can do, and is interfered with by the state only at the point where his action appears too patently to hinder the like freedom of another. But in practice this means that the state will interfere very seldom, since the economically strong will control the state, and, when it does interfere, it will often do so to compel the economically weaker to submit to exploitation by the strong, whose instrument the state has become. The fallacy in this doctrine of police power lies in its assumption that the public or moral life can be controlled by force. It is an instance of the "power state," and its final form will be military.

3. POLITICAL ACTIVITY SHOULD FURNISH FURTHERANCE AND GUIDANCE

On the other hand, the theory that the state should furnish guidance and the furtherance of his purposes to the citizen is coming to the fore again. It has never been lost since Plato constructed the theory out of the practice of the Greek democracies and has since been kept in a sort of suspended animation in the idealism of the Christian movement. It assumes that the state, operating in the name of the moral whole and to the end of the whole good, will present to each person a setup of positive opportunity, acceptance of which by the person, and with faithful action on his part, will guarantee to him the attainment of his ends. Not any ends the person's caprice may anticipate but any end admitted within the whole of ends by the wisdom of the whole. Whatever substance there may be in the individual's caprice will find embodiment in the end, and wisdom will find it there. Such a theory recognizes the many difficulties in the practical application of its ideas, but it also knows that no significant moral achievement is attainable on any other assumption, since moral ends have been attained in human life only in the proportion that they have been approached by principles identical essentially with its own. That is to say, so far as any moral purpose has found significant expression in human history, it has done so to the degree that it has accepted the principle of the whole good as expressed in the agencies of positive opportunity and freedom and as recognized by the total wisdom of the race. The organization of these moral agencies around the basis of the concept of the whole good is the political state, which becomes therefore the major concept of moral practice and the fundamental principle of moral theory.

B. Types of Political Order

As we have already seen, the type of order or organization the moral whole will assume depends primarily upon the systems of ideas and purposes which make up the political content of the whole. To a lesser degree the type of order will be dependent upon the sort of circumstance within which it is formed. This circumstance consists of the natural environment, the geographical and other features of the natural system, together with the cultural environment or systems of human institutions. The type of order originally accepted by the United

States, for example, was determined in the cultural systems and ideologies of western Europe, as modified by the different natural conditions which the American continent afforded. What we are concerned with here, however, is to point out the various general moral ideas or attitudes that may furnish the motive of control to the political order, and of these we may name four.

I. BASED ON POWER

Perhaps the earliest, certainly the most primitive, but yet the most common, form of political order is that based on power. Power may be one of a number of varying forms, and the best way to designate these forms is by the type of institution the form takes substance in. Thus the power order may be personal, as depending upon the extraordinary capacity of a strong individual, or it may be familial, as based upon the principle of respect developed in the family organization. Again, the order may derive from the dominance of the religious institution, in which case a deeply cultural personal relationship holding among individuals will be objectified in a set of aesthetic forms and rituals which tend strongly to magnificence. It is the awe of magnificent form which gives to the religious policy its power; and, so far as a power state can be a moral state, it is effected most perfectly in the religious state.

Or the form of order may be determined by "social" factors of prestige and display and dignity, the highest form of which is the order based upon honor, which is recognition of assumed or actual worth in the persons who implement the idea in the governing system. Something like this was perhaps realized in the Athens of Pericles, and a modern instance may be cited in the British nobility, which has tended toward an aristocracy of dignity and personal worth. The bad instance of the social power state is the economic, where mere mass possession is the medium of control. This becomes institutionalized in the business system, which most nearly suggests the military.

But the prime instance of the power state is, historically, at least, the military and is the form toward which all other power forms tend. The military state is however perhaps less dangerous than some other forms, since its avowal of the power idea is conscious and deliberate. It is in any case the best illustration of the negative moral value of the power state, since the contradictions of the power motive clearly demonstrate that no state can approach the good through the use of force. Force has in no case a direct moral function, that is, it can never be used with reference to ends but only in the technical process of shaping means or instruments. We can employ explosives to "blow" stumps or to break rocks or to drive machinery, but, if the force is ever to come to grips with ends, it will be through having surrendered the direction to intelligence. There is nothing good in power as such, and to direct it to the good requires the highest skill of intelligence.

There is, however, a still more dangerous instance of the power state than the military. It has developed out of a combination of the military with the economic state, by an exaggeration of one of the methods common to both. The military state consciously employs deception and openly avows its use. The economic state employs deception, but under the guise of truth, and more or less unconsciously deceives itself and its victims as to the fact that it employs deception. Combining these two features, the commercial or propaganda state consciously and deliberately employs deception as an instrument by which it may deceive itself and its victims. This is an instance of the power state in that it is based upon psychological force, and the method of fraud, which is psychological force, is developed into a fine art. This type of "order" is of course not important, since it can but destroy itself in a relatively short time. Its significance lies in the fact that its influence is purely negative, and it is dangerous in the fact that it can exist only through the destruction of essential moral institutions. It illustrates perfectly the contradictory character of the power state, the inherent weakness which makes those who resort to the sword perish by the sword.

2. BASED ON FREEDOM

Another type of moral order as politically set up is the order based on freedom. What it has historically meant is freedom from restrictions imposed upon personal action by any of the forms of the power state. It is thus essentially a denial of the power state, and, as we shall see, its weakness lies in this negative character. In modern times its earliest expression was in the form of a revolt against religious absolutism and was only partially successful. It failed to weaken the absolutism it was in revolt against, and itself developed the power attitude from its acceptance and adoption of the methods which it used against power. But the negative motive continued to express itself in revolt and was more successful against the legal and social absolutisms which had begun to contest the religious in its assumed right to use absolute power. This revolt against legal and social absolutism worked itself out in the revolutionary movement which established political democracy throughout the world and which has been universally acclaimed as the embodiment of the principle of freedom in political society.

But it has not been so universally recognized that the movement has been throughout essentially negative. There is a strong resemblance to the power idea in the attitude of revolt which has characterized the freedom movement, and the method of freedom has become characteristically the resort to force. Its "removal of hindrances" became a destructive tendency in the "social reform" movement later, and with the industrialization of society the principle was openly acknowledged in the theory of competition. This was blessed by the much-touted scientific spirit of the time, which found it true, as it supposed, in the "fact" of struggle and survival. This was followed by the acceptance of survival and the minimum of subsistence as ends, and the self-contradiction in the idea of freedom negatively interpreted was made complete and final. Its fundamental weakness lies in its tacit acceptance of the methods and aims of the power state, which has appeared with devastating clearness in the business system.

3. BASED ON INTELLIGENCE

The political order as a moral phenomenon may be based upon intelligence, and this may mean a number of things. The idea of the rational state is at least as old as Plato and has even figured in the thought of the modern power state and the state of freedom. There are two forms of the doctrine of the rational state, which differ in the way in which they conceive the application of intelligence to the facts of the moral life. In the one case intelligence is applied to the facts as represented ideally, and in this case intelligence is supposed to furnish the order and constitution of the state ready-made and in advance of the state's existence. This attitude is supposed to have reached its fullest development with Plato and the utopians, but in strictness of statement it is best represented in modern constitutionalism. Thus the United States got its constitution imposed upon it in advance and made out of the abstractions of eighteenth-century speculation, and its character, which is predominantly negative, was taken from the negative freedom attitudes that were dominant at the time. That is an instance of the "planned" state, but it is the state as completely perfected in idea without too much reference to the concrete matter that must enter into the abstract scheme. On this point it recognizes that politics has no peculiar content, and it came dangerously near assuming that the state had no content at all.

But there is another sense in which the state may be said to be based upon intelligence. This combines intelligence as the idealizing capacity with intelligence as the capacity for observation, and implements both capacities in the methods and techniques of experiment. This means, of course, that the object arrived at is rationally determined, but it does not mean that it is ideally determined in advance of its existence. Experimentalism is only timidly recognized as yet as a valid political method, and its full ethical significance must await its fuller development in practice. But it assumes that any use of intelligence will keep close to the facts to which it refers and relates, and that, while political order has no content of its own, it is capable of accepting any rational content and must have a concrete content if it is to determine the ends of morality.

4. BASED ON SPECULATIVE ACTIVITY

Another type of order which as yet is not fully worked out in its modern form is the speculative. This represents a synthesis of the two uses of intelligence in the previous sections. It defines speculation as experimentation under logical conditions, and corresponds to practice as the use of intelligence in experimentation under temporal conditions. The combining of the two methods as the mode of expression of our practical attitudes is what is meant here by the speculative method. The practical object that results from the use of this method is what is meant by the speculative order of the moral life and is the image at once of the ideally perfect state and the replica of the most perfect political organization attainable under given conditions. Its full statement calls for a reformulation of the whole system of political ideas and would constitute the subject matter of political philosophy.

The conclusion here, then, with respect to the problem of the content of the political order, that there is no specific or peculiar kind of content, no experience that can be isolated and identified as the political experience as such, but that all types of experience, either personal or institutional, and regardless of their specific form or classification, are embraced within the political order. Politics then refers to the order and organization of life with regard particularly to the way in which institutions are to be related functionally to each other, and tends to ignore the question as to what specific sort of experience is best, which probably cannot be answered at all.

III. PROBLEMS OF POLITICAL STRUCTURE

Whatever may be the structure of the state in actual fact as distinguished from its abstract paper structure instanced in constitutionalism and other theories, it will in any case follow closely and be largely determined by the peculiar sort of content that is the dominant matter of the state. There is a general substance or matter of the state in the activities of persons behind all the forms of content, and this substance varies according as the natural and cultural environments of life vary. As represented in political thought, this substance is what is commonly pictured as the "purpose" or end of the state, or as some form of experience or some objective condition to be attained; and of this purpose there are three types or forms, usually represented as proprietary goods, as interests, or as welfare. With respect to this *object* of the state the types or forms of political order will be either (A) democracy-anarchy, (B) monarchy-absolutism, or (C) socialism-communism.

A. DEMOCRACY-ANARCHY

This form of political society may be distinguished, in its extreme developments, at least, as either democracy or anarchy; it conceives of goods or property and the experience of possession, as the matter or substance-content that is to be ordered and organized in the state. Democracy and anarchy will differ as to the nature and extent of the control that is to be exercised over property and the processes of production, distribution, and consumption, as well as to the character and extent of the privileges that are to be protected in possession; but it is this circle of ideas centering around the conceptions of property and possession that constitutes the stuff of the good life and the content of the state for both types of theory.

The theories fail to comprehend both the nature of the problem of property and possession and the control which is to be exercised over them by the state. If it is true, as both theories assume, that property and possession are essentially matters of the relation between objective goods and the person who is to use and enjoy and control the goods, then the state would have no right of control over goods and their possession, and the negative theory of the police state would be final, since the state could do nothing but exercise a general oversight to prevent conflicts. But both property, or goods, and possession are correctly defined not with reference to the individual person or persons who use and enjoy them but with reference to the state as the moral whole and the representative of all persons. And the forms of reference which goods and possession bear to the state are legal relations and are promulgated by the state as fundamental principles of law governing both goods and persons and determining the possessory relations between goods and persons. The state through law defines goods, persons, and possession, that is, the state by law creates all these entities so far as the order of the whole is concerned. Their content is determined for them in the moral structure of the world, but their form and the relations that shall be possible to them are matters to be determined by and within the state.

B. Monarchy-Absolutism

For the monarchy-absolutism theory of political content, what is at once accepted as the substance of the state and the content of the good is interest. Here the objective and material aspects of the good are regarded as incidental to the subjective and personal and also instrumental to the subjective and personal. Even persons themselves have their value in the reference they make to a specialized person or class of persons; hence all forms of the good are reducible to the reference to a subjective and personal source. And this reduction of all value to a subjective status is what is meant by interest.

It is, of course, evident that such an interest state as monarchy and the absolutism it tends always to become can maintain itself only because it does not adhere strictly to its principle. It is not possible to continue to regard objective good as merely incidental and instrumental to subjective good or states of mind. And when objective forms of the good assert themselves and force a recognition of their status as substantial good, as will always be true of property, the pure interest state, which is normally a power state of the personal type, begins to degenerate into oligarchy, and interest is identified with wealth. Thus the state when based on pure subjectivity is shown to be contradictory just as is the property state of democracy.

C. Socialism-Communism

In the socialism-communism theory there is recognizable an effort to avoid the contradictions of the other two theories by conceiving the substance of the state and the moral good as a synthesis of property and interest. This seems to be the meaning of the abstract notion of the "general welfare" which all these state-forms claim to be the content and substance of the good, and whose realization is the function of the state. It appears to rest on the simple assumption that subjective interest and objective good are interchangeable; that interest as a subjective fact is identical with goods as objective. On this assumption it is easy, in theory, at least, to build up a state in which all the conflicts about property and possession can be overcome and reconciled in a uniform state of mind that can be maintained in all persons indefinitely. This assumption is the basis of contract. And the method of politics, as the order of objective life, is identical with the method of maintaining order within the subjective life; it is itself a subjective method. Hence all types of political thinking which show the influence of this conception, as all modern types clearly do, will resort to subjective methods. Thus democracy accepts the method of education, monarchy the method of fear, etc., and in so far as they have been influenced by religious motives all accept the hortatory method or the method of persuasion.

The difficulty with all these conceptions lies in the fact that they attempt to force a concrete and specific content into the politico-ethical form. The substance of the good and the content of the political state is neither goods nor interests nor human welfare. The ultimate content of the political structure is the *order* of all objective goods, and the place and function of subjective goods are incidental to the main principles by which the order of objects is determined. The traditional theories—democracy, monarchy, theocracy, anarchy, socialism, etc.—are all wrong in that they assume that the content of political order is always persons and subjective elements like interest, welfare, etc., while the real content of politics is the system of real goods and the law of their order. It is of course true that persons constitute one kind of object in the system of all other kinds, are, for purposes of politics, objects in the same sense that other ultimate values are objects, and are to be disposed in the same ways. The position of the person is not unique or peculiar so far as the order of the whole is concerned. The person as an ethical concept is to be treated as in the same case with any other ethical concept, is to be regarded as an object whose place in the ultimate whole is to be determined. The fact that all other objects are objects *for* the person gives to person a specialized place in the theory of ethics regarded as a purely logical discipline, but in determining the ultimate object which ethical thought contemplates the person has merely a place among others in the structure of that object.

The overlooking of these fundamental ethical distinctions has tended to divorce politics from ethics and thus to release it from the control which ethics, as the doctrine of the good, has inherent and a priori right to exercise. The state has come to be interpreted subjectively as the "society of persons" in which persons are conceived to occupy a place unique and distinct from the other objects which constitute the objective world. But this abstract subjective notion of a collectivity of persons is social theory or sociology and is concerned merely with what may be the phenomenology of ethics, but it is not politics at all. Its primary conception of the mass of persons brought into a harmonic whole whose constitutive principle is the similarity of their instincts, the uniformity of their ideas and beliefs, and the identity of their convictions—in brief, the subjective like-mindedness of individuals, is a heritage which came upon the Western mind as the culmination of the religious movement and is in direct contrast with the original objective meaning of politics with Plato and Aristotle. In its real and original intent the political system is the orderly arrangement and organization of the things and objects of culture along with the things and objects of nature in an objective whole, and the constituent content of this whole was the order and law which applied indifferently to the persons and things involved. There is a suspicion of this truth in the major emphasis given in modern law to the law of contract as the order of persons and to the law of property as the order of things. But even of these conceptions there has been a subjective interpretation, the original compact or contract becoming a subjective meeting of wills, and the theory of property, as good things experienced, becoming the subjective doctrine of possession. Politics is, however, the objective order of the goods of life, with a basis in material goods. Politics is the order of all acts as acts are objectified in persons and property. Its basic principle is ethical law.

IV. PRACTICAL PROBLEMS OF POLITICS

These are problems of transforming the essential institutions of life in such ways as are necessary to the creation and maintenance of the goods which morality designates as representing the meaning of life. It is implied that institutions may be changed, either in structure or organization or in arrangement and distribution of content. The problem is to work out the methods and procedures through which institutions may the better be adapted to attain the ends they are designed to attain. It is also assumed that the task of effecting needed transformations and adaptations is one for politics. Among such procedures are the following.

A. The Modernization of the Family

It is still true that in our ideas of the family and the forms by which we represent those ideas there are many antiquated elements. The

marriage customs and ceremonies, the legal forms of the family relations, the methods of divorce and the provision for the care of individuals made helpless by the dissolution of the family, the moral rules
and social customs governing the conduct of members of the family—
all these are confused by remnants of past custom and superstition
which should be eliminated. Great strides have been made in recent
years, for example, involving the freedom of the wife, and these ad-
vancements have for the most part yet to be properly co-ordinated
with the other relations within the family. Also in the methods for
dealing with children of broken homes we seem still to have much to
improve. It is not possible to set a fixed standard as to what the organization of the family shall be for the future, but its corporate form
appears to be a biological and cultural necessity. All that appears possible is a general maxim to the effect that the family must change in
detail of organization as time goes on so as to fit with other institutions into the total scheme of the good life. It may, for example, be
necessary so to arrange the family as to permit the wife to work in
order that the family may co-operate with the institution of industry.
But it would appear safer to effect changes in industry such that the
wife's work will not be needed there. A rule of still broader scope
contemplates all the institutions as factors in the structure of culture
and requires of all of them the necessary adaption to each other and
to the whole to guarantee the most significant content for the whole.
These maxims which we have laid down will therefore apply to all
institutions and need not be repeated.

B. The Rationalization of Industry

While a large proportion of mothers must leave the home to work,
while a great number of children must leave school before their capacities are developed, while a great many men must idle their time away
seeking work while their children starve, while immature girls are
driven into a public life in factory and office, while many young
men and young women of undoubted capacity for the higher reaches
of culture are driven to cynicism and despair because of lack of opportunity which under the present scheme can only be guaranteed by a
share in the rewards of industry—while such conditions exist, it would
seem that some changes may be called for in our industrial organization. There is no purpose to argue that industry is further out of step
than other institutions, but the very emphasis that is placed upon it
suggests that its present structure might well be made the subject of
serious thought. In any case great and momentous forces are now

operating to transform industry, and it appears probable that a new institution may be in course of formation. What appears to be the case at present is that industry is now in the midst of the process of taking on the new corporate form. This is probably the meaning of the "industrial age," that the functions of work, production, distribution, etc., are being wrought into their corporate organization, just as in an earlier age the functions of worship, etc., were incorporated into the institution of religion. It is probably true that industry has never been, strictly speaking, an institution, and we may now be in the process of creating an institutional or corporate form for the desultory processes by which we maintain our existence and create material values. It is the lack of this corporate solidity in many industrial activities that brands them as chaotic and lawless. When these processes are properly set up in corporate form, it will be possible to think of industry as a corporate whole and as a real institution, and its place and function in the good life may appear more clearly to us. A great part of industry now has the physical and mechanical basis of incorporation fairly well accomplished. What is needed is to find and fit into its ponderous body the cultural principle of publicity which will complete the process of incorporation and institutionalization. It will then be possible to harmonize its activities with the other institutions of culture in the whole system of the good life. The fact that industry is taking on the form of the corporation is hopeful, for if it can be manipulated it can be managed. What is required now is the principle. It is the moral task of politics to find this principle and establish it and co-ordinate it with the system of the whole.

C. The Realization of Religion

We have already learned that religious motives tend to express themselves in characteristic and appropriate objects. They have innately the tendency to corporate form and organization. What seems necessary to emphasize is then a change from the excessive subjectivism which, in recent times, tries to realize religious ideas in mere mental visions and inward abstractions. So far has this subjective tendency gone that religion keeps aloof from and has little part in the actual work of the world, and it appears to be the accepted conviction that religion should have no relation to politics and the state or to business and industry, or with legal and aesthetic institutions and values. Consequently, we have a double, at least a confused, standard of the good with reference to religion on the one side and "worldly" affairs on the other. But if we can accept the principle that religious ideas, like all others, must find objectification if they are to carry moral force, then we shall see the essential fallacy in the attitude of spirituality and aloofness. And if religion is to justify its claim to speak in the name of morality, it will be obliged to show that its motives are capable of coming down into the thick of the fight and taking concrete form just as other motives do. Otherwise its interest in the moral good will be recognized as passive and subjective, and its judgments on moral questions futile. It would seem desirable, in view of the moral claims of religion, that it make solid corporate connections with politics, industry, and business so that it might find its appropriate form of body in which to express itself. We have noted its apparent preference for the aesthetic object, and here suggest that it might find political or industrial objects appropriate to many of its motives. In any case if the institution of religion is to take its natural place in the good life it will have to come to terms with politics, for it is the business of politics to furnish form and order to the good life and to determine the place in the whole of the various cultural factors.

D. The Demobilization of Education

We have seen all along that an act implies an object and that the kind of object determines the nature of the act; in fact, the act is precisely what, when realized, is the object, the object is the act as objectified. This principle determines the type of process involved in education, since the process of learning is an act. Then it is true that the type of person demanded by morality should determine the educative process as to both form and content. It is also true that objective considerations should control the act in each specific case—the object should be the act as realized in the instruments through which it is effected. A competent knowledge of a language will thus be the issue of study in connection with the language, reading it, writing it, constructing it in syntactical forms, and exploring it in grammatical analysis. The same is true in the more "practical," even the "manual" arts—the kinds of activity required are predetermined by the nature of the object they issue in. What acts I am required to perform in making a table are predesigned in the table; the outline and plan of the table are in detail the model and pattern of the acts I am to perform.

Then if the acts of the educative process are to be determined by the nature of the object to be produced, the acts of the learner cannot be dictated by the teacher. Hence the teacher is not a boss, and the educative process has no need of directors, supervisors, principals, etc. Such officers may look after the externals in equipment, etc., but they have no business interfering with the actual process of learning, which, under their negative influence, becomes the hopeless process of "instruction." The principle is that the educative process is a system of acts determined only by the nature of the objects which they contemplate, and any interference in the action is a perversion of education as a function in the good life. The problem of education as a moral question is to find the nature of the object which the educative process is to produce and to suggest the type of organization for education that will best fit it into the good life. It is clear that now the latter is the most pressing problem. It is generally agreed that the educational system has an organization that is rigid and unwieldy; that the system is not properly incorporated within the public purpose and, as a consequence, is out of harmony with other interests. Since it is the peculiar function of politics to look to the order of life, it should face the question of a better-organized education. This does not necessarily mean an increase in organization; in fact, an intelligent survey of the question would probably show that organization is now excessive. What is required is a change in quality and principle. It is precisely the meaning of our American insistence upon the public character of education that the public or political power should find for it its place in the scheme of the whole.

E. The Sanctification of Art

It is obvious that the proper place and the value of art in the good life have never been generally recognized. That place and value are determined simply by the fact that art and beauty are intrinsic and inherent aspects of the good, and this implies that no good is whole or complete that lacks the character of beauty. This, it is to be emphasized, is its moral function—it satisfies all requirements of morality when it merely exists as beauty, since, as such, it is a constituent of the good. This does not mean that art should be "moral" but merely that it should be art, for, in being what it is, it is right and good, and its contribution to the good life is completed. It is possibly true that the objects of beauty may be of any kind—industrial, religious, even moral—but their beauty is not because of the nature that thus classifies them. That is, an object is not beautiful because it is a religious object or an industrial object; its beauty, if it has any, is entirely independent of any such classification. Objects have their own unique requirements and characters by which they are beautiful, and these characters have nothing to do with religion, industry, or even moral-

ity. If a beautiful object is found useful or effective in religion, industry, or morality, so much the better, perhaps; but its beauty is independent of such utility or effectiveness.

That art should fulfil its function in morality, or, better, should
stand in its appropriate relations to morality, it should be demoralized.
That is, the principle that art has a function of its own and needs to
borrow no dignity from other concerns should be clearly and universally recognized. It does not depend on morality, or religion, or
anything else; it has a nature of its own, and its morality lies in merely
possessing that nature and in occupying the place in the whole good
which is determined for it by that nature. But the giving effect to
these principles in the actual world is the task of politics. It is the business of politics to find the order of the good life, and this order is constituted of the relations among the institutions. So the relation of art
and beauty to the whole through its corporate connections with the
other institutions it is the function of politics to determine.

F. The Publicization of Politics

By this awkward phrase we mean to insist that the moralization of
the world, which is the task of politics, has its first necessary prerequisite in the complete separation of the political function from
private interest. The institutions described above are the chief instruments of morality, and their effective functioning as individual instruments and their proper co-ordination to the moral purpose is the
charge that gives to politics its peculiar nature and purpose. When I
say that it is the task of politics to free itself from private interest,
I mean that every active function is to be directed *by politics* toward
the whole good; and by excluding the private interest I mean that all
specialized reference of an act to an isolated person or thing is to be
prevented. Of course it is true that in the technical process this special reference is essential; but this means that we must clearly distinguish the technical process from the moral act. The looking to the
total relations of life as institutionalized in the cultural world, and
the maintaining them in a perfect harmony and consistency with each
other, is the task of politics in the fulfilment of which it itself becomes
moralized.

It would be the task of political philosophy to work out in principle how this is to be effected. But we may say here that this concept
of a harmony of the cultural institutions effectively appropriated to
the system of nature, in the dynamic aspect implied in its maintenance, is the ground of the principle of right, which is the dynamic

form of the good. The function of politics is then the maintenance of right as order in and among the instruments of morality. It is not the province of the political state to concern itself with private morality or the lives of individuals as such. This is the function of the institution of law. It is rather the domain of politics to look to the universal principles of right and to see that they are adequately formulated in terms of the ideas and facts of each generation of persons. This is the process of legislation, the continuous exercise of which is the life of the state. This in detail will consist of a continuous reinterpretation and reassertion of the elementary concepts implied in the good life, and this reinterpretation and reassertion of the elements of morality is what is meant by the publicization of politics. The moral function of the political state is then continuously to institutionalize the primary forms of actions of men and to individuate these forms into the structure of the good life. It is the function of politics to supply the *wholeness* of the good life.

Chapter *XXII*

The Moral Life as End-Object

WE SHALL discuss here the moral life as the ultimate or perfect object, that is, as representing all in the way of meaning that can be required of an object considered as an end in the act of a person, and shall try to justify the conception of perfection as a moral category. For this justification it would seem to be necessary merely to state the sense in which the word is to be used. The perfection of an object implies that the object is an end, and this involves that the object has a history or a career, that it passes through processes of change in which it appears successively in a variety of forms. It is also implied that there is a first form of the object or a form with respect to which any antecedent form would have to be designated a different kind of object and as possessing a different nature. Also, there must be a last form, in the sense that any further development would involve a change of type.

To be an object at all implies a form which distinguishes the object within a type and a general nature which sets the bounds of the type. This nature is a group or synthesis of characters which the object must possess; any instance of the object will have and manifest all of the qualities or characters represented in this group. The form of the object will be the order of these characters; and this order may vary within the limits of possible combination and also within limits determined by the possibilities of degree of the characters as indicated in the mode of their appearance in any instance of the object. Thus an individual tree may be regarded as a perfect specimen when there is a form which, as an order of qualities, determines it an ash, and a nature which includes all (theoretically) of the characters which an ash tree can have under the limitation that each character must be specified as to degree.

In other language a perfect object is one that has a history or a career and whose qualitative appearance in a given form makes it obvious that it is, in the form in which it appears, a synopsis of that history. Only, it is to be understood that history does not refer merely to the stretch of time backward from the appearance of the object, its actual history, but also to its possible history as indicated in the series of forms which the object can have in the future. Perhaps it is better to speak of this total history as the object's career; then a perfect object is a typic object which in each instance of its appearance expresses its full career, or an object that is all that it can be. Or, if we like an apter rhetoric, we may call the perfection of an object its "destiny." We would thus accept Green's phrase that a perfect object is one that is all that it has in it to become, but would add that the object has within it now all that it ever has been. An object's history and destiny are parts of its being as fact, and a reference to that history or destiny is a characterization of the fact.

With these distinctions in mind the question of the ultimate objectivity of the moral life is one of asking for a statement of the factual implications of the central concepts of morality when these concepts are regarded as categories of perfection. Thus, in terms of our definitions, the question of the nature of the ultimate moral object becomes one of the meaning of a perfect person, a perfect world, a perfect act, together with a perfect end as the synthesis of the meanings of all of these taken in their total interrelationships. These we shall take up in their order.

I. THE PERFECT PERSON

A large part of this work (Part II) has been devoted to the explanation of the concept of person and to description of the person in his character as fact. Here we wish to consider the person as having attained all that the moral law requires of him, living in a world which is what it ought to be as a consequence of his act, which act is in itself regarded as complete and as satisfying all the conditions laid upon it by moral law. The good life we wish to consider as the eternal moral act which continuously creates and maintains the unity of this person with this world, thus constituting the end for which there is no further issue.

In chapter ix we gave a summary statement of the characteristics of the person. These we saw to fall into two groups, one enumerating the physical and conscious capacities that belong to the person when taken by himself; the other describing the civil, legal, and social capacities, those which depend upon the necessary relations that in fact hold between such individual persons. These relations have their primary meaning determined largely by the nature of the corporate social structure rather than by the individual persons between whom they hold. Thus what freedom is to mean in a given case is a question of what kind of people exercise it; if we think of the freedom of savages or degenerate civilized people, it will consist of acts that are simple and of a low order. On the other hand, the freedom of cultivated people will be made up of acts that are complex and delicately formed. Again, the community or state that can be explained as made up of the relations of individual persons, or of "groups" of persons, will be loose-jointed and unstable and composite. It was, however, this descriptive notion of the person and the composite community that came to be the presuppositions that determined the meaning of the concepts of traditional ethics. Right, duty, conscience, freedom, responsibility—all the categories on a basis of which the prevailing ethical thought has been built up—get their meaning from the assumption that all the capacities of the person are functions of the person as an isolated individual together with the assumption that all relations of persons are nothing but expressions of these distinct capacities. As a corollary from these premises there is the composite state or community, which is conceived to be a mere aggregate or collection of persons brought together in some unexplained way by the individual expression of their capacities and held together by subjective bonds of interest or patriotism or "respect for law" or whatever other subjective motive might be the prevailing theory of the time.

Such is the person and the world (community) of individualistic and collectivistic ethics. The mistake that is common to these two supposedly different points of view lies in the kinds of assumptions which both make with respect to the nature of the person and to the kinds of relations that can hold among such persons. These assumptions compel an interpretation of all the ethical ideas in strictly subjective terms. All these ideas are either forms or states, or traits, or habits of mind, and the theoretical explanation of any one idea lies in finding and describing the state of mind with which it is identified. Duty is thus the sense or feeling or conviction of the individual that he is bound to a certain course of action, for example, that he owes something to somebody or to some cause. Freedom is the consciousness of the absence of hindering bounds or of the capacity to surpass or transcend those bounds and always refers to the individual as either alone or collected in groups. Obligation is the sense or feeling, or rational conviction, on the part of the individual person, of the necessary and inevitable character of the bonds of duty; or the psychological motive that functions as the rational acceptance of a more or less definitely fixed place or status within the group. All these concepts are then either individual or "social" in nature, but all are in any case subjective states or states of mind when the question is asked as to the facts upon which they depend for their meaning.

The practical consequences of these mistaken assumptions have been disastrous. For ethical science they have resulted, for the most part, in psychological analysis and description, or logical analysis, of mental states, apparently assuming that if we know the states of mind of the individual, all that we need to know about his actions will somehow be added unto us. Also, in the examination of action all that is needed to reveal to us the meaning of an act is to find the mental state upon which it depends and out of which it flows. Given the individual's "motive" or "intention" or "purpose" in a particular case, the act involved is immediately explained; and the method is also suggested by which the state of mind may be approved or condemned. Also, approval or condemnation of the state of mind, which is supposed to establish it or destroy it, is assumed to be the essential part of the moral judgment upon the act or the moral estimate of the act; the actual objective circumstances and relationships of the act being, for the most part, overlooked. The relationships of the act, if judged bad, are overlooked because it is assumed that the change that is effected in the antecedent state of mind by the bad relationships is a safe guaranty against recurrence of the act. And if there is too much doubt that the guaranty is safe, the erring individual will be subjected to punishment in order that the chastened state of mind may be maintained.

Thus has grown up, out of these subjectivist presuppositions, the fundamental practical "principle" that significant results can be obtained in the moral world by a mere change of mind. To cure the thief, we should develop in him a peculiar state of mind which we will call the conviction of the evil of stealing; or we will put fear into him by threats of punishment, and this fear will deter him. If he lapses after our operations upon his mind, we will put him in jail or subject him to other tortures in order to maintain in his mind the proper state or attitude out of which righteous acts are to flow, and the presence of such proper states or attitudes will inhibit or prevent the recurrence of the state which made the act of stealing inevitable. Upon this sort of thing are based not only our ethical convictions and precepts but also our theory as to the practical application of these precepts. Thus our system of criminal law in its theory is a confusion of subjective monstrosities and in its execution the scandal of the age. It plays with hypothetical states of mind and constructs a system of toys and tools by which these states of mind may be manipulated or created or destroyed or maintained, blissfully ignorant of the essential fact that an act, which is the subject matter of our problem and even the essence of the states of mind, is a fact hard and stubborn in the objective external world. Hence no act can be "corrected" in the sense that it can be changed into its opposite or made less of a fact than it is, and any effort in this direction will be hocus-pocus. The only thing that can be *done* about acts is to anticipate and prevent them, and this anticipation and prevention of the act is only possible by control of the objective world in which alone the act can occur as fact. The only thing that can be done about states of mind is their ordering in thought, and this is not an act in the sense contemplated in ethics. That is, an act is a state of mind only when we think it, only when we are intelligent about it; yet our thinking and intelligence are not supposed to result in an act but in the law of an act. And the prevention of an act can mean only such a determination of objective conditions by the law of the act as will render the act unnecessary or impossible, the impossibility and lack of necessity being merely descriptive names for objective situations. Hence we are at every and all points dealing with objective situations of fact when we deal with acts, whether we deal with them in the theoretical way in thought or in the practical way in conduct and the order and control of life.

The outstanding instance of the breakdown of our ethical concepts because of their subjectivity is the case of international relations. The desire for peace and orderly relations seems to be practically uniform and unanimous among men. Yet war and commercial confusion and conflict are the prevailing condition. The mere desire for peace cannot effectually establish peace, nor is there any conviction or any other state of mind that can directly or indirectly determine the conditions of peace. Yet we do not see this. The statesman, even the politician, laments the fact that there is no peace. The statesman, however, gives the wrong reason for this fact in every case—that peace must await the general acceptance among men of a common conviction as a state of mind. But the common conviction or state of mind is already generally accepted. The fact that determines international relations, as well as interpersonal relations, is the objective system of instruments within which our characteristic forms of action are implemented. We trade with other peoples, and our trading creates and embodies itself in a system of tools and instruments. Our acts are thus objectified in permanently fixed structures, and these structures become the causes and conditions of future action. Thus we fight, and our fighting in war objectifies in munitions. Munitions become permanently established in the armaments industry; the armaments industry can thrive only on continued war, and wars come. Or we trade with and deceive each other. Deception is objectified in business as the instrument of trade; as objectified in this instrument, it becomes a fixture of culture—commerce. Commerce, business, thrives only on deception, and deception comes. But the armaments industry and commerce are not states of mind, and we can do nothing about either by changing our minds.

It is only therefore as states of mind become objectified and realized in the instruments through which they are expressed that they have *any* real part in action. They are not "motives," if by motives we mean originators of movement, for these are largely organic conditions determined by situations external and objective to the organism. Mental life becomes realized therefore only in the systems of instruments through which and by means of which it is expressed, and these systems of instruments, as elements of public or "social" structure, become again the ground and condition of further ideas and further actions.

The subjectivist interpretation of morality, the theory that morality can be formulated in states of mind or "ideas," is hopelessly inadequate. When we realize this, then psychology can no longer masquerade as ethical method, and we shall have to go back to logic. The first consequence of this is that the theory of the individual as the basic ethical concept must be given up. This will entail a complete reinterpretation of the system of ethical concepts. But when we give up individualism, then the theory of "interpersonal" relations is done for. And with this will go all reference to the "social," and ethical method will have nothing to do with sociology.

What we require to see now is that the systems of objectified acts—acts realized in their means of expressions—are in reality the persons that morality and ethical thinking contemplate, for it is these objectified acts that form the substance of institutions, and man lives only in and through institutions. The real person of morality is therefore the corporate person, the man enthroned within the system of his institutions. These institutions furnish means, conditions, and ends for his acts; they furnish him with his motives and purposes; and, since a man's morality is the man, they furnish to him the very substance of his being. They are his body; in them he is incorporate. And it is this corporate person that is contemplated by all the categories of morality, since it is through and by reference to it that they have their meaning. They all find their universality in their reference to the corporate person as end—the man living in a scheme of institutions which adequately and perfectly express his purposes and ideas. It is to this person that all moral ideas refer, even when we include the states of mind of individuals within the system of moral ideas; for the idea or state of mind of an individual that cannot find objective place within the structure of the world cannot be true and can never be real. The man then as objectified in and instrumented through institutions is the corporate person, the person of morality.

We shall be interested in the following four or five chapters to give an account of the virtues of the corporate person, or what we shall call the "objective virtues"; but before we go on to that task we must consider some other fundamental concepts in their relation to the person. Just here we shall indicate that what we have called the moral world is this system of institutions, which we have already described individually as the family, industry, education, religion, art, and politics. The relations among these institutions are the "personal relations" of ethical theory.

II. THE PERFECT WORLD

It has already been explained that the moral world is, in our view, the system of human institutions. The world is therefore the objective meaning of the person. And we have already shown that each of these institutions represents the organization and embodiment, by human effort, of some typical object which experience has found to be an essential form of the good. Each represents therefore a universal good as determined in the concrete in the experience of men; and taken together they constitute the good as law, the final object in which life through action has embodied itself. Each institution is thus the corporate whole of the instinct, feeling, and knowledge of men with respect to some major aspect or object of life, which action and will have, through the instruments of nature, realized as a permanent element in the structure of culture. In this vast process of creating the good, individual effort has co-operated with individual effort, with the result that the total effect of action has been the realizing of the creative power of culture as the joint product of all human forces and resources. It is thus that the private and personal energies of men have been collected, synthesized, and transcended in the public power or public act, the act of culture which continuously creates the good and maintains it in the structure of its institutions. It is true that analysis finds that, in heroic instances, the creative act may begin in the great individual, but it does not do so necessarily, and the individual act bears a relation to the total public act of culture similar to that which a single cell bears to the organism in which it has its life.

It is to this total structure of the good that each of the concepts of morality has the relation that determines its peculiar character as a moral concept. It is only by analogy to this living whole that the "individual" gets its character as a person. And the relation in which the life-urgency of the individual stands to the creative urge of the cultural whole characterizes the individual urge as an act. Taken by itself and in its local relations to its environing objects, the individual's "act" is properly described as a movement. It acquires meaning only through its relation to that whole in which it is ended, and only from the viewpoint of the whole does it become properly an act. It is within this relation to the institutional whole that the idea of end has the meaning which distinguishes it from the mere limit or point where action stops and from the mere result which marks the point where movement ceases. Right as a quality of acts has its meaning in the consistency with the whole which the act manifests in its structure. The act is wrong or bad because of its lack of consistency with the whole of the good. And the moral qualities which we tend to attribute to the person as the originator of acts have their meaning only from their relation to the whole. Thus obligation, which we commonly try to explain by reference to the states of mind of the individual as actor, is a quality of the relation of the act to the whole and is found in the necessity that the act be consistent with the whole if it is to be a moral fact. Obligation is thus an objective fact, an attribute of the act, and its relation to an act can be determined without reference to the individuality of the actor. It is thus a "universal," and we can say of acts that they are obligatory for any person who finds himself in the situation where the obligation is determined. Even such facts as intent, purpose, desire, etc., which we are accustomed to regard as mere states of mind, are not mere psychological facts when we think them in relation to an act but objective aspects of a relation determined by the nature of the whole. Freedom is the character impressed upon an act by the act's being made obligatory by the demand of the whole good. And a similar "deduction" is possible for every moral concept.

It is thus within man's corporate or institutional connections that moral concepts have their meaning, since the whole good is the total synthesis of institutions. We shall illustrate this by an instance taken from each of the major institutions, showing how each act to which we attribute the moral quality carries with it a reference to the whole good and how its moral quality depends upon this reference.

Let us take the family first, and in the family the duty of the parent to care for his child, and the reciprocal phase of the same relation of duty on the part of the child to respect the parent.

The reason why a parent should support and care for his child is not that such conduct is to the interest either of the parent or of the child. For under ordinary conditions, where the element of chance is large, this tendency to consider the interests as final will result in the sacrifice of one of the persons to the interests of the other. It is probably true that in a majority of cases in family relations at the present time the child is being handicapped with respect to his future by the necessity to help support the family. This we attempt to explain and justify on the ground of the child's duty; but the child has no such duty, and, if such support be required of him beyond a certain limit, he is being sacrificed, his future usefulness is being drawn on and expended before he has a chance to realize his capacities. On the other hand, if such a situation is interpreted in terms of the interest of the child, then under normal conditions the parent is sacrificed. If it be argued that sacrifice is the lot of mankind here below, the answer is that it is such so far as life is not yet moral. But there is no moral quality in mere sacrifice. Then the sacrifice of the parent in the interest of the child is an instance of elementary evil, and the tragedy of modern life lies in the fact that a large percentage of parents are broken beyond recovery by the time they have reached forty in a hopeless effort to give some degree of cultural opportunity to their children. It is still more tragic in the fact that the effort rarely succeeds, since the child also breaks under the strain when to his own duty there is added the burden of his parent's failure. It is probably true that in modern society the vast majority of children realize only a small part of their natural and cultural possibilities, for the reason that they must assume the duties of adults before they are old enough to understand them. And there seems no way out of the difficulty on the principle of the interests of parent and child.

The duty of the parent has nothing to do with his interest or with the interest of the child. The parent's support and care of the child are his duty because it is good that parents care for children, and it is good that parents care for children because in so doing they maintain and perpetuate the conditions of parental care and filial respect. That is, in the exercise of the function which corresponds to the duty the parent and the child contribute to the creation and maintenance of the institution of the family, and the family is the sum of all conditions necessary to parental care and filial respect. That is to say, the argument becomes circular not because of faulty presuppositions but because the argument is itself the statement of an ultimate presupposition—it states, that is, the presupposition of the family as the objective condition of all moral relations between parent and child. It is thus a corporate judgment.

But the family as presupposition is final because it is a miniature of the whole cultural structure. It is the world. Then the relations of the family are ultimate aspects of the good because each of them corresponds to its counterpart in the total structure, and the relation which in an earlier connection we called "analogy" is now seen to be a relation of identity. Parental care and filial respect are then good because there is nothing in the whole of the good that can be demanded beyond them which is the same with them in quality. This long argument can be summed up in the statement that family relations are intrinsically good, goods that are good not because of dependence upon anything other than themselves in quality but because their quality is itself a factor of the world and a presupposition of life and culture.

We have already shown (chap. xviii) that industry is the organization of work, and so far as it is moral, it is so in that it is a product of the elementary reason that is implied in the phenomena of human action. What we want to show here is that industry represents for us a part of the objective good, a part of the world which every act assumes. To do this we shall show that the moral meaning of work is derived from the relation between the work activity and the moral whole and that it has nothing of consequence to do with the private and special characters of the situation where action takes place. As in the case of the family relation it is easy to show that the morality of work has nothing to do with the interests of individuals or with any other specific relation in which individuals may stand. The description of work in terms of interests and needs and wants is an economic description and derives whatever consistency it has from the presupposition of gain. But morality can accept no such presupposition. What makes work a moral function, when it is a moral function, is the fact that it tends to create and maintain the natural-cultural whole in which work will always be possible. It is this circle in the proof which is the evidence of its intrinsic good, a fact which the economic instinct feels but fails to understand and hence perverts in the repetitive productive process. For it is the moral purpose of work to create and maintain in an eternal process the conditions under which work may successfully be performed, and the successful performance means such performance as will make work eternally possible. The evidence of successful performance in the individual case is the perfection of the object created. But this means that work is an objective good, a part of the total whole which is the presupposition of all moral distinctions. The work activity then objectifies itself in the nature of things and for this reason becomes a good for which there is no further reason. Work becomes incorporate in the institutional system, and its "necessity" is thus moral. What in detail the existing work process will have to become in order to meet these moral conditions is the task of politics in discovering the grounds of harmony among the essential institutions. But this is in any case clear, that work as a moral function is in no sense an economic necessity. In the existing economic "system" labor is compulsory, and it is the prostitution of work under our peculiar economic superstitions that stands in the way of accomplishing even the simplest elements of moral good in the sphere of material things.

Thus the institution of industry as the moral organization of work so as to perpetuate its conditions is an objective good and a part of the world that is implied in every act.

We have in the case of education the same problem of insistence upon the objective or institutional aspect of the function. And, as in the case of the family and industry, education as it is in fact is pretty much what morality could not sanction. But there is in the existing education one sound instinct at least; the educative process must be institutionalized. The fact that our expert educationists, in attempting to follow the instinct, merely succeed in mechanizing the function does not argue the instinct perverse but merely demonstrates that instinctive activity requires the direction of reason and good sense if it is not to go wrong. The fact then that the educational activity is smothered in administrative mechanism means not that education should be disorganized by merely getting rid of the machinery but that its mechanism should be transformed into rational organization. Our instinct of a universal, public, free school system was wiser than we knew when we adopted the theory, since we did not see clearly how universality, publicity, and freedom were to be incorporated in the institution; could not anticipate the type of corporate body these ideas require to give them power. As a consequence the ideals of universality, publicity, and freedom have been corrupted; especially has the corruption of the public function of education proved disastrous. We have to keep in mind the fact that the act is the means by which the objective reality of anything is maintained, that it is through the act alone that, as individuals, we achieve a real continuity with that in which we ourselves are realized. And as the function of learning-teaching is an act, its very essence lies in its publicity, its being a part of the objective wholeness of things. The education system is then a part of our total world, a necessary body within which essential types of activity are carried on. And the process to which it gives body is an act in which the individual realizes his objective continuity with the good world.

A similar review would show that art and religion are corporate orders of typical acts, that they represent an aspect of the good that can be realized in no way other than by their appropriate institutions, that they require to be objectified in public systems, and that as objectified they constitute each its unique phase of the ultimate good. In fact, the sense of realization of the good, as exemplified in perfect objects, is perhaps stronger in religion and art than in any other institutional form of the good. So far, at least, as realization is to be measured by the immediate consciousness, there can be no doubt of this, particularly when we remain on general ground. In the sense of possession these have closer contact with the good than educational activity or work, and it cannot be denied that immediacy of possession of the good is itself a good. In education and work, and most moral activities, the hold on the good is postponed, deferred, ideal, and there is a sense in which morality itself rests upon this deferment. For an act implies that something is *to be* accomplished, is not yet within the scheme of existence, and it is the purpose of the act to bring the object into existence. Thus it seems that the possessory attitude is nearer the good than those which merely anticipate it; but we shall have to learn that the possessory and the anticipatory attitudes are not exclusive when they are understood consistently with moral requirements.

But no further argument is required to show that religion and art are objective facts and thus parts of the world of the good.

There is a difference of character to be noted when we come to discuss the objective morality of politics. We have seen that other institutions of the good are each described as a part of the good. But it is the nature of politics to represent, or in some sense to be, the good as the whole. This we saw in finding that there is no peculiar content for politics, that its content is the *order* of the moral institutions when that order is complete to the extent that the harmony of the whole is maintained. What is peculiar about politics is therefore that it objectifies and incorporates and implements the *order* of institutional life. As this order is, in principle, ideal, there will be a large element of symbolism in the structure which it builds up; and this symbolic structure has the disadvantage that it is not visible to the ordinary individual but is real only to those of a certain capacity of imagination. As a consequence the *object* we call "politics" is confused with the instrument by which politics works, viz., government. But we have ourselves identified the object of the act with the instrument of its expression. What is meant here by differentiating them is that we can distinguish the instrument as object when it appears in its character as end and as instrument merely when it appears as primarily means. But the distinction is perhaps not important practically; it is only necessary when theory requires exactness and adequacy.

For practical purposes the object of politics, the instrument in which it objectifies, is government. This is the form then in which the whole good appears as concrete; and its immediate material is the *res publicae*, the public affairs in which the highest form of action is attempting objectification. This activity consists, for the individual, in all acts of his which directly or remotely affect the total structure of life. As all acts to some extent have this character, all acts are public, and it is in this character that we can qualify them as good.

The world which morality implies is, then, the total world which becomes objective in public relations, and for this we have the name "politics." Politics is then the final instrument of morality, and while it is true in the particular case that "you can't legislate morality," yet morality can legislate the good through political action; and this is finally the only way that the good is to be achieved. The good is a corporate product of all our activity, but it is so only as this activity is properly organized and instrumented in public agencies. Morality is thus the only thing that can be legislated or can legislate; and, if we mean by legislation the corporate act of the whole by which the good is objectified, then it is the ultimate moral act. It is the perfection of the state that gives the law, and the law objectifies in the good of human relations. The ultimate moral object is thus the state, even the state that is the actual embodiment of our perfection and our imperfection, as well as the state as it is implied in the eternal process of the act.

We have now to inquire as to what, as a last word, it is that constitutes this ultimate act, or the act which we have called "perfect."

III. THE PERFECT ACT

We have just seen that it is through political or public instruments that an act is, in the end, made real. And we have noticed that it is the essential meaning of an act that it connects a person with, and realizes him in, his world. The ideal standard of acts, or the perfect act, is then the idea of the dynamic whole in which the perfect person, as representing all subjective values, and the perfect world, as representing all external values, are united and harmonized in an objective whole of good. This implies the fulfilment of all the requirements with respect to both the person and the world that were laid down (chap. iv) in the law of morality. Thus it was stated that the good life implies a person "endowed by nature and culture with all the capacities and capabilities that are possible to him, living in a world so organized and ordered as to give to the person full and free access to all the means to the achievement of his purposes." The "perfect person" and the "perfect world" are no more and no less than the fulfilment of these requirements, and the perfect act is any act in which the two are brought into harmony and union. Perfection is thus the standard by which we measure the degree to which any act tends to unify and articulate the person with his world, and it represents the aspect of universality which we identify as the moral quality itself. Thus we say that an act is moral, immoral, right, wrong, etc., in so far as it does or does not tend to establish the individual person in the substance of his world. But this does not imply the "adaptation" of the person to his world or the modifying of the person to make him fit into his world. It implies rather that the world and the person are to be made over so as to conform to the ideal and objective values which it is the special function of the person to create through his unique powers of experience in thought and feeling.

It is in such terms that we have defined the meaning of an act. "An act," we have said, "is the assumption of the possibility of a real relation between a person and his world," or, "the assumption that such a relation conceived in idea can be made real through the efforts and capabilities of the agent when in possession of the necessary external means." We say the act is an assumption because it must always be designed and decreed ideally in thought before it can be realized; it must exist in plan and design before it can exist in fact, and the transformation of this design into an object is precisely what is meant by an act. By a perfect act we mean, therefore, the idea of an act as implying all that the act can be in terms of unity and harmony between the actor and his world, with this idea of the fulfilled act taken as a standard by which the moral quality of all acts of the same kind are judged. The perfect act of honesty is, therefore, the idea of the unity of all personal values with all external values in so far as this unity is to be maintained by paying debts, etc. That is, the perfect act is the idea of the act as having become all that it can be, or the act as realized and objectified in its necessary external conditions. The idea in its subjective ideality is what traditional theory means by "intention" and the "good will," while the sum of its necessary objective conditions is probably what is meant by "results."

IV. FORMS OF THE PERFECT ACT

The act, then, incorporates the person, as the synthesis of cultural values, into the world, as the sum of natural values. It thus creates the individual. Or, since it is the individual that acts, the act is the process by which the individual creates and maintains itself. This it does in effecting the unity and harmony between persons and the external conditions upon which persons depend for their objective realization. Work, for example, is the act by which the person guarantees to himself, through the whole implied in the idea of the act, material sustenance and effective energy. Worship is the act through which the person objectifies in symbols his ideal designs. But the forms of the act that connect with the individual as its peculiar modes of expression are not, as we have just seen, all that the act can mean. The act is, as objective, the process of self-expression in and through which the institutionalized forms of the good maintain themselves in the whole which they create. There is a sense then in which the moral act may be described as the peculiar form of expression of an institution, and it is this expression that represents all that can concretely be meant by the universality which is attributed to the act. It is possible then to speak of generalized acts and of institutions expressing themselves as persons through these generalized acts.

The types of these generalized acts are what we shall call the "objective virtues." They are virtues in the sense that they have all the characters of personal expression. They are objective in the sense that they are incorporated in the fixed structure of the world. They represent, therefore, the intelligence, feeling, and active tendencies of persons as realized in the course of history and as substantiated in the structure of culture. We shall name the characteristic objective virtues here and shall discuss them in their order in the succeeding chapters.

When the knowledge of persons which has been acquired in the process of their historic experience has become incorporate and effective in the systems of science, it separates itself from individuals and becomes impersonal and, in becoming impersonal, becomes also the ground of what is true as such and independently of specific conditions. It is thus that knowledge becomes an active force incorporate in human culture and acts without directly involving the individual. It rather furnishes the cognitive background within which the individual acts and in whose substance the individual shares. This is what we call the "objective virtue of wisdom." It is institutionalized knowledge. And as we say that behind all the subjective virtues there lies knowledge as their foundation, so in the case of objective virtues, wisdom, which is institutionalized knowledge, is found to be their uniform basis.

The life-activities and life-functions, both biological and psychological, undergo a similar institutionalization in the instruments through which, as natural tendencies, they are directed and controlled. Life, in the form of instincts and natural tendencies—sex, hunger, security, dignity, etc.—comes to be organized in its objects with reference to objectives—the family, church, school, etc.—and becomes a significant organ in the structure of culture. This we call the "objective virtue of temperance."

Even tendencies to types of acts become generalized and objectified in fixed forms, and these forms we know in the individual as established active attitudes. When these active attitudes are publicly organized into the structure of culture, we may speak of the objective virtue of courage.

The function of intelligence in understanding these virtues as generalizations of all aspects of experience, and in organizing them into a consistent whole, when incorporated in instruments appropriate to its nature as intelligence, the judicial system, we may call the "objective virtue of justice."

Finally, when from the point of view of action we contemplate the future of the good life as the moral whole and idealize it with respect to its possibilities, we are exercising the virtue of holiness, which is a final synthesis of the subjective virtues with the objective virtues in the aesthetic imagination. But this carries us beyond morality into the fields of religion and art.

We shall in the next part give a chapter to the explanation of each of the objective or moral virtues.

Part V

The Objective or Perfect Virtues

Chapter XXIII

Wisdom or Objectified Knowledge

W E HAVE in Part IV described the types of institutions in which human action is realized. Action, we saw, seeks means of expression appropriate to it and, in constantly using this means, attaches itself to it in so intimate a way that the means may be said to come to embody the form of the action or to be the structure of which the action is the function. It is because of this character of action that the world may be contemplated as a whole, since it is only within the unity of means constituted by the act that the discordant and opposing subjective and external factors can be reconciled. It is in this sense also that action has what are called "metaphysical" or "cosmic" implications, in that not only does its nature necessitate that it take on substance or be real but the nature of everything else that can be real is such that it can be thought only as an element of order through the integrating force of action. Then a world can exist or be thought only in so far as experienced fragments of reality are brought to terms of consistency with each other through action. And it is the system of the forms of action implied here which, after being embodied in appropriate means, constitute the substance of culture; and this substantial culture in its dynamic expression takes various forms. It is to these forms of embodied action that we give the name of "objective virtues." To these we now turn.

I. WISDOM AND KNOWLEDGE

We found in the discussion of subjective virtue that knowledge is the most important moral accomplishment of the individual or isolated person, and we expressed this fact by saying that the first and basic obligation of the individual is the obligation to know. Here we are to see that knowledge is only the beginning of wisdom in the active experience.

Knowledge becomes wisdom through the corporate activities of individuals, these activities being always implemented in the established structures of culture. For instance, *knowledge* of politics is attained through the efforts of individuals by private study, and this knowledge is co-ordinated and corrected by the scholarly exchange of opinion among workers in this field. But this knowledge will remain without effect so long as it is buried in the science of politics in books and in the minds of men. It is only when this knowledge is solidified and embodied in the instruments of politics and government that it gives effect to the purposes of men in any practical way, since it is only by such instrumentation that knowledge becomes a concrete good. Political knowledge therefore becomes political *wisdom* when it is made practically effective in and through the forms of political and civil organization, since in this form it gives body to habits and customs, and so becomes an actual part of the acts and purposes of men. So long as such knowledge is mere science, classified and organized knowledge, it is a product of the abstract intellect and is yet to be given meaning in terms of experience by actual application. The application is effected by giving it means of expression in political machinery, and as thus expressed it acquires meaning in terms of the active and feeling experiences out of which as impulse the knowledge grew. We have noted that experience has a content only as it finds material in feeling, and it is this feeling intelligently organized and instrumented in the tools and objects of action that becomes the permanent stuff of culture. As such it is there as a fixed and permanent good, organized into the texture of institutions, available to any who care to make use of it; and we recognize it as the "wisdom of our fathers" because it comes to us as a heritage.

It is so with all types of knowledge; only in so far as they are capable of embodiment in the public structures of life can they exert that influence upon the lives of men that we associate with wisdom. Knowledge must be tested and seasoned in the experience of the race before we can say unqualifiedly that it is good, and the test of its being seasoned is the fact that we find it available to all in the objective form of institutions. As an example of what we mean by wisdom defined as objectified knowledge we may take an instance where knowledge fails of appropriate objectification and note the effects upon the cultural life. The best instance is the case of technique, where knowledge is expressed in a mere tool which does not become a proper objective instrument. This includes all the processes and products used in the private production and control of goods in the economic life. All such techniques require to be organized for use as public instruments to a public good if they are to be made consistent with moral principle. We may cite as a further example the use of knowledge of chemistry in the production of the instruments of war, in inventing and perfecting poisonous gases, explosives, etc. Such knowledge cannot become wisdom, since there is no way by which it can be incorporated in the public instruments of culture. To attempt to organize into the structure of life the use of poison gas will prove contradictory at once, since the very effect of the use of the gas is to disintegrate the social whole of culture in whose benefit it is supposed to be used. It is only when and where such things can be implemented to a constructive purpose that they can be conceived as moral agencies, and by a constructive purpose we mean one that makes an essential contribution to the public good in the total life of man. And the knowledge that invents and controls such instruments and processes is of no moral significance, and so not strictly true, until it is embodied in public means and directed to a public end.

A generalized instance of the moral fallacy involved in technique is the case of machinery. The evils of machinery are frequently pointed out, but it is doubtful whether its real moral weakness is often fully or correctly perceived. The fatal weakness of machinery, as employed in the production of goods, appears in the imperfection of the product, which in no case will fit rightly into the system of the good. Into the creation of the goods that are to become the content of the good there must go some elements of life itself. Ordinarily this factor of life is provided in the knowledge and purpose of the agent who directs the activities that create the good. We have noted that the content of the good will always represent experience and that experience becomes the content of the good by fitting to itself through action an object or body which it fabricates out of the things of nature and culture. These things of nature and culture, in their order and system, are the wisdom that constitutes the medium in which life-activity takes place. Now in the operation of machinery this element of life or experience is absent. The process of forming materials is blind, and the nearest approach to a life-element in the operation of the machine is in the design that created the machine. There is none in the product. But this design is rigidly hardened into the structure of the machine, and with respect to the product it becomes a mere pattern, which necessitates that every product shall imitate it exactly in every detail. Consequently, the element of life that is necessary in every good object is not to be found in the machine product, since it is not knowledge that directs the processes of its production but the mere mechanism of fixed routine. Such a product will never satisfy, for no object will equate with life in the way of satisfaction that does not have within it an element of life itself; that is to say, an element of the life that produced it. Only from life itself can life come, and the final criticism of machinery and its product is that they are lifeless and hence have no direct relation to the good. The knowledge that creates life in a public object is wisdom, and the only perfect instance of a completed moral act is the work of art.

But the machine and its product may have an indirect relation to the good. They may contribute to the good while they will never be any part of the good. We have seen that they cannot be goods because they are never perfect instances of that objectified life which is wisdom. How they are to be made indirect contributors to the good is a question of special technical knowledge for each type of machine and product; what the good demands is that they must bear some final reference relation to the whole in their structure and design, for in the absence of such relation the goodness of any object is only partial and potential. Whether an automobile is to have this "instrumental" goodness depends upon whether or not an ultimate reference to the whole good is cast into its design and materialized in its structure. That such a reference to the good is not now a factor in the automobile is sufficiently evidenced in the excessive speed, noise, stench, and aesthetic formlessness which now characterize it. And in this case, as in all cases, perhaps, the test of the presence or absence of goodness in the strict moral sense is the aesthetic test; an object or an act the idea or design of which is not strictly consistent with aesthetic feeling as objectified in form—and by consistency here is meant that an object must perfectly express and embody the feeling—is an object or act which cannot appropriately articulate with the whole good and is thus not a moral good. But a good hammer, although it may be cast or forged by machinery, may be so ground to form and so balanced on the handle that it is a moral necessity to the hand that fits it, and life could not be complete without it.

We see in these examples what is meant by wisdom. That knowledge is wisdom which completely and permanently objectifies and embodies itself in the instruments of life and then co-ordinates these instruments in such a way that each expresses a final relation to the whole, so that all of them in their unity constitute the whole. Wisdom is objective and real then in institutions, for institutions are *realized* experience. And experience, which is essentially affective or emotional and active in content, is capable of realization, and becomes realized, through the spontaneity of the knowing function operating as form within it. The substance of institutions is then life and will and feeling, while their form is intelligence. And as the controlling factor in experience is always knowledge, the primary form of objective virtue will be wisdom, since wisdom is knowledge realized in its objects and incorporated in the structure of the good. As such, wisdom is the substance of culture and represents the content and meaning of obligation, the central conception of morality. Culture is to be understood as the real medium in which the active life of the moral agent is lodged, and, in so far as it is constituted of wisdom, it becomes the directing force which guides the efforts of the individual.

II. WISDOM AND OBLIGATION

It was noted above that wisdom is the accumulation of human thought and feeling objectified by *action* in the institutions of life and that as such it is the stuff or substance of culture. We wish now to emphasize that this substantial wisdom is historically continuous, and this introduces us to the very important question of growth. This idea of growth is simple enough when considered as an aspect of natural objects and relations but becomes increasingly complex and difficult when applied to cultural objects and relations. It is easy to see that a moving and growing environment is involved as the medium in which the individual agent lives and moves and has his being, for it is a necessary postulate of individual life when life is interpreted in terms of action. Since life in the individual can never be adapted to its environment, action, which is always the attempt to complete this adaptation, involves an end deferred or postponed to the future as the imagined real expression of the plan or design now present in the actor's purpose but, as now held, recognized as unreal and as realizable only through action. That is, a growth situation, as one in which two or more phases of the same object that are divergent in time are nevertheless unified in a present fact, is the essential objective presupposition of an act, is the objective situation in the absence of which an act is inconceivable and indistinguishable from a movement.

The fact that the individual person is thus *bound* to his objective world through the fact that his life is conditioned upon action is what is meant by obligation. Obligation is thus the objective necessity that is logically presupposed in the idea of an act. The acting agent is continuously under this moral necessity because of his intelligence; when he knows the objective conditions to action, he recognizes them as necessary to his being as a moral person, and he has no choice with respect to the form his action is to take. He *can* choose a different form, but he *may* not, for he knows that such a choice will negate the conditions of existence upon which choosing itself depends, and this is, in the end, impossible. The only "free," that is, obligationless, *act* of an agent would be the act by which he denies the conditions of his own existence, by which, that is, he destroys himself. So if freedom is to be conceived as thus inconsistent with obligation then such freedom will have to be given up, for obligation is objective fact and cannot be ignored except at the cost of self-contradiction, which in this case is self-destruction. This is, of course, not a denial of freedom but a recognition of the fact that the conditions of freedom will have to be determined within bounds that are set by obligation.

We have little difficulty, therefore, in recognizing that obligation is "personal" in the sense, at the least, that by it, considered as the general conditions upon which action in the individual depends, the individual is determined to a unique and separate existence but is also morally bound to the cultural whole by a logical and natural necessity. As a consequence of this cultural relation, we are now to see that wisdom or obligation is "social," or, as we prefer to say, public and objective. And it is the objectivity of wisdom that gives to our concept of obligation its character of universality and thus invests moral principles with the logical necessity that is the basis of their moral authority. And this, of course, puts moral freedom outside the "universe of discourse" of scientific determinism.

But when we say that obligation is public, we mean that wisdom, which we saw is the substance of culture, is also the basic or material ground of the *order* of societies, the common matrix of organized human life. It is upon this foundation that the whole fabric of organized society rests, and we thus see the moral basis which lies behind the institutions of politics and law. And the importance of law and politics lies expressly in the fact that they recognize the public and objective character of the obligatory relations with which it is their function to deal. A very simple and in part mistaken expression of this fact is to be observed in those theories of society which rest upon the ideas of "contract," "compact," "agreement," "consent," "covenant," etc. All these theories are faulty because they depend upon an interpretation of the obligatory relation that implies that the substance to be organized and united is the mental states of men, or experience in its particular and accidental characters. It is true that what is organized is in the last analysis experience, but it is experience only when expressed in the objects of life and thus objectified and become universal. Prior experience, or "past" experience, in the sense of the actual processes of individual life, does not exist and so does not admit of order or organization. The obligatory relation is not a subjective relation, and the consciousness of obligation is not a feeling or any other state of mind but the apprehension of an instance of logical necessity exemplified in a concrete situation which sets the conditions for action. It is not a relation among the states of mind of an individual; this is the fallacy of "individual responsibility." Nor is it a relation between the mental states of one man and the mental states of another man or any number of men; this is the fallacy of "social responsibility." The essence of the obligatory relation involves persons and states of mind, to be sure; but it is always of these states of mind and personalities as objectified in the structures of life, since it is only as such that relations have those stable points of reference which give them universality as objects of thought. There is a sense of course in which obligation is personal and a sense in which it is social, but it is the sense in which both the concepts of person and social derive their meaning from their relation to obligation; it is not that obligation gets its meaning from them. So neither personal obligation nor social obligation is capable of complete logical support, and both have what truth they have from their dependence upon and assumption of the proposition that moral obligation is objective.

But there is here the possibility of two errors which it is well to avoid. One interpretation of the statement that obligation is objective is to make it involve merely a reference to the external, in which it is identified with necessity in the natural sense. The other interpretation is to limit it to mere logical objectivity, where logical objectivity is conceived in terms of those universal conditions required to satisfy abstract thought. This is perhaps the meaning of Kantian objectivity, in which the reality of a relation is guaranteed in the consistency of the ideas in which it is expressed.

The first of these is easily identified as naturalism. This form of the conception of obligation had great success in destroying the old notion of "freedom of indifference," since all it was required to do to win the triumph was to demonstrate the necessity of law, even in the simple sense that is implied in the idea of uniformity. But it has no effect with a completer conception of freedom, with which the notion of law is thoroughly consistent, since it involves a law that goes far beyond the reach of the naturalist. This is true even of the ambiguous concept of "scientific law," which is shown to be an implicate of freedom in all cases where it can be given a strict logical meaning. Consequently, all morality has to do to make its peace with naturalism is to show that obligation implies law; and this makes it necessary to express law in a form that is consistent with freedom. But it is a chastened naturalism that emerges from the demonstration. This confusion of obligation with the idea of an external relation is thus easily disposed of. What is true of the point of view is, of course, the insight that all real relations are external in the sense that all imply something outside and beyond the states of mind in which they are conceived, so that the relation does not disappear in its own terms. But the insight nevertheless failed to see that, to be external and public and "out there," it is not necessary to be a material thing but may be a relation whose meaning is not exhausted in the content of the terms between which it holds.

But in the other case where obligation is expressed altogether in terms of internal relations the case is somewhat different. Here apparently the requirements of logic are met, and obligation is explained as a function of the internal relations of ideas. It is then final to find those states of mind in which we are "conscious of" obligation, since immediate apprehension of it is the only form of our access to it. Then the psychological description of the state of mind can follow upon the identification of it, and this description, together with a strong recommendation of the fact couched in appropriately enthusiastic rhetoric, constitutes the theory of obligation. When we therefore find and recommend the "good will" or "sense of duty," we have located obligation by tracing it to the original substance from which it springs, and no further questions can be asked. It is thus perfectly consistent with the abstract and rhetorical ideal spiritual personality which does not require to possess a body in order to act but only a soul with which to create. But this explanation of a relational fact by tracing it to its subjective original is itself an instance of the magic of creation, even if it is sweetened to palatability by calling it "scientific causation." Such psychological and scientific abstractions no longer satisfy, and a logic whose consistency is limited to the mere agreement of mental states will have trouble whenever facts involving ontological relations are presented. The logic which finds obligation can be only the logic which makes its peace with metaphysics, since, if obligation is not objectively real, there is no reality of any kind within the moral sphere, and this is equivalent to a denial of all reality in a complete skepticism.

Assuming, then, that obligation is real and that with it the reality of the moral life is established, the significance for reality of the essential moral concepts may be demonstrated. This will be true especially of the concepts which appear to represent states of mind and, if so, will enable us to give to these concepts a substantial ground which they could not have when they were regarded as the originals from which obligation itself was derived. That is, subjective categories in ethical thinking derive their meaning from objective obligation and not vice versa.

We cannot say, therefore, that obligation is a feeling or sense of duty or conscience or that it is a function of the will or of "free" will or that it is the "good will"; in fact, we cannot identify obligation with any act or state of mind whatever. On the other hand, we can say that conscience, duty, the consciousness of freedom, and the feeling of ought are elementary moral concepts and represent the realities of moral experience because they have a ground in the objective fact of obligation, in the fact that the whole situation in experience that gives rise to such moral ideas as duty, ought, etc., is constituted of the relation between the agent and the world of his environment in nature and culture. It is to this objective fact that the individual is bound, and, because he is bound to it, his sense of being bound or his consciousness of being bound are "true," since they are genuinely and truly objectified.

All the categories, that is, get their meaning from the fact that they each express some aspect of the relation of the individual agent to the system of nature and culture as unified in the institutions of culture. This ultimate relation is obligation. As a further consequence the categories of obligation, in their larger connotation, can be identified as political, religious, industrial, aesthetic, familial, or whatever other institutional forms we may be concerned to recognize, since any access, or other essential relation we may have to the good, will fall within the industrial, political, etc., aspect of the ethical system in this wide sense. That is, politics, law, religion, etc., "have their basis in ethics" because they are of the content of ethics when ethics is taken in its full comprehension—the comprehension that is wide enough to permit a genuine logical deduction of its categories from a formulation of their metaphysical or cosmic implications.

Conscience, duty, ought, are, then, not mere states of mind. They are logically objectified cognitive attitudes, objectified in the various aspects of the relation which the moral agent experiences as binding him to his world. They, therefore, have a status in "existence" beyond the narrow sphere of the individual mind and within the system of reality which includes mind along with whatever else there may be in the universe that is real. They are even "physical" categories in the new sense which that term has recently acquired. As such they are presuppositions of knowledge of whatever kind and not products of knowledge as it functions in experience. From them knowledge is derived; they are not derived from knowledge. They are "given" in experience and are not results of experience, except as experience is embodied as wisdom in the historical process, nor are they accidental or any other results of our sensuous contacts with nature. Even our sensuous contacts are derived from the real relation which they all connote and are thus intellectual concepts. They are not, however, knowledge, but wisdom; for wisdom is the substance to which they, as relations, connect the individual mind and all its categories of experience.

But sensuous contacts are, also, something more. They are historically fixed emotional attitudes having an origin within the meaning quality of the relation of the agent to his world as that relation has been experienced in the course of the evolution of human life and objectified in aesthetic form. It is this that gives them their drive, their efficacy for action, which is seated in the universal wisdom and which makes them effective in the creation of the good. The sensuous contacts are the precipitate of the history of human feeling and represent all the content of meaning and value that reality has had for man. They therefore furnish the substance and material for ends, and it is out of them—felt individually and anew as conscience, duty, ought— that the moral consciousness shapes the good in each object pursued. They therefore furnish ideal direction, and upon this character of action and the good all categories of order in human affairs are based. It is upon these and such categories that speculation will dwell in such immediately practical connections as politics and law. It is enough for ethics that the ground of all systems of practical categories has been secured. And this ground of all practical categories has been supplied in the concept of objective obligation, the reality behind which is the wisdom of the ages as incorporate in the institutions of life.

Wisdom is a *virtue* because it is, in its effects upon the individual's action, a *type* or *form* of action; that is, it imposes a typical character upon the individual's acts because it is the substance and medium in which every act must occur. The control of the direction of the act and the inspiration of the individual's inclination toward the good are its peculiar functions with respect to particular acts. Wisdom is an objective virtue because it establishes types of action in the substance of life and culture from which the individual draws the suggestion and the plan of his active career.

III. WISDOM AND CULTURE

In the sense that wisdom is the whole product of man's experience, in that it represents all that as a race he has done and been, it is culture. But wisdom, used in this broad sense, has wider meanings than are comprised in ordinary cognitive or knowing experience. We have seen that wisdom is knowledge institutionalized; but, in the process by which knowledge takes on the established form of institution, many elements other than knowledge enter into the whole. The system of science and the realm of the abstract is the proper sphere of knowledge in the ordinary sense of the term, but it is one small segment of the whole of wisdom, which includes along with the realm of knowledge proper the region of practical activity as well as the total sphere of feeling. It is proper therefore to speak of culture as representing the whole domain of values, where the scheme of values includes some objects at least that are not produced in experience. Thus along with the systems of knowledge and science, and serving as the objective basis of these systems, there are all the structures of practical life in the institutions of politics, industry, religion, etc., together with the higher and more refined structures of the fine arts. These are assumed to rest upon nature, a system of valued objects not produced in experience.

If we now ask in what aspect of these systems we are to find the essence of value, or what quality or character distinguishes values, regarded as the works of man and as also the more elementary products of nature, we shall find that it is their peculiar relation to feeling. Feeling is then the primary substance of value, as the universal to which all objects are referred as individual, when regarded as the basis of culture; and we must now ask in what its logical characters and its nature and status in the value system consist. The question is a difficult one and, like so many questions in ethics, borders close on to the confines of metaphysics. Let us then inquire as to the elementary modes by which feeling is related to the system of values.

We may at the beginning lay down the hypothesis which we shall accept. Feeling is the material substance of all value. Of values there are two main types, cognitive and active, when we think of values purely and narrowly in their relation to experience. The experiences of feeling do not constitute a separate third system. Feeling is, from the point of view of experience, the unity and synthesis of the other two, the synoptic and ordered unity of cognition with action. In more general terms, feeling is the objective ground in which both cognitive activity and practical activity and their respective objects are fused into a complete and harmonious whole. Feeling is the substance which makes possible the unity of thought and action in an end as realized. This gives to feeling a duality of meaning: that of its primary subjectivity as an actual experience within a concrete situation dominated by "mind" and that of its primordial objectivity as the logical substrate upon which feeling *experience* is distinguished from, or discerned within, its ground. This latter is the subject matter of aesthetics, and we cannot go into it here. But we shall assume, from the relation which this feeling substrate bears to the cognitive and the active experience, that all values have their ultimate reference to reality in the relation in which they stand to this primary feeling substance.

Culture is the same, then, with this general scheme of values. But it is within this general scheme of values that wisdom may be defined as that portion of the whole scheme which consists of the objects of value that have been created more directly through the agency of the active intelligence. In this sense wisdom represents the institutionalized form which common intelligent action takes as it comes to be expressed in objects. It for this reason corresponds to the knowledge function in the individual. And for similar reasons to those by which we were led to say that to know is the first obligation of the individual and the summation of subjective virtue for the individual, we can now say that wisdom represents all that the objective or public activity of man can mean. Wisdom, in that it is the peculiar object-instrument of values, is thus distinguished from knowledge, as the individual function, on the one side; and from culture, as the total product of the common or mutual activity of men, on the other.

It is clear, then, that wisdom is not an individual characteristic and that it is only in a figurative sense that we may speak of a wise man. We do not mean in describing a man as wise to indicate a quality of the man but to suggest a universal relation in which he stands to the whole system of things human. Or we may regard it as a quality of the man if we think of it as this relation objectified. The wise man thus is the man who has a significant connection with the scheme of culture or a place in the scheme by which his activity is able to further the ends of culture; and, by so doing, incidentally to furnish to himself the opportunities through which his good is to come to him in a higher quality of himself. This place in the scheme does not imply a high position or an exalted station; it means merely that wisdom dictates that the man have a place within the scheme of life which offers him the materials, means, and opportunities through which he may produce a good commensurate with his capabilities and that the good thus produced rebound upon the man with further opportunities for action and fresh satisfactions. In more ordinary language it implies a world of institutions so ordered that each person shall have a "job," that this job be of the kind that brings into play all his major types of capacity both physical and mental, and that as a consequence of his remaining faithfully "on the job" he be supplied with the means by which the job may be most effectually done. It is doubtful whether, under these conditions, it would ever occur to a man to inquire if he is "happy" or "satisfied."

This, of course, raises the question as to just what place in such a situation has the "satisfactions" of the man and of the persons directly dependent upon him. We shall answer immediately that the question is simple and that it has been enormously complicated by approaching it from the viewpoint of questionable assumptions. The most doubtful of these assumptions is just that which asserts the dependence of the good of one agent upon his own act or the act of another agent, as, for example, the "happiness" of the child upon the "care" of the parent. But we have seen in numerous connections that the good of the person or agent is objectified within the cultural structure and thus not dependent upon any other person or any number of persons, except that the maintenance of the structure as an objective whole is a responsibility of all agents acting as a corporate whole. This assumption of the one-to-one correspondence of acts to satisfactions is implicit and never discussed. Most discussion is devoted to the assumption that a "satisfaction" may be the object or end toward which an action is directed or that it may be the key factor or object within a plan of action as contemplated in advance of performance. It seems that the simple answer to the proposition that a satisfaction may be the object or result toward which an act is directed lies in the reflection that it is perhaps never consciously or deliberately so. A person is perhaps never conscious that he is directing his action toward the feeling of pleasure or a satisfaction as an object. What he does aim at is some objective physical or ideal situation which he imaginatively presents to himself as a value, and the feeling which is to be the substance of the value when realized is not yet, or so long as he is *acting* with reference to the object will not be, any part of his experience. That the feeling content of an end cannot be anticipated is shown in the fact that an end when attained seldom gives us the feelings which we had experienced as incident to the action while in pursuit of it.

The meaning of directed action is, therefore, not that some psychological state must be found which operates as a cause of the act but that some object must be prefigured as that into which the act may issue and express its finished form. Direction of action is thus a function of intelligence and implies the world of objects, not the furniture of mind or experience. That these objects are values when contemplated as constituted with a feeling content is an aesthetic fact and is observed after the action that creates the object has been completed. Morality implies direction and direction implies intelligence operating through objects. But it is doubtful whether, say, an automatic "act" to satisfy hunger can be said to be intelligible in any sense, since, if nothing operates to produce the "act" except the urge of hunger, the situation would properly be described as purely automatic and mechanical. And a causal situation is not internally and intrinsically intelligible, since it is only as a causal situation is included within a larger whole that its meaning as a cause can be understood. The intelligibility of a causal situation therefore is not a character of that situation but a character referring to the relation of the situation to a whole; it is this relation which constitutes the intelligibility of the situation.

But this means that satisfactions and pleasures and such states of mind are as such more properly described as factors within situations that involve intelligence on other grounds and that they are not projected beyond the situation in the way that is implied in saying that they are ends of action. They are not therefore objects or objective facts contemplated by intelligence as having a status beyond experience toward which experience may be directed. They are thus not ends; the object of a genuine act is never a state of mind. We act with ideas as ends only when ideas are taken not in the psychological but in the Platonic sense as genuine realities, when ideas are taken to be the same with objects. As such "objects," pleasure and satisfactions may *have* qualities, but they *are* not qualities. Real objects may be thus projected and, as such, become the substance of our plans and, when realized, become elements in the solid fabric of culture which is both object and medium of every act. It is this system of objects that is the end toward which every act is directed in so far as it is intelligent and significant, that is, so far as it is an act, or is moral; and there is nothing that is more remote from the consciousness of a person performing a significant act than the states of satisfaction that may result when the act is completed. The full intent of the actor, all his states of mind, are completely exhausted in the processes through which the object passes in its development while serving as plan or end of action and in the processes necessary to control the techniques essential to the adequate expression of the act at each of its stages. There is no mind left with which to contemplate a possible satisfaction or any other sort of result. And, if a satisfaction appears anywhere in the situation, it is either a mere incidental factor indicating the adequacy or accuracy of the technical processes, and thus external to the act itself, or it is a mere impulse out of which grow the physical phenomena of the act. But an impulse never results in an act; unless to the impulse there is superadded an element of intelligence, no act will result, but the situation will remain describable as a mere movement.

Culture is, then, the system of intelligible objects, and within it the objects which involved intelligence and direction in their creation constitute the system of wisdom. It is within this system that the good man lives and acts, and the more perfect degrees of articulation with the system entitle the good man to be called wise. But it is to be emphasized that wisdom is not a *possession* of the wise man, not an intrinsic character which distinguishes him, or a form or type of object external to him which he controls. Wisdom is that objective whole of human achievement in which good men all share, the total wealth of culture which intelligence has prepared as the heritage of every person equipped and permitted to enjoy it. Our traditional notion that the wise man is one who possesses some mystic capacity of insight into the good is at bottom sound; only it tends to an individualistic and subjective interpretation of the facts which distorts the fundamental meaning of wisdom. But by wisdom as translated into terms of the facts of active experience we mean the common matrix of cultural reality within which we all live so far as we are equipped with capacity and opportunity to take advantage of it. And the person's identification of himself with this common ground constitutes his moral salvation, his moral obligation, and the fulfilment of his moral destiny. Realizing the good, or self-realization, consists in attaining a recognizable place within it, and the fact that such realization is for every person only partial indicates that it is for practical purposes a mere possibility depending on the intelligence of the actor in choosing his ends and means and on the fortune that adequate means and "chances" are available and accessible to him. It appears once more that the good life is an adventure, and the wisdom or insight that guides us aright through its tortuous course is a form of the faith which leads or impels us to act where we cannot see and to see where we cannot act.

Chapter XXIV

Temperance—the Organization of Life

I. THE DEFINITION OF LIFE

BY LIFE in its most inclusive sense we mean all the forms and forces of active nature. While we distinguish it from the forms and forces of intelligence, yet we imply a close connection with the sphere of mind. Possibly we regard life as that developed nature out of which mind and consciousness grow, or upon which, in some way we do not make clear to ourselves, mind and consciousness depend. But it is clear that life lies somewhere between mere physical existence, on the one side, and mind, on the other, and there is a sense in which the term includes in its meaning all that lies between these extremes.

The fact that makes the problem of the relations of life and consciousness difficult is that of direction in their expression. Direction, in the sense in which we are using it here, has two elements of meaning which we must carefully distinguish. There is the sense in which direction indicates a line of distinction within the structure of an order, and this refers to a situation in nature; and there is the sense in which direction involves this and the element of control, where the reference is to some cultural situation. Direction in the first sense is regarded as predetermined by something either within or outside the structure involved, while in the other it is supposed to be "free." We shall make use of both of these senses, and the problem that is implied in making direction and control intelligible with respect to life is the problem of temperance.

The problem is in the first case one of what it is that is controlled. This is complicated with the further problems of the end of control and the means of control. But, as life for us implies spontaneity, the answer is that it is life itself as it is expressed in instinct and impulse and the urges of nature that is to be subjected to control. These facts are present at the inception of any active situation, since an act has its existential ground in movement; and this has led the theory of ethics to consider whether the acts of persons are causal processes arising

392

from the phenomena of impulse and thus are events capable of simple scientific explanation. But the fact that human beings can and do, on occasion, break the connection between the instinctive and impulsive events and the act which normally follows them would appear to indicate that the relation is not causal; and the further fact that the act through its conscious phenomena may turn upon the instincts and impulses and change them in various ways, at least raises the question whether a causal or any kind of fixed relation holds between the act and its antecedents.

In any case the latter fact, viz., that consciousness may intervene to change the effect of impulse and instinct with respect to the inception and direction of action is the generally accepted basis of our belief in the power to control our acts and the antecedent facts out of which acts arise. Thus the subject of direction and control, the fact upon which the processes of control are directed, is in this view the type of impulse and instinct which appear uniformly at the origination point of action. We are to control our impulsive and instinctive tendencies, so the theory goes, and it is through this exercise of control over them that the morality of the agent is to be built up. This is the question of temperance or self-control, as it has been formulated in ethical thinking. We shall see that with respect to control it implies a mysterious power which can operate upon the vital facts of impulse and instinct directly, or through a means which the controlling power develops for each occasion. In any case the question as to how and by what means control of the active life is to be effected is the problem which we have here under review, and this is the problem of temperance.

II. DIRECTION AND THE SPONTANEITY OF INTELLIGENCE

From the point of view of one type of theory the control of the "lower nature" lies in the hands of intelligence directly and without mediation. This means apparently that it is of the essential nature of intelligence to exercise control, pretty much as it is of the nature of water to wet and of fire to burn. Hence just as nobody would expect or require an answer to the question as to why or how fire burns, it would never occur to anyone to ask why and how or by what means intelligence can control impulse. The intelligence has a power of directly originating changes in impulse and instinct, and this power is sufficiently understood when it is given a name. So it is called "spontaneity," "will," "free will," etc., and the name is taken to explain the fact without further discussion.

But there are distinguishable factors or moments of both nature and culture involved in the capacity of control by intelligence. This would then demand a scientific knowledge of the world, including both nature and culture, since both aspects of the world are to be found together in any situation involving action. The world of action would appear as a system of forces corresponding to what the scientist calls laws, and such forces would appear in particular forms in mental and bodily processes. Thus at least the chief condition of effective control would be laid down in the knowledge system that would ultimately be built up, and there would be left nothing but to ask how in detail this knowledge of an abstract system of theoretical forces makes contact with the facts in such a way as to effect real changes.

In other words, the attempt to make a connection between intelligence and the world of fact through the knowledge systems leaves the problem of control exactly where it was before. Out of this fact comes the universal feeling that knowledge is powerless to effect any real change in the world, which leads to the search in other directions for the power that is distinctive of control. Also it requires that the originating source of control be sought in other directions.

Here we may refer to the other character of direction in which a specialized agency is supposed. In this view direction is anticipated or in some way represented in the mental process in advance of action, and the act of anticipation is most commonly given the special name of "will." With this name, and with the tendency to make a thing out of an act when it is named, the will has the power, through mere mental process and in advance of the fact, to compel the facts to conform to the anticipatory representation of them. Thus the vexatious question as to how the intelligence is to make active contact with its object is solved by including the power to do this within the definition of intelligence in terms of will. But the obvious impossibility of any such solution forces the concession that the object cannot be made actually to conform with precision to the form that was willed but only ideally and in the way that a physical object conforms with the pattern by which it was made.

By this procedure the problem is of course merely postponed again, unless some more literal interpretation can be found. The belief that the act and its object will conform closely to the idea through which it was envisaged in plan is difficult to avoid. But if and in so far as we speak of ideas and a plan, the problem of action is reduced to pure rational terms, and if impulse is controlled by ideas there is no excuse for the appeal to a will. And in some sense it appears that it must be necessary to appeal to ideas; otherwise any degree of success in following out a plan in action would be purely accidental. It is obvious that in experience the objects we set up in idea, in advance of action as the design which the act is to take on, do actually appear in reality after action has taken place; so again there seems to be no point in assuming that the specialized function of will is involved. The house I build in fact will closely resemble the plan I had formed of it in idea, and it does so uniformly enough to indicate that there is some elementary connection running from plan through action into the object which is created. That is, the belief that by "taking thought" we can modify the nature of the world, or our own nature, seems well grounded in experience, and the problem as to just how the effective power of intelligence is hitched up in action so as to connect really with things and our own inner forces cannot be evaded. We may as well face it therefore and see what we can do with it.

III. THE RELATION OF INTELLIGENCE TO LIFE

We shall suggest here by way of beginning that the reason the problem of direction and control persists without final solution in ethical thought lies in the false terms in which the problem has been formulated. As we have noted, the discussion has been altogether of processes and events in individual experience. Will, so the theory goes, is a process or function within the isolated person, and the plan or idea is a fact within an individual mind. And even the processes of action and the means suggested are phases of inner experience, and the object that results gets its entire character from its relation to the individual who is supposed to have created it. It is not necessary to pronounce judgment upon this view. No statement of it has had any important relevance to the facts of life since the time when life took on a pronounced degree of complexity. It would therefore seem at least reasonable to inquire if there is another view that will give some insight into the complexity of life in its active phases, and we shall undertake to state the rudiments of another view.

We shall begin by stating baldly the doctrine which we wish to present. The basis of control of action, even of individual action, does not lie in the mystic depths of the individual, nor is it to be discovered within the immediate facts of the action involved. It is not a question, in any important way, of individual will. At least in so far as will is involved, it is a question of learning just how the will itself came to be established in the individual character by the cultural influences under which the individual grows up. Thus to cite the mere possession of a will is not an explanation; what we want to know is how we come to possess such a power as will is supposed to be. All genuine control of action, as we shall show, is corporate and objective and public, and it is within this process of control that the will itself comes into being. That is, the "individual will" is created and its powers and characters determined by the cultural forces within which the individual develops. Control by the will is then a matter of affecting the various directions of incidence of these public cultural forces. And to understand this we must analyze typical forms of action and describe them in terms of the cultural conditions by which they are determined. And the degree and quality of control which we shall be able to exercise over action will obviously depend upon how fully we understand the cultural conditions within which action is initiated. This is the problem of technique to which we now turn.

The primary question is: How and by what means and instruments is intelligence made effective in determining the direction, point of impact, intensity of effort, etc., of action, and how can intelligence determine the character of the object that results from action? It is in such matters as these that the meaning of control lies, unless we are to resort to mystical powers whose relation to the facts can never be determined. And accordingly the answer to the question is to be sought through the methods of those disciplines whose special business it is to deal with such facts.

Ordinarily, we go to the physical and biological sciences for the solution of these questions. Impacts and intensities and efforts and effects are physical phenomena; hence physics tells us all we know or can know of them. But note that it is not with these processes as such that we are concerned. What we want to know is: Under what conditions do such processes begin? The natural sciences will describe them after they happen. But the ethical question is: Why do they happen? We have on our hands a question of origins, and with such a question the natural sciences are not competent to deal. We shall therefore appeal to the social sciences. Or, if we resort to psychology on the ground that it stands between the two systems of sciences, all it can tell us is that the idea always tends to express itself, that the act or expression can be regarded as a part of the fact which we designate the idea. But this means that the question is dodged by assuming the answer in the statement of the question. The act is a part of the idea, and explaining the idea includes the explanation of the act. So nothing is to be got from this source, and we shall appeal to the cultural disciplines. Hence we should look to the doctrines of law and politics and legislation for the adequate discussion of these questions, and, in so far as these sciences are to be treated as means to the good life, they become essential content of ethics. When such disciplines are regarded as instruments to the creation and maintenance of the good life, they become matters of the technique of morality, and it is to morality that we must turn for the principles that govern their technical use. We shall therefore ask about the principles of the governance of action which are presupposed by the legal and political and legislative processes, and shall regard them, when and if found, as the basic principles of moral control, and as constituting the essential meaning of temperance considered as an objective virtue.

Let us repeat that we are facing this large and difficult question of control with the assumption that it can be most effectively handled through a study of the techniques and means involved. Now the technical means employed uniformly by law and politics and legislation is that of authority. All the motives to control depend in the last resort upon authority as the instrument through which they are to be made effective. It will be desirable therefore to look into the concept of authority, and to note its use and the various forms in which it may be expressed.

The first thing to be noted is that authority, when considered as a means to the control of human action, is a subjective instrument, and hence subject to the limitations that subjectivity discloses in any case. In its most elementary sense it is a unique power of right that inheres in the "subject" from which issue law and legislative enactment and political activity of every kind. It is thus an inherent and innate right and power to control the actions of men, resident in the subject who exercises it, and it belongs to this subject either because of his nature or position or both. But these presuppositions of "divine" or "natural" right, and of the metaphysical "subjects" in which they inhere, have been given up pretty generally by legal and political theorists, and it is only in ethics that such conceptions are still defended. Here the assumption takes the form of the moral "personality," and the discussion becomes wishful expression in bad rhetoric. Legal and political theorists have long ago discovered that authority in any form is a purely subjective motive, and as a consequence its "command" has no power of effectiveness within actual human relations. The "authority" of the law cannot make itself effective in enforcement, and the "sovereignty" of the political state is helpless as against the normal institutional growth within the content of the state. It is from such situations as this that the adage "You can't legislate morality" is seen to be true. But the perception of this fact fails to discover the real reason for the failure of legislation in morality. There are a number of possibilities; it may be that you cannot legislate morality because of "human nature" which is assumed to be fixed. It may again be because morality is not the sort of thing which lends itself to legislative influence. Or it may be that legislation itself has by nature distinct limitations. These questions are worthy of brief discussion.

If it is true that human nature is fixed, then you cannot legislate morality, for the simple reason that you cannot legislate anything, since none of the terms would have any meaning. Obligation, responsibility, attainment of ends—all of the essentially moral concepts are meaningless at once if we accept a deterministic view of human nature. But not only the moral conceptions are false; all the categories of culture, the motives of industry and education and religion and politics and law, are nonsense unless there are possibilities of advancement and enrichment within what is known as human nature. So this dogma of the fixity of human nature is easily disposed of.

In the case of the second argument, that morality cannot, because of its ethereal and spiritual nature, be given objective form within the crude conditions of life, we are dealing with a proposition that is true only after we have accepted a particularly limited view of morality. But it is nevertheless a view held by perhaps a majority of men. If morality means in every case an abstract ideal of right which is constituted in opposition to ordinary natural conditions, or without regard to natural conditions, or if morality is nothing more than the subjective visionings of saintly souls whose moral attitude is itself a disdain of the world, then it will not submit to legislative enactment because it refuses objectification in any form. And the prevailing attitude toward morality in the popular mind, as well as the dominant conviction among theorists, is that morality is really a matter of states of mind. If this is so, then you cannot legislate morality; that is, you cannot objectify moral ideas and moral ideals, for you cannot by methods of legislation, or by any other method, determine the states of men's minds in any objective direction. It is not supposed to be the function of legislation, which I am assuming here is the process of realizing moral ideas, to determine men's minds; "free thought" and "free speech" are the bases upon which a rational legislation itself rests; and this means that thought and speech and conscience are "free" because they are not the kinds of things that can be given objective form by legislation, or full objective form by any power whatsoever.

This leads to the other question of technique, the third one above. This is to the effect that legislation has its own limitations and that these preclude the objectification of moral ideas. This is also true in a sense, but only in a sense which depends upon a false notion of legislation. It is of course clear that legislation cannot objectify or "enforce" a moral or any other idea if legislation is merely the speculative enactment of abstract rules or principles, merely "passing laws." That is to say, if legislation is itself merely a subjective process concerned only with the formation of empty general injunctions about conduct, then it could not objectify a moral idea because it is so constituted as not to be able to realize ideas at all. But we shall see a little later that this is a very inadequate notion of the nature and function of legislation. We may assume then that it is at least possible that moral ends may be attained through legislation. But not if legislation is merely the expression of the abstract fiat of authority. So authority does not express the relations of intelligence to life, and therefore has nothing to do with real direction and control.

This consequence is perhaps generally recognized in legal and political connections, but it seems clear that the fallacy persists in moral thinking. In politics and law it is realized that a mere expression of authority is ineffective. Consequently, since it does not seem possible to lawyers and statesmen to give up the concept of authority, the attempt is made to supplement it by sanctions, and these suggestions have developed a wide variety of theories which we here can have space only to note, since we must get on to the development of a positive theory.

Generally, subjective authority has supported itself by the appeal to force. And force of any sort may be utilized, as force of every kind has been at some time or place utilized. In the earlier stages of history physical force was resorted to perhaps most freely, although "subjective" force was not unknown. An ancient monarch generally maintained his authority by the military, but as a supplementary force there were employed the subjective forces of pomp and glory and majesty with which to awe the citizenry into subjection. Religion was generally the instrument of this type of force. These are forms of external force; even the psychological forces are to be recognized as external relations. But modern forms of organization have tended more to depend on internal relations as the substance of public order, and the subjectivity of authority has accordingly appeared in another form. In this case the basis of authority and the conditions of "enforcement" lie in the internal relations of life, viz., in "assent" or "agreement" or "contract," all of which are, however, in legal theory at least, translated into objective terms of "instruments" in order to endow them with authority. Politically, assent or agreement or contract will objectify in constitutions either written or solidified in custom, while legally these ideas assume objective force only when translated into "facts productive of legal consequences." It is these two conceptions of the objectification of ideas through their appropriate instrumentation that furnish the technical basis of the objective theory of virtue, which in this view is the most significant of ethical concepts. Before leaving this problem of the subjective basis of authority it may be worth while to point out that any theory of internal relations is likely to degenerate into some form of propaganda, which is the pure instance of subjective force and the denial of moral reality in every connection.

The fundamental weakness of all theories of the relation of intelligence to life, and of the techniques through which the relation is mediated, is to be found in the subjectivism which infects the whole of modern thought. It is suggested that the apparent total collapse of the practical affairs of men now prevailing throughout the world is due fundamentally to the subjective basis upon which men have, through the past few centuries, attempted to rest the practical structures of culture. The politics, religion, industry, government, education, art, and the familial relation of the present are magnificent in superstructure, but they all nevertheless rest upon a false basis in the assumption that in the end all reality is a state of mind, and that in the proximate relations of life solid structures may be built upon subjective motives. It is through this fallacy that civilization and culture at the present time are near the point of dissolution, and the occurrence of a few major shocks—themselves due to the same elemental weakness—in war and industrial conflict will bury the whole edifice in the sands upon which it was built.

It has appeared clearly that in the virtue of temperance we have a fundamental problem. Let us see if any constructive suggestions may be found for its solution or at least for its restatement in terms that will give promise of advance.

IV. TEMPERANCE AND SELF-CONTROL

As we have noted above, the subjective virtue of temperance reaches its perfection in self-control. And this, in prevailing theory, means that we should, through the instrumentality of one part of our nature, take control of other parts and of the whole of our nature with the purpose to direct our effective powers upon the attainment of the ends of the good life. And the method by which our "higher" nature is to control the "lower" is that of inhibition. But in so far as this "higher" nature is a function of mind, or a form of intelligence, its subjectivity and contradictoriness have been pointed out. Also, by implication it was shown that the possession of a power either to inhibit or to redirect is a myth in so far as such a power is assumed to give effect to itself directly. Yet in popular belief and in ethical theory there is assumed a "rational will" that is able by mere fiat to inhibit or suppress any tendency to action or to direct it into different channels from that which it normally follows.

But no such specific "power" can be found, and the assumption of a "moral will" is a remnant of an old superstition, if we mean by it that there is a thing there which exerts force. It perhaps arises from the fact that there is a feeling of freedom which accompanies action under appropriate conditions. This feeling has possibly a sensory basis or source in the movements involved in the direction of the body among environing objects. This would give it a factual basis sufficient to justify the idea of a spontaneous will, provided we mean by this nothing more or less than that action itself is the elementary fact which we must take for granted. And if we assume, as we have done, that the act itself is the original fact, we do not have to go behind it for its cause in a subjective state but have a genuinely objective basis for a will which can be described in terms of the facts.

The question is one as to the nature of the assumptions which can legitimately be made from the facts in a situation described as an act. That is to say, there is a situation made up of objects, events, and relations, and it is a question of the characters of the objects and events and of the nature of the relations. Specifically, what is wanted is to know whether there is some circumstance which can be regarded as the key to the explanation of all the other facts, or one from relations to which all other facts can be given their characteristic meanings. Without going into the question here, it appears that no such specific fact is discoverable. The question then remains as to whether there may not be some character of the situation as a whole which will account for the persistence of "will." We are to keep in mind that by will we are not permitted to mean some specialized entity or thing which exerts power, for that has been answered by a reference to the facts. No specific point can be located from which energies or causes take their origin. The movements and acts therefore which we connect with a situation must be functions of the relational wholeness of the situation. But, if we examine this idea, we find that this is merely taking the situation itself as the center from which flow its energies; we are therefore considering it as a "will" or cause and have accepted the position which we have just criticized. We have merely accepted the "situation" as a sort of absolute, in the regular pragmatic fashion, or we have taken over the idealistic "whole," which seems to be pretty much the same thing. In any case, there is no advance beyond the simplest atomism so long as we accept a situation of whatever dimensions as containing all its important qualities and relations within itself.

What must be seen in this connection is that there are no situations of the kind supposed. It is obvious, of course, that a situation cannot contain within itself its own relations to other things, and it is equally clear that a situation is the basis of its qualities only in a sense which permits the qualities to have references to terms outside the situation itself. Now it is these relations of reference, and characters that cannot be confined within a given complex, that are the most suggestive for the theory of will. And this involves the notion of "a situation as a whole" in contradiction, for there can be no such thing, if it is meant that the situation is self-explanatory. That is, a situation can possess the aspect of being whole only on the basis of a reference to what is not the situation or its wholeness. The wholeness insists on going beyond the situation, and we should find that it admits of no limitations whatever if we followed it through. Then the wholeness which can be attributed to a given situation is a universal character and not a defining characteristic; it connects all situations by a common bond and indicates that the secret of the situation's internal "will" or tendency to initiate, inhibit, or redirect action is to be found in a basis of objects outside and beyond the situation. The will that manifests itself in a man is therefore a center of externally conditioned relations, and these relations are determined in their effective character by the terms which lie in the indefinite circumstance which environs the man.

The "spontaneity" of the man's will, then, consists largely in the fact that many determining factors in its total effectiveness are unknown until action brings them forth, and the unpredictability of his action, upon which the assumption of spontaneity rests, is premised upon ignorance of these factors. But not altogether upon ignorance, since otherwise we should have to regard his acts as caused. Some of the factors *cannot* be known, either in advance of the act or after its occurrence, for in the system of relations constituted by the total circumstance the event related to the man's present will may change. Consequently, it could not be and never can be known.

What we mean by will, then, in terms of objective fact, is the total effect of all relational connections with the circumstance, and this assumes that the wholeness which is important is the relation of universality in which an event stands. The will of a man therefore is the synthetic effectiveness of all the relations in which he stands to his world, this total world being unlimited as to space and time and history. The facts that are important then, in consideration of the problem of control, are the systems of circumstances within which the object of control is normally set. A man is ensconced in a matrix of institutions which are of extraordinary complexity, and his "will" is his and is free in the fact that it is the will uniquely conferred upon him by his relations to his natural and cultural circumstance. The mechanism of control in human relations, both individual and general, is this system of institutions. Through it such changes are made in human life and human nature as can be made, and the problem of temperance or the control of life is a problem of understanding the methods of operation and *modus vivendi* of these institutions. We control *ourselves* through these institutional instruments, and the "social" and "political" control that is possible is effected through the same institutions. We can illustrate this doctrine of objective will and objective control by use of the sex "instinct" and the family.

Left to itself as the procreative urge of the individual, the sex "instinct" would express itself without reference to its object, its end, or any consequence. This we see is what happens in the case of the animals. The individual man often, however, does not control his sex instinct, and it is probable that few men would "control their lusts" if their only means of control were their capacity to think. Relieve the man of the influence of the home, the club, the church, the professional or industrial connection, and his reason will be a poor support under temptation. Without this institutional support a mere idea, no matter how attractive or how demonstrably true, will sooner or later disappear; and with a competent institution behind it a mere superstition persists indefinitely.

The conclusion from these facts is, then, that what has traditionally been called "self-control" is of relatively little consequence as a constructive force in the good life. If we ask what it is that enables the average individual to maintain his character, we shall find the largest element in the fact that he has had no occasion to do otherwise. No strong "temptation" has come to him, by which we mean that his activities have fitted satisfactorily into his environment, and the conditions of his environment have not radically or suddenly changed. As a consequence he has had no unusual "wants." If he is a mature person and has a family and a home of his own, it perhaps does not occur to him that he has a sex instinct, so evenly runs the course of his life. His "wants" and interests and desires are being satisfied, or being proved unworthy of satisfaction, so quietly that they do not occur to him with such insistence as to require serious or prolonged attention. He seldom "thinks," for his life is very largely reduced to routine, and there is no occasion for him to dwell long or painfully upon any moral question. The average person therefore maintains his character largely because he has not had occasion to lose it, or because all or most occasions in his experience have been such as to demand that he hold on to it.

The important question, then, is what these occasions are which determine whether the person shall hold on to his character or lose it. In the case of the person who does not maintain his character, we shall find almost invariably that something has gone wrong within his institutional connections somewhere. In the case of sex disturbance within the family, there may be cases of biological incompatibility. But, if this is the case, there is nothing that the individual can do about it by resort to his own powers and capacities. He has no control of the situation, and there is nothing to do except to regard himself as unfortunate. The only thing that is to be done is a dissolution of the family if there are not other grounds that demand that it be maintained. If there are children who cannot otherwise be properly cared for, to maintain the family appears an absolute obligation in spite of sexual or any other form of dissatisfaction. The point is that the remedy for sex irregularity is such a setup of the family and other institutions as will permit of normal exercise of the function. Where there is no opportunity for normal exercise of the function, there will be perversion of it in some form.

A similar account is to be given of persons of maturity who are unmarried. Whether a childless "family" in which both parties work is the remedy remains to be seen. A looser arrangement which permits of occasional and varied contacts, without the restraints of the marriage bond, seems to be developing as a possibility among young people. But the older idea of a permanent union is doomed unless there can be more assurance than now exists of opportunities to economic and other forms of security and at the same time a reasonable access to the higher forms of culture.

The essential principle in the morality of sex is that there must be such an institutional organization of life as will permit of a normal development and exercise of the function. It is folly to expect a sexually pure society from the mere restraints of self-control under unfavorable institutional conditions. A community living in extreme poverty or extreme wealth will rot in sexual corruption. And a community in which excessive strictness is enjoined by social custom or religious or "moral" tradition, and conformity expected through self-control, will find occasional individuals requiring readaptation which can never be effected under the conditions. A cultured existence is not possible where there is a violent conflict between nature and culture, and such conflicts can be avoided only through institutional control, by which we mean the adaptation of the institutions of life to the adequate and appropriate exercise of all functions natural or cultural.

As a moral virtue, then, temperance is an objective or public function. The "restraint" that is to be exercised over the individual is effected by furnishing to him a full and free expression for every normal capacity, thus leaving him no reason or excuse for falling into excess or undesired or undesirable forms of action. The instruments to expression are all essentially public agencies, and in the nature of the case cannot be provided for the individual by himself. Together these agencies constitute the substance of culture, and they are the content of the political life. Politics is then morality given objective or real form in institutions as the material from which the individual draws the stuff of his life. Self-control does not mean control of the individual self by the individual self; in this sense it is merely contradictory and denies all meaning to spontaneity. It is not a negative or restrictive or prohibitive function. It does not assume that there is in the agent something that is essentially bad that is to be got rid of; it is the positive effort to provide the agent with the means and instruments by which his acts may be made significant. Self-control refers to the part which the individual is to play in the work of establishing effective institutions through which action can be made real. I control myself when I act in a way which tends to create and maintain a competent family, school, church, industrial system, and political state, and when these institutions support me in the effort. And as such temperance or self-control is an objective or public virtue and is best understood and exercised through the institutions which have been created in the interest of its adequate expression.

Chapter XXV

Courage—Institutionalized Active Attitudes

I. DEFINITION

COURAGE in the traditional sense refers to the attitude of steadfastness with which the individual meets situations involving uncertainty and danger. Its typical instance is the soldier who stands firm in the midst of fire or the person who performs some feat at the risk of his life. It is the character perhaps most celebrated in the history of mankind and was of great usefulness both to the individual and to the group during the ages when men's lives were passed constantly in the presence of physical danger. And as there probably never will be a time when men are altogether free from physical dangers, something like courage will always be a highly prized quality. But the form in which danger confronts us has changed greatly in the past and has been matched by corresponding changes in men's reactions to it; so as dangerous objects and situations change in the future, the form of our courage must be expected to change accordingly. In earlier periods situations calling for action required mere physical strength and endurance, but we are now, for the most part, able to meet such situations without hardships and danger by effectively implementing our reactions to them.

At a relatively early stage of development of men courage ceased to be essentially an individual virtue. Considered as an individual virtue, it presupposes man living as an individual among conditions which call upon him to face the dangers of life alone. But a little reflection will show that man never could have lived in such conditions, and an occasion upon which an individual is left to meet dangers alone is now unusual and temporary and accidental. He may become separated from his fellows in battle or in hunting, but he is quickly united to them again or perishes. Not only will his physical strength prove unequal to his enemies, but by himself he is not capable of supplying himself with the tools and instruments necessary to preserve his life.

Consequently, by the time man has reached a distinctly human stage, and certainly before his morality has reached any degree of refinement, the virtue with which he meets the dangers of life will have become a characteristic of the organization of men in corporate bodies and will be embodied in and expressed through his corporate action and mediated through means that are common and public. As far back as we can go in actual history we find courage regarded as a quality of the clan or tribe, although it may be symbolized in the person of a great individual.

II. IS COURAGE A SUBJECTIVE VIRTUE?

Courage is therefore not primarily an individual virtue. It is a corporate virtue, an aspect of the peculiar strength and power that resides in an organized body of men. Courage is also not a state of mind, or an individual attitude, although there are states of mind that appear to be closely bound up with it. As an expression of the individual, courage is essentially fear, and as a form of fear individual courage has no special moral significance, the moral obligation connected with it being the obligation to destroy the conditions that occasion it. There is a profound sense in which it can be said that the very purpose of the moral life is to overcome fear and to destroy the occasions where fear is normally felt. It is extremely unlikely that a normal man would assume an aggressive attitude to danger or would expose himself to danger if not stimulated to do so by a fear which overpowers his judgment. In any case the exposing one's self to danger unnecessarily is a mere instance of folly, and it is difficult to conceive of a dangerous situation as being necessary in the conditions of modern civilized life. Any aggressive attitude to danger on the part of the individual appears therefore as mere rashness or foolhardiness, and virtue does not under any circumstances require such attitudes.

As an individual trait with genuine moral significance courage is best described as presence of mind. This does not necessarily mean the capacity to act quickly or vigorously; in fact, it does not so much refer to the specific act of "will" as to the prevailing state of the individual's character, which may be conceived to be the source of the act. It is a reference to a made-up character and indicates that the mind and will have been active on previous occasions in building up habits of action and are acquainted with the type of situation that is presented. It is this intelligent perception of the nature of a presented situation that is the meaning of presence of mind. An intelligent mind, a mind built into a character which knows, as against a quick will, is best capable of perceiving its duty in a given case. It is also best able to determine from the nature of the situation what form of action is best fitted to meet the obligation that is imposed upon the character by the presence of the situation. The best "courage" with which to meet the responsibilities of life is a competent mind seasoned in a broad experience, which develops in the individual the power of interpretation by which the characteristics of circumstances are clearly seen in relation to the requirements of action.

Courage as an individual function is, then, a phase of the knowledge which is the basis of all the subjective virtues. And the broader and more inclusive the knowledge, the more spontaneous and ready to act will the person be. What for the most part makes us hesitate in a difficult situation is not cowardice but ignorance of the nature of the facts before us and the consequent lack of suggestions from the facts as to what can be done. For, as we have seen, the possibilities of action in any case are prefigured in the form and structure and relations of the objects before us. What I *can* do is spread out before me in the qualities and relations of the facts before me, and what I *should* do is similarly contained in outline in my past experience and knowledge as organized in my character. It is this organized mind, a mind structured upon a basis of a competent knowledge, that constitutes a proper courage for the individual person. But as so organized it is woven into the texture of public life.

III. COURAGE AND INTELLIGENCE

It is for this reason that Plato's definition of courage is perhaps the best—a "knowledge of things that are to be feared and of things that are not to be feared." This means that, if a situation which calls for action is understood, some type of worthy action will be indicated in the nature of the situation, and the degree of worth of our act will depend upon the quality of our interpretation and the extent of our knowledge. Where our knowledge is imperfect, our action will be hesitant and awkward or possibly impulsive and disastrous but, in any case, inappropriate to the end which would be indicated to us if we saw more clearly. What we are likely to call "cowardice" is thus rather stupidity or ignorance and, in the most favorable interpretation, an unfamiliarity with the nature of the circumstances where action is called for. When we know a situation fully, some significant form of act will be suggested to us by the nature of the fact, and, where we do not know, we are left helpless if action is made compulsory.

The "things that are to be feared," then, are things demanding time and effort to acquire a competent knowledge of, and, if action is forced in advance of proper knowledge, it is likely to be inappropriate and "wrong." It of course may by accident be right and proper, and useful results may follow; but as action and results rest on no dependable knowledge there is no guaranty for future exigencies of a similar type. Nothing therefore makes action safe and sure except valid knowledge, and where such knowledge is not attainable there is no obligation. Similarly, the "things that are not to be feared" are simple cases where the actor possesses a competent knowledge, and where action may be rational and deliberate in spite of the fact that it may have to be quick and decisive.

But if it is true, then, that courage in the acting person merely indicates an adequate knowledge and the fixed attitudes that knowledge involves, bravery, as ordinarily described, merely means ignorance. To rush in regardless of the consequences does not indicate a moral attitude but rather an untrained character. And to "stand firm" in the presence of known danger indicates that the mind is not properly functioning, perhaps from fear or other form of excitement. Even if I have dedicated my life to a cause, there is no reason why I should hasten to deliver it up, and the longer I can evade the final offering the more likely I am to further the cause. There is no way to interpret courage as a genuine moral virtue which does not lay down knowledge as its basis, and action on any other basis has no assurance as to the nature of its results. Of course it is true that the very best of our knowledge is sometimes inadequate, as where the facts are beyond our comprehension in the nature of things, and in many cases of this kind we are obliged to act. But this situation we have already provided for in recognizing that there is an element of adventure in the life of action which in our present state of knowledge cannot be overcome. And it may be that the finer values of morality depend upon the uncertainty thus made essential in experience, as making necessary the creations of the imagination as ideal patterns of what may be possible to the will when acting under the impetus of pure speculation. In any case there is a ground here for the curiosity that makes possible a life directed by reflection, as well as a life of creative activity in art, religion, and politics.

It is practice in reflection upon these critical instances of the creative act of the imagination that develops in the person his special moral or practical reason. The patterned acts which I can build up in imagination come to be moral rules for me, and their status in my character is best represented by saying that they are an organized system of active attitudes. Taken in their system, they constitute the character of the person. These attitudes are our previously attained intellectual insights into common situations rendered permanent in us by having become strongly emotionalized and then firmly established by habituation. They thus throw the mass or volume of feeling, which is the total content of many of our ideas and the partial content of all of them, into the balance in doubtful cases, and in this way determine the direction of perception and mark out the course for action. As fixed attitudes they are the source of all our acts in so far as acts may be said to have a source in the actor, and the nature and direction of an act will be determined largely by the emotional content of the attitudes. Feeling is the matter or stuff of ideas in any case and constitutes the substantial body which makes it possible for knowledge to be true and permanent. These attitudes can be cultivated, and their creation and maintenance in a system representing our typical values constitute the exercise of moral courage for the individual. They represent the person's active integrity and thus constitute the basis of his character.

IV. COURAGE AN OBJECTIVE VIRTUE

The one thing that is essentially true in the common conception of courage is that it is the virtue in which is expressed the peculiar connection of the moral agent with the moral *world* of persons. Courage is thus the basis of the character as a political and social agent and thus of the responsibility to the objective whole which the person feels as his deepest obligation. It refers us to our civil and public obligation and demands of us that such a social and political structure shall be maintained as will permit of the full exercise of the function of obligation. It now has nothing to do with danger and supposes such an objectified moral world as will eliminate fear from our nature and the conditions that occasion fear from the cultural structure. It functions now through knowledge and thus outlines in imagination the plan by which the moral state may be constructed and maintained as a political order. Thus the civil and political character of courage was early recognized.

In this objective sense courage represents the type of action through which our established active attitudes, as described above, are institutionalized or expressed and embodied in objects so as to form the structure of the moral world. It is the peculiar function of courage to give objective expression to all our active attitudes, and it becomes the special executive power in the moral person. It is then the practical capacity of the agent or person. But it is as a public and objective factor in the good life that its importance appears. What in the last analysis we mean to achieve by courage is a world in which the essential institutions are all of them materializations of the virtues, where each institution is an embodiment of one of the characteristic active attitudes. What this means is perhaps best expressed in illustrations, and we shall give a number of instances.

The first that ordinarily comes to mind in connection with courage is what is commonly called "bravery," or the capacity to meet obstacles effectively. When we think it through, we see that it is not merely meeting and overcoming obstacles that interests us. When I go to war, what I mean is, ideally, at least, that I am willing to do something in the interest of seeing that justice is done, that obligations are met, that oppression is stamped out, or that any wrong and evil condition that happens to exist in institutional life may be corrected and thus may become the occasion and the stimulus to the worthy expression of an active attitude. I do not want to fight, and I certainly do not want to commit murder; but I may accept these if they can be conclusively shown to be necessary stages in the process of putting into existence the objective conditions through which justice may be done. Courage therefore implies that the existence of such an institutionalized political structure is a claim upon the will prior to all other claims; such a structure will make the course of justice easy and sure; and being courageous and acting upon the urge of courage means that I am doing something calculated to create and maintain such a system of political order. As an objective virtue courage is the objectification of the will to justice, honesty, probity, industry, thrift, generosity, or any impulse that can be justified on moral grounds. Courage is the determination that there shall exist an objective world in which the virtues may be realized, when we think of it as a subjective "spring to action"; but in its proper objective sense it is that world as actually created and existing and functioning as the stage upon which men may act significantly. This is the meaning of courage in its most universal sense.

We can see a concrete instance of real courage in the work-life. Work is the demand of the moral will to execute itself in utility and beauty. Here courage means the process by which the work activity is fitted into its appropriate external instrument or set up in its proper institutional agencies. Courage is then not a separate and peculiar virtue but just the ideal demand that work shall be what it ought to be and can be. And the giving objective expression to the work process, the setting-up of the work activity in appropriate tools and means, and with the right relations to other systems of activity, this is the courageous life with respect to work. Courage is in this connection the institutionalization of the creative attitude and refers to the system of objects in which past instances of this attitude have been expressed and which now stand ready to instrument any creative purpose. In work this system of objects is industry, which consists for the most part of the multitude of tools and machines that as yet we only imperfectly know how to use, since we lack the courage to give them their proper function in systems of public instruments.

This virtue could be illustrated in any of the characteristic types of activity. "Moral" courage in religion and education and civic activity, in any of the normal functions of life, consists in the creation and maintenance of a corporate system of objects through which an appropriate expression of these activities is possible.

V. COURAGE AND SAFETY

It was noticed above that it is not, under modern conditions, the special function of courage to deal with danger and that its relation to fear is negative, a relation that implies the elimination of fear. But the elimination of fear does not involve the acceptance of the attitude of safety. The motive to safety is worthy within its proper limitations, but it has unfortunately been made to include a number of motives which are at least questionable. It is probable that it has cultivated an overemphasis upon caution and the excessive carefulness which prevents the normal adventuresomeness necessary to the beginning of new projects. It has carried hesitancy beyond the ordinary limits of prudence and has checked enterprise where it should perhaps have stimulated it. Safety, if it is to be a moral attitude, must not involve inaction, since action in the interest of securing unknown ends is the basic meaning of morality. Morality is not a static condition in the practical world any more than it is a "state" of mind in the individual.

What is probably intended in the mistaken motive to safety is such a correlation of the activities and instruments of life as will prevent unnecessary loss of life in accidents. This is of course a valid motive, and it shows the objective character of courage in the reference to the machinery and instruments of practice as important elements in the moral world. But there has apparently been included in the idea of safety the condition of settled inactivity which is often mistaken for peace. The instinct for peace is perhaps innate in us, and the ideal of a worthy peace is a perfect representation of the ultimate end which human action sets before itself. But it certainly does not exclude activity and change and danger, for change and uncertainty are inherent in the very nature of action. There is therefore no such thing as moral certainty, at least in the matter of the results and consequences of action, and courage as a virtue implies the acceptance of a problematical existence and the corporate organization of active attitudes in institutions designed to cope with its problems.

VI. COURAGE AND PEACE

It is at this point that courage appears as representing the whole meaning of morality. It has been already noticed that any of the virtues, taken in its total meaning and along with all that it implies, comes to the same thing as morality itself. This is what is meant by "the unity of the virtues." Develop each of them to its fullest stature, and it covers the whole of the good life. So in this case the concept of peace to which courage leads gives us the idea of the moral world corporately organized under the control of our active attitudes and erected into a perfect whole. This whole includes and harmonizes the realm of nature with the system of human culture, the order of which is continuously maintained by political activity implemented and institutionalized in governmental machinery. It is in this sense that courage is properly regarded as a public virtue and as involving the relations of the person to the state. It implies that the person lives with the dominant attitude to maintain the good in the form of the institutions of human culture and the special values of which it is made up and to know and appreciate the significance of the whole.

Chapter XXVI

Justice—the Order of Culture
under Law

I. DEFINITION

VIRTUE completely developed in a wise and temperate and courageous public life and established in appropriate institutions is
culture. Culture organized and unified within the political state and
given effective power by and in law is justice. The discussion of
justice thus involves little more than a review of the various elements
of culture, with emphasis on their unity, and a statement of their more
important bearings on the practical relations of life within the public
order. The more fundamental of these elements of culture have been
described, and it is only necessary here to emphasize the importance
of their interdependence, the one upon the other and each upon the
whole. It would be impossible to overestimate the importance of the
instinct-life and its realization in the family, and it is just as necessary
to understand the importance of the relations between the family, on
the one side, and industry and religion and art, on the other.

We have seen that these relations of interdependence become the
factual basis of the objective virtues, and it is only possible to comprehend the meaning of wisdom, courage, and temperance by seeing
them objectified in these relations and hardened down into the institutions through which they find appropriate expression. The relations
of life which we call "instinctive," and which we sum up in the
attitude of love, find their embodiment in the family and their characteristic active expression in the virtue of temperance. But the moderation and balance which we learn in the family is what we mean by
temperance; it extends all the way through our world and in this way
becomes a factor in the whole balance of culture which we call "justice." In a similar way we find objective meaning for our physical
relations to the world in the institution of industry; these relations are
extended and idealized until they set up a creative attitude to the
whole and thus supply another element to justice. Our faith attitudes

first become realized and objective in institutional religion and then by extension become the elements of steadfastness in the whole structure of justice. And, finally, we see wholeness in harmony in the concrete and actualized instance for the first time in the work of art, and this becomes by extension the principle and pattern upon which we idealize the perfect harmony of life as a whole which we call justice. Justice is then merely the fulfilment of all the virtues; it is the idea of them as all harmonized into a whole and set up as a principle and standard for the guidance of life and a pattern of the constitution of things.

But this indicates that there are peculiar weaknesses in our commonly accepted ideas of justice, and we may notice some of them. For instance, we speak of "doing justice," as if justice were a peculiar type of act or a special quality or thing which we may produce by our act. But it is to be recalled that justice is not a quality of any particular thing and not an aspect of any act taken by itself. There is no act of any kind which we could call "just" by way of distinguishing it from other kinds of act, and the same act may in one case be just and in another case unjust. Justice is not a character or quality that belongs to or inheres in an act of any kind; it makes no direct reference to the act as taken by itself. It is rather the name of a relation in which an act stands to other things. It is specifically that relation of harmony or consistency in which a given act stands to the system of relevant acts and which, by equating them, constitutes them a finished whole. Then justice is rather the universal form of a relation which states the principle by which an act is made capable of being incorporated with other acts in a whole of right or good.

When I "do" justice, therefore, I perform an act which is principled with consistency to a system of acts which, taken together, constitute a good. My act is a contribution then to the reality that gives to justice its claim to finality and authority. I must do justice therefore because the constitution of things enforces it upon me. It does not compel me, but I cannot do otherwise without denying both my own reality and also the reality of the world. The idea of not doing the just act is self-contradictory, and I negate my rational existence when I assent to its not being done by me. Doing justice, then, is realizing my act in the world whose own characters determine the conditions of the act, including the conditions we call the "motive" or "intention" by which we initiate the movements through which the act is expressed.

There is a similar fallacy in the common expression, "get or obtain justice." From what has been said it is clear that justice is not a thing or condition which could be "got" or "had," and there are two possibilities as to what the expression means. We may mean by "getting" justice the bringing-about of the condition in which all acts will be performed with full conformity to the principles laid down above. In this case getting justice would refer to the establishment of a set of rules and the determination of a type of object and would mean the same as the total life of action in which justice is to be realized. On the other hand, it is to be feared that in the general use of the phrase "getting justice" is meant the securing of the special interest of the persons who thus use the phrase. Going to court thus to get justice often means nothing except that the person who goes to court intends to realize his interest in the matter in controversy, and his interest may have no relation to moral justice. It is evident that in this commercial age everything with which we may be in any way concerned is likely to be evaluated largely by simple reference to the special interests of the person who does the valuing. An interest in the "just" conduct of a business, then, means the desire to get for one's self whatever one can out of it, or at least one's full share as against the shares of other interested persons. An interest in the "just" management of a church will mean such a management as will increase the influence of the interested person. But all this is "subjective" and has only a very limited and at best a negative moral significance. The tendency of the demand to "get justice" is therefore to place it upon a basis of barter, and this interpretation comes to be recognized in the legal theory of justice as the process of "matching interests." It is largely this commercial interpretation of justice as what can be got from a matching of interests of "prudent men of business" that has thrown civilization into chaos, and the correction of the errors involved in the viewpoint appears to involve problems which are, at the present moment, beyond the capacity of statesmen to comprehend. There will be no adequate comprehension of fundamental questions of public life as ethical problems, and thus no basis for valid rules either of law or morality, until we see that there is no possible positive relation between interest in any of its forms, and right as defined by moral principles. Justice and interest mean as nearly as is possible exactly opposite things; they are as near as possible a concrete instance of pure practical contradictories. What is just is never an interest, and an interest is never just. Of course the theory of interest gets a degree of plausibility from the ambiguity in the definition of the term. But the theory that can call my concern about my bank

stock and my concern about art both "interests" needs detain us no
longer. There can be no "matching" or trading in the moral world,
and what refers exclusively and only to me can never be right or good.
So far as justice is an ideal of existing political order, it is a purely
negative concept, and its influence in the world of action will be
negative and destructive until it is reformulated upon an exactly opposite basis. The essential basis of justice involves four ultimate concepts,
which we proceed to discuss—freedom, law, peace, order.

II. FREEDOM AND JUSTICE

A. POLITICAL FREEDOM

As a consequence of the negative interpretation of justice, the concept of freedom has a badly ambiguous use and meaning. What has in
recent centuries been called "political freedom" is one of the meanings of the term. It is the negative freedom of distributive justice and
is based upon the utilitarian or commercial interpretation which confuses justice with interest. In this view freedom means merely the
absence of external restraint upon the action of the individual and
conceives the individual as alone in the universe depending upon his
own powers to collect from his environment the means necessary to
his existence. His freedom means that no one will be permitted to
interfere with his conquest of his environment—that all will be required to stand out of his way. It seems to assume that there will be
no relations at all between persons, that all strictly interpersonal relations are unreal, and that only those relations are real which connect
the person with his world. It further assumes that the only environment of the free man is the natural environment and that this natural
environment is both instrument and object of all his acts—that he
never acts except it is the natural environment which is the tool, the
stage, and the object of his act.

The tragic weakness of such assumptions is, of course, seen in the
fact that many of the acts of the person are directed upon another
person as object or are mediated through another person as instrument. Or, in general, the environment within and upon and by means
of which the person acts is quite often, if not always and necessarily,
the cultural environment, and there are few if any genuine acts in
which the actor is not involved with other persons as means. The
final perfection of the theory of negative freedom was achieved in
the famous injunction never to use the moral person as a means but
always as an end. But this rule appears to contemplate a condition

which could not exist in fact. Developments in the actual world of men within the past generations have demonstrated the futility of this doctrine, and no argument is necessary. A cultural existence is not possible where men are engaged in exploiting nature and following their independent interests, for no power, not even the apotheosized assumptions of individualism, can keep them from each other's throats.

B. Positive Freedom

Freedom is therefore a positive conception, and we must indicate briefly what it means. For the man who has abstract "political" freedom in the protection against interference by others, but who nevertheless has no access to the tools and materials necessary for successful action, freedom is not likely to mean much. What therefore is meant by positive freedom is just such access to whatever is necessary to enable the person to perform significant acts. This is so fundamental that it is incorporated in the very law of morality, which is a description of the major factors in the good life. And we have already named some of the most important elements of freedom in the description of the applications of that law. In general terms, the free person must have connections in a competent family, in order to develop appropriate instincts and sensibilities; must have the privileges of an educational system which is capable of developing his intellectual powers; must be empowered by an industrial system to meet all his material requirements; must have the capacities and the opportunity to enrich his nature in a religious institution; must be endowed with the capacities for and have access to the instruments for the creation of beauty and the ability to create other types of valued objects; and, as a synthesis and harmony of all these, must live in a state where justice is the law and principle of guidance of the life that is full and whole.

It is not necessary, perhaps, to go into details as to what positive freedom means; nearly everybody mature enough to appreciate a description of the facts has already had direct experience of them in his own life. The young man or woman who has had to struggle unduly for the chance of a college education need not be told the terms of positive freedom in that connection. The father and mother who must see their child die for want of food or medical care do not require the experience restated to them in doctrines. The parent who stands by helpless while his son goes down in crime and degradation knows by its absence what freedom means. And there are coming to be enough people who suffer under the fact that the mass of men and women are denied the merest indispensables to a reasonable degree of health and comfort, and a minimum of the opportunities to worthy action, that provision will have to be made to remedy the situation. Our civilization is at this moment facing the necessity of ordering its affairs upon principles almost the exact opposite and reverse of those upon which affairs previously rested. We have sought the good life from the point of view of the isolated person; we shall have to give up that viewpoint. The good life is not now, and perhaps never was, available to the individual through his own efforts and capacities. The fundamental moral person of the future, indeed perhaps of the present, is the corporate person—the individuality composed of all the personal powers and capacities embodied and instrumented within an institutional form. The industrial corporation, the family, the church, the school, and, over and above all, the state which incorporates them in a single body, politic and public, constitute the moral person through whose genius our positive freedom is to be accomplished. Industry has abolished want or will have done it when freed of private control; education has eradicated, or, when rescued from private interest, is prepared to eradicate, ignorance; the church will throw the businessman out of the temple and thus rapidly conquer superstition; art has enthroned beauty and has abased the ugly and the foul and the unclean. The complete and full harvest of all these advantages now awaits the final perfection of the political methods and forms upon which the good life depends. With the new state established, culture will pass from the state of mere empty promise, which our institutions now offer, to the fulfilment of the reality of positive justice where we shall indeed be free.

III. JUSTICE AND LAW

The instrument through which we shall accomplish our positive freedom is a just law exercised by the moral authority of a corporate state. We wish here briefly to point out what are the essential characters of such a law.

In the first place, there is a good deal of confusion as to what law is and what are its functions in the moral world. It is not necessary to discuss the various theories as to the nature of law; each of them represents some important aspect of the law and, like most theory, mistakes this aspect for the whole meaning. Until quite recently, and for the most part still, the American lawyer regards the law as the "command of the sovereign," merely the order issued by the prevailing authority which the citizen must obey or may disregard at his peril. The judge in adjudicating a case under the law has the task merely of interpreting an instrument and making mechanical application to the facts. This is of course too simple to have any real correspondence with the facts and is perhaps an interpretation which has been adopted because it simplifies administration. But simplification of method has trouble when it undertakes to deal directly with the facts, so that administration under this method often results in grave injury and injustice. This "positivism" is of course a crudely false interpretation of the meaning of law; yet the insistence on the necessity to face the facts in the interpretation of law, and the recognition that only from the point of view of fact can law have meaning, indicate a profound insight. The law has its very essence in the facts of human experience and is grounded in human relations.

But these facts and relations are vastly more complicated and obscure than the legal positivist ever dreams. Just precisely what the facts and relations are is a question for the legal theorist to decide; but we may suggest that the principle upon which it will be decided is that which states the relation of the individual moral person to the corporate moral person and shows at the same time that the relation is constitutional to the corporate person and identifies with the relation between corporate persons as the foundation principle of the state. Such an interpretation is made necessary by the fact that morality is the content and the intent of the law and will therefore determine its form. Thus a simple positivism is as naïve and inadequate as the "scientific jurisprudence" which gives an account of it. The relation of the law to fact is not a simple matter and is in the first instance a problem for philosophy. But the relation of law to fact is the essence of the meaning of the law.

It was noted above that the ultimate fact of the law is that it states the relation of the moral person, considered as an individual, to the moral person contemplated as corporate and universal. This statement gives us a basis for the explanation of two other difficult concepts common to the law and to morals. These are the concepts of authority and obligation. Indeed, all the concepts of ethics and all the substantial notions (as opposed to the procedural devices) of the law have their meaning in that phase or aspect of this relation of the individual person to the corporate person to which they each give expression. This relation grounds the fundamental principle of all practical philosophy. The concept of authority is the viewpoint which interprets the relation which the law expresses, interprets the law, that is, from the point of view of its bearing or incidence upon the corporate moral person; that is, the viewpoint that sees the law as universal. Its inter-

pretation is therefore a categorical imperative, since it states the fact
of the law as it *is* and therefore as it must and shall be. What the law
is, however, is not merely what it is by statutory enactment; its positive basis is metaphysical.

Obligation, on the other hand, is an interpretation of the law
(which has its ground in the relation between the individual moral
person and the corporate moral person) as expressing the meaning and
essence of the individual, and this it finds in the "ought" which expresses the logical dependence of the individual upon the corporate
whole. The fact that the legal relation (through its moral content) is
statable only in personal terms, that it holds always between a person
and a person, gives rise to the question whether the two terms (persons) may not on occasion be identical or the same person; in any
case, this is the basis of justification of the democratic principles of
self-government and self-determination. We have here the basis of
the meaning of the elemental concepts that are common to ethics and
law; and, as it is easier to see their meaning from the legal angle, the
law becomes in practice the interpreter not only of morality but also
of the theory about morality.

It is rather obvious, when we see the complexities that lie at the
bottom of the relations of law and justice when interpreted in terms
of their moral content, that the positivist approach to the problem of
justice, in spite of its emphasis upon the facts, has yet failed to find out
what the essential nature of the facts really is. We shall find a good
deal more willingness to go to the bottom of things when we discuss
the "natural law doctrine."

We noticed in discussing the "facts" that the facts tell us nothing
about justice until we look behind them or follow up the suggestions
which their relations exhibit. And then, in order to get any consistent
meaning from them, we must go far beyond their mere appearance
and immediate character. What this amounts to is that we are called
upon, by the nature of the facts themselves, to go beyond the facts to
the principles which can be derived from their relations. There is no
justice, no morality, in the world of fact as it appears; and we must go
back to the "nature of things" to find a basis for moral principles.
And the nature of things is, from this point of view, just the system of
external realities conceived as animated by a principle of reason, a
principle which is as objective and external as the objects of nature
themselves. It at one time appeared to be the notion of cause or force
endowed with a kind of intelligence, and as this "natural reason"
picked its way through the devious possibilities which the world of

fact presented to it, it could be regarded as an expression of will. The pronouncements of this will are law, and in this view they are law for the reason that they present, in the form of plan or pattern, a portion of the fixed structure of the universe. As such these laws are not so much obligatory and authoritative as they are necessary and inexorable, and this makes a difficulty with the question of freedom. As a consequence of the doctrine of freedom there is also a difficulty about justice, which comes to take on many of the characters of fate. But there are compensating elements here, for, while justice is rigid and incorrigible, the same qualities prevent the overseasoning with mercy or corrupting interest, and the law maintains a dignity which it never attains under any other system.

The profound ethical significance of this natural law theory of justice lies in its recognition that justice is not in any circumstances a quality or character of a particular situation but is a function of the substantial element of the whole as this is expressed in the particular situation. This is to say it is the cosmic implication given as an element of the whole presented in the situation, when it is a question of "doing" justice in conduct, or in "the determination of what is just" in adjudication. The presence of the substance of justice as the ultimate reality of things in the concrete case makes collapse of the law difficult in the process of administration of justice, and this fact that it does not fail endows the law with the power to compel respect for its integrity. The respect for law dies out at once in the positivism which makes it depend upon "the law and the evidence," and judicial empiricism buries it in confusion. The doctrine of respect for law produces a law that is not respectable, for the simple reason that it makes law depend upon purely subjective bases. These characters of dignity and integrity and respect have, however, been of enormous importance in the historical development of legal and moral institutions and have been the instruments through which the moral authority and obligatoriness of the law could maintain itself against untoward natural conditions. They have been therefore of the greatest value in the development of culture. They have emphasized the truth that all moral concepts are objective, and show that the *virtue* of justice lies in the objective and obligatory tie with which it binds the moral person to his universal and absolute self conceived as the basis of the corporate person of the state, and that the substance of justice is the system of cultural institutions through the functioning of which the tie of obligation is made the essence of the agent's good and is hence incorporated into the structure of the world.

It is not necessary to go on with further discussion of the concept of

justice in its legal aspects. Suffice it to say that the discussion proves
(and statement of other legal notions would prove it more abundantly) that morality, when it comes to principle, has nothing to do with
the states of mind and feelings and opinions of individual men. That
morality appears *within* these states of mind and feelings and judgments is an accident of the natural constitution of man; but that
morality should get its meaning or value from this accident is absurd.
Whatever value attaches to these states of mind and feelings and
judgments derives from the elemental relations which constitute the
individual a person, and these relations are the texture of reality itself.
Morality or good is not a type of value; it is the type from the nature
of which value itself derives its significance. For as the act of a person
morality incorporates value within and into the structure of existence—this is the meaning of an act—and in the absence of the funda-
ments of existence value is the sounding brass of abstract mentality
and inward mystic states of mind. What merely happens in mind is of
the least importance (value) in the world; unless its happening there
has other grounds than its mental circumstance, it is as nothing; its
roots must rest in the dark elements of nature before it can ever see
the light of mind, and both light and darkness are phases of the incorporate whole. Justice will be done *or* the heavens fall.

IV. JUSTICE AND PEACE

The realization on the part of the person of the ultimate significance
of his obligation as exemplified in objective justice establishes him in
his place within the moral whole. This *establishment* of the person
within the objective substance of morality (the state) is peace, and
its moral significance lies in the fact that it gives stability to the reign
of justice and embodies it in the institutions of life. Peace then is the
condition of equilibrium between the moral person and his world, the
person in perfect relations with his world, and when the state is so
organized as to furnish him the opportunity to act, and a vantage
point from which to act, it has done all that can be expected of it or
that can be done for him. And recalling that the state is the symbol and
synthesis of all the institutions of life, in which all the various types
of action are expressed, the requirements of morality are all fulfilled
when the balance between the person and his world is established in
the state.

V. JUSTICE AND ORDER

The condition in which the *active* life of the person is objectified
in the institutions of his world, and harmonized with the system of
the whole in the state, is what is called the moral order. The phrase

means no more than has been described already but emphasizes the wholeness and balance and unity of the life of action and its objective character as expressed in the things and processes of nature and culture. The moral or just order means, to the individual person, that there is for him at least an opportunity for any act, consistent with the right, which he may desire to perform. And it means at the most that there is accessible to the person who wishes to act all and every means he may need, so far as his proposed act is consistent with moral principles as laid down. These moral principles are simply directions as to how to act in the way to create and maintain the whole good, the latter itself being the system of the objective conditions to action. The agent acts in order that it may always be possible for agents to act. It is in connection with this conception of the good that our theory and practice are most deficient. We have misrepresented the idea to ourselves in the phrase the "good of the whole" or "the greatest good of the greatest number"; but these conceptions are easily seen to be deficient. The good of the whole has been taken to mean merely the sum of the goods of individuals, with the individual holding the possessory relation to the goods, that is, with the assumption that what is the good of one cannot be the good of another. Both expressions have uniformly been interpreted as expressing the individual person's ownership of the good, the idea being that the good of one man is distinct from the good of another.

This is the most profound fallacy of modern moral life—the assumption that the moral quality can be expressed in terms of ownership, that the person does his duty when he owns. It was perhaps stated first in the Puritan "virtue" of thrift and, as prudence, has been accepted in our commercial age as representing the whole of duty and the completion of moral living. The good consists in the individual's owning and holding a share of the whole good, and this is taken to justify him in *withholding* what he owns from contributing to the whole good in so far as the whole good may be perceived to benefit another.

Modern society is thus built upon the idea that what I have you may not have, that what I use you may not use; and this has come to mean that, whether I have a thing or use it or do not have it or use it, what I can control you are excluded from in every particular. It is this false notion of exclusive control of the good that has prevented any significant degree of moral order in modern times. The good is not an object of control in any sense, and the moral good in a commercial age has become the multitude of physical goods defined by the process of barter. The first condition to a moral order, as the final idea of justice, is a revision of our notions of the relation of the person to the good; we must learn that what can be possessed and controlled is not and cannot be the good; that what is exhausted in the use (as food) or used up is never in any case anything but a means. The good is beyond our control; we can create it, but, once having given it being, it pronounces destiny for us. We can attain it, but we cannot possess it, can reach it but not hold it. The good is real, and men must comport themselves accordingly.

Chapter XXVII

The Corporate Person and Objective Virtue

I. SUBJECTIVE VIRTUE AND THE NATURAL PERSON

THERE are as many virtues as there are typical forms of action. We have defined virtue as any typical or characteristic form of action because action is the elementary fact of life. All the moral categories therefore get their meaning from their relation to action and are distinguished from the categories of other subjects because of their peculiar relation to action. But we may for practical purposes classify virtues or designate kinds of them by reference to something other than their direct reference to action, and on this ground we designate as subjective virtues those that are given expression through the natural person.

Forms of action, therefore, which get their distinctive character from the backward reference to the type of agency they are expressed through are subjective virtues, as, for example, an act described as generous is so described by referring it to a quality of the character of the agent who performs the act. It is clear that there will be a certain correspondence between the qualities and attributes of the natural person and the characteristics of the act performed by him. But the nature of subjective virtue and of the natural person have been discussed in previous chapters. Here we want to show the subjective virtues in relation to the objective virtues and to correlate the corresponding natural person of the subjective virtues with the corporate person of the objective virtues and then exhibit both in their relations to the whole of the good life.

We selected (Part III) four subjective virtues as typical, but with the definitions of virtue and of subjective which we have accepted there might have been named a different number and a different list of virtues, since all that is required of the list is that it should be representative. Yet there seems a certain propriety in our list when we note their peculiar nature. Sympathy, we saw, is an expression of the elementary sensitivity of the natural person and is the most elementary of the conditions upon which the moral character depends. In the absence of this quality a moral nature is absolutely precluded; it is the one necessary condition of a moral nature, the original seed out of which all cultural possibilities grow. And the person who is insensitive or dense is shut out completely and forever from the higher spheres of life. The importance of sensitivity is shown also in the hypersensitive person, whom the ordinary impacts of the environing life are enough to drive to desperation or to poetry. For the hypersensitive person the picture of a starved child or a crippled animal or a ruthlessly crushed flower or a neglected old person, or a person whose mind cannot follow the thread of his life, is an unutterable tragedy and the cause of immitigable suffering. But, on the other hand, the person of highly and finely developed sensitivity, particularly when balanced with knowledge and good sense, makes the highest contributions, in the way of content, to the good life in every field. So the virtue of sympathy, which we define by reference to a quality of the agent's character, also is definable in terms of the fineness of the corporate culture which it produces.

In the case of generosity also the richness of meaning of things known and felt and created by the sensitive person is shared with his fellows in so far as its nature permits. When a sensitive nature has apprehended the elementary values of art and religion, and of material and social relations and objects, the next step in moral worthiness appears to be the attempt to share these rare value-contents with other persons, and where the generosity is expressed in the selection of beneficiaries the attitude approaches a great nobility. And where I can be completely indifferent toward whom I shall direct my generosity, if this is possible, I appear to have attained to complete "disinterestedness" and objectivity. I seem to attain the "universal love" in those cases where I project my goodness out upon all beings regardless of nature or status, and generosity has been justly praised as representing one of the highest of possible moral attitudes. The activities in which I attempt to extend to others the good that I experience are indeed as perfect in moral quality as any that I can as an individual perform or plan and, within the limitations of "personal" experience, represent again a type of action of which it can be said that none are higher.

And when we objectify our generosity and spread it over so as to include a great number of people whom we think of as thereby embodied in a unitary life, we again appear to have reached the highest spheres of moral experience. Nothing can present itself to our imagination which is more attractive than the image of ourselves living peacefully and respectfully and lovingly among a number of admiring and admired friends in a sort of garden of Epicurus; and the corporate neighborhood made up of contented homes which we can find in any community in prosperous times furnishes a picture of life that is close to what the ordinary human being will describe as representing the "larger" life which he conceives and appreciates in the moments when he can forget his own little personal affairs. It is difficult to overestimate the value of these friendships when we think of them as embodied in a public corporate life, where life is thought of in terms of experience content for the individual. These pictures of subjective qualities hardened down in community substance have entered largely into all our ideals.

The sensitive person who is generous and capable of a large friendship—in short, the person who is whole and complete in the sense that he is all that a person can be or can be expected to be, whose relations to other people are all satisfactory and agreeable—this person is the ideal of thousands of years of thought and struggle and hope and at last is real and exists in many human beings everywhere. That is to say the good man is here; he came with Socrates and Jesus and Buddha, but he also comes with the millions of men who every day attain to friendliness and generosity and who exhibit in their acts and the things they create the sensitivity that fulfils all that can be required or expected of men. The good man is an actuality, corporately writ large in his community, and it is hard to interest the ordinary human being in pushing the limits of personal goodness further. What he now wants is a world in which all men may be good men, a world in which it is neither necessary nor inevitable that the majority of human beings born into it are already, at the moment of their birth, cut off and denied any access whatever to significant forms or degrees of goodness. For the majority of persons the good life is not yet even a hope; its inaccessibility to them is the only certainty they have. That these persons, as persons, are subjectively good is demonstrated; that they should remain good in any sense is inconceivable.

That is to say, we have attained the good man, but we have not the good life. It is impossible to argue that peace and plenty and happiness and prosperity and blessedness are not already accomplished and accepted in the "wills" and "hearts" of men. It would be absurd to ask that men should value them more than they do already. Furthermore, peace and plenty and happiness and prosperity and blessedness—goodness—are also already accomplished in the perfected individual acts and completed individual objects of our culture. How are we to see that our wills and hearts are given body and substance in these acts and objects, that the world which we desire may be created? There is probably nobody who desires war and poverty and disease and filth and confusion, for men have been convinced as to these things for ages. And it is mere fatuity to argue that we do not want peace and prosperity and happiness and blessedness badly or "hard" enough. And yet all these evils are here in greater intensity and raw brutality than ever before, and the moral sensitivity and brotherliness and generosity of men appear to be absolutely powerless to do anything about it.

We have a morality complete and perfect in our hearts and our states of mind, and we have the objective conditions for its realization in our industrial and religious and artistic and legal and political achievements; and yet the good life is prostrate and as yet unable to be born. Why?

The answer lies in the imperfections and limitations of the virtues upon which hitherto we have attempted to build our systems of morality and the consequent and corresponding weakness of the instruments through which we have attempted to give expression to these virtues. Our good wills and our good hearts fail to find solid substance in which to embody themselves, and remain flabby and helpless; likewise our industrial and religious and political instruments fail in spirit and remain brutal and lifeless and hard things. How shall we vivify these dead instruments with the spirit of our good will—how shall we implement our will to goodness? The answer is the new agent, the corporate person. Meanwhile, precisely what is wrong with our virtues?

Brief comment on each of the virtues will make their weakness and failure clear. And our comment may take the form of citing facts. Sympathy and "love" contribute little to the making of the good life. Sympathy does nothing toward carving a farm out of the wilderness or making a home. It will not hold a job or feed a child. Thus in spite of all our charity the child life is dying for lack of opportunity to the good life. There is no need to argue the point further; in the simplest and most immediate of moral relations our primary virtue has very little if any part. And in the greater relations of the good life it is conspicuously absent. Where is it in the working of a bank or in the operations of our larger corporate practical agencies? How much does it influence the food market, or oil, or steel? Where is it present in the workings of the law courts and the other agencies of government? Are court decisions wrought out in pity and love for the innocent young men and women who can find no work and must steal bread? With love of our neighbors in our hearts do we build up systems of international friendship and comity? Is the principle on which we deal with each other confidence and love and faithfulness, or is it suspicion and fear and deception? And yet these are precisely the things and relations and agencies which men everywhere have accepted as the fundamental elements of the good life. It is true, of course, that men claim to "hold" to "higher" things; but, reflecting that the ultimate fact of morality is action, what do men as a fact and in their every act hold as the best or highest good? We have fashioned our moral concepts with a lofty "idealism" and have perfected them in spiritual abstraction as instruments of the individual consciousness and will; but at the same time our action was building a system of corporate acts and corporate concepts more solidly into the texture of our life, so that what we actually do and live, and what we merely think, are moving in different and sometimes opposite directions. And our corporate bents and purposes, and the objects they involve, are what we really and actively regard as good; and what we say and believe we regard as good we have abandoned long ago.

This is the reason these larger corporate agencies of the good life appear to us to be evil. There are two alternatives. They may actually be evil; this is the theory we have followed for many years—in fact, until quite recently. But it is to be observed that they prospered in wickedness under our efforts to "moralize" them; and remembered also with humility and shame should be the ridiculous effort we made to find their moral perversity in "bad men." Through a couple of generations we looked for the wicked man in the "trust" and fondly and solemnly hoped we could correct the trust if we could catch and punish the "bad man" who was "behind" it. But we found no bad man; we found ordinary human beings motivated by the desire to send a son or a daughter to college or to be provided for in their old age. Men in "trusts" are no more wicked than they are out of them; they are the same sensitive or dense, generous or grumpy, friendly or hostile, intelligent or boneheaded, human beings they are elsewhere. The difference is that in the corporate organization men are able to act with respect to purposes and objects that are altogether out of the reach of the individual and to act with the power of ten thousand individuals. But in these acts it is never the wills or purposes of individual agents that get expressed; it is the public or corporate will that is expressed, the will to the whole good, and this public purpose or end is only perverted when we try to infuse into the corporate act our good will and our right heart. The consequence is that we must face the fact that, with respect to the larger goods of life, the individual is powerless to act either alone or in groups; until he learns to implement aright the corporate public act, his larger ends will float in the uncertain and imaginary sea of his ideas and ideals with constant danger of wreck upon the rock of chance and hard circumstance.

So if we cannot find badness in the man, may it not be that we do not find goodness in the man?

The other alternative is that we may have an entirely false notion of what is evil. There is a derived and secondary and metaphorical sense in which it is true that evil resides in the wills of men. But, in order to find or prove it there, we have to exhibit its grounds in the facts and circumstances of their action, that is, we must find it realized in the public objects and concerns of men. But in that case we have only such knowledge of good and evil as we have from objective facts, and the reference to the will is not necessary, so long as the will is considered the private mystery of the person's inner life. Evil, then, if it is real, is not a state of mind; or, if it is only *a state of mind*, it is not real, and so is practically unimportant. The evil that we are concerned about, moral evil, evil that is defined by reference to action, lies in those objective conditions of existence and culture upon which the good life as an objective fact rests. We find evil in poverty, but poverty is not evil because it makes us sad or hungry; hunger in itself may not be bad, we enjoy it in anticipation of a good dinner, and sadness writes itself into great poetry or great music. Poverty is evil because it is a limitation and curtailment of our action; it distorts and deforms the objects we create. And, as such, that is to say as a moral phenomenon, poverty is a simple objective or external fact. Its squalor and sordidness and filth and suffering, considered as facts within the internal economy of individuals, are aesthetic phenomena and become moral objects characterizable as good or evil for us only when we act with respect to them and create objects on their account. As states of mind they are not moral facts and are neither good nor bad. Poverty as real evil is distortion and distraction in the corporate organization within the natural-cultural system, of objective agencies which have blindly set themselves up out of the spontaneous movement of life, because that movement has failed to get appropriate direction from intelligence. Moral evil comes into existence by our default.

Good and evil are, then, as real, conditions of our natural and cultural existence which facilitate or interfere with our capacities to act, or with the objects of our acts, when referred to the perfection of the objects of nature and culture. In so far as states of mind, ideas, attitudes, convictions, intentions, etc., can be called good or evil, they are so only when regarded as objective aspects of the natural or cultural world when the natural-cultural world is considered in relation to the perfection of the objects to which they refer. Otherwise they are abstract psychological existences, existences, that is, without worth. As qualities or states referring to isolated agents, or to agents in their strictly personal or "social" relations, they are incomplete and imperfect, and actions dominated by them are subjective virtues. As such subjective facts we shall discuss them in the following sections; but before we go on to that we may offer examples of the contradictoriness of the subjective virtues.

Take the supposedly good man in a bad world. The man is a saint, but he lives in poverty and filth and rags. His attitudes and intentions and motives all ideally contemplate beautiful and exalted ends, while he rots in hopeless inaction, or strives only to fail. But what *can* he *do* about it? As a shoemaker, statesman, saint, no act that he can perform is significant from the viewpoint of the ends he contemplates. He has no access to proper tools or means or materials. Nor is the matter helped if he joins his neighbors to commiserate and "co-operate" and "share" in the mater. The tools are out of his reach; there is nothing he can do. He is not a good man. He is, we will believe upon inferences based upon his expressed attitudes, the sort of man who would be good *if* the conditions of his life made it possible, and we will respect and pity him. Nor can ten thousand of his kind contribute anything to goodness by social effort or co-operation so long as they lack the essential means in the natural and cultural structures of life. The saintly attitude is beautiful, sometimes, and always impressive; but not everything that in any way interests us may be called moral or good. Morality and goodness and evil are questions of action, and action always implies objective or external means. What states of mind or attitudes are connected with action are accidental, that is, circumstances of the actor's subjective history, and the feeling qualities are even more remote than accidental and are properly described as phenomenal. What I feel with respect to morality is, so far, of the least possible consequence; it is of little consequence in any connection except in aesthetic considerations, and here it is important only as hypostatized into a material with respect to which certain kinds of action may be realized.

It is in this mistaking our aesthetic or other feelings for elements of morality that the present collapse of civilization may be explained. It is doubtful whether there is one person in the million who does not accept the proposition that the total meaning and essence of good and evil are, for him, identifiable with his states of mind. Even so far as the objects of nature and culture have significance, that significance is supposed to have been loaned to the objects by our states of mind. Thus we degrade and demoralize the institution of property by interpreting it in terms of needs and wants or enjoyment and power—states of mind to which real property has no determinate relation. The entire structure upon which life depends is consequently crumbling beneath us; we retire into our Epicurean garden, and the world goes to pieces about us. We are charged with being a materialistic people; we are not materialistic, but in our moral imbecility we undertake to transform the material universe into satisfactions and enjoyments and other moonbeams of our diseased imagination. We overlook and ignore the material world, the world of things, which alone may be valuable; as a consequence the world of things organizes itself outside morality. We merely entangle ourselves within its blind and insentient processes and are crushed.

Actions in the interpretation of which is required the backward reference to the person who acts are subjective virtues and do not express the whole meaning of morality.

II. OBJECTIVE VIRTUE AND THE
CULTURAL PERSON

We have noted that the "good man" theory is a subjective myth, and the effort to give body to its vagueness in "social" relations is equally a superstition. These vagaries of moral thought depend upon the assumptions of the subjective virtues, which however have not been examined, but have merely been impressed upon us by the peculiar accidents of our history. They have been so universally accepted in the Western world that the civilization and culture of the West have been attributed to them. This is an obvious mistake, and the question is rather whether civilization and culture have not developed from and under other causes and, in many citable instances, in spite of the opposition of the subjective virtues. The culture of western Europe was obviously not built up under the influence of charity and generosity and magnanimity. It was equally not the product of hate or anger or greed or of other hostile attitudes. It was not because of any of the characteristic feeling attitudes of the human mind that we have a significant culture resting upon a substantial civilization. Culture is not made or composed of states of mind, which are incidental to it in every way.

This has been made obvious in the history of democracy and perhaps with even more emphasis in the history of Protestantism. Democracy is the assumption that the outward structure of life can be created and maintained by the persistent operation of our states of mind. It forces a purely subjective meaning upon the institution of agreement, contract, compact, and a psychological interpretation upon all the concepts of action, which, after all, represent the continuity and substance of life and culture. The fallacy here is the assumption that men may be held together and integrated into cultural wholes by means of their states of mind. But the fact is that no integration can be effected by such means that is not extremely impermanent, which in fact lasts only so long as the state of mind is being maintained by means of persuasion. It should be obvious, just now, that our states of mind are pretty much out of hand, that they mean much less and very different things from what they have been supposed to mean, and that further dependence upon them as a basis of culture is likely to prove fatal to the entire structure.

As a matter of fact the good man is likely to be a person whose states of mind are satisfactory or interesting neither to himself nor to others and have no characteristic relation to his own action or to that of other people. He may be "unsocial," or even "antisocial," as perhaps the best men, those who make substantial contributions to culture, usually are. He may not have any close connection with his "group," since it is just the influence of the group to prevent him from doing anything above or different from the average.

The man who lives the good life cannot be identified by his states of mind. Men live equally good lives whose inner experiences are of exactly opposite characters so far as their feeling quality is concerned. The part of the man's mentality that is real is the part which becomes realized in what is not a state of mind in any sense. And it is those objects and processes through which mind is realized that are important in the cultural career of men. Aside from the instinctive and aesthetic objects and processes of early family life, the most important element in the moral structure of the person is his job, his work. But this does not mean to exalt "industry" and "prudence," which is a crass viewpoint limited to economic and property motives. The work of the person may be play or art or thought, anything that constitutes his characteristic activity and allows him to embody his act in a significant object. It is through this function that the person builds himself into the structure of his world which he uses as his larger body or builds the objects of his immediate world into his own structure as the instrumental means to his act. He thus obliterates the line which divides him from his world, even from other persons; the "others" of subjective morality are by him regarded as parts of that world, in that he must consider them in intending or planning any act. There is probably no act of his which appears to him to be centered upon another person as subject of interest in the act; yet the other person may loom so large as an object in his act as to overbalance other factors. But the other person is peripheral after all, and the person who designs the act remains the design of the object that is to be realized in the act. This is the reason egoism can maintain itself against all subjective arguments, and the reason altruism will always be required to justify itself; but it is also the reason why neither egoism nor altruism are important as moral theories.

The person's morality, therefore, begins with his work. We want to insist that by work we do not mean the process by which he gains his "living." We mean that aspect of his active life by which he appropriates the objects of the environment to himself and appropriates himself to those objects, the act by which he as agent becomes realized in his world of objects. It is this form of act that constitutes his objective virtue, acts which effectively and completely integrate the person with his world. We have noted that this is the definition of an act—that it perpetually creates and maintains the continuity between the person and his world. We also noted that the act thus defined is the ground of institution.

Mutual inclusion of persons by each other in the world in which each acts is the basis of "association." It never, as a moral situation, means that one person intends to consider another as an objective or end and to act with or for him, and it involves no necessary or characteristic feeling attitudes of the one person to the other. Association merely means, where its meaning has any reference to fact, that the other person is there as a part of the objective design of the act and is recognized as such. It involves no subjective attitudes in the determination of fact. This is the fallacy of sociology, which assumes that we can co-operate each other into the Kingdom, pretty much as the religious tradition assumed we could love each other into the Kingdom. In fact, the association is not a product of the person's will; he does not create it, but it is there as the institutional condition of his act and as a part of the objective structure of things. It is a fact that is given, a characteristic of the world of objects. It is for this reason that Aristotle's dictum that "the state is natural" is true, and for the same reason the modern political doctrine of contract is false. We are only lately beginning to learn that the notion of a subjectively formulated contract is not an important legal concept. But for the same reason also the Stoic doctrines of an "assent" grounded in the reason of things, and of a natural law expressing the objectivity of that reason, are true and become the metaphysics upon which the theory of human "association" will always rest. It is at this point that we can see clearly the objective and corporate structure of the moral agent or person.

That is to say, the essence of the person considered as a moral agent is just this system of objective relations, relations whose terms are parts of the structure of things, to which he gives expression in his acts. The person therefore becomes identified and identical with the institutions of life, which are the common body of the multitude of persons regarded as active agents. Culture therefore is this system of persons as they have made themselves corporate in their objects. It is the medium in which the individual lives, and the instrument through which he acts, and in the absence of which his act can never be real. If the person as individual is to act, if, that is, he is to be a moral being, the source, the means, the materials, and the end of his act will be found within this corporate medium. It is the ultimate object of every act—every act intends or is designed to create and maintain this medium as the condition and ground of all action. An act thus creates its own ground, and this is what is meant by spontaneity and the basis of any consistent theory of freedom. Virtue is thus objective in that it is objectified and realized in its ultimate means, and, operating through these means, constitutes value or significance in corporate form, and this value is the essence of the end—the system of institutions. The person as moral agent thus identifies with the institution in which he lives, becomes, that is, the corporate person.

III. MORALITY AND THE CORPORATE PERSON

The nature of the corporate person has been indicated in a number of connections throughout our discussion. Corporeity is the principle of the moral person, and all persons are persons by virtue of their embodying this principle. There is then no "natural person"; the "individual" of modern ethical theory has no existence and never had existence. It is not even true that the assumptions of individualism apply to the body of the moral agent, for the recent theory of the organism has shown the individual contradictory and as having no resemblance to the facts of existence. What we wish to point out here is, however, that *in fact* in our existent culture the effective or active or moral person has the corporate form and that the nature and structure of the act are correspondingly different from what it has been supposed to be. There is in existence no such thing as the act of the isolated person which ethical theory presupposes. It cannot exist, and the attempt to find its "origin" in psychological "springs to action" has been the shame of modern ethical theory.

The moral person is the corporate person, and the moral act is the corporate act. The only person that can act *really* is the corporate person. The act is objective, exists in its own right when the expression of the corporate person, and the attempt to ground it in the spontaneity and subjective "intention" of an exclusive person is something less than an adequate expression of the least and simplest aspects of its nature. We have shown in another connection that the isolated "individual" cannot act in the constitutive meaning of the term and have there pointed out that the characteristic act of the "individual" is the imperfect and abortive act of thought; and that, if such an act is to objectify in actuality and so become real, it must incorporate in the objective circumstance of culture. And we have noted in an earlier chapter that the primary moral obligation of the "individual" is the obligation to know and that his attempts at action will always be subjective and incomplete. We are now emphasizing the fact that every act is effected or realized or comes into its object or end only when it implements itself in corporate structures. In a negative and rhetorical way all religions have recognized this fact, which they express in terms of the limitation or "weakness" of the individual as he stands alone and apart from the support of the ritual, and they find the overcoming of these defects in the whole institutional structure as objectified in God. But the most immediate examples are to be found in industry.

Practically every act in modern industrial life that comes anywhere near completion is the act of some corporate body, even those acts which are immediately implemented in the individual. What I do either as employer or as employee in an industrial organization is designed and determined by the organization, and my "freedom," whether I am doorkeeper or owner, consists in the alternative to do what is assigned me or lose my connection with the organization.

What I do is not my act but the act of the corporate body in which I live and move and have such being as it allows me. And something of the same sort is true almost equally in every other connection. Each of us is bound within the system in which his peculiar work is determined; the freedom of the individual is the larger freedom of the corporate bodies with which he is connected and is genuine when the structure of the corporate whole is complete. The ultimate moral authority of acts also is a prerogative of the corporate person, in that the corporate person expresses the purposes of the cultural life. This primacy of the corporate person in the moral life has been in process of legal and political establishment for a long time, and its position of dominance in the industrial sphere has been secure for the last fifty years. It is tragic that we have as yet not seen that the corporate person is the basic concept of political, legal, and ethical theory. The effects of this dominance have not as yet been fully realized; only its minor and negative and adverse influences have come into full notice. But the structure of the corporate body indicates the form which the culture of mankind will take on for the future and dictates the directions the thought of the future must follow.

As was noticed above, the corporate personality came into being when in the development of life and complex practical purposes the execution of certain types of plans and designs became impossible for the individual. The formulation of plans and the creation of designs, because these are necessarily ideal or thought structures, are the unique function of the individual as a thinker and knower, and the plans and designs represent the last and final product of the knowledge function, and the last ultimate that the individual can *do*. But the carrying-out of these plans into execution, their realization in concrete objects, is a problem not for knowledge but for wisdom, and wisdom, as we have seen, is the function of the corporate wholeness of culture. Thus the public corporation, the state, came into being to give objective reality to ends created and designed by individuals, but which individuals were powerless to give body and expression. Similarly, the United States postal system came into being to accomplish ends that individuals had designed but were incapable of realizing. And that failure is objectified in the private express systems. The modern utility corporation was called into being to do the purposes and wills of individuals, purposes beyond the power of the individual to secure. It is unfortunate that in their present stage of development they are still left in the hands of individuals, but the incompetence of the individual to direct them has been so abundantly demonstrated of late that their completer development into genuine moral persons is assured. Such bodies are designed to express the wisdom of the cultural whole, and this wisdom we are coming to recognize in the public purpose.

It is futile to undertake to say in any detail what the form of the good life is to be in the future. Yet it is clearly the tendency for the future to look to the corporate person for the achievement of all large ends. And it begins to be more or less obvious that in the not distant future all moral or practical purposes will get their realization through the corporate agency and in the corporate form. The processes of education and politics are already ostensibly completely corporate and acknowledgedly public functions. Religion and art and the family seem corporately organized in nature almost before cultural development begins. The fight is now on to determine whether the industrial function shall be fully organized in the corporate form. But the outcome seems inevitable if it is not to have a different position from that of other human activities, and the result can be awaited with some confidence. It is the tragedy of our ignorance if industry cannot be moralized without a catacylsm of blood.

That men should have food, shelter, a reasonable degree of comfort, recreation, intelligence, books, love, truth, beauty, it is necessary that these should be organized as public obligations, since they are beyond the competence of the individual person to provide. They constitute in their active aspects the moral life, and the moral life is the public life, the life that man lives outside the narrow confines determined by his mental limitations. Within this narrow sphere of his mentality all is private and peculiar to the individual and, as such, is unmoral at best and immoral at the ordinary. The ultimate ends that men can think out for themselves cannot be left to the limited capacities of individual men to be accomplished; they are too important to rest upon a basis so weak. They are therefore tasks for the corporate body and can be accomplished only by corporate agencies.

IV. THE CORPORATE PERSON AND THE GOOD LIFE

The corporate person is the good life. So far as the good life is possible to the individual, it is so in the fact that the individual's functions may all be fitted into the operation of the corporate person and may thus share in its accomplishments. Thus both in the knowing function and in the active function the fulfilment of life for the individual is found to be effected only in the harmonizing of the individual function and the corporate function in the corporate person. What makes

the conception difficult is the fact that we have for so many ages demanded an ideal end for the good life in terms of private feeling, thus
confusing the moral problem with the aesthetic problem. But we
have seen already in the discussion of beauty and religion that the
moral aspect of feeling is provided for in the *form* of the act, that
all that feeling can claim of morality is met when the moral act takes
on a perfect form as in ritual, etc. Hence the proper demands of feeling are satisfied in the acts of the corporate person, since these acts
possess the form that results in the perfect object.

The difficulty, then, comes from confusing the demands of the
natural individual with those of the corporate individual. Feeling has
its requirements met for both the natural and the corporate individual
when it is acknowledged that the good act must meet certain requirements of form. But feeling makes a demand of the individual for satisfaction in terms of its content, and if this demand is to be recognized
then the corporate person is not a moral person, for there is in its
structure no possibility of providing for a feeling-content other than
that of the aesthetic object which the moral end includes. But there
is another alternative. There seems no reason to believe that satisfaction in terms of feeling-content is a legitimate requirement to be
made by the individual person. It is not possible consistently to require that the individual should be "happy" or that he should be
guaranteed any type of feeling-content. The content of feeling therefore seems to have no moral significance, it has no place, except in
an aesthetic object, in the scheme of the good life for the corporate
person, and the place it has in the individual life appears to have no
relation to morality. We have suggested that the content of feeling
can be provided for only in aesthetic theory, and here we may be
content to leave it as one of the special problems of aesthetics.

If we are to concede that the good life is of the form of an experience, which we decline to do, then we may have to change our notions
about what is a typical experience. The content of consciousness and
the content of feeling obviously are not uniformly present in experience and are therefore not the universal element that experience is
supposed to represent; and every other aspect of experience will be
seen to take place readily within the corporate form. The form of
feeling, which is its value aspect as is shown in aesthetic theory,
knowledge, wisdom, beauty, truth—all these are phases of the existence and action of the corporate person; and, as they constitute goodness, they are the "experience" of the corporate person which is objectified in institutions, so that the corporate person becomes itself

objective reality. Then and in this form the good person lives as a permanent element of the world and views the good of man as individual in terms of its possibilities for the future. In this attitude the good is complete—a person endowed by nature and culture with all the capacities and capabilities that are possible to him, with these capacities developed to the highest degree possible to them; living in a world which is so constituted and organized as to guarantee to the person full and free access to all the means and conditions necessary to enable his act to complete itself in satisfying objects.

Bibliography

Bibliography

The following works recognize that the life of action has a significant place as objective fact in the nature of things and that its interpretation involves metaphysical principles in the sense that its meaning lies in its relation to the world as a whole and not in its relation to the actor.

PLATO. *The Dialogues; Republic; Laws*
ARISTOTLE. *Works; Ethics; Politics; Metaphysics*
EPICTETUS. *Discourses*, trans. LONG
MARCUS AURELIUS. *Meditations*, trans. LONG
LUCRETIUS. *De rerum natura*, trans. MUNRO
The New Testament, King James Version
AUGUSTINE. *City of God; Confessions*
THOMAS. *Summa theologica; Ad Gentiles*
MACHIAVELLI. *The Prince; History of Florence*
HOBBES. *Leviathan; Elements of Law*
SPINOZA. *Ethics*
HEGEL. *Philosophy of Right*, trans. DYDE

The following works representing the modern period explain action in terms of experience and so are based on subjectivist assumptions as implied in the analysis of experience; with the final result of skepticism. The last five in the list issue in the irrationalism that is inherent in the subjectivist position.

DESCARTES. *Discourse on Method; Meditations*
LOCKE. *Essay concerning Human Understanding*
HUME. *Treatise of Human Nature; Essays*
ROUSSEAU. *Social Contract*
KANT. *Critique of Practical Reason*, trans. ABBOTT
SCHOPENHAUER. *The World as Will and Idea; Basis of Morality*
NIETZSCHE. *Beyond Good and Evil; Genealogy of Morals*
KIERKEGAARD. *Either/Or*
BERGSON. *Introduction to Metaphysics; Creative Evolution*
FREUD. *A General Introduction to Psychoanalysis*, trans. HALL; *Interpretation of Dreams*, trans. BRILL

The following works represent the attempt to confine ethical thought to the field of "fact" and science and experience, with "principles" that are purely practical in the technical sense.

445

BENTHAM. *Deontology; An Introduction to the Principles of Morals and Legislation*
MILL. *Utilitarianism; Principles of Political Economy*

The last heroic effort of the subjectivist motive is represented in

BRADLEY. *Ethical Studies*
GREEN. *Prolegomena to Ethics*
SIDGWICK. *Methods of Ethics; Elements of Politics*

The following historical works are useful:

HICKS. *Stoic and Epicurean*
LECKY. *History of European Morals*
SIDGWICK. *History of Ethics*
STEPHEN. *The English Utilitarians*

Index

Index

Absolute, good and bad as, 50, 51, 269

Absolutism, 349

Act: of cognition, 120; defined, 17; embodied, 19; as form, 101; as intelligence, 156; as judgment, 127–28; and movement, 35, 58, 64, 67, 70, 81, 94; not a cause, 23; as original fact, 29; as perfect, 371–72; as plan, 18; as standard, 176; as substance, 14; of thought, 18; of will, 117; as worship, 323

Action: analysis of, 17; and meaning, 25, 28; and movement, 24; not a cause, 29, 34; as objective, 35, 38, 105, 108, 114, 124, 250, 251, 255, 377; as real, 18, 24; as subject matter, 5, 17; as substance, 9, 13

Advantage, 136–37

Adventure, 27, 40, 41, 47, 114, 125, 166, 242, 322, 391

Aesthetics: and ethics, 7; as philosophy of value, 12, 38, 45; as standard, 92, 100, 101, 116, 265

Affective faculties, 114, 115, 116

Agency, 119, 120, 122

Agent, 8; as origin of act, 16, 26, 80, 97, 119, 120, 246

Ambiguity, 75, 201, 224, 225, 293

Analogical identity, 75, 77, 78, 236, 367

Analogue, 75

Analysis, of action, 17, 77, 122

Animal, 112, 134

Appreciation, 325

Appropriateness, 56, 71

Aristotle, 24, 181, 196, 268, 351, 436

Art: appreciation, 325, and beauty, 324–37; function of, 328, 334, 355, 369; as moral, 324; as objective, 45

Assumption: reflex as, 95, 118, 119, 122, 123, 142, 277; tropism as, 95

Attitude, 70, 87, 92, 406–13

Authority, 9, 10; based on fact, 64, 88, 163, 165, 305, 382, 397, 399; of moral law, 62–63

Autonomy, 95

Bad, 21, 25; as real, 49; as absolute, 50, 51

Balance, 57, 148, 414

Beauty, 102, 150, 324–37; its comprehension, 326; and education, 334; and the family, 328; and morality, 337; and politics, 336; and religion, 334

Belief, 70, 316

Benevolence, 213

Better-worse, 49; as maxim, 51

Biological capacities, 86–102

Body: as active, 86, 94; as agent, 95; as end, 98; as good, 99, 115, 116, 123, 141; as ground, 143, 267; as objective, 36, 37; as person, 142

Category: practical, 41; theoretical, 28

Cause, 95, 115, 116, 252, 253

Chance, 65, 69, 70, 71, 83, 114, 125, 253, 319

Change, 5, 71, 83, 252

Character, 14, 15; as ideal, 36; objectified, 38, 68, 128, 129, 147, 165

Charity, 214

Choice, 43, 45, 47; and chance, 47; as concept, 48, 67, 71, 127, 155

Circumstance, 55, 66, 125

Civil person, 160

Cognition, 115, 242

Cognitive act, 117

Common, 57, 142

Communication, 303

Community, 57, 160

Compulsion, 69

Concept: of freedom, 43; of obligation, 51

Conduct, 107

Conflict, of institutions, 283, 284

Conscience, 23, 148

Consciousness, 8, 23, 96, 112, 124, 241, 242

Consistency, 57, 63

Constitution, 267

Content: of ethics, 6, 13, 17, 182; of politics, 339

449

Continuity, 112, 114, 126, 240
Contract, 200, 293
Control, 3, 10; of body, 99, 113, 119, 121, 136, 276, 287, 298, 309, 342; by inhibition, 401, 403; logical, 14, 40, 41, 89, 91; by power, 344, 393–94, 397–98
Conviction, 24
Co-operation, 273
Corporate judgment, 80
Corporate person, 84, 97, 123, 127, 129, 130, 141, 142, 241
Corporate property, 144, 145
Corporate whole, world as, 34, 37, 57
Corporate will, 190, 233, 242, 254, 269, 286, 309, 332, 353, 363, 437
Correct-incorrect, 51, 53
Cosmic, the, 7
"Cosmic element," 11
Cosmic implication, 140, 217, 377, 385, 422
Cosmic relation, 39
Cosmic unity, 77
Cosmopolitanism, 210, 230
Courage, 373, 406–13; as fear, 407, 410; as "moral," 341; and peace, 413; and safety, 412
Criterion, 26, 78, 153, 263
Culture, 4, 5, 71, 110, 129, 254, 381; and wisdom, 387, 414, 433–34, 436
Custom, 5, 97

Democracy, 201, 207, 348
Design, 68, 70, 82, 113, 116, 152, 228, 267, 268, 380
Desire, 120, 121
Direction, 4, 67, 68, 95, 118, 259, 390, 393
Discipline: cultural, 12, 61; practical, 4; thoretical, 10, 11
Disinterestedness, 54, 55, 71, 136, 216
Duality, 130, 388
Duty, 70, 71
Dynamic, acts as, 39

Economics and ethics, 6, 33, 54, 110
Education, 271, 301–13, 303, 304, 305; beauty and, 334, 354, 368; its method, 308; organization, 310; public, 306; universal, 306
Egoism, 208
Emotion, 91, 158
Empirical concepts, 51, 126
Empiricism, 128, 208
Empiricist, 30, 170

End: as ground of preference, 26, 35; as moral concept, 318, 358–73; object as, 9; world as, 37–38, 43, 109, 122, 143, 263, 266
Environment, 32; as content of acts, 55, 124, 125
Ethics: its content action, 6, 13; and law, 8; as philosophy, 40, 13; as practical, 4, 5; and religion, 7; as science, 3; subject matter of, 14, 15; theory of, 28, 50, 128
Evil, 284, 431–32
Exercise, 100, 101
Existence, 13–14, 116, 117
Expediency, 51, 55
Experience, 14, 59, 75, 78, 118, 138
Experiment, 41, 54

Fact, and value, 75, 77
Faith, 70, 314, 316, 320
Family, 270–87; and beauty, 328, 351, 366; as body, 274; breakdown of, 272; as corporate, 285; functions of, 279, 280; its future, 285–86; as history, 271; as political unit, 281; as spirit, 275; and work, 277
Feeling: as end, 314; as ground of law, 60, 115, 132; as objectified, 218; of obligation, 56; as passive, 227, 314; and value, 387
Fictive persons, 83, 84
Fitness, 56
Food, 87, 99, 134
Freedom, 10, 31, 43; ground of, 48, 65; of indifference, 65; and order, 297; as property, 144, 164, 177, 229, 253, 292, 296; of will, 66, 69
Friendship, 218–32; as virtue, 230, 428
Future: of family, 285–86; of the good life, 439

Generosity, 204–17, 205, 218, 427
Goal, 106
God: as ground of law, 60; as rationality, 64, 71, 76, 155, 167, 241, 437
Good: as absolute, 269, 292, 295; art as, 325, 327, 336, 340, 349, 378, 380, 424; and bad as absolute, 50; as a corporate function, 100, 110, 147, 181, 182, 269; as desire, 185; as experience, 183; as feeling, 184; as goods, 200, 207; as happiness, 190; highest, 187; as judgment, 25; not a mental state, 190; objective, 297; as objective and uni-

versal, 16, 21, 32; as pleasure, 184; as property, 200, 210; as real, 49; as reason, 189; as relative, 51, 64; as sense, 186, 187; as subject, 36; as whole, 27, 305, 313; as will, 187
Good-bad, 43, 48
Goodness, 27, 39; as cosmic relation, 50, 58, 63, 64; as a public function, 99, 150
Goods, 292, 295, 379
Grace, 151
Ground: as law, 232; of moral judgment, 141; of moral law, 59; of validity, 61, 116, 121, 128
Group, as corporate body, 139
Growth, 124, 253, 381
Guidance, 343

Habit, 96; its function, 97
Harmony, 9, 148, 234, 277, 328, 337, 415
Health, 87, 92, 148–49; of mind, 235; as public, 149, 234
Hedonism, 62
Heredity, 127, 128
History, 47, 83, 112, 125, 127, 358
Holiness, 373
Human, the, 123
Human institutions, 128
Humanitarianism, 210
Hygiene, 99
Hypothesis, 21, 121, 123

Idea, 6, 18
Ideal, 7; act as, 18, 82, 106, 262
Idealism, 35, 38, 128
Identity, 55, 56; by analogy, 79; of means and end, 267; and obligation, 56, 71
Imagination, 113, 116, 315
Imperative, 71, 87, 281
Impersonal world, 69
Impersonal zealot, 71
Implication, 115, 317
Impulse, 258
Incorporation, 19, 267
Indifference, 65, 215, 253
Individual, 76; collective, 82, 83, 116, 123, 171, 212, 363, 372; person, 80; as thinker, 8
Individualism, 23, 31, 56, 64, 85, 118, 123, 207, 292
Individuality, 80, 267, 269
Industry, 33, 88, 288–300; and politics, 297, 352, 367
Inference, 24, 25

Instinct, 127, 220, 270; family and, 270–87, 274
Institution, 5, 37, 110, 123, 144, 223, 227; as principle, 228, 254, 270, 281, 307, 328, 363, 403
Instrument, 34, 35–36
Integrity, 63, 119, 120, 233–44, 235, 243
Intelligence: and control, 10, 116, 216, 233, 238, 240, 255, 301; and life, 395
Intelligibility, 25, 60, 77, 80, 107, 112, 250, 251
Intention, 12, 39, 181, 259
Interest, 134, 136, 137–38, 221, 223, 224, 349, 366
International society, 163, 231
Interpretation, 15, 20, 25
Irrationality, 69, 70, 106

Judgment, 21, 26; corporate, 80, 107, 127, 138, 207, 257, 367; of individuality, 80
Justice, 373, 414–25, 416; and freedom, 417; and law, 419; and peace, 423

Kant, 196
Knowing, 3, 6, 114, 120; as obligation, 156, 302
Knowledge, 3, 10, 21, 103, 103–30, 114, 156, 302, 315

Law, 8, 46, 58, 68, 139, 163, 170, 229, 231, 291, 300, 330, 414, 419, 421
Legislation, 67, 398–99
Liberality, 209, 211, 421
Life, 12, 13, 38, 47, 94, 115, 123, 231, 253, 325, 379, 392–405
Logic, 6, 25, 41, 223
Love, 91, 214, 277

Meaning, 8, 15, 19, 21, 25, 76, 77, 79, 257
Means, 107, 108, 182, 251, 266, 268
Mechanism, 32, 98
Metaphysics, 12, 31, 76, 78, 127, 130
Method, 24; logic as, 25; speculative, 117, 307–8
Mind, 12, 13, 16, 96, 235, 308
Moral act, 117
Moral faculty, 121
Moral judgment, 57, 138
Moral quality, 118
Moral will, 117
Morality, 6, 10, 16, 27, 60, 80, 128, 139,

242, 256, 269, 319, 337, 437; and art, 324, 326
Motive, 9, 39, 117, 121, 125, 128, 259, 261
Movement, and action, 24, 67, 94, 106, 115, 122
Mutual implication, 76, 77
Mutuality, 76, 133, 274
Mysticism, 30, 206

Naturalism, 31, 32, 383
Nature, 4, 5, 77, 81, 249
Necessity, 66, 177, 329
Need, 6, 23, 194

Object, 9, 12, 18, 38, 39, 40, 103, 107, 228, 236, 258, 264, 265, 267, 269, 286, 291, 302, 309, 317
Objective, 9, 11, 44, 80, 109, 119, 122, 175, 247, 288–300, 372
Objectivity, 56, 218, 262, 325
Obligation, 10, 30, 41, 43, 51, 55, 57, 68, 168, 171, 233, 301, 365, 381, 382, 384
Opinion, public, 200
Opportunity, 37, 88, 212, 255
Order, 124, 126, 128, 170, 238, 243, 252, 275, 291, 322, 328, 341, 346, 356, 382, 423
Organic theory, 32, 97, 115
Organism, 81, 87, 97, 222
Origin: in fact, 60, 61, 396; in God, 60; of moral law, 59–60
Others, 149, 205, 209, 212, 213, 243
Ought, 40

Partial virtues, 173, 179
Passion, 115, 120
Passive feeling, 115, 116
Past, 111, 112
Perfect specimen, 358
Perfect type of act, art as, 324, 325
Perfection, 62, 358, 368, 371
Person, 9, 14, 16, 26, 28, 30, 41, 58, 78, 80, 81, 83, 98, 119, 140, 142, 145, 147–72, 246, 270, 288–300, 302, 333, 359, 363, 419
Personality, 129; corporate, 130, 141
Philanthropy, moral, 129, 215
Physical activity, 86, 93, 97, 99, 101, 139, 148
Plan, 17, 18, 82, 113, 262
Plato, 24, 128, 196, 268, 346, 361
Play, 92, 93

Pleasure-pain, 62, 100, 101, 184
Political body, 10; relation, 90, 110; as unit, 161, 229
Politics, 10, 37, 139, 227, 241, 297, 336, 338–57, 341, 347, 351, 356, 369
Possible relations, 3, 18
Power, 295, 344, 345
Practical categories, 42
Practical interests, 4
Practical life, 312
Prediction, 41, 126
Preference, 6, 25, 43, 45
Principle, 15, 46, 124, 129, 228, 277, 291, 330, 332
Private interests, 306
Private will, 145
Probability, 70, 125
Production, 99, 330
Property, 38, 97, 143, 145, 211, 294, 297, 309, 329, 348
Psychology, 23, 30, 103, 118, 169, 222, 363
Public, 97, 136, 138, 300, 306, 332, 356, 364, 382, 439
Purpose, 3, 51, 52, 89, 105, 121, 226, 261, 297

Quality, 15, 23, 25, 78, 96, 101, 104, 112, 120, 126, 176, 250, 256, 259, 266, 309, 326, 327, 340
Quantity, 187

Rationalist, 30, 117, 156
Rationality, 64, 152, 158, 190
Real, good-bad as, 49, 77
Reality, 76, 77, 84, 85
Reason, 60, 114, 159, 235
Reform, 38, 39, 195
Relation, 8, 17, 113, 119, 122, 124, 129, 134, 142, 147, 218, 223, 250, 273, 303
Relative terms, "good" and "bad" as, 51
Relativity of ends, 46
Religion, and ethics, 7, 84, 85, 232, 314–23, 317, 319, 322, 353, 369
Responsibility, 41, 71, 154
Restitution, 86, 92
Result, 23, 70, 118, 119
Rewards, 62, 63
Right, 20, 31, 36, 51, 56, 57, 110, 114, 147, 167, 212, 217, 257, 365
Ritual, 318, 322, 334

School, 227, 228, 301
Science, 3, 81, 129
Self-control, 393, 400, 403
Sensitivity, 20, 54, 204, 205, 213, 238, 242
Shelter, 100, 134, 135
Significance, 15, 92, 93, 118, 130, 275, 322
Situation, 21, 25, 124
Skepticism, 30
Social, 23, 60, 82, 97, 131–32, 139, 169, 383
Sociology, 131, 170, 363
Speculation, 24, 40, 41, 347
Spirit, 7, 95
Spontaneity, 31, 95, 127, 393
Stage, 34, 35
Standard, 21, 92, 100, 263, 291, 314
State of mind, 16, 38, 79, 162, 282, 300, 343
Structure, 8, 46, 68, 70, 77, 96, 123, 143, 267, 328, 348, 365
Subject matter of ethics, 14, 17
Subjective, 11, 23, 118, 121, 123, 132, 169, 175, 178, 213, 247, 360–61, 400
Sympathy, 192–203, 194, 196, 197, 200, 202, 218, 426

Technique, 311, 378, 396
Temperance, 373, 392–406, 400, 403, 405
Theory, 4, 22, 27, 118, 129, 153
Thing, 14, 35, 37, 104, 143
Thought, 18, 81, 133, 309
Time, 126, 127
Tool, 32, 107, 251, 266, 298

Type: of action, 5; of ethical theory, 128; of persons, 80; of political order, 343

Uncertainty, 41, 69
Unity, 9, 39, 79, 112, 118, 120, 124, 128, 142, 148, 237, 303, 308–9, 338
Universal judgment, 80, 112
Universality, 56, 240
Urgency, 66, 68, 108, 120
Utilitarianism, 31, 32, 176

Validity, 59, 61, 291
Value, 12, 13, 45, 75, 77, 131, 197, 225, 267, 278, 313, 387, 423
Virtue, 5, 180, 182, 217, 372, 426–41, 433
Volition, 45, 96
Voluntarist, 117, 156

Whole, 5, 8, 10, 34, 100, 102, 149, 161, 181, 210, 226, 230, 252, 291, 313
Wholeness, 326, 332, 402, 424
Will, 23, 31, 66, 68, 95, 108, 116, 119, 144, 155, 156, 165, 188, 395, 403
Wisdom, 14, 103, 156, 233, 373, 377–91, 380, 381, 386, 387
Work, 86, 88, 90, 152, 157, 177, 288–300, 289, 290, 291, 292, 329, 339, 330, 331, 367, 372, 411, 435
World, 22, 34, 37, 41, 125, 245–73, 247, 251, 254, 256, 269, 272, 277, 278, 294, 299, 309, 364
Worth, 22, 25, 50, 78, 180, 197, 226
Wrong, 20, 57, 241, 257